地道荷兰

"游译"生活

刘德强 编著 韩刚 审译

中国纺织出版社有限公司

图书在版编目（ＣＩＰ）数据

地道荷兰："游译"生活：汉、英、荷 / 刘德强编著；韩刚审译. --北京：中国纺织出版社有限公司，2020.1

ISBN 978-7-5180-6681-0

Ⅰ. ①地… Ⅱ. ①刘… ②韩… Ⅲ. ①英语—汉语—对照读物②散文集—中国—当代 Ⅳ. ①H319.4：I

中国版本图书馆CIP数据核字（2019）第206764号

责任编辑：郭　婷　　责任校对：韩雪丽

责任印制：储志伟

中国纺织出版社有限公司出版发行

地址：北京市朝阳区百子湾东里A407号楼　邮政编码：100124

销售电话：010—67004422　传真：010—87155801

http://www.c-textilep.com

中国纺织出版社天猫旗舰店

官方微博 http://weibo.com/2119887771

三河市宏盛印务有限公司印刷　各地新华书店经销

2020年1月第1版第1次印刷

开本：787×1092　1/16　印张：19.5

字数：350千字　定价：49.00元

前　言

　　近年来，中国人出境游的数量急剧增加，而出行的路线也由最初的"新马泰"逐渐延伸到欧洲大陆。荷兰作为欧洲游的主要目的地之一，在中国游客行程单中出现的越来越频繁。然而，中国人对荷兰的了解仍然仅仅局限在风车、郁金香、木鞋等传统的宣传形象。作为一名旅荷华人，作者从中国人的角度出发，对荷兰的多个方面都进行了较为详细的介绍。荷兰有着悠久的历史文化，拥有众多国际知名品牌，从这本书中我们可以了解到在荷兰吃、喝、玩、购、行等多方面的知识及旅游生活建议。

　　在编写的过程中，作者亲历了绝大部分推荐目的地，并对本书所有篇章中的人物、事件、数据等都查阅和考证了相关的荷兰语文献资料，力求展示出一个地道真实的荷兰，把荷兰的美推荐给来荷旅游、学习或对荷兰文化感兴趣的读者，这也是作者编写此书的主要目的。

　　为了让本书有一定的学习价值，书中全部内容以中英双语形式呈现，并特别邀请国内翻译界大咖韩刚先生作为审译者，对英文部分进行润色，使本书语言更为流畅和地道。作者在每章附上中、荷、英三国语言的旅游口语例句，并配音，读者可非常方便地学习到常用荷兰语发音。

　　特别感谢美文苑公司为本书提供的大力支持。

目　录

低地之国

The Low Countries

The Netherlands not only is a small country, but also lies below sea level. That is why people often call it the "Low Countries". This nickname is actually a translation of the Dutch name for the Netherlands (Nederland). About half of the Netherlands lies below sea level, and the lowest point in the Netherlands lies near Nieuwerkerk aan den IJssel, east of Rotterdam, at 6.76 meters below sea level. "Vaalserberg", the highest point of the whole territory, is only 323 meters above sea level and lies near the south of Maastricht. The harsh natural environment of the Netherlands and the constant fight to keep the North Sea at bay led to what is now known as "the golden age", because it forced the Dutch to be inventive, making brilliant achievements in water control, agriculture and many other fields such as culture and science.

荷兰，不止国家狭小，海拔还在海平面以下，所以人们经常称它为"低地国家"，这实际上是荷兰人对"Nederland"这个名字的翻译。荷兰有一半的国土都位于海平面以下，最低点位于鹿特丹东边的艾瑟尔河畔尼沃凯尔克，海拔为－6.76米。整个国家的最高点只有区区的323米，位于马斯特里赫特南部，被称为"瓦尔斯堡"。荷兰恶劣的自然环境，对北海的不断围堵，造就了举世闻名的荷兰"黄金时代"，使荷兰在治水、农业以及文化、科学等领域都取得了辉煌的成就。

1. 国家概要
Country Profile

※ Geographical Location

The Netherlands, a nation in western Europe, is bordered by the North Sea in west and north. In the east by Germany and in the south it is bordered by Belgium. At sea the country also shares maritime borders with France and the United Kingdom.

The Netherlands is a low-lying country with around a quarter of its territory at or below sea level, with an area covering 41,543 square kilometres it is just slightly larger than for example Switzerland (41,285 km²), it is about half the size of the state of South Carolina in the U.S.

Dutch Dependencies used to consist of the Caribbean islands of Aruba, and the Netherlands Antilles, but on 10 October 2010 the Netherlands Antilles has been dissolved and its constituent islands have acquired a new status within the Kingdom of the Netherlands. Curaçao and St Maarten are now autonomous countries, but as said they still remain within the Kingdom of the Netherlands. The beautiful islands of Bonaire, St Eustatius and Saba have become special municipalities of the Netherlands.

※ The Economy

The Netherlands has a rather developed economy and has been playing a special role in the European economy for many centuries. For many years it has also been one of the best countries to do business. Since the 16th century, shipping, fishing, agriculture, trade, and banking have been leading sectors of the Dutch economy, this is largely because a high level of economic freedom.

Key trading partners of the Netherlands are Germany, Belgium, the UK, the United States, France, Italy, the Peoples Republic of China and the Russian Federation. The Netherlands belongs to the top 10 of the world's leading exporting countries. Other major industries include the chemical industry, metallurgy, machinery, electrical goods, trade, the service industry and tourism.

The Dutch agricultural sector is highly developed and mechanised, it has a strong focus on international exports. The agricultural sector employs about 4% of the Dutch labour force but produces large surpluses for the food-processing industry and accounts for 21 percent of the Dutch total export value. The Dutch rank second worldwide in value of agricultural exports, only behind the United States.

※ History

● The Netherlands in ancient and medieval times

Agriculture arrived in the Netherlands somewhere around 5000 BC. At first farmers made tools and weapons of stone. However after 1900 BC they started to use bronze. Around 750 BC the use of iron was introduced.

In the 1st century BC the Romans conquered the areas that now belong to Belgium and the southern Netherlands, they built roads and towns. However they did not succeed in colonising the northern part of the Netherlands. As the Roman Empire started to fall apart in the late 4th century, the Romans withdrew and left the Netherlands to the Germanic tribes, Franks, Saxons and Frisians. In the 8th century AD the Franks conquered most of the area and put it under their rule. Meanwhile the area converted to Christianity although not all tribes were willing to converted to the new religion. The Frisians, for example, put the missionary Boniface to death in 754 and he is therefore considered a martyr by the Roman Catholic church.

In 768 the great Charlemagne became ruler of the Franks and he created a great empire in Europe. Under him the Netherlands was divided into different cantons, each of these cantons was ruled by a count. When Charlemagne died in 814, his empire was divided into three parts, roughly modern France, Germany and the region in between. At first the Netherlands was part of the Middle Empire, but in 925 it was absorbed into the German Empire.

Although the Netherlands, as many other countries suffered from violent Viking raids during the 9th and 10th century, town life and trade flourished during the Middle ages. In the 14th century Dutch towns, compared with other places, enjoyed considerable freedom. During in the 15th century the Dukes of Burgundy gradually took control of the region.

● The Netherlands from the 16th to the 18th centuries

4

Eventually the Low Countries including the area currently called the Netherlands became the possessions of the powerful Habsburg family. In 1555 Phillip II of Spain became ruler of the Dutch, but the Dutch ended up despising him.

Meanwhile the Reformation despite rigorous and violent persecution was sweeping the Netherlands. Calvinism, the teachings of John Calvin became popular in many Dutch towns. In 1566 Calvinists destroyed religious art in many churches in a movement called the Iconoclastic Fury (De beeldenstorm in Dutch).

This provoked the fury of Phillip II and in 1567 the King sent his servant the Duke of Alva with an army to suppress the Calvinists uprise and ordered the Duke to impose the king's will on the inhabitants of the unruly area. Alva set up the infamous Council of Troubles, which tried and condemned to death more than 12,000 people for taking part in the riots of 1566. This invoked anger among the population and led to the rise of Prince William of Orange, familiar known as William the Silent whom became the champion of Dutch fight for freedom. In 1572 William led pirates called the Sea Beggars, or Geuzen in Dutch, against the Spanish. From the sea they sailed up rivers and captured Dutch towns. The Dutch flocked to join the rebellion, the Spanish retaliated and a terrible war ensued.

This resulted in the signing of the Union of Utrecht in 1579 by seven provinces of the Low Countries signed and in 1581 they declared independence from Spain. In 1588 they formed the Republic of the Seven United Netherlands. The Spanish were not just going to let this happen and fought to hold onto the region and in 1584 William the Silent was assassinated in Delft. In the

meanwhile the English supported the Netherlands and Spain got also struck a heavy blow by the defeat of the Spanish Armada by the English in 1588. Phillip finally died in 1598.

During this time the Netherlands became a prosperous trading nation, this was helped by a 12 year truce with Spain from 1609 to 1621. The Dutch East India Company was formed in 1602. The Dutch West India Company was formed in 1621 and in 1625 the Dutch founded New Amsterdam (now known as New York). In 1652 they also founded a colony in south Africa. In the 17th century Dutch sailors undertook many long voyages to explore unknown areas, In 1606 Willem Jansz discovered Australia, which was then named New Holland, and in 1642 Abel Tasman discovered Tasmania.

In 1648 the Spanish finally recognized the independence of the Netherlands at the Peace of Westphalian, which effectively also ended the European wars of religion.

Dutch trade rivalry with England led to the three wars in 1652-1654, 1665-1667 and 1672-1674. William of Orange, Stadholder (ruler) of the Netherlands made peace with England and married Princess Mary of England and 1688 William became king of England.

The late 17th century was an era of great developments in science, art and philosophy in the Netherlands, but during the 18th century The Netherlands as an economic and political power went into decline. The Dutch were involved in the War of the Spanish Succession against the French. This long war exhausted the resources of the Netherlands. Increasingly Britain and France took over the position of the Netherlands and started to dominate world trade.

● The Netherlands in the 19th century

At the end of the 18th century Europe was thrown into turmoil by the French Revolution. The French invaded The Netherlands in 1795 and founded the Batavian Republic. In 1806 Napoleon made his brother Louis king of the Netherlands, but in the end the brothers fell out and Louis was forced to abdicate in 1810 and The Netherlands was absorbed into the French Empire.

However by 1813 Napoleon was facing defeat and in that year William of Orange whom was is exile in England returned to the Netherlands and in 1814 he was made King William I. In 1815 Belgium and The Netherlands were joined together as one country under King William I. However the two countries were too different to be united and 1830 the Belgians rebelled against Dutch rule and in 1839 the great powers forced William I to give the people of Belgium the independence they longed for.

William I died in 1840, his son who succeeded the crown in1848 introduced a new liberal constitution. For the rest of the 19th century the Netherlands was a prosperous and stable country. However not everybody has his or her share in the prosperity. Some industrial growth took place, (In 1839 a railway was opened from Haarlem to Amsterdam) but work conditions in 19th century factories in the Netherlands were terrible, and inhumane.

● The Netherlands in the 20th century

During the First World War The Netherlands remained neutral and in the end the last German

Emperor and King of Prussia William II, fled to the Netherlands in 1918 and was granted asylum there.

During the 1930s, like the rest of the world, the Netherlands suffered from the Great Depression and there was mass unemployment. Yet despite the depression, living standards rose during the 1920s and 1930s.

When the Second World War began, Dutch again chose to remain neutral but soon was forced to face the reality of war, as 10 May Hitler's Germany started the invasion of the Netherlands. On 14 May, 1940 Nazi Germany cowardly bombed Rotterdam and The Netherlands was forced to surrender to avoid more casualties of it citizens. Her Majesty Queen Wilhelmina and important members of the government managed to escaped to the United kingdom, where she established a government in exile to coordinate the resistance against Nazi Germany.

During World War II the Netherlands suffered terribly. Thousands of Dutch men were deported to work in Germany and 23,000 people who resisted the Nazis were shot. The worst suffering was during the Winter of Hunger in 1944-1945 when the Germans looted the Netherlands of food, reducing the people to near starvation. Furthermore the Nazis murdered a huge number of Jews. In 1940 about 140,000 Jews lived in The Netherlands but less than 25,000 survived. After the liberation of the Netherlands by the allied forces, the Netherlands recovered from the war and a new welfare state was created. In 1949 the Dutch colony of Indonesia became independent and was followed by Suriname in 1975. Meanwhile the Netherlands was a founder member of the EU in 1957. In 1999 the Netherlands joined the Euro.

● The Netherlands in the 21st century

Like the rest of the world, the Netherlands got its fair share of the financial crises in 2009 but it soon recovered. Today the Netherlands is a highly developed capitalist country and one of the top ten economies in Western Europe, it also the second most important agricultural exporter in the world (the USA being number one) and one of the countries with the highest NHI (National Happiness Index) in the world.

Dutch society with its population of 17 million inhabitants is a patchwork of different ethnic groups: in addition to the native Dutch population, there are many other ethnic groups from Indonesia, Turkey, Suriname, Morocco, the Caribbean, Asia and other regions.

※ 地理位置

荷兰是西欧的一个国家，它的北面和西面濒临北海，东面和南面分别与比利时和德国接壤，在海上疆域还与法国和英国共享海上边界。

荷兰是一个低地国家，其领土的四分之一都位于海平面以下，面积为41 543平方公里，仅比瑞士的41 285平方公里略大一些，大约相当于美国南卡罗来纳州的一半。

荷兰的属地过去由加勒比海的阿鲁巴岛和荷属安的列斯群岛组成，但在2010年10月10日，荷属安的列斯群岛已被解散，其部分岛屿在荷兰王国内获得了一个新的身份地位；库拉索岛和圣马丁岛现在是自治国家，但仍然属于荷兰王国；而美丽迷人的博奈尔群岛、圣尤斯特歇斯岛和萨巴岛则已成为荷兰的特别行政区。

※ 经济

荷兰有着相当发达的经济，几个世纪以来都在欧洲经济中扮演着重要的角色。荷兰多年以来也一直是商业发展最好的国家之一。自16世纪开始，航运、渔业、农业、贸易和银行业一直是荷兰经济的主导部门，这在很大程度上归功于荷兰高度发达的自由经济。

荷兰主要的贸易伙伴是德国、比利时、英国、美国、法国、意大利、中国和俄罗斯联邦。荷兰属于世界领先的10个重要出口国之一。其他主要的工业包括化工、冶金、机械、电器、贸易、服务业和旅游业。

根据库肯霍夫郁金香公园的信息提示，荷兰郁金香球茎出口份额排名第一的是美国，在2016年已经达到1.1亿欧元，对中国出口列居第五位，为4200万欧元。

荷兰的农业高度发达并且机械化，对国际出口依存度极高。农业部门雇用了大约4%的荷兰劳动力，但却为食品加工工业创造了大量的盈余，占荷兰出口总值的21%。荷兰在全球农产品出口额中排名第二，仅次于美国。

※ 历史

● 古代与中世纪的荷兰

大约在公元前5000年，荷兰就出现了农耕活动。起初，农民制造工具和石制武器，但到了公元前1900年以后，青铜器具开始被人们运用。公元前750年左右，人们开始使用铁器。

在公元前1世纪，罗马人征服了现在属于比利时和荷兰南部的地区，修建道路，建造了城镇。但是荷兰北部地区却没有被他们成功占据。在公元4世纪晚期，罗马帝国开始瓦解，罗马人从这一地区撤退并把荷兰留给日耳曼部落、法兰克人、撒克逊人和弗里斯兰人。公元8世纪，法兰克人征服了大部分地区，并将其置于他们的统治之下。与此同时，这个地区皈依了基督教，尽管并不是所有的部落都愿意皈依新的宗教。例如，弗里斯兰人在754年杀死了传教士圣卜尼法斯，也正因此，其被罗马天主教认为是殉道者。

公元768年，伟大的查理曼大帝成为法兰克人的统治者，在欧洲建立起一个伟大的帝国。在他的统治下，荷兰被划分为不同的州，每一个州都由一名伯爵进行统治。当查理曼大帝在814年去世时，他的帝国被分成了三个部分，大致上是现代的法国、德国以及中间的地带。开始，荷兰是帝国中间区域的一部分，但在公元925年被并入到了德意志帝国。

尽管荷兰和其他许多国家一样在公元9世纪和10世纪遭受到了残暴的维京人的袭击，但在中世纪，城镇生活和贸易依然兴盛起来。14世纪的荷兰城镇，与其他地方依然享受自由。在15世纪期间，勃艮第公爵逐渐控制了该地区。

● 16世纪到18世纪的荷兰

最终，包括现在被称为荷兰的地区在内的低地国家成为哈布斯堡家族的财产。1555年，西班牙的腓力二世成为一个让人畏惧的荷兰的统治者。

此时，宗教改革尽管遭到严厉的暴力迫害，但却席卷了整个荷兰。加尔文主义，来自约翰·加尔文的教义在荷兰的许多城镇中广泛流传开来。1566年，加尔文主义者把很多教堂里的宗教艺术加以毁坏和摧残，这一运动被称为"破坏圣像运动"。

西班牙的腓力二世是个暴虐的统治者

这项运动激怒了腓力二世，他于1567年派遣其追随者亚尔伐（Alva）公爵率领军队压制高涨的加尔文主义，并下令公爵将国王的意志强加给那些不守规矩的地区的居民。亚尔伐成立了臭名昭著的"血腥委员会"，又或称"麻烦委员会"，审判并处死了参加1566年暴乱的人员超过12 000人。这激起了民众的愤怒，从而也导致了威廉·奥伦治亲王的崛起，他被称为"沉默的威廉"，成为荷兰自由斗争的捍卫者。1572年，威廉率领被称作"海上乞丐"（荷兰语叫作Geuzen）的海盗与西班牙人对抗。他们从海上起航，占领了荷兰的城镇。荷兰人成群结队地加入到了叛乱当中，西班牙同时展开了疯狂回击，一场可怕的战争随之而起。

这场战争促使了1579年乌得勒支同盟条约的签署，这是由七个低地国家签署的，1581年他们宣布从西班牙独立。1588年，他们成立了"荷兰共和国"。西班牙人当然不会允许这种事情发生，并且会努力坚守这一地区，于是在1584年威廉在代尔夫特被暗杀。在英国人支持荷兰的同时，西班牙也因为其海上无敌舰队在1588年被英国击败遭受到沉重的打击。腓力二世最终也于1598年去世。

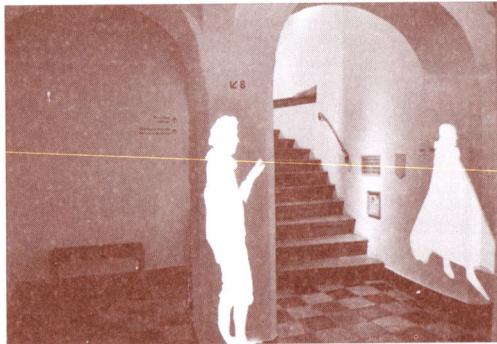

沉默的威廉就是在这里被刺杀，现今是亲王纪念馆，就在这个台阶处，纪念馆利用声光技术还原了当时的情景。图为亲王纪念馆荷兰国父被刺杀处。

在此期间，荷兰已成为了一个繁荣的贸易国家，这得益于从1609年到1621年与西班牙12年的休战。1602年，荷兰东印度公司成立。1621年，荷兰西印度公司成立。在1625年，荷兰人建立了新阿姆斯特丹（即现在的纽约）。1652年，他们还在南非建立了殖民地。在17世纪，荷兰水手进行了许多远洋航行，去探索未知的地区。1606年，威廉·扬茨发现了澳大利亚，后来被命名为"新荷兰"，1642年，阿贝尔·塔斯曼发现了塔斯马尼亚岛。

1648年，西班牙人最终签署了"威斯特伐利亚和约"，承认了荷兰的独立，这也在一定程度上有效地结束了欧洲的宗教斗争。

荷兰与英国的贸易竞争导致了1652～1654年、1665～1667年和1672～1674年的三次战争的爆发。荷兰的统治者威廉·奥伦治与英国达成和解并与英国的玛丽公主结婚，1688年威廉成为英国国王。

17世纪晚期是荷兰科学、艺术和哲学伟大的发展时期，但在18世纪，荷兰作为一个经济和政治强国却开始走向没落。荷兰人参与了西班牙对抗法国人的王位继承战争，这场旷日持久的战争耗尽了荷兰的资源。英国和法国逐步替代了荷兰的位置，开始主导世界贸易。

● 19世纪的荷兰

在18世纪末，欧洲陷入了法国大革命的混乱之中。法国于1795年入侵荷兰，建立了"巴达维亚共和国"。1806年，拿破仑让他的兄弟路易斯做了荷兰的国王，但最终兄弟俩分道扬镳，路易斯在1810年被迫退位，荷兰被并入法兰西帝国。

然而到了1813年，拿破仑面临失败，那一年流亡英国的威廉·奥兰治回到了荷兰，于1814年成为威廉一世。1815年，比利时和荷兰在威廉一世国王的统治下成为一个国家。然而两国国情不尽相同，难以团结一致，1830年比利时人开始对抗荷兰的统治，1839年国内强大的对抗力量威逼威廉一世给予比利时人民所渴望的独立。

威廉一世于1840年去世，他的儿子在1848年继承了王位，并提出了新的自由主义宪法。在19世纪剩余的时间里，荷兰繁荣而稳定。然而，并不是每一个人都能够坐享这种繁荣。工业出现增长——1839年，从哈勒姆到阿姆斯特丹的铁路开通，但是19世纪荷兰工厂的工作条件非常糟糕，而且不人道。

● 20世纪的荷兰

在第一次世界大战期间，荷兰保持了中立，末代德意志皇帝和普鲁士国王威廉二世于1918年逃往荷兰，并在那里获得了庇护。

在20世纪30年代，像世界其他地方一样，荷兰遭受了大萧条的摧残和影响，并且出现了大量失业的现象。然而尽管萧条，荷兰人的生活水平在20世纪20年代到30年代间仍旧有所提高和改善。

第二次世界大战开始之际，荷兰人再次选择了保持中立，但很快就被迫面对战争的现实，因为希特勒在1940年5月10日发动了对荷兰的袭击。5月14日，纳粹德国卑鄙地轰炸了鹿特丹，为了避免无辜平民在战争中伤亡，荷兰最终被迫投降。威廉敏娜女王和一些政府的重要成员设法逃到了英国，并在那里她建立了一个流亡政府，以组织协调抵抗纳粹德国。

第二次世界大战期间，荷兰经历了严重的磨难。数千名荷兰人被驱逐到德国进行辛苦劳作，23 000名反抗纳粹组织的人员被枪杀。最严重的苦难发生在1944年至1945年的饥荒期间，当时德国人劫掠了荷兰的食物，使人们徘徊在饥饿的生死边缘。此外，纳粹还杀害了大量犹太人。1940年，生活在荷兰的犹太人约有14万，但只有不到25 000人幸免于难。被盟军解放之后，荷兰从战争中逐步复原，重新建立起一个新的福利国家。1949年，原荷兰殖民地印度尼西亚独立，紧随其后，苏里南在1975年也独立。彼时，荷兰在1957年成为欧盟的创始成员国。1999年，荷兰加入了欧元区。

● 21世纪的荷兰

和世界上其他地区一样，荷兰在2009年的经济衰退中遭受到了重创，但很快就恢复了元气。今天的荷兰是一个高度发达的资本主义国家，是西方十大经济体之一，也是世界上第二大农产品出口国（美国是世界上最大的农产品出口国）和世界上国家幸福指数最高的国家之一。

除了本土荷兰人之外，来自印度尼西亚、土耳其、苏里南、摩洛哥、加勒比和其他地区的民族共同构成了荷兰的1 700万人口。

Tijd voor Nederlands 荷兰语时间

● 单词+短语

荷 Nederland	荷 land	荷 overheid
英 the Netherlands	英 country	英 government
译 尼德兰（荷兰）	译 国家	译 政府
荷 openbaar vervoer	荷 gisteren/vandaag/morgen	荷 lente (voorjaar)/zomer/herfst (najaar)/winter
英 public transport	英 yesterday/today /tomorrow	英 spring/summer/autumn/winter
译 公共交通	译 昨天/今天/明天	译 春/夏/秋/冬
荷 klein/groot	荷 koud/warm	荷 nat/droog
英 small/big	英 cold/warm	英 wet/dry
译 小的/大的	译 冷的/暖的	译 潮湿的/干燥的
荷 mooi	荷 weer	荷 regenen
英 beautiful/ good/nice/fine/ pretty	英 weather	英 rain
译 漂亮/好的	译 天气	译 下雨

● 例句

荷 De Nederlandse overheid zit in Den Haag.	荷 Het openbaar vervoer in Nederland is erg handig.
英 The Dutch government is in The Hague.	英 The public transport in the Netherlands is very convenient.
译 荷兰政府位于海牙。	译 荷兰的公共交通非常方便。
荷 De lente in Nederland is zeer prettig.	荷 De winter in Nederland is koud en nat.
英 Spring in the Netherlands is very comfortable.	英 The Netherlands often rains.
译 荷兰的春天非常舒适。	译 荷兰的冬天又冷又湿。
荷 Het is mooi weer vandaag.	荷 In Nederland regent het vaak.
英 It's nice weather today.	英 Winter in the Netherlands is cold and wet.
译 今天天气不错！	译 荷兰经常下雨。

10

2. 人口和宗教
Population and Religion

※ Population

The Netherlands is the 68th most populated country in the world, and as of the end of 2017, it has a population of more than17,000,000, and although many people consider the Netherlands a calm and quiet country, many Dutch people consider their country busy and crowded. The Netherlands is the thirty-first most densely populated country in the world. The 17,000,000 Dutch men, women and children are concentrated on an area of 41,526 km²; this means that the country has a population density of 409 per km².

The Netherlands is at an ageing stage of the population. Furthermore, life expectancy has increased because of developments in medicine, and in addition to this, the Netherlands has seen increasing immigration. During the first six months of 2017 about 100 thousand immigrants settled in the Netherlands, about the same as in the same period in 2016. A total of 69 thousand people emigrated away from the Netherlands. Among the immigrants, the number of new asylum seekers from war-torn areas such as Syria, Iran, Libya, etc., decreased. The most immigrants mainly came from Asia, followed by Europe. The number of Asian immigrants dropped from 19,500 in the first half of 2016 to 15 thousand of 2017. The number of immigrants from other European countries increased from 8,500 to 12 thousand. Among the European immigrants, particularly the number of people from newer EU states like Bulgaria, Romania, Latvia and Lithuania increased.

According to Eurostat, in 2010 there were 1.8 million foreign-born residents in the Netherlands, corresponding to 11.1% of the total population. Of these, 1.4 million (8.5%) were born outside the EU and 0.428 million (2.6%) were born in another EU member state, those primarily being Belgium, Germany, Poland and the United Kingdom.

※ Religion

Over the years Dutch society has become increasingly secular. According to the government's Social Cultural Planning Bureau, church membership has declined in a steady pace from 76% in 1958 to 41% in 1995 and continues to decrease. Only about 26% of all members are active in their religious community. The Dutch Reformed Church, whose membership has declined by more than 50% since 1900, is the largest Protestant denomination and is strongest in the province of Drenthe, in neighbouring Groningen, and in Overijssel. Other reformed churches are particularly strong in Friesland and Zeeland. Roman Catholicics are mainly found in the south, this denomination of Christian belief is widespread in North Brabant and Limburg. Other Christian denominations include Baptist, Lutheran, and Remonstrant.

There were 850,000 Dutch residents who identified as muslim in 2006. Of this 38% were ethnic Turkish, 31% were Moroccan, 26% were other Asian/African, 4% were European (Non-

Dutch) and 1% were native Dutch. 40,000 of the Muslims were Pakistanis, 34,000 were Surinamese, 31,000 were Afghan and 27,000 were Iraqi. At the end of 2012 the Dutch Central Bureau of Statistics estimated the number of Muslims in 2010-2011 to be around 4% of the total Dutch population. Because of the influence of refugees from the Arab region in recent years, the number of inhabitants that consider themselves muslim will grow substantially.

Hinduism is a minority religion in the Netherlands, with around 215,000 adherents. Most of these are Indo-Surinamese. There are also sizable populations of Hindu immigrants from India and Sri Lanka. The Netherlands has an estimated 250,000 Buddhists or people strongly attracted to this religion, mainly ethnic Dutch people. There are about 45,000 Jews in the Netherlands.

※ Languages

The official language is Dutch, which is spoken by the vast majority of the inhabitants. Besides Dutch, West Frisian is recognised as a second official language in the northern province of Friesland.

The Netherlands has a tradition of learning foreign languages, formalised in Dutch education laws. Some 90% of the total population indicate they are able to converse in English, 70% in German, and 29% in French,

The Netherlands as an non-native speaking country has the highest English-proficiency in the world: narrowly beating Denmark and Sweden, according to the English Proficiency Index (EPI). Some nine in 10 Dutch people speak English as a second language. According to the EU language report (2012), 94 percent of Dutch people are able to speak two or more languages, well above the EU average of 54 percent. Taking into consideration that more than half of the population also speaks German, many Dutch people are able to speak at least three languages. The Netherlands belongs to the top countries where residents are more likely to learn a language at school, around 91 percent, and through conversation.

※ 人口

荷兰总人口数量居全球第68名，截止到2017年年底，荷兰的人口超过了1 700万，尽管很多人认为荷兰是一个宁静祥和的国家，但是许多荷兰人自己认为荷兰繁忙且拥挤。荷兰是世界上人口密度第31高的国家。1 700万的荷兰男男女女及儿童拥挤在这片41 526平方公里的土地上，其人口密度相当于每平方公里409人。

荷兰正处于人口老龄化的阶段。由于医药的发展和进步，人口的预期寿命增加了。另外，荷兰的移民人数也处在上升阶段。在2017年的前6个月内，大约有10万新移民移居到荷兰，与2016年同期大致相同，从荷兰移出的人数为69 000人。移民当中，来自叙利亚、伊朗、利比亚等战乱地区的新庇护人数有所减少。移民主要来自亚洲，其次才是欧洲。亚洲移民的人数从2016年上半年的19 500人下降到2017年上半年的15 000万人。来自其他欧洲国家的移民人数从8 500人增加到12 000人。在欧洲移民中，特别是来自保加利亚、罗马尼亚、拉脱维亚和立陶宛等欧盟国家的人数一直在增加。

根据欧盟统计局的数据，2010年荷兰居民中在国外出生的人数有180万，相当于总人口的11.1%。其中有140万人（8.5%）出生在欧盟以外的国家和地区，有42.8万人（2.6%）出生在其他欧盟成员国内，这些国家主要是比利时、德国、波兰和英国。

※ 宗教

在过去的许多年间，荷兰社会已经变得愈加世俗化。根据政府社会文化规划局的数据，荷兰教会成员的人数持续减少，信教人员的比例从1958年的76%下降到1995年的41%，并且这一比例仍在下降中。在宗教团体活动中较为活跃的成员大约只占26%。荷兰归正教会，荷兰最大的新教教派，在德伦特省、格罗宁根省和上艾瑟尔省是最强大的，自1900年以来，其教徒数量已经减少了50%以上。其他改革教堂在弗里斯兰和泽兰地区尤为强大。罗马天主教主要分布在南方，其信徒在北布拉班特省和林堡省广泛存在。其他的基督教派别还包括浸信会、路德宗和抗辩派。

图为鹿特丹市郊一处清真寺，这是荷兰穆斯林人口数目比较庞大的地区之一。

2006年，有85万荷兰居民自称是伊斯兰教教徒，其中38%是土耳其人、31%是摩洛哥人、26%来自亚洲和非洲地区、4%是非荷兰欧洲人、1%是荷兰本土人。信徒的人数中有40 000是巴基斯坦人，34 000苏里南人，31 000阿富汗人，还有27 000伊拉克人。荷兰中央统计局在2012年底估计，2010年到2011年的穆斯林人数约占荷兰总人口的4%。近几年由于受到阿拉伯地区难民问题的影响，荷兰穆斯林信徒的数量应该大有增加。

印度教是荷兰的少数民族宗教，大约有215 000万信徒。其中大部分是印度苏里南人，还有相当一部分是来自印度本土和斯里兰卡的印度教移民。据估计，荷兰的佛教徒大概有250 000万，其中包括一部分对此宗教充满兴趣的本土荷兰人。而在荷兰的犹太人约有45 000名。

※ 语言

荷兰的官方语言是荷兰语，这也是绝大多数居民所使用的语言。除了荷兰语之外，弗里斯兰语被认为是荷兰北部弗里斯兰省的第二官方语言。

荷兰有学习外语的传统，这在荷兰的教育法中有明文规定。大约90%的荷兰人表示自己可以熟练使用英语交流，70%的人会说德语，会说法语的人占29%。

据英语水平指数（English Proficiency Index, EPI）的研究表明：在母语非英语的国家中，荷兰以微弱优势领先丹麦和瑞典，是世界上英语水平最高的国家，大约有90%的荷兰人把英语作为第二语言。根据2012年欧盟语言报告，94%的荷兰人能够说两种或两种以上的语言，远高于欧盟54%的平均水平。考虑到一半以上的人口还会讲德语，因此很多荷兰人至少能说三门语言。从居民有更大概率在学校通过日常交流学成一门语言这方面来看，荷兰算得上顶尖国家，91%的人都能由此途径学习语言。

13

Tijd voor Nederlands 荷兰语时间

● 单词+短语

荷 meneer/mevrouw 英 sir/madam 译 先生/女士	荷 Nederlands 英 Dutch 译 荷兰语	荷 gezin 英 family 译 家庭
荷 man/vrouw 英 man or husband/woman or wife 译 男人（丈夫）/女人（妻子）	荷 kind 英 child 译 孩子	荷 zoon/dochter 英 son/daughter 译 儿子/女儿
荷 bedankt/dank u wel 英 thanks/thank you 译 谢谢/谢谢你	荷 komen 英 come 译 来	荷 wonen 英 live 译 居住
荷 spreken 英 speak 译 说	荷 vragen 英 ask 译 问	荷 begrijpen 英 understand 译 明白
荷 getrouwd 英 married 译 已婚的	荷 lang 英 long/tall 译 长的/高的	

● 例句

荷 Ik ben Zhang Hua, ik kom uit China. 英 I am Zhang Hua, I am from China. 译 我是张华，我来自中国。	荷 Nederlanders zijn erg lang. 英 The Dutch are very tall. 译 荷兰人很高。
荷 Dank u wel! Veel plezier! 英 Thank you very much! Have fun! 译 非常感谢！玩儿得开心点儿！	荷 Ik begrijp het, ik spreek een beetje Nederlands. 英 I understand, I speak a little Dutch. 译 我能理解，我会说一点儿荷兰语。
荷 Ik kom uit een groot gezin, en jij? 英 I come from a big family, and you? 译 我来自一个大家庭，你呢？	荷 Ik ben getrouwd, ik woon in Beijing met mijn vrouw. 英 I am married, I live in Beijing with my wife. 译 我结婚了，我和我的妻子住在北京。
荷 Ik heb twee kinderen, een zoon en een dochter. 英 I have two children , a son and a daughter. 译 我有两个孩子，一个儿子，一个女儿。	荷 Hallo meneer! Mag ik wat vragen? 英 Hello sir! May I ask you something? 译 先生您好！我能问您点儿事吗？

第二章
Chapter 2

创新型的荷兰

The Innovative Netherlands

*T*he Netherlands is an innovative country, which has a lot to do with the support of the government in addition to its own conditions. The Netherlands is a relatively small country with one of the highest population densities in the world, which requires the Dutch to take a different approach to innovation. The government supports companies that develop innovative products through tax benefits, innovation credit and grants. There are also a number of EU grant schemes for innovation. Innovative businesses can help develop solutions to major social issues like global food security, ageing populations or life-threatening diseases. By developing new products they can also gain access to new markets. Innovation boosts economic growth and creates jobs. That's why the government provides financial support for innovative enterprises. So businesses can bring their innovative products and services onto the market more quickly.

The Netherlands' innovative top sectors are among the world's best. The government wants to further strengthen their international position. The Netherlands has nine top sectors: Horticulture and Propagation Materials, Agri-food, Water, Life Sciences and Health, Chemicals, High-tech, Energy, Logistics, Creative Industries.

荷兰是一个创新型的国家，除了自身的条件外，它与政府的支持有很大的关系。荷兰是一个相对较小的国家，却是世界上人口密度最高的国家之一，这就要求荷兰采取不同的创新方法。政府通过税收优惠、创新信贷和赠款对开发创新产品的公司进行支持。另外还有欧盟的一些创新资助计划。创新企业可以帮助解决诸如全球粮食安全、人口老龄化或威胁生命的疾病等重大社会问题。通过开发新产品，他们也可以进入新的市场。创新促进经济增长，创造就业机会，这就是为什么政府为创新型企业提供财政支持的原因，这样一来，企业可以更快地将他们的创新产品和服务推向市场。

荷兰的顶级创新产业是世界上最好的，政府希望进一步加强其在国际中的地位和影响力。荷兰有九个顶级行业：园艺和繁殖材料、食品、水、生命科学与健康、化学制品、高科技、能源、物流、创意产业。

1. 发明与创造
Invention and Creation

The Netherlands has had a considerable part in the making of modern society. The Netherlands and its people have made numerous seminal contributions to the world's civilisation, especially in science, technology and engineering, economics and finance, cartography and geography, exploration and navigation, law and jurisprudence, thought and philosophy, medicine and agriculture. The Dutch, in spite of their relatively small number, have a significant history of invention, innovation, discovery and exploration.

荷兰在现代社会的建设中占有相当大的份额。荷兰人民为世界文明尤其是科学技术与工程、经济与金融、制图与地理、勘探与导航、法律与法学、思想与哲学、医学与农业等领域做出了许多开创性的贡献。尽管荷兰人口数量相对较少，但却拥有非常重要的发明、创新、发现和探索历史。

Agriculture 农业

The Netherlands is a small country with limited land area for production, but the Netherlands is one of the world's leading exporters of agricultural products. The Dutch agricultural sector is highly mechanised, and has a strong focus on international exports. It employs about 4% of the Dutch labour force but produces large surpluses for the food-processing industry and accounts for 21 percent of the Dutch total export value. The Dutch rank first in the European Union and second worldwide in value of agricultural exports, behind only the United States [The data source: The Economist. Sevenum: The Economist Group. 23 August 2014. Retrieved 29 August 2014.] with exports earning €80.7 billion in 2014,up from €75.4 billion in 2012.

There was a time, that the Netherlands supplied one quarter of all of the world's exported tomatoes, and now one-third of the world's exports of chilis, tomatoes and cucumbers go through the country. The Netherlands is also the world's largest producer of cheeses and a major potato producer.

Aside from that, a significant portion of Dutch agricultural exports consists of fresh-cut plants, flowers, and flower bulbs, with the Netherlands exporting two-thirds of the world's total. And the agricultural contributions of the Netherlands don't end here.

※ Orange-coloured carrot (16th century)

The orange carrot is probably the most common, but originally the colour of the carrot was way more colourful. They were black, purple, white, brown, red and yellow. Probably orange too, but this was not the dominant colour. Orange-coloured carrots appeared in the Netherlands in the 16th century. Dutch farmers in Hoorn bred this colour carrot. They succeeded by cross-breeding pale yellow carrots with red carrots. It is also very likely that Dutch horticulturists actually found an orange rooted mutant variety and then worked on its development through selective breeding to make the plant consistent. Through successive hybridisation the orange colour intensified and the orange carrot became on our table the most dominant species of carrots.

※ Flower auctions

Holland is famous for its exports of cut flowers, plants and bulbs. More than 60% of the complete world trade in flowers and plants takes place through flower auctions in Holland. So it is not strange that Royal FloraHolland, established more than 100 years ago, is the biggest flower auction in the world. Royal FloraHolland, has several auctions spread across the country: Aalsmeer (the biggest), Rijnsburg, Naaldwijk and Eelde. Also auction Rhein-Maas (Herongen, Germany) belongs to FloraHolland and is a collaboration with Landgard.

Every workday around 43 million flowers and 4.8 million plants from almost 50 countries are being sold on the flower auctions in Holland. This is almost 95% of the total sales in the country. To do this, the companies located on the auctions use 12 million flower buckets, 5.5 million plant trays and 800,000 flower boxes. In total around 650 flower and plant wholesale and exporter companies are located in Holland, mainly located at FloraHolland (Aalsmeer). The flowers will be exported all across the world. For Holland, the biggest export country is Germany, followed by the United Kingdom, Italy, France, Belgium and Russia. But the flowers will also reach the Baltic states, the United Arab Emirates, USA, China and a lot more. Popular flowers in Holland are roses and tulips. Mainly in Noord-Holland there are many tulip growers and that's why the tulip is also one of the national symbols. More than 80% of the flowers are being exported to other countries.

A typical example. Growers harvest roses for export to the United States by mid-morning on any given day. By mid-afternoon, machines will have sorted the roses by as many as 200 varieties, and by the length of the stems. These roses are gathered, labelled for quality, and packed in uniform plastic tubs for transport. By 10 pm, the flowers arrive at the auction house where they are placed in cold storage overnight. The next morning at 4:30 am, they are transported to the collection hall, inspected, assigned lot numbers, and assembled onto "stapelwagens" or uniform carts for transport into the auction hall. The stapelwagens are then towed into the auction halls where their contents are auctioned, and the auction begins at 6:30 in the morning in auction rooms with up to 500 buyers. The computerised auction clocks in the room provide the buyers with information on the grower, product, unit of currency, quality, and minimum purchase necessary.

Once the auction is completed, each lot of flowers is tagged with a computer printout of the sale and distributed to the buyer's area in the auction house where they are repackaged and boxed for air or land transport (in case of distribution in mainland Europe). Flowers exported to New York are transported on a special eight-hour flight, which departs Schiphol airport at 7:10 pm and arrives in New York at 8:10 pm local time. The cargo is then unloaded, inspected, cleared by customs and shipped to nearby warehouses or to other wholesalers for distribution the next day. Thus roses from an Aalsmeer greenhouse can be sold in New York within 48 hours after they are cut.

※ Improved fruit variety—Belle de Boskoop/Elstar

Dutch exports of agricultural goods reached a record level of 91.7 bn euros in 2017, exceeding

the previous record in 2016 by more than 7 percent. This is reported by Statistics Netherlands (Dutch:CBS) and Wageningen Economic Research on the basis of joint research commissioned by the Ministry of Agriculture, Nature and Food Quality.

The Netherlands is the world's leading supplier of vegetables, dairy products, meat and fruit, has its roots in Dutch experimentation and innovation in agricultural technology. Unlike other agricultural exporters, the Netherlands is a small country with limited arable land, and the Dutch need to work on land production per unit area. China, for example, is the world's largest exporter of apples, but the average yield per unit is far lower than in the US and Europe, and even less than half of Brazil and Chile. The Netherlands has greatly improved the apple cultivation through cultivated in greenhouses and making use of dwarf rootstock, which greatly reduces the use of arable land area but at the same time greatly improving the average yield of fruit trees per unit area. According to the Statistics Netherlands (Dutch:CBS) : Between 1950 and 2015, the output of fruit and vegetables per square metre in the Netherlands has been growing. In 1950, the Netherlands produced six tons of apples per hectare, compared with 44 tons in 2015.

Here are two varieties of apples cultivated by the Dutch, among them Elstar is still very much welcomed in the European market.

Belle de Boskoop is an apple cultivar which, as its name suggests, originated in Boskoop, the Netherlands, where it began as a chance seedling in 1856.

There are many variants: Boskoop red, yellow or green. This rustic apple is firm, tart and fragrant. Greenish-gray tinged with red, the apple stands up well to cooking. Generally Boskoop varieties are very high in acid content and can contain more than four times the vitamin C of 'Granny Smith' or 'Golden Delicious'. This apple tree responds well to plenty of water and is very strong but cannot stand frost (fruits tend to burst) or dry soil. The apple stores well after harvest.

The Elstar apple is an apple cultivar that was first developed in the Netherlands in Elst in the 1950s by crossing Golden Delicious and Ingrid Marie apples. It quickly became popular, especially in Europe and was first introduced to America in 1972. It remains popular in Continental Europe, but less so in the United Kingdom.

The Elstar is a medium-sized apple whose skin is mostly red with yellow showing. The flesh is white, and has a soft, crispy texture. It may be used for cooking and is especially good for making apple sauce. In general, however, it is used in desserts due to its sweet flavour.

荷兰是一个小国家，耕地面积有限，但荷兰却是世界上最大的农产品出口国之一。荷兰的农业部门是高度机械化的，并且非常重视国际出口。荷兰的农业部门雇用了大约4%的荷兰劳动力，但却为食品加工工业生产了大量的盈余，占荷兰出口总值的21%。荷兰的农产品出口额在欧盟排名第一，在全球农业出口总值中排名第二，仅次于美国，出口额从2012年的754亿欧元增长到2014年的807亿欧元（数据来源：《经济学家》，检索2014年8月29日）。

曾经有一段时间，荷兰供应了世界上四分之一的西红柿出口，世界上的辣椒、西红柿和黄瓜出口量的三分之一都是来自于荷兰。荷兰也是世界上最大的奶酪生产国和最主要的土豆生产国。

除此之外，荷兰农业出口的很大一部分是由鲜活的绿植、花卉和鲜花球茎构成的，其出口量占世界上总出口量的三分之二。但荷兰在农业上的贡献还不止于此。

※ 橙色的胡萝卜（16世纪）

橙色的胡萝卜应该是最常见的了，但最初胡萝卜的颜色要鲜艳得多。胡萝卜有黑色的、紫色的，还有白色、褐色、红色和黄色的。当然还有可能是橙色，但它并不是主要的颜色。16世纪，荷兰出现了橙色的胡萝卜。这是由荷兰的农民培育出来的颜色，他们通过把淡黄色的胡萝卜和红色的胡萝卜进行杂交培育出了这种橙色的胡萝卜。也很有可能是荷兰的园艺家发现了一种橙色的变种，然后通过选择性育种来达到了植物的一致性。通过连续杂交，橙色特征得到强化，最终橙色胡萝卜成为世界各地人们餐桌上非常常见的一种食物。

※ 花卉拍卖行

荷兰花荷花卉拍卖行在荷兰有几处，在德国也有分支，市场上的大部分鲜花都是从这里分销出去的。图为分门别类准备包装的鲜花。

荷兰以出口切花、绿植和鲜花球茎而闻名。世界上60%以上的花卉和植物贸易都是通过荷兰的花卉拍卖行来完成的。因此，成立于100多年前的皇家荷兰花荷成为世界上最大的花卉拍卖行并不足为奇。荷兰花荷花卉拍卖行在荷兰全国范围内有几场大的拍卖会：最大的有阿斯米尔鲜花拍卖市场、艾恩斯堡、纳尔德韦克和埃尔德鲜花拍卖市场。另外，德国赫隆根的莱茵-马斯拍卖市场也隶属于荷兰皇家荷兰花荷花卉拍卖行，与德国兰德花草公司是合作关系。

每个工作日，来自近50个国家的大约4 300万朵鲜花和480万株的植物会在荷兰的花卉拍卖行上被拍卖，这几乎是全国销售总额的95%。为此，在拍卖会上的公司要使用1 200万个花篮、550万个植物托盘和80万个花箱。大约有650个花卉植物批发和出口公司驻扎在荷兰，主要位于阿斯米尔。这些被拍卖的花卉将被出口到世界各地。对荷兰来说，最大的出口国是德国，其次是英国、意大利、法国、比利时和俄罗斯。再往远处，这些花卉也会销到波罗的海国家、阿拉伯联合酋长国、美国、中国等。在荷兰比较畅销的花是玫瑰和郁金香。在荷兰北部地区有许多郁金香种植者，这也是为什么它是荷兰国家的标志之一。这些种植的鲜花中有超过80%都被出口到了其他国家。

举个例子。比如随便某一天的清晨，花卉种植者要采摘玫瑰以出口到美国。在下午三点钟左右，机器将会按照茎的长度把多达200个种类各异的玫瑰进行分拣。这些玫瑰被收集起来，贴上质量标签，然后用统一的塑料桶打包运输。到晚上十点，这些鲜花会被送至拍卖行，然后放置在冷藏室里过夜。第二天早上四点半，玫瑰被运送到采集大厅，接受检查，分配批号，然后装配到堆放车或统一的推车上，以便运送到拍卖大厅。接着，堆放车被拖进拍卖大厅，人们将装配好的鲜花进行拍卖，拍卖在早上六点半开始，拍卖大厅里的买家能达到500家。正式拍卖时，大厅的电子钟会为买家提供与鲜花相关的信息，包括鲜花种植商、拍卖产品、货币单位、花卉质量和最低购买量等。

一旦拍卖完成，每批鲜花都被贴上电脑打印出来的标签，并分发给拍卖行的买家所在的区域，在那里鲜花被重新包装并装箱以供空运或陆路运输（在欧洲大陆销售）。出口到纽约的鲜花是通过专门的"八小时航班"来运输的，该航班将于荷兰当地时间晚上七点十分离开史基浦机场，然后在美国当地时间晚上八点十分抵达纽约。鲜花抵达之后进行货物卸载、检查、海关清关，然后再运送到附近的仓库或其他批发商那里，以便第二天进行分发分销。整套流程下来，来自阿斯米尔温室的玫瑰在被采摘后的四十八小时内就可以在纽约出售了。

※ 水果改良Belle de Boskoop/Elstar

荷兰的农产品出口在2017年达到创纪录的917亿欧元，超过2016年的出口纪录的7%。这是由荷兰统计局（CBS）和瓦格宁根经济研究所根据农业、自然和食品质量部委托进行的联合研究报告。

荷兰是世界上领先的蔬菜、乳制品、肉类和水果供应商，其根源在于荷兰的试验和农业技术创新。与其他传统的农业出口国不同，荷兰是一个耕地有限的小国，荷兰需要在单位面积的土地生产上做努力。举个例子，中国是世界上最大的苹果出口国，但每单位面积的平均产量远低于美国和欧洲国家，即使跟巴西和智利相比，中国也不及它们的一半。荷兰通过温室栽培和矮化砧木大大改善了苹果的种植，减少了耕地面积的使用，同时大大提高了果树的单位面积平均产量。根据荷兰统计局的报告：1950年到2015年间，荷兰每平方米的水果和蔬菜产量一直在增长。1950年，荷兰每公顷土地产出6吨苹果，而2015年的单位公顷产量为44吨。

这里是两种由荷兰人培育出来的苹果品种，其中埃尔斯塔尔在欧洲市场至今都非常受欢迎。

博斯科普美女果是一个苹果品种，顾名思义，它起源于荷兰的博斯科普，是在1856年很偶然繁殖出来的果树幼苗。

博斯科普美女果有许多变种，红色博斯科普、黄色博斯科普或绿色博斯科普。这种平淡无奇的苹果果肉很结实、味酸但却芬芳。灰绿色的果实微微带着点儿红，用于烹制果酱和甜品非常好。博斯科普的酸含量通常非常高，其果实含有的维生素C可以达到澳洲青果或金冠苹果（又名黄金帅、黄香蕉等）维生素C含量的四倍以上。这种果树喜水，树木强壮，但遇霜冻果实会裂，也不适应干燥的土壤，收获后储藏非常便利。

埃尔斯塔尔也是一种苹果品种，是20世纪50年代在荷兰的埃尔斯特由金冠苹果和英格丽玛丽苹果杂交培育出来的。埃尔斯塔尔很快就在市场中流通起来，特别是在欧洲，并于1972年首次引入美国。时至今日，埃尔斯塔尔果在欧洲大陆仍然很受消费者的欢迎，但在英国的状况要差些。

埃尔斯塔尔果大小中等，果实表皮的颜色主要是红黄色。果肉呈白色，口感绵柔而酥脆。埃尔斯塔尔果可用来于烹饪，特别适合制作苹果酱。但是因为果实口感偏甜，所以人们多用它来做甜点。

Communication and Multimedia 通信和多媒体

※ Compact cassette (1963)

For many people born after the 90s, compact cassette can be a stranger, but for anyone born in the 70s or 80s this was the most important entertainment partner of their youth.

The Compact Audio Cassette (CAC) or Musicassette (MC), also commonly called the cassette tape or simply tape or cassette, is an analogue magnetic tape recording format for audio recording and playback. It was released by Philips in 1963. Compact cassettes come in two forms, either already containing content as a pre-recorded cassette, or as a fully recordable "blank" cassette. Both forms are reversible by the user.

From the early 1970's until the late 1990's, cassette tape was one of the two most popular pre-recorded music storage formats during which its rival changed from the original compact disc to the later CD. In Western Europe and North America, the market for cassettes declined sharply after its peak in the late 1980's. Most of the major U.S. music companies had discontinued production of cassette tapes by 2003.

※ Compact disc (1982)

Compact disc (CD) is a digital optical disc data storage format that was co-developed by Philips and Sony and released in 1982. The format was originally developed to store and play only sound recordings but was later adapted for storage of data (CD-ROM). The first commercially available Audio CD player, the Sony CDP-101, was released in October 1982 in Japan.

At the time of the technology's introduction in 1982, a CD could store much more data than a personal computer hard drive, which would typically hold up to 10 MB. In 2004, worldwide sales of audio CDs, CD-ROMs and CD-Rs reached about 30 billion discs. By 2007, 200 billion CDs had been sold worldwide. By 2010, hard drives commonly offered as much storage space as a thousand CDs, while their prices had plummeted to commodity level.

From the early 2000's CDs were increasingly being replaced by other forms of digital storage and distribution, with the result that by 2010 the number of audio CDs being sold in the U.S. had dropped about 50% from their peak; however, they remained one of the primary distribution methods for the music industry.

※ DVD (1995) Blu-ray (2006)

DVD (an abbreviation of "digital video disc" or "digital versatile disc") is a digital optical disc storage format invented and developed by Philips and Sony in 1995. The medium can store any kind of digital data and is widely used for software and other computer files as well as video programs watched using DVD players. DVDs offer higher storage capacity than compact discs while having the same dimensions.

In 2006, two new formats called HD DVD and Blu-ray Disc were released as the successor to the DVD. HD DVD competed unsuccessfully with Blu-ray Disc in the format war of 2006–2008. A dual layer HD DVD can store up to 30 GB and a dual layer Blu-ray disc can hold up to 50 GB. By 2009, 85% of stores were selling Blu-ray Discs. A high-definition television and appropriate connection cables are also required to take advantage of Blu-ray disc.

DVDs are also facing competition from video on demand services. With increasing numbers of homes having high speed Internet connections, many people now have the option to either rent or buy video from an online service, and view it by streaming it directly from that service's servers, meaning that the customer need not have any form of permanent storage media for video at all. By 2017, digital streaming services had overtook the sales of DVDs and Blu-rays for the first time.

※ LED lighting (2009)

Before the introduction of LED lamps, three types of lamps were used for the bulk of general (white) lighting:

Incandescent lights, which produce light with a glowing filament heated by electric current. These are very inefficient, having a luminous efficacy of 10-17 lumens/W.

Fluorescent lamps, which produce ultraviolet light by a glow discharge between two electrodes in a low pressure tube of mercury vapour. These are more efficient than incandescent lights, and are widely used for residential and office lighting. However their mercury content makes them a hazard to the environment.

Metal halide lamps, which produce light by an arc between two electrodes in an atmosphere of argon, mercury and other metals, and iodine or bromine. These were the most efficient white electric lights before LEDs, are not used for residential lighting, but for commercial and industrial wide area lighting, and outdoor security lights and streetlights.

The first high-brightness blue LED was demonstrated by Shuji Nakamura of Nichia Corporation in 1994. The existence of blue LEDs and high-efficiency LEDs led to the development of the first 'white LED'. China further boosted LED research and development in 1995 and demonstrated its first LED Christmas tree in 1998.

In the USA, the Energy Independence and Security Act (EISA) of 2007 authorised the Department of Energy (DOE) to establish the Bright Tomorrow Lighting Prize competition, known as the "L Prize", designed to challenge industry to develop replacements for 60 W incandescent lamps and PAR 38 halogen lamps.

Philips Lighting ceased research on compact fluorescents in 2008 and began devoting the bulk of its research and development budget to solid-state lighting. On 24 September 2009, Philips Lighting North America became the first to submit lamps in the category to replace the standard 60 W A-19 "Edison screw fixture" light bulb, with a design based on their earlier "Ambient LED" consumer product. On 3 August 2011, DOE awarded the prize in the 60 W replacement category to a Philips' LED lamp after 18 months of extensive testing.

※ 盒式磁带（1963年）

对于许多20世纪90年代以后出生的人来说，盒式磁带可能是一个陌生的事物，但对于20世纪70或80年代出生的人来说，这可是这一代人们年少时最重要的娱乐伙伴。

Compact Audio Cassette（简称CAC）或Musicassette（简称MC）通常被称为盒式磁带或磁带，是一种模拟磁带录音格式的音频录制和播放设备，它是由荷兰的飞利浦公司于1963年开发的。盒式磁带有两种形式，一种是已经包含内容的预先录制的磁带，另一种是完全可记录的"空白"盒式磁带。这两种形式的磁带都可以逆向使用（指消除已经灌入音频内容的录制磁带到空白状态，和将空白磁带灌入音频内容）。

从20世纪70年代初到90年代末，盒式磁带是两种最流行的预录音乐存储格式之一，在市场竞争中，对手从原来的光盘变成了后来的CD。在西欧和北美，盒式磁带市场在20世纪80年代末达到高峰后急剧下降。到2003年，美国大多数主要音乐公司已经停止生产盒式磁带。

23

※ 光盘（1982年）

光盘，也就是我们常说的CD，是一种数字光盘数据存储格式，由飞利浦和索尼公司在1982年共同研发。这种格式最初是用来存储和播放录音的，后来被改编并用于存储数据。第一个商用音频CD播放机，索尼CDP-101，于1982年10月在日本发布。

在1982年这种技术刚推出之际，CD可以存储比个人电脑硬盘还要多的数据，通常可以达到10MB。2004年的时候，全球音频CD、CD-ROM和CD-R的销量达到了300亿张。到2007年，全球已经售出了2 000亿张CD。但到了2010年，硬盘驱动器通常提供的存储空间相当于1 000张CD，而它们的价格却已经跌到了商品级水平。

从21世纪初开始，CD逐渐被其他形式的数字存储和分配所取代，在2010年，在美国销售的音频CD的数量已经从峰值下降了约50%，但即便如此，它们仍然是音乐产业的主要发行方式之一。

※ DVD（1995年）蓝光（2006年）

在20上世纪末，CD和DVD这种新型产物可谓给我们带来了难以忘怀的娱乐生活，而它们都是飞利浦的发明。

DVD是"数字视频光盘"或"数字多功能光盘"的缩写，是由飞利浦公司和索尼公司在1995年发明并生产的数字光盘存储格式。这种介质可以存储任何类型的数字数据，并广泛应用于软件和其他计算机文件以及使用DVD播放器观看的视频节目。具有相同尺寸的DVD可提供比CD光盘更高的存储容量。

在2006年，又有两种新格式的高清光盘（HD DVD）和蓝光光盘作为DVD的后继版被发布。HD DVD在2006～2008年与蓝光光盘的格式大战中竞争失败。双层HD DVD最多可以存储30GB，双层蓝光光盘最多则可以容纳50GB。到了2009年，85%的商店都在销售蓝光光盘。高清电视和匹配的连接电缆也需要利用蓝光光盘。

DVD也面临着来自视频点播服务的竞争。随着现在拥有高速互联网连接的家庭数量不断增加，很多人可以选择租用或购买来自在线视频的服务，并通过直接从该服务的服务器流式传输来查看，这意味着客户不需要任何形式的永久存储视频的媒体。2017年，数字流媒体的服务首次超越了DVD和蓝光光盘的销售。

※ LED照明技术（2009年）

在引入LED灯之前，一般（白色）照明主要使用三种灯：

首先是白炽灯，通过电流加热发光灯丝产生光。但这些效率非常低，仅具有10～17流明/瓦的发光率。

第二种是荧光灯，它通过汞蒸气低压管中两个电极之间的辉光放电产生紫外线。这种荧光灯比白炽灯更有效，广泛用于住宅和办公室照明。但是，荧光灯的汞含量会使其对环境造成危害。

还有一种是金属卤化物灯，在氩气、汞和其他金属以及碘或溴的大气中，通过两个电极之间的电弧产生光。这种灯是LED之前效率最高的白光电灯，但它们并不用于住宅照明，只用于商业和工业领域的大面积照明以及户外安全灯和路灯。

1994年，日亚公司的中村修二首先演示了高亮度蓝光LED。蓝光LED和高效率LED的存在促成了第一个白光LED的发展。中国在1995年进一步推动了LED研发，并于1998年展示了其首款LED圣诞树。

在美国，2007年的能源独立与安全法案（EISA）授权能源部（DOE）建立"光明未来照明奖"竞赛，称为"L奖"，旨在挑战开发60瓦白炽灯和PAR 38卤素灯的替代品。

飞利浦公司照明系统在2008年停止了对紧凑型荧光灯的研究，开始将其大部分研发经费用于固态照明。2009年9月24日，飞利浦照明北美公司成为第一家提交此类灯具的公司，以其早期的"Ambient LED"消费产品为基础的设计取代标准60 WA-19"爱迪生螺丝灯具"灯泡。 2011年8月3日，经过18个月的广泛测试，美国能源部将该奖项颁发给了飞利浦设计的用于替换60瓦白炽灯LED灯。

Economy and Finance 经济与金融

※ Dutch East India Company

The Dutch East India Company (Dutch :Verenigde Oostindische Compagnie, or VOC), founded in 1602, was originally established as a chartered company to trade with India and Indianised Southeast Asian countries, when the Dutch government granted it a 21-year monopoly on the Dutch spice trade.

※ First capitalist nation-state (foundations of modern capitalism) —17th century

Economic historians consider the Netherlands as the first predominantly capitalist nation. The development of European capitalism began among the city-states of Italy, Flanders, and the Baltic. It spread to the European interstate system, eventually resulting in the world's first capitalist nation-state, the Dutch Republic of the seventeenth century. The Dutch were the first to develop capitalism on a nationwide scale (as opposed to earlier city states). The economic primacy of the Dutch Republic in the 17th century is considered by many a world-systems theorists as the first capitalist hegemony in history world history.

There are now stock markets in virtually every developed and most developing economies, with the world's largest markets being in the United States, United Kingdom, Japan, India, China, Canada, Germany (Frankfurt Stock Exchange), France, South Korea and the Netherlands.

※ 荷兰东印度公司

荷兰东印度公司（荷兰语：Verenigde Oostindische Compagnie，简称VOC）成立于1602年，最初是作为一家与印度和东南亚国家进行贸易而成立的特许公司，当时荷兰政府授权它可以在21年的时间内独占荷兰的香料贸易。

※ 第一个资本主义民族国家（现代资本主义的基础）——17世纪

经济历史学家通常认为荷兰是第一个主要的资本主义国家。欧洲资本主义的发展开始于意大利、佛兰德斯和波罗的海地区的城邦。它蔓延到欧洲的洲际体系，最终导致了世界上第一个资本主义民族国家的形成，即17世纪的荷兰共和国。荷兰是第一个在全国范围内发展资本主义的国家（相对于早期的城邦而言）。荷兰共和国在17世纪的经济首要地位被许多世界体系理论家认为是世界历史上第一个资本主义霸权。

现在几乎所有发达国家和大多数发展中国家都有股票市场，全球最大的股票市场在美国、英国、日本、印度、中国、加拿大、德国（法兰克福证券交易所）、法国、韩国和荷兰。

Foods and Drinks 食品和饮料

※ Gibbing (14th century)

Gibbing is the process of preparing salt herring (or soused herring), in which the gills and part of the gullet are removed from the fish, eliminating any bitter taste. The liver and pancreas are left in the fish during the salt-curing process because they release enzymes essential for flavor. The fish is then cured in a barrel with one part salt to 20 water.

The invention of gibbing is important because the invention of this fish preservation technique led to the Dutch becoming a seafaring power.

The process of gibbing was invented by Willem Beukelszoon, a 14th-century Zeeland Fisherman. Sometime between 1380 and 1386, Willem Beukelszoon of Zeeland discovered that "salt fish will keep, and that fish that can be kept can be packed and can be exported".Buckels' invention of gibbing created an export industry for salt herring that was monopolised by the Dutch. They began to build ships and eventually moved from trading in herring to colonising. So you could say the modern day the Netherlands was built on herring.

The Emperor Charles V erected a statue to Buckels honouring him as the benefactor of his country, and Queen Mary of Hungary after finding his tomb sat upon it and ate a herring.

To this day, herring is still very important to the Dutch who celebrate Flag Day each spring, as a tradition that dates back to the 14th century when fishermen went out to sea in their small boats to capture the annual catch, and to preserve and export their catch abroad.

※ Gin (1650)

Gin (Dutch: Jenever), also known as Gin in China, is a neutral spirits base made from fermented and distilled cereals and flavoured with spices.

It may come as a surprise to many, but gin was not invented by the British. Gin can trace it roots back to the Netherlands and is the ancestor of many modern spirits. Its earliest use was medicine, not a casual drink. In the mid-17th century, numerous small Dutch and Flemish distillers popularised the re-distillation of malt spirit or malt wine with juniper, anise, caraway, coriander, etc., which were sold in pharmacies and used to treat such medical problems as kidney ailments, lumbago, stomach ailments, gallstones, and gout. Gin emerged in England in varying forms as of the early 17th century, and at the time of the Restoration, enjoyed a brief resurgence. When William of Orange, ruler of the Dutch Republic, occupied the British throne with his wife Mary in what has become known as the Glorious Revolution, gin became vastly more popular, particularly in crude, inferior forms, where it was more likely to be flavoured with turpentine as an alternative to juniper.

The Dutch physician Franciscus Sylvius is often falsely credited with the invention of gin in the mid-17th century, although the existence of Jenever is confirmed in Philip Massinger's play The Duke of Milan (1623), when Sylvius would have been about nine years old. It is further claimed that English soldiers who provided support in Antwerp against the Spanish in 1585, during the Eighty Years' War, were already drinking Genever for its calming effects before battle, from which the term Dutch Courage is believed to have originated.

※ Cocoa powder (foundations of modern chocolate industry) (1828)

Chocolate is probably one of the most popular sweets in the world. According to the relevant data, global chocolate sales in 2016 reached us $982 billion, with the highest annual consumption per capita.

Cocoa powder, the basis of chocolate production, originated in the Netherlands in the 19th century. In 1815, Dutch chemist Coenraad Van Houten introduced alkaline salts to chocolate, which reduced its bitterness. In the 1820s, Casparus van Houten, Sr. patented an inexpensive method for pressing the fat from roasted cocoa beans. He created a press to remove about half the natural fat (cacao butter) from chocolate, which made chocolate both cheaper to produce and more consistent in quality. This innovation introduced the modern era of chocolate. Van Houten developed the first cocoa powder producing machine in the Netherlands.

Van Houten's machine—a hydraulic press—reduced the cocoa butter content by nearly half. This created a "cake" that could be pulverised into cocoa powder, which was to become the basis of all chocolate products. The press separated the greasy cocoa butter from cacao seeds, leaving a purer chocolate powder behind. This powder, much like the instant cocoa powder used today, was easier to stir into milk and water. As a result, another very important discovery was made: solid chocolate. By using cocoa powder and low amounts of cocoa butter, it was then possible to manufacture chocolate bar.

※ 腌鱼技术（14世纪）

Gibbing是制作咸鲱鱼（或腌制鲱鱼）的一个过程。只切除鱼鳃和部分食道，消除鲱鱼的所有苦味，但鱼的肝脏和胰腺仍然留在体内，在腌制过程中，这些部分可以释放一种特殊的酶而产生独特风味，最后再把鱼放到比例为1份盐20份水的盐水中腌渍。

鲱鱼腌制方法的发明至关重要，因为这种鱼类保存技术的发明促使了荷兰人成为航海大国。

Gibbing腌制技术的过程是由14世纪的泽兰渔民威廉

荷兰人发明了鲱鱼技术，还发明了鲱鱼的吃法，一口吞一定是荷兰人演示给你的最正确的吃法。

姆·贝克尔斯通所发明的。在1380年到1386年，泽兰的威廉姆·贝克尔斯通发现"咸鱼可以进行保存，并且保存好的鱼还可以进行包装再出口"。贝克尔斯通鲱鱼腌制技术的发明造就了一个由荷兰人垄断的盐鲱鱼出口产业。人们开始建造大量船只，并最终从鲱鱼贸易转向全球殖民统治。所以也可以说，现代荷兰是建立在鲱鱼的基础之上的。

为了表彰贝克尔斯通对国家的贡献，查尔斯五世还为其树立了一座雕像，以纪念他成为国家的恩人，匈牙利的玛丽皇后在找到他的坟墓后，还坐在上面吃了一条鲱鱼。

时至今日，鲱鱼对荷兰人来说仍然非常重要，每年春天人们都要庆祝国旗日，这一传统可以追溯到14世纪，当时渔民们乘着小船出海捕获第一批鲱鱼，保存起来并出口到国外。

※ 杜松子酒（1650年）

Gin（我们常称之为"金酒"或"琴酒"）在荷兰语中叫Jenever，也叫杜松子酒，是一种中性的烈酒，由发酵的和蒸馏的谷物制成，并加香料调味。

很多人可能会感到惊讶，但杜松子酒确实不是由英国人发明的。杜松子酒的出现可以追溯到荷兰，它是许多现代烈性酒的"祖先"。杜松子酒最早是用来当作药物使用的，而不是休闲饮料。17世纪中叶，荷兰和弗拉芒的许多小酒厂开始推广用杜松、茴芹、香菜、芫茜等制成的麦芽酒和再蒸馏麦芽酒，这些酒主要在药店进行出售，用于治疗诸如腰痛、胃痛、胆结石和痛风等肾脏疾病。在17世纪早期，杜松子酒以不同的形式出现在英国，在王政复辟时期曾短暂兴起。当荷兰共和国统治者威廉·奥兰冶与他的妻子玛丽一起在被称为光荣革命的时候登上英国王位时，杜松子酒变得更加盛行起来，特别是一些伪劣酒大量出现，因为杜松很容易用松节油调味来代替。

荷兰医生弗朗西斯·西尔维乌斯在17世纪中期经常被误认为是杜松子酒的发明者，尽管在菲利普·马辛格已经在他的剧作《米兰公爵》中对其进行了证实，那个时候西尔维乌斯大概只有9岁。还有人声称，在1585年安特卫普抵抗西班牙统治的八十年战争中，英国的援军士兵为了在战斗前能够镇静下来已经在喝杜松子酒，因此可以考究，荷兰语中的"Dutch Courage"一词便来源于此，意为"荷兰人的勇气"，也就是指酒后之勇。

※ 现代巧克力工业的基础——可可粉（1828年）

巧克力可能是世界上最受欢迎的甜食之一了。根据相关数据，2016年全球巧克力销售额达到了9 820亿美元，人均年消费量创历史新高。

可可粉是巧克力生产的基础，起源于19世纪的荷兰。1815年，荷兰化学家库恩纳德·范·豪登在巧克力中引入了碱性盐，以便减少巧克力的苦味。在19世纪20年代，卡斯帕罗斯·范·豪登获得一种用廉价方法来压制烤可可豆中的脂肪的专利，他发明了一种榨汁机，将巧克力中大约一半的天然脂肪即可可脂去掉，这使得巧克力的生产成本更低，质量也更稳定。这种创新技术被引入到现代的巧克力时代。范·豪登在荷兰开发了第一个可可粉生产机器。

范·豪登研发的机器——一个液压机，将可可脂的含量减少了近一半，形成了一个可以粉碎成可可粉的"蛋糕"，这些粉碎的巧克力"蛋糕粉"是生产所有巧克力产品的基础。通过挤压压榨，可可豆中的可可油脂被分离出来，留下的是更加醇厚的可可粉。这种粉末就像人们今天使用的速溶可可粉，更容易跟牛奶和水搅拌混合。但结果又有一个意外的惊人发现：被挤压后形成的固体巧克力。通过使用可可粉和少量可可脂，就可以生产巧克力棒了。

Law and Jurisprudence 法律和法学

※ Marriage equality (legalisation of same-sex marriage) (2001)

Same-sex marriage is a marriage between people of the same sex, either as a secular civil ceremony or in a religious setting. The term marriage equality refers to a political status in which same-sex marriage and opposite-sex marriage are considered legally equal.

In the late 20th century, rites of marriage for same-sex couples without legal recognition became increasingly common. The first law providing for marriage of people of the same sex in modern times was enacted in 2000 in the Netherlands and came into force in 2001. By the end of 2017, same-sex marriage is legally recognised (nationwide or in some parts) in the following countries: Argentina, Australia, Belgium, Brazil, Canada, Colombia, Denmark, Finland, France, Germany, Iceland, Ireland, Luxembourg, Malta, Mexico, the Netherlands, New Zealand, Norway, Portugal, South Africa, Spain, Sweden, the United Kingdom, the United States and Uruguay.

※ Legality of euthanasia

In 2000, the Dutch House of Representative had passed the "euthanasia" bill by 104 votes to 40, making the Netherlands the first country in the world to legalise euthanasia. In fact, 20 years ago, the Netherlands began to condone the practice of "euthanasia", which is mainly implemented in two ways. One is the medicine that doctors give patients to terminate their lives, and the patients take it by themselves. Second, doctors use drugs to help patients end their lives. In 1999, there were 2 216 cases of "euthanasia" in the Netherlands.

Euthanasia laws in vary in the countries where it is allowed. The British House of Lords Select Committee on Medical Ethics defines euthanasia as "a deliberate intervention undertaken with the express intention of ending a life, to relieve intractable suffering". In the Netherlands and Belgium, euthanasia is understood as "termination of life by a doctor at the request of a patient". The Dutch law however, does not use the term "euthanasia" but includes it under the broader definition of "assisted suicide and termination of life on request".

Euthanasia is categorised in different ways, which include voluntary, non-voluntary, or involuntary. Voluntary euthanasia is legal in some countries. Non-voluntary euthanasia (patient's consent unavailable) is illegal in all countries. Involuntary euthanasia (without asking consent or against the patient's will) is also illegal in all countries and is usually considered murder. In some countries there is a divisive public controversy over the moral, ethical, and legal issues of euthanasia. Passive euthanasia (known as "pulling the plug") is legal under some circumstances in many countries. Active euthanasia however is legal or de facto legal in only a handful of countries (e.g. Belgium, Canada, Switzerland) and is limited to specific circumstances and the approval of councillors and doctors or other specialists.

※ 婚姻平等——同性婚姻合法化（2001年）

同性婚姻指的是同性别之间的婚姻，无论是世俗的民间仪式还是宗教场合。婚姻平等一词指的是一种政治地位，即同性婚姻和异性婚姻在法律上是平等的。

在20世纪后期，没有法律认可的同性伴侣结婚仪式变得越来越普遍。2000年，第一部同性婚姻法在荷兰颁布，并于2001年生效。到2017年底，同性婚姻在以下国家（全国或部分地区）和地区已经合法化：阿根廷、澳大利亚、比利时、巴西、加拿大、哥伦比亚、丹麦、芬兰、法国、德国、冰岛、爱尔兰、卢森堡、马耳他、墨西哥、荷兰、新西兰、挪威、葡萄牙、南非、西班牙、瑞典、英国、美国和乌拉圭。

※ 安乐死的合法化

2000年，荷兰众议院以104票对40票通过了"安乐死"法案，使荷兰成为世界上第一个将安乐死合法化的国家。事实上，荷兰在20年前开始对"安乐死"的做法保持宽恕的态度，这主要是通过两种方式实现的：第一种是医生给病人终止生命的药物，病人自己服用；第二种是医生使用药物来帮助病人结束生命。在1999年，荷兰进行"安乐死"的行为已经有2 216例。

在允许安乐死的国家，法律也各不相同。英国上议院特别委员会将安乐死定义为"一种有意识的干预，旨在结束生命，缓解顽疾"。在荷兰和比利时，安乐死被理解为"医生在病人的请求下终止其生命"。然而，荷兰法律并未使用术语"安乐死"，而是将其纳入"辅助自杀和应要求终止生命"这一更广泛的定义之下。

安乐死分为不同的方式，包括自愿、非自愿或无意识地。自愿安乐死在一些国家是合法的。非自愿安乐死（无法获得患者同意）在所有国家都是非法的。无意识安乐死（不征得患者同意或违反患者意愿）在所有国家也是非法的，通常被认为是谋杀。在一些国家，对安乐死的道德、伦理和法律问题存在分歧性的公共争议。被动安乐死（被称为"拔塞子"）在许多国家的某些情况下是合法的。然而，只有少数国家（例如比利时、加拿大、瑞士）主动安乐死是合法或事实上合法的，并且仅限于特定情况以及议员和医生或其他专家的批准。

Medicine and Biology 医学和生物

※ Clinical electrocardiography (first diagnostic electrocardiogram) (1902)

In the 19th century it became clear that the heart generated electric currents. The first to systematically approach the heart from an electrical point-of-view was Augustus Waller, working in St. Mary's Hospital in Paddington, London. In 1911 he saw little clinical application for his work. The breakthrough came when Willem Einthoven, working in Leiden, used his more sensitive string galvanometer, than the capillary electrometer that Waller used. Einthoven assigned the letters P, Q, R, S and T to the various deflections that it measured and described the electrocardiographic features of a number of cardiovascular disorders. He was awarded the 1924 Nobel Prize for Physiology or Medicine for his discovery.

※ Rotating drum dialysis machine (first practical artificial kidney) (1943)

The first successful artificial kidney was developed by Willem Kolff in the Netherlands during

the early 1940s. Kolff was the first to construct a working dialyser in 1943.The procedure of cleaning the blood by this means is called dialysis, a type of renal replacement therapy that is used to provide an artificial replacement for lost kidney function due to renal failure. It is a life support treatment and does not treat the disease.

※ Foundations of modern reproductive biology (1660s–1670s)

In the 1660s and 1670s the Dutch Republic-based scientists (in particular Leiden University-based Jan Swammerdam and Nicolas Steno, and Delft-based Regnier de Graaf and Anton van Leeuwenhoek) made key discoveries about animal and human reproduction. Their research and discoveries contributed greatly to the modern understanding of the female mammalian reproductive system. Regnier de Graaf is seen by many as the founder of modern reproductive biology.This is due essentially to his use of convergent scientific methods: meticulous dissections, clinical observations and critical analysis of the available literature.

※ Microscope(1590)

The early simple "microscopes" which were only magnifying glasses they could usually only magnify an object about 6x-10x. One thing that was very common and interesting to look at, were fleas and other tiny insects, hence these early magnifiers called "flea glasses".

Sometime, during the 1590's, two Dutch spectacle makers, Zaccharias Janssen and his father Hans started experimenting with these lenses. They put several lenses in a tube and made a very important discovery. The object near the end of the tube appeared to be greatly enlarged, much larger than any simple magnifying glass could achieve by itself!

Their first microscopes were more of a novelty than a scientific tool since maximum magnification was only around 9X and the images were somewhat blurry. Although no Jansen microscopes survived, an instrument made for Dutch royalty was described as being composed of "3 sliding tubes, measuring 18 inches long when fully extended, and two inches in diameter".

It was Antony Van Leeuwenhoek (1632-1723), a Dutch scientist, and one of the pioneers of microscopy who in the late 17th century became the first man to make and use a real microscope.

He made his own simple microscopes, which had a single lens and were hand-held. Van Leeuwenhoek achieved greater success than his contemporaries by developing ways to make superior lenses, grinding and polishing a small glass ball into a lens with a magnification of 270x, the finest known at that time (other microscopes of the time were lucky to achieve 50x magnification). He used this lens to make the world's first practical microscope.

Antony van Leeuwenhoek considered to be the world's first microbiologist as he used his invention to analyse the composition of lots of things around him from cheese to the eyes of bugs and is credited with a vast number of discoveries including that of the sperm cell.

※ 临床心电图——第一诊断心电图（1902年）

在19世纪，人们发现心脏可以产生电流。第一个系统性的从电生理学角度研究心脏活动的人是

31

奥古斯都·沃勒，他在伦敦帕丁顿的圣玛丽医院工作，但是直到1911年，他仍然没有看到这项技术应用于临床的前景。因为沃勒以前使用的是毛细管静电计，后来在莱顿工作的威廉·埃因托芬使用敏感度更高的弦振镜时发现有了突破性的进展。埃因托芬将字母P、Q、R、S和T分配给它测量的各种偏转，并描述了一些心血管疾病的心电图特征。也因这项发现，埃因托芬被授予1924年诺贝尔生理学或医学奖。

※ 转鼓式透析机——首次实用性人造肾脏（1943年）

第一个成功的人造肾脏是20世纪40年代早期由荷兰的威廉·科尔夫研发的。科尔夫于1943年率先建立了一台工作的透析器，通过这种方法清洗血液的过程被称为透析，这是一种肾脏替代疗法，用于为因肾功能衰竭导致的肾功能丧失提供人工替代疗法。这是一种生命支持治疗，不是疾病治疗。

※ 现代生殖生物学基础（1660～1670年）

在17世纪六七十年代，荷兰的科学家们，特别是莱顿大学的扬·斯瓦默丹和尼古拉斯·斯丹诺以及代尔夫特的雷尼尔·德·格拉夫和安东尼·范·列文胡克，对动物和人类的繁殖研究方面取得了重大发现。他们的研究和发现极大地促进了现代对雌性哺乳动物生殖系统的理解。雷尼尔·德·格拉夫被许多人视为现代生殖生物学的奠基人，这主要是由于他使用了收敛的科学方法：细致的解剖、临床观察和对现有文献进行批判性分析。

著名的科学家，来自代尔夫特的安东尼·范·列文胡克。

※ 显微镜（1590年）

早期的最基础的"显微镜"只是放大镜，它们通常只能放大6～10倍。有一点非常常见而且有趣，那就是放大镜早期常用于观察跳蚤和其他小昆虫，因此这些早期的放大镜被称为"跳蚤眼镜"。

在1590年的一天，两个荷兰眼镜制造商撒迦利亚·扬森和他的父亲汉斯开始用这些镜片做尝试，并有了一个非常重要的发现——靠近管子末端的物体看起来要大得多，比任何一个简单的放大镜都要大得多。

他们的第一个显微镜还说不上是科学工具，只是一些新鲜尝试，因为最大放大率只有大约9倍，而且图像有些模糊。虽然扬森最初的显微镜没有被保存下来，但这台为荷兰皇室制造的仪器被描述为"它由3根滑动管组成，当完全伸展时为18英寸长，直径为2英寸"。

荷兰科学家安东尼·范·列文胡克是显微镜的先驱之一，他在17世纪后期成为制造和使用真正的显微镜的第一人。

列文胡克制作了自己的一个简单的显微镜，这台显微镜只有一个透镜，而且是手持的。列文胡

克比他同时代的人取得了更大的成功，他发明了制造高级透镜的方法，将一个小玻璃球磨成一个透镜，放大率为270倍，这是当时最著名的（当时的其他显微镜能达到50倍的放大倍数）。他用这个透镜制作了世界上第一个实用的显微镜。

安东尼·范·列文胡克被认为是世界上第一个微生物学家，他利用自己的发明分析了从奶酪到昆虫眼睛周围的许多东西的成分，并获得了包括精子细胞在内的大量发现。

Special Equipment 专用设备

※ Fire hose(1673)

Until the mid-19th century, most fires were fought by water transported to the scene in buckets. Original hand pumpers discharged their water through a small pipe or monitor attached to the top of the pump tub. It was not until the late 1860s that hoses became widely available to convey water more easily from the hand pumps, and later steam pumpers, to the fire.

In Amsterdam in the Dutch Republic, the Superintendent of the Fire Brigade, Jan van der Heyden, and his son Nicholaas took firefighting to its next step with the fashioning of the first fire hose in 1673. These 50-foot (15 m) lengths of leather were sewn together like a boot leg. Even with the limitations of pressure, the attachment of the hose to the gooseneck nozzle allowed closer approaches and more accurate water application. Van der Heyden was also credited with an early version of a suction hose using wire to keep it rigid.

The earliest fire hose made of canvas, but not durable enough, and later switched to leather sewing.Around 1890, unlined fire hoses made of circular woven linen yarns began to replace leather hoses. Until modern industrial production, the material of fire hose has been changed many times, and the performance of anti-exposure and corrosion has been greatly improved.

※ Traffic enforcement camera(1958)

The Dutch company Gatsometer BV, which was founded in 1958 by rally driver Maurice Gatsonides, produced the "Gatsometer". Gatsonides wished to better monitor his average speed on a race track and invented the device in order to improve his lap times. The company later started supplying these devices as police speed enforcement tools.The first systems introduced in the late 1960s used film cameras to take their pictures. Gatsometer introduced the first red light camera in 1965, the first radar for use with road traffic in 1971 and the first mobile speed traffic camera in 1982.

※ 消防水带（1673年）

直到19世纪中期，大部分火灾的救助用水都是以水桶的形式运送到现场的。原始的手泵通过连

33

接在泵桶顶部的小管道或监测器排出水，直到19世纪60年代末，水管才被广泛应用，以便更容易地将水从手泵和后来的蒸汽泵中喷洒向火苗。

在荷兰阿姆斯特丹，消防队负责人扬·范德·海登和他的儿子尼古拉斯在1673年采用第一支消防软管进行消防工作。这些长度为15米的皮革像靴子一样被缝在一起，即使受到压力的限制，胶管与鹅颈管的连接也可以实现更近距离和更精确的供水喷水需求。早期版本的吸水软管使用金属丝保持其刚性，也被称为范德·海登。

最早的消防水带由帆布制成，但不够耐用，后来改用皮革缝制。大约1890年，用圆形亚麻纱线制成的无衬里的消防水带开始取代皮革软管。在现代工业生产之前，消防水带的材料已经几经变化，抗暴露和腐蚀的性能得到了很大的提高。

※ 交通执法相机（1958年）

由职业赛车手毛利兹·哈桑尼德在1958年成立的荷兰嘉素公司制作了速度检测器"Gatsometer"。哈桑尼德希望能更好地监测他在赛道上的平均速度，于是发明了这个装置以提高他的圈速。后来，嘉素公司开始把这些设备提供给警察作为快速执法工具。20世纪60年代末，使用胶片相机拍摄照片被第一次应用于装置当中。Gatsometer检测器系列在1965年推出了第一台红光照相机，在1971年推出第一台用于道路交通的雷达装置，在1982年推出了第一个移动式交通摄像头。

马路上的交通摄像头每天监视着无数车辆往来，这源自荷兰赛车手毛利兹·哈桑尼德早期的速度检测器。图片为资料翻拍，左边的人为毛利兹·哈桑尼德。

Tijd voor Nederlands 荷兰语时间

● 单词+短语

荷 agrarisch	荷 bedrijf	荷 collega
英 agricultural	英 company	英 collage
译 农业	译 公司	译 同事
荷 vergadering	荷 haven	荷 zaak/bedrijf
英 meeting	英 port	英 business
译 会议	译 港口	译 业务，商业

续表

荷 handel	荷 exporteren/importeren	荷 belangrijk
英 trade	英 export/import	英 important
译 贸易	译 出口/进口	译 重要的
荷 ontwikkelen	荷 samenwerken	
英 develop	英 cooperate	
译 发达的	译 合作	

● 例句

荷 De agrarische industrie in Nederland is zeer ontwikkeld. 英 The agricultural industry in the Netherlands is very developed. 译 荷兰的农业很发达。	荷 China heeft vier belangrijke uitvindingen gedaan. 英 China has made four major inventions. 译 中国有四大发明。
荷 China en Nederland hebben veel handelscontacten. 英 China and the Netherlands have many trade contacts. 译 中国和荷兰有很多贸易往来。	荷 Nederland importeert veel producten uit China. 英 The Netherlands imports many products from China. 译 荷兰从中国进口很多产品。
荷 Rotterdam is de grootste haven van Europa. 英 Rotterdam is the largest port in Europe. 译 鹿特丹是欧洲最大的港口。	荷 We moeten een heel belangrijke bijeenkomst in Den Haag bijwonen. 英 We have a very important meeting to attend in The Hague. 译 我们在海牙有一个很重要的会议要出席。
荷 Wij zijn een zakelijk bedrijf. 英 We are a business company. 译 我们是一家商业公司。	荷 Dit is onze partner, we werken al heel lang samen. 英 This is our partner. We have been working together for a long time. 译 这是我们的合作伙伴，我们已经共事很久了。

2. 荷兰设计
Dutch Design

There are two points worth mentioning about the importance of Dutch design in the world:

Designers have a more relaxed self-play space. The government or the client in order to let the designers perform their duties, do not interfere in the designers' work. They have a very flexible approach to cooperation.

Furthermore, the Dutch government has a long-standing policy of patronage for cultural undertakings. The earliest traces can be traced back to the "Golden Age", when wealthy Dutch merchants donated money to artists for creative purposes. Since the early 20th century, large Dutch companies have been very active supporters of Design projects in the Netherlands, and the government has also established a special fund (referred to as the BKVB, which is the Netherlands Foundation for Visual Arts, Design and Architecture) to sponsor artists and designers.

Dutch design can find its roots in the movement "De Stijl", Dutch for "The Style", also known as Neoplasticism, and was a Dutch artistic movement founded in 1917 in Leiden. De Stijl consisted of artists and architects. In a narrower sense, the term De Stijl is used to refer to a body of work from 1917 to 1931 founded in the Netherlands. Proponents of De Stijl advocated pure abstraction and universality by a reduction to the essentials of form and colour; they simplified visual compositions to vertical and horizontal, using only black, white and primary colours.

De Stijl is also the name of a journal that was published by the Dutch painter, designer, writer, and critic Theo van Doesburg that served to propagate the group's theories. Along with van Doesburg, the group's principal members were the painters Piet Mondrian, Vilmos Huszár, and Bart van der Leck, and the architects Gerrit Rietveld, Robert van't Hoff, and J. J. P. Oud. The artistic philosophy that formed a basis for the group's work is known as Neoplasticism—the new plastic art (or Nieuwe Beelding in Dutch).

Today, works by De Stijl members are scattered all over the world, but De Stijl-themed exhibitions are organised regularly. Museums with large De Stijl collections include the Gemeentemuseum in The Hague, Amsterdam's Stedelijk Museum and the Centraal Museum of Utrecht.

The movement later inspired the design aesthetics of Rumyantsevo and Salaryevo stations of Moscow Metro opened in 2016.

关于荷兰设计在世界上的重要性，有两点值得一提：

设计师有更宽松的自我发挥的空间。政府或客户为了让设计师最大化地遵循自己的设计理念，不会干涉设计师的设计工作。他们有非常灵活的合作方式。

此外，荷兰政府长期以来一直赞助文化事业。最早的踪迹可以追溯到荷兰的"黄金时代"，当时富有的荷兰商人们向艺术家捐资以表达他们对艺术创作的支持。自20世纪初期以来，荷兰的大公司也非常积极地支持荷兰的设计项目，政府还设立了一个特别基金——荷兰视觉艺术、设计和建筑基金会，简称BKVB，对艺术家和设计师进行资金援助。

荷兰的设计可以从"De Stijl"（即我们常说的"风格派运动"）运动中找寻到根源，这是"The Style"的荷兰语表示，也被称为"新塑造主义"，是荷兰的一项艺术运动，于1917年在莱顿兴起。"De Stijl"由艺术家和建筑师组成。狭义上来说，"De Stijl"这个词是指从1917年到1931年在荷兰建立的一个工作机构。"De Stijl"的支持者主张通过减少形式和色彩的本质来提倡纯粹的抽象和普遍性；他们将视觉构图简化为垂直和水平，只使用黑色、白色和原色。

"De Stijl"风格最典型的人物和作品风格就是蒙德里安。

"De Stijl"也是由荷兰画家、设计师、作家和评论家西奥·范·多斯伯格出版的一本杂志的名字，该杂志旨在宣传该组织的创作理论。与多斯伯格一起的主要组织成员有画家皮特·蒙德里安、威摩斯·胡萨尔、巴特·范德·莱克，以及建筑师格里特·里特维尔德、罗伯特·范特·霍夫和J.J.P.奥德。形成该团体工作基础的艺术哲学被称为新塑型——新塑造艺术（或荷兰语Nieuwe Beelding）。

今天，"风格派运动"成员的作品遍布世界各地，但会定期举办"风格派运动"，即"De Stijl"主题的展览活动。收藏大量"风格派运动"作品的博物馆有海牙的市立博物馆、阿姆斯特丹的国立博物馆和乌特勒支的中央博物馆。

2016年莫斯科地铁开放的Rumyantsevo和Salaryevo两个车站的美学设计也是受"风格派运动"的启发。

Graphic Design　平面设计

Dutch graphic design is very advanced, its avant-garde position in the world is nurtured by factors, such as, a loose design environment without intervention, respect for individualism, private enterprises and full funding for the works of the designers by government departments attaching importance to the design industry.

※ NKF-Piet Zwart

When talking about Dutch design, most people pay attention to the "De Stijl" movement. In fact, Dutch independent design plays a very important role in modern Dutch design, and one of the important designers is called Piet Zwart. He contacted "De Stijl" in 1919 and began to associate with the modern design group, but he did not join the group.

Piet Zwart was born on May 28, 1885 in Zaandijk, in North Holland. He was trained as an architect, and began graphic design projects at the age of thirty-six. He was influenced by the De Stijl movement, which focused on the essentials of form, colour and line, but later moved to a more functional design aesthetic.

In the early 1920s Zwart received his first typographic commissions from Laga, a flooring manufacturer. Later, he began to work for Cable manufacturers Nederlandsche Kabelfabriek (NKF) in Delft. While working for the company, he learned the principles of printing, experimented with upper and lower case letters, lines, circles and screens, and free letter composition. He produced 275 designs within a decade, and then after he moved on to interior design, industrial design and furniture design.

Zwart began using photographic images in his compositions in 1926. He first worked with commercial photographers. Thus creating a balance between the two-dimensional type and the three-dimensional image. The photographs that he integrated into his work have high contrast, negative images, and are overprinted with coloured ink and cropped into geometric shapes. In 1928, he bought himself a camera and taught himself the photographic techniques. Zwart's admiration for repetition, structure, lines and planes, and balance show throughout his photographs.

In 1930, Piet Zwart was asked to design Het boek van PTT. The book was aimed at teaching school children how to use the Dutch postal service. He created two main characters for the book: 'the Post' and 'J Self'. He did not adhere to traditional typography rules, but used the basic principles of constructivism and "De Stijl" in his commercial works. His works can be recognised by its primary colours, geometrical shapes, repeated word patterns and an early use of photomontage. The book was finally published in 1938.

※ New Alphabet-Wim Crouwel

Wim Crouwel is another founder of the Dutch graphic design. From 1947 to 1949, Wim Crouwel studied art at the Minerva School in Groningen, the Netherlands. In addition, he also studied typography at the Gerrit Rietveld Academie in Amsterdam.

In 1963, he was one of the founders of the design studio Total Design (currently named Total Identity). From 1964 onwards, Crouwel was responsible for the design of the posters, catalogues and exhibitions of the Stedelijk Museum in Amsterdam. In 1967 he designed the typeface New Alphabet, a design that embraces the limitations of the cathode ray tube technology used by early data display screens and phototypesetting equipment, thus only containing horizontal and vertical strokes. Other typefaces from his hand are Fodor and Gridnik. In 1970 he designed the Dutch pavilion for Expo '70 (Osaka, Japan). Later, Crouwel designed the Number Postage Stamps for the Dutch PTT, well known in the Netherlands during its circulation from 1976 to 2002.

During the years that Crouwel worked for Total Design, he designed many geometric wordmarks, one of which is the wordmark for the Dutch Rabobank, designed in 1973.

In addition to his work as a graphic designer, he was also active in the educational field. From the 1950s to the 1990s, he was a teacher at the Royal Academy of Art and Design in 's-Hertogenbosch, and was a distinguished professor at Erasmus University Rotterdam. In the years 1985–1993 he was the director of the Museum Boijmans Van Beuningen in Rotterdam.

※ Dutch guilder-Ootje Oxenaar

Not many will remember the Dutch Guilder now that the euro is completely integrated in the Netherlands. The Dutch guilder was the currency of the Netherlands before the euro, and the design of the Dutch guilder was an outstanding example of international graphic design. It was designed by Ootje Oxenaar.

Ootje Oxenaar was a student at the Royal Academy of Art, The Hague and graduated in 1953 with honors. He later was a lecturer at the Royal Academy of Fine Arts in The Hague between 1958 and 1970 and taught as Professor of Visual Communication at the Delft University of Technology between 1978 and 1992.

As Head of the Art and Design Advisory Bureau at the Dutch Postal and Telecommunications (PTT/KPN) from 1976-1994, he was responsible for the commissioning of art and design for the largest Dutch public concern, and served as an aesthetic advisor to the Dutch National Bank, the Ministry of Justice in the Netherlands and the Danish Ministry of Transport. His influence on the next generation of designers was extensive as a commissioner, teacher, and international lecturer, in the Netherlands, Europe, and the US.

From 1964-1987, Ootje Oxenaar was commissioned two series of banknotes by The Nederlandsche Bank (DNB) and was responsible for the revolutionary design of the "snip" (100), the Sunflower (50) and Lighthouse (250) banknotes which were internationally celebrated as the most beautiful and least countrified money in the world. His banknotes stayed in circulation from 1964 until being replaced by the Euro in 2002.

Ootje Oxenaar was also a prolific designer of acclaimed posters, books, and postage stamps. His graphic design work is represented in various collections, including Center Georges-Pompidou in Paris, Gemeentemuseum Den Haag, Museum of Modern Art and Stedelijk Museum Amsterdam.

Ootje Oxenaar was knighted in the Orde van Oranje-Nassau, and the recipient of the Medal of Honor for Art and Science in the House of Orange, bestowed by Queen Beatrix in 2004.

※ SHV Think Book-Irma Boom

Irma Boom has been described as 'the Queen of Books'. She is a Dutch graphic designer—who specialises in book making, having created over 300 books and is well reputed for her artistic autonomy within her field.

Irma Boom loved painting since childhood, but later changed her interest, she gave up painting and joined the graphic design department. Boom attended the AKI Art Academy in Enschede later, where she pursued a B.F.A in graphic design. During this time she interned at various offices including the Dutch Government Publishing and Printing Office in The Hague, Studio Dumbar, and The Dutch Television (NOS) design department.

Boom got her first job as both an editor and designer during her time at the Dutch Government Publishing and Printing Office. It was here that she was noticed by Ootje Oxenaar, a designer of Dutch banknotes, who invited her to design two catalogues for a special edition of postage stamps in the years 1987–1988. It was a great opportunity, her design style was outstanding and the result was very successful and established her as a designer to a certain extent. In the 1980s, Irma Boom became acquainted with Paul Fenter van Vlissingen who would invite her to design the SHV Think Book—a book which eventually elevated her status to a design star.

The book's entirely white cover reveals a title as it dirties with use over time. An alternate version comes in black. Transparent adhesive had been typographically applied to collect dust and fingerprints. Creating a book with a blank cover alarmed publishers at the time but their unease presumably disappeared after the book's release, as it elevated Boom to international design stardom. The anniversary book was one of her biggest and designed to be distributed worldwide. Four thousand copies were printed in English and five hundred in Chinese. It has been described as an international icon of Dutch design. It is part of the permanent collection of MoMA.

For Chanel's 2013 exhibition at the Palais de Tokyo in Paris, Boom created a book filled with solid white, textural pages. The 300-page book was printed devoid of ink, instead embossed with text and image creating a semi-invisible narrative for Gabrielle "Coco" Chanel. The book structure is housed in a black box. The concept behind the book was inspired by the nature of perfume—it is best understood in an olfactive, not visual, manner—and relies on lesser dominant senses to convey the essence of the Chanel N°5 fragrance. It won the Dutch Design Awards in 2013 and is part of the permanent collection at MoMA.

Irma Boom has won numerous awards in her career. Many famous brands are her clients, Rijksmuseum in Amsterdam, The Museum of Modern Art New York, Prince Claus Fund, Fondazione Prada, Maserati, Yale Press London, Serpentine Gallery, Chanel, Paul Fentener van Vlissingen, Museum Boijmans, Ferrari,United Nations, Aga Khan Foundation and so on. Her works are permanent collection by The Museum of Modern Art, Centre Pompidou, Musee national d 'arty Modern, Library of The University of Amsterdam, etc.

※ Miffy-Dick Bruna

Miffy is a cute little bunny with small eyes and Iconic, two tall large ears, even in China, children are no strangers to this little rabbit called Miffy. But some information about Miffy is not known to many people, that is, Miffy from the Netherlands, and otherwise known as Nijntje, is a small female rabbit in a series of picture books drawn and written by Dutch artist Dick Bruna.

Dick Bruna was a Dutch author, artist, illustrator and graphic designer, best known for his children's books which he authored and illustrated, numbering over 200. His most notable creation was Miffy (Nijntje in the original Dutch), a small rabbit drawn with heavy graphic lines, simple shapes and primary colours.

Miffy was created in 1955 after Bruna had been telling his one-year-old son, Sierk, stories about a little rabbit they had seen earlier in the dunes, while on holiday at Egmond aan Zee. Miffy became a female after Bruna decided that he wanted to draw a dress and not trousers on his rabbit. Depending on the story, Miffy can range in age from being a baby to being four years old.

At first Miffy looked like a toy animal with floppy ears, but by 1963, she started to look the way we see her today, a stylized form of a rabbit. Miffy is drawn in a graphic style, with minimalist black graphic lines. Bruna chooses to only use black, white, the primary colors (red, yellow and blue), green and orange. It is his use of primarily primary colours that makes Miffy instantly recognisable, and also popular with pre-schoolers, because of her bright and intense simplistic colours.

Bruna's books have now been translated into more than 50 different languages, and over 85 million copies have been sold all over the world. He has won many awards for his books, such as the Golden Brush in 1990, for Boris Bear and the Silver Brush for Miffy In The Tent in 1996. In 1997, he was awarded the Zilveren Griffel for Dear Grandma Bunny, a book where Miffy's Grandmother was sick and died.

In addition to the image of the Miffy rabbit, Dick Bruna also created stories for characters such as Lottie, Farmer John, and Hettie Hedgehog, and illustrated and designed book covers, posters and promotional materials for his father's publishing company A.W. Bruna & Zoon. Well known among his designs are those for Simenon's Maigret books, typified by graphic silhouettes of a pipe on various backgrounds.

荷兰平面设计在世界上是非常前卫的，这离不开以下因素，如不加干预的宽松的设计环境，对私人企业和个人的尊重，政府部门对设计师作品的充分资助和对设计行业的重视。

※ NKF电缆公司——皮特·兹瓦特

当谈到荷兰设计时，大部分人会关注"De Stijl"运动。事实上，荷兰独立设计在现代荷兰设计当中扮演着非常重要的角色，其中有一个非常重要的设计师叫作皮特·兹瓦特。他在1919年与"De Stijl"组织取得联络，并与现代设计团队建立了联系，但他并没有加入该团队。

皮特·兹瓦特于1885年5月28日出生于北荷兰省的赞代克。他接受过建筑师培训，36岁开始从事平面设计项目。他的设计受到了"风格派运动"的影响，该派别注重形式、色彩和线条的本质，但他后来又转向实用性更强的设计美学。

20世纪20年代初，兹瓦特从一个地板制造商Laga那里收到了他的第一批排印佣金。后来，他开始在代尔夫特的电缆制造商NKF工作。在为公司工作之际，他学习了印刷原理，尝试用大小写字母、线条、圆圈和阴影以及随意的数字组合。他在10年内创作了275款设计产品，之后又转向室内设计、工业设计和家具设计。

1926年，兹瓦特先是与商业摄影师合作，开始在他的作品中使用照片图像，从而在二维图像和三维图像之间建立一个平衡。他整合到作品中的照片有很高的对比度，使用底片，并用彩色墨水渲染覆盖或裁剪成几何图形。1928年，兹瓦特自己买了一部相机，自学了摄影技术。他的摄影作品追求重复性，讲究结构、线条和平面在图像中的完美平衡。

1930年，兹瓦特受委托设计《PTT手册》（Het boek van PTT），这本书的目的是教学生如何使用荷兰邮政服务。他为这本书创作了两个主要角色："邮差"和邮政服务享用人，第二人称的"你"。他没有遵循传统的排版规则，而是在他的商业作品中使用了建构主义和"风格派"的基本原则。他的作品可以通过原色、几何形状、重复的文字图案和早期使用的蒙太奇图像来识别。这本书最终在1938年得以出版。

※ New Alphabet字体——维姆·克劳威尔

维姆·克劳威尔是荷兰平面设计的另一位创始人。从1947年到1949年，维姆·克劳威尔在荷兰格罗宁根的密涅瓦学校学习艺术。此外，他还在阿姆斯特丹的格里特·里特维尔德学院学习印刷术。

1963年，维姆·克劳威尔作为创始人之一成立了Total design工作室（现在的名称是Total Identity）。从1964年起，克劳威尔负责阿姆斯特丹国立博物馆的海报、目录和展览的设计。1967年，他设计了New Alphabet字体，该设计受到了早期数据显示屏和照排设备所使用的阴极射线管技术的局限性，因此只包含水平和垂直笔画。另外，Fodor字体和Gridnik字体也是出于他之手。1970年，他设计了日本大阪世博会荷兰馆。后来，克劳威尔为荷兰邮政服务公司PTT设计了号码邮票，在1976年到2002年期间在荷兰被广为流传。

维姆·克劳威尔为荷兰合作银行所设计的文字标识和其设计的New Alphabet字体。

在克劳威尔为Total design工作的多年间，他设计了许多几何文字符号，其中便包括了1973年为荷兰合作银行设计的文字标识。

除了平面设计师的本质工作，他在教育领域也很活跃。从20世纪50年代到90年代，他曾是斯海尔托亨博斯皇家艺术与设计学院的老师，也是鹿特丹伊拉斯谟大学的杰出教授。1985年至1993年，他还曾担任鹿特丹博曼斯·范·博宁恩博物馆的馆长。

※ 荷兰盾——乌杰·奥克斯纳

欧元已经完全融入荷兰社会，现在大概没有多少人记得起初的荷兰货币——荷兰盾了。荷兰盾是荷兰在通用欧元之前的货币，荷兰盾的设计是国际平面设计的杰出代表，它是由乌杰·奥克斯纳设计的。

乌杰·奥克斯纳是海牙皇家艺术学院的学生，1953年以优异的成绩从那里毕业。后来，他在1958年至1970年期间担任海牙皇家美术学院的讲师，并在1978年至1992年期间担任代尔夫特理工大学视觉传播学教授。

在1976年到1994年奥克斯纳作为荷兰邮政和电信艺术和设计顾问局（PTT/KPN）的领导人期间，他负责这个荷兰最大公众企业的艺术和设计委员会，并任职荷兰国家银行、荷兰司法部和丹麦交通部的美术顾问。作为荷兰、欧洲和美国的委员、教师和国际讲师，他对下一代设计师产生了深远的影响。

乌杰·奥克斯纳所设计的50面值的荷兰盾，颜色非常鲜艳，被誉为最美丽的货币设计，但早在2002年就停止了流通。

从1964年到1987年，乌杰·奥克斯纳受当时荷兰银行的委托设计两组钞票，于是便诞生了100荷兰盾（鹬图案）、50荷兰盾（向日葵图案）和250荷兰盾（灯塔图案）革命性的设计，这些钞票在国际上被誉为世界上最美丽、最质朴的货币设计。他所设计的荷兰盾从1964年一直流通到2002年，直到被欧元取代。

乌杰·奥克斯纳是一位多产的设计师，他还设计海报、书籍和邮票。他的平面设计作品被收藏到各处，包括巴黎的蓬皮杜中心、海牙市立博物馆、阿姆斯特丹市立博物馆/现代艺术博物馆。

乌杰·奥克斯纳被授予"奥伦治拿骚"勋章，并于2004年由贝娅特丽克丝女王颁发奥伦治之家"艺术与科学荣誉勋章"。

※ SHV Think Book——伊玛·布姆

伊玛·布姆被形容为"书籍女王"。她是一位荷兰平面设计师，专门从事书籍制作，她创作了超过300本书，并因其艺术领域的自主性而闻名。

伊玛·布姆从小就热爱绘画，但后来她的兴趣变了，她放弃了绘画，加入到平面设计领域。她后来到了恩斯赫德的AKI艺术学院，在那里就读平面设计艺术学士。在这期间，她在多个部门实习过，包括海牙的荷兰政府出版和印刷办公室、Dumbar工作室和荷兰NOS电视设计部。

在荷兰政府出版和印刷局任职期间，她的第一份工作是担任编辑和设计师。也正是在这里，她被荷兰盾的设计师乌杰·奥克斯纳注意到，奥克斯纳邀请她在1987~1988年设计了两本邮票的特别目录。这是一个千载难逢的机会，布姆的设计风格非常出色，结果也异常成功，这在一定程度上确立了她作为设计师的地位。20世纪80年代，伊玛·布姆结识了保罗·芬特纳·范·弗利辛恩，弗利辛恩邀请她设计SHV Think Book——就凭着这本书，伊玛·布姆最终成为一个设计明星。

这本书的封面是全白色的设计，但这样也会存在一个问题，因为随着时间的推移封面也变得越来越脏。其中还有一个黑色的版本，已经采用透明胶黏剂封存起来，以隔绝灰尘和指纹。这样一本全白封面的书让出版商们很是感到震惊，但在这本书发行后，他们的不安也就随之烟消云散，因为正是源于这本书的独特设计，布姆上升成为一个国际设计巨星。这本书的周年纪念版是伊玛·布姆最伟大的作品之一，旨在向全球发行。包括用英文印刷的4 000本和中文印刷的500本。它被描述为荷兰设计的国际性标志，是纽约现代艺术博物馆（MoMA）永久收藏的一部分。

布姆还为香奈儿2013年在巴黎东京宫的展览创作了一本书，内页纯白而有质感。这本300页的书没有用墨水，内页的文字和图像都是凸印的，为嘉柏丽尔"可可"香奈儿创造了一个半隐形的故事。整个书被装在了一个黑色的盒子里。布姆这本书的设计受到了香水本质的启发——用嗅觉才是最佳的理解方式，而不是视觉——并且依靠较少的主导感官来传达香奈儿No.5香水的精髓。这个设计在2013年赢得了"荷兰设计大奖"，也被现代艺术博物馆永久收藏。

伊玛·布姆在她的职业生涯中获奖无数，许多著名的品牌都是她的客户，如阿姆斯特丹国立博物馆、纽约现代艺术博物馆、克劳斯亲王基金会、普拉达、玛莎拉蒂、耶鲁出版社、蛇形画廊、香奈儿、保罗·芬特纳·范·弗利辛恩、博曼斯·范·博宁恩博物馆、法拉利、联合国、Aga Khan基金会等。她的作品成为纽约现代艺术博物馆、蓬皮杜中心、法国国家现代艺术博物馆、阿姆斯特丹大学图书馆等的永久收藏。

※ 米菲兔——迪克·布鲁纳

米菲兔是一只长着一对小眼睛竖着一对高高的标志性的大耳朵的小兔子，即使在中国，孩子们对这只叫米菲的小兔子也并不陌生。但是有一些信息可能并不是尽人皆知的：米菲来自荷兰，也不叫Miffy，而是叫Nijntje。她是荷兰艺术家迪克·布鲁纳所绘制的一系列图画书中的主角，一只女性小兔子。

迪克·布鲁纳是荷兰作家、艺术家、插画师和平面设计师，他最著名的是所编著的儿童插画读物，已经创作了200多本。其中最知名的形象便是米菲，也就是荷兰的Nijntje，用粗粗的线条、简单的形状和基本原色绘制的小兔子。

米菲的形象创作于1955年，当时布鲁纳给一岁大的儿子西尔克讲他们之前在埃蒙德海边度假时看到的沙丘上一只小兔子的故事。布鲁纳决定要给这只小兔子画一条裙子而不是裤子，这样米菲就成了一个小姑娘。根据这些图书中故事的发展线，书中米菲的年龄设置是从婴儿时期到四岁。

起初，米菲看上去就像一只耷拉着耳朵的玩具动物，但到了1963年，她变成了我们今天所看到的样子，一只兔子的造型。米菲的形象是由极简主义的黑色线条绘制出来的。布鲁纳选择只使用黑色、白色、原色（红、黄和蓝三种颜色）、绿色和橙色。但他使用最多的还是原色，使米菲的形象立刻跳脱出来，因为色彩明亮而又强烈，也很受学龄前儿童的欢迎。

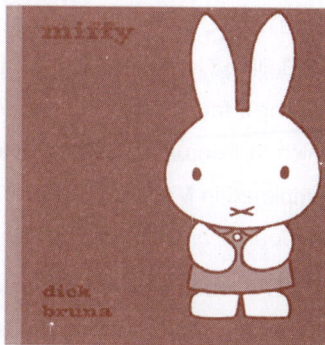

米菲的形象非常可爱，绘图非常简约，其形象在成人世界中也同样受到欢迎。

布鲁纳的书现在已经被翻译成50多种不同的语言，在全球销售了超过8 500万册。他为他所创作的图书赢得了许多奖项，比如1990年《小熊鲍里斯》获得"金画笔奖"、1996年《米菲在帐篷里》获得"银画笔奖"。1997年，《亲爱的兔奶奶》又被授予"银笔奖"，这本书描写了米菲的奶奶生病去世了。

除了米菲的形象，迪克·布鲁纳还为Lottie、农民约翰和刺猬赫蒂等人物创作了故事，并为他父亲的出版公司A.W. Bruna & Zoon设计图书封面和插画、海报和宣传材料。在他的设计中，为大众所熟知的是他为乔治·西姆农的Maigret探长系列丛书设计的在不同背景下的管道图形轮廓。

涨 Architectural Design 建筑设计

The Dutch architecture industry is one of the most innovative in the world and is influenced by the lack of space, the regard for sustainability, the increasing influence of users and the problems associated with water. Dutch architects are renowned worldwide for their social engagement, use of innovative materials and sustainability.

The Dutch architectural tradition is known for more than just its building design but for its total approach to urban planning and complex restructuring. Dutch architects are increasingly obtaining a central role throughout the entire building process (supply chain director). There were about 15,000 architects registered in the Netherlands in 2014. This group included architects, interior architects, urban planners and landscape architects, many of whom are renowned designers around the world, such as Rem Koolhaas and Ben van Berkel. At the same time, these projects are distributed all over the world, even in China, there are many cities with buildings designed by Dutch designers.

※ CCTV Headquarters-Rem Koolhaas-OMA

CCTV Headquarters, or CCTV's new office building, is probably the most controversial building in Beijing, the controversy started from the drawing of the design and lasts till today, this mainly because Beijing has never been the centre stage for such a unfamiliar but eye-catching design.

The CCTV Headquarters is a 234-metre, 44-story skyscraper on East Third Ring Road in the Beijing Central Business District (CBD). Ground breaking took place on June 1,2004 and the building's facade was completed in January 2008. The further construction was delayed by a fire which in February 2009 engulfed the adjacent Television Cultural Centre, the headquarters was completed in May 2012. The CCTV Headquarters won the 2013 Best Tall Building Worldwide from the Council on Tall Buildings and Urban Habitat.

The building was designed by The Office for Metropolitan Architecture (OMA) in the Netherlands and Rem Koolhaas is one of its founders.

Rem Koolhaas is a Dutch architect, architectural theorist, urbanist and Professor in Practice of Architecture and Urban Design at the Graduate School of Design at Harvard University. He studied at the Architectural Association School of Architecture in London and at Cornell University in Ithaca, New York. Rem Koolhaas is the founding partner of OMA, and of its research-oriented counterpart AMO based in Rotterdam. In 2005, he co-founded Volume Magazine together with Mark Wigley and Ole Bouman.

He is widely regarded as one of the most important architectural thinkers and urbanists of his generation. In 2000, Rem Koolhaas won the Pritzker Prize. In 2008, *Time* put him in their top 100 of The World's Most Influential People.

The Office for Metropolitan Architecture (OMA), created by Rem Koolhaas and three other architects, has now opened offices in New York, Beijing, Hong Kong and Doha. Its projects are carried out all over the world, and many projects are very characteristic and representative, such as: The Kunsthal, Rotterdam (1992), Embassy of the Netherlands, Berlin (1997), Seattle Central Library(1999), Leeum Samsung Museum of Art (2004), Casa da Música in Porto (2005), Edouard Malingue Gallery in Hong Kong (2010), etc.

※ Tianjin Binhai Library-MVRDV

The Tianjin Binhai Library, nicknamed the Eye, was completed in 2017 and is probably one of the most frequently occurring Chinese buildings on social media such as Instagram in 2017.

Tianjin Binhai Library is a five-storey building, and has a total space of 33,700 square metres. It features floor-to-ceiling, terraced bookshelves able to hold 1.2 million books, and a large, luminous sphere in the centre that serves as an auditorium with a capacity of almost 100 people. The library is nicknamed 'the Eye' because the sphere, which appears like an iris, can be seen from the park outside through an eye-shaped opening.

The first and second floors contain mainly lounge areas and reading rooms. The floors above have computer rooms, meeting rooms, and offices. There are also two rooftop patios. Because of a decision to complete the library quickly and a conflict with what was officially approved, the main atrium cannot be used for book storage; the rooms providing access to the upper tiers of shelving were not built and book spines were printed onto the backs of the shelf space for the opening-day photographs.

The library was designed by the Rotterdam-based architectural firm MVRDV along with the Tianjin Urban Planning and Design Institute and opened in October 2017.

MVRDV is a well-known Dutch design team, founded in 1993. The name is an acronym for the founding members: Winy Maas, Jacob van Rijs and Nathalie de Vries.

The products of MVRDV's unique approach to design varyingly, ranging from buildings of all types and sizes, to urban plans and visions, numerous publications, installations and exhibitions. Built projects include the public broadcasting corporation VPRO in Hilversum (the first commission in 1997), Dutch Pavilion at the Hannover World Exhibition Expo 2000 (2000), the boutique shopping building Gyre in Tokyo(2007), the iconic Mirador and Celosia housing in Madrid (2005-2009), the international bank headquarters in Oslo(2012) and the Rotterdam Market Hall which is billed as the world's most beautiful vegetable market.

Current projects in progress or on site include various housing projects, office buildings and cultural centres in the Netherlands, China, France, India, the United Kingdom, the United States and other countries, a cultural complex in Roskilde, a public art depot in Rotterdam, a mixed use building in central Paris. MVRDV is also working on large scale urban masterplans in Bordeaux and Caen, France and the masterplan for an eco-city in Logroño, Spain. Larger scale visions for the future of greater Paris, greater Oslo, and the doubling in size of the Dutch new town Almere are also in development.

※ Erasmus Bridge-Ben van Berkel-UNStudio

Even if they have never been to Rotterdam, many people are still familiar with this Bridge, they probably don't know its name, but a bridge with such a graceful body that looks like a swan leaves a deep impression on many. The Erasmus Bridge is truly a jewel in the crown of Rotterdam. In the chapter "cities and sights in Rotterdam", we already introduced the Erasmus Bridge, a famous landmark of Rotterdam, which has become one of its most popular tourist attractions.

Its designer Ben van Berkel was born and grew up in the Netherlands, he is the founder and principal architect of UNStudio. He studied architecture at the Rietveld Academy in Amsterdam, and at the Architectural Association in London, receiving the AA Diploma with Honours in 1987.

In 1988 he and his then wife, Caroline Bos, set up an architectural practice in Amsterdam named Van Berkel & Bos Architectuurbureau. In 1998 they relaunched their practice as UNStudio, where UN stands for "United Network". Erasmus Bridge is just one of his many works, and Ben van Berkel has built several projects since UNStudio was relaunched, for example, Arnhem Central Station (1996), Mercedes-Benz Museum in Stuttgart (2001), Raffles City in Hangzhou (2008), Doha Metro Network (2012), Beethovenhalle in Bonn (2014), Chicago Museum of Film and Cinematography (2014), Schiphol terminal1 (2017), and etc.

Also, Ben van Berkel won many awards for his designs, such as for his design for the Arnhem Central Station (1996) which won The Zumtobel Group Award for Urban Developments & Initiatives and the German Design Award 2018 for Urban Space & Infrastructure; The Galleria Centercity in Cheonan (2008) won the RIBA International Award 2011 and the Lane 189,Shanghai (2013) won the MIPIM Asia Gold Award for Best Retail Development, also the Wafra Tower in Doha (2015) won the Best Residential Green Building for 2017 from QGBC.

Ben van Berkel has lectured and taught at many architectural schools around the world, such as the Berlage Institute in Rotterdam, Architectural Association in London, Städelschule in Frankfurt, and he was a visiting professor at Columbia University, Princeton University and Harvard University. In 2011 he was appointed the Kenzo Tange Chair at the Harvard Graduate School of Design.

Ben van Berkel has received many personal awards and affiliations, such as the Eileen Gray Award (1983); the British Council Fellowship (1986); the Charlotte Köhler Award (1991); Member of Honor of the Bund Deutscher Architekten (1997); the Charles Jencks Award (2007); the Honorary Fellowship AIA (2013); and the Kubus Award (2016).

荷兰的建筑业是世界上最具创新精神的行业之一，它受到空间缺乏、对可持续性的重视、用户影响力的增加以及与水相关的问题的影响。荷兰建筑师因其社会参与度、创新材料的使用和可持续性方案而享誉全球。

荷兰的建筑传统并非仅以其建筑设计而闻名，它还以其对城市规划和复杂结构调整的总体方案而闻名。荷兰建筑师越来越多地在整个建筑过程中承担着重要角色（供应链总监）。2014年在荷兰注册

的建筑师约有15 000万。这个在册人员包括建筑师、室内设计师、城市规划师和景观设计师，他们中的许多人都是享誉世界的著名设计师，比如雷姆·库哈斯和本·范·贝克尔。与此同时，这些出自荷兰建筑师的项目在世界各地均可见踪影，即使在中国，也有许多城市项目是由荷兰建筑师设计的。

※ 中央电视台总部大楼——雷姆·库哈斯——OMA

CCTV总部，或者叫CCTV的新办公楼，可能是北京最具争议的建筑，从设计蓝图出来一直持续到今天，争议几乎就没断过，这主要是因为北京从来都不是一个这样陌生但又引人注目的设计的中心舞台。

中央电视台总部大楼位于北京中央商务区，在东三环边上，是一座高234米的44层摩天大楼。该项目于2004年6月1日破土动工，建筑外墙在2008年1月竣工。在2009年2月，一场大火将附近的电视文化中心吞没，大楼的建设被迫推迟，直到2012年5月才竣工。央视总部大楼荣获2013年高层建筑与城市居住委员会"全球最佳高层建筑"的称号。这个项目是由荷兰大都会建筑事务所（OMA）设计的，雷姆·库哈斯是其创始人之一。

雷姆·库哈斯是一名荷兰建筑师、建筑理论家、城市学者，同时也是哈佛大学设计研究院建筑与城市设计专业的教授。他曾就读于伦敦的建筑联盟学院和位于纽约州伊萨卡的康奈尔大学。雷姆·库哈斯是大都会建筑事务所，以及鹿特丹以研究型为导向的AMO工作室的创始合伙人。2005年，他与Mark Wigley和Ole Bouman共同创办了*Volume*杂志。

他被普遍认为是他这一代最重要的建筑思想家和城市主义者。2000年，雷姆·库哈斯获得"普利兹克奖"。2008年，《时代周刊》将他列入世界上最有影响力的100人之列。

大都会建筑事务所是由雷姆·库哈斯和另外三位建筑师创建的，如今已在纽约、北京、香港和多哈开设了办事处。事务所的项目遍布世界各地，许多项目都极具代表性，如：鹿特丹昆莎美术馆（1992年）、荷兰驻柏林大使馆（1997年）、西雅图中央图书馆（1999年）、Leeum三星艺术博物馆（2004年）、波尔图音乐厅（2005年）、香港马凌画廊（2010年）等。

※ 天津滨海图书馆——MVRDV

天津滨海图书馆昵称"滨海之眼"，于2017年完工，它可能是2017年在Instagram等社交媒体上最常见到的中国建筑之一。

天津滨海图书馆是一座五层建筑，总建筑面积33 700平方米。它具有落地式梯田般层叠的书架，可容纳120万册藏书，中庭是一个发光球形报告大厅，可容纳近百人。该图书馆被昵称为"滨海之眼"，因为球体看起来像虹膜，可以通过眼睛形状的开口从公园外看到。

图书馆的一楼和二楼主要是休息区和阅览室。上面的楼层有电脑室、会议室和办公室。还有两个屋顶露台。由于紧迫的施工周期和完工时间要求，以及和官方批准有冲突，使得部分设计概念未能实现，主要的中庭暂不能用于图书存储；可供进入上层或搁架的房间也没有建成，最终上方书架全部由印刷书本图案替代了真实书籍，以便图书馆开放之日可以看到它应有的样貌。

图书馆是由位于鹿特丹的MVRDV建筑公司和天津城市规划设计研究院共同设计的，于2017年10月对外开放。

MVRDV是荷兰非常有名的设计团队，成立于1993年。该名字是创始成员Winy Maas、Jacob van Rijs和Nathalie de Vries名字首字母的缩写。

MVRDV独特设计的作品风格各异，从各种用途和规模的建筑作品到城市的总体规划和愿景，以及众多的出版物作品、设备装置和展览。已经建成的项目包括Hilversum VPRO公共广播公司（1997年）、汉诺威世界博览会荷兰馆（2000年）、东京Gyre精品购物大楼（2007年）、马德里标志性的Celosia住宅楼（2005～2009年）、奥斯陆国际银行总部（2012年）和被称为"世界上最美丽的菜市场"的鹿特丹缤纷市场或拱廊市场。

目前正在进行的或已经建成的项目还有荷兰、中国、法国、印度、英国、美国和其他国家的各种住宅、办公大楼和文化中心项目，以及丹麦Roskilde的文化综合体、鹿特丹的公共艺术基地、巴黎市中心的混合建筑。与此同时，MVRDV也参与到多项城市大规模的整体规划中，如法国波尔多和卡昂的城市总体规划以及西班牙洛格罗尼奥（Logroño）生态城设计。规模更宏远的项目如大巴黎、奥斯陆未来都市构想以及将在旧城基础上双倍扩建的荷兰Almere新城市规划项目也同时都在进行之中。

※ 伊拉斯谟大桥——本·范·贝克尔——UN工作室

这是人们对鹿特丹最熟悉的一个地标建筑，连接着中心城区和港口区。

即使从来没有到过鹿特丹，很多人仍然对这座大桥很熟悉，或许你并不知道它的名字，但这座身躯如天鹅般优雅的大桥给很多人留下了深刻的印象，这就是伊拉斯谟大桥，鹿特丹王冠上一颗璀璨的宝石。在"鹿特丹的景点和地标建筑"这一章中，我们也会介绍这个鹿特丹著名地标——伊拉斯谟大桥，它已经成为这座城市最受欢迎的旅游景点之一。

这座桥的设计师本·范·贝克尔在荷兰出生并长大，他是UNStudio的创始人和首席设计师。他曾在阿姆斯特丹的格里特·里特维尔德学院和伦敦建筑联盟学院学习建筑学，并于1987年获得AA荣誉证书。

1988年，他和当时的妻子卡罗琳·博斯在阿姆斯特丹成立了一个名为范·贝克尔与博斯的建筑事务所。1998年，他们重启了UNStudio的实践项目，这其中UN代表"联合网络"。伊拉斯谟桥只是贝克尔诸多作品中的一个，自从UNStudio重新启动，他已经设计了数个项目，例如阿纳姆中央车站（1996年）、斯图加特梅塞德斯－奔驰博物馆（2001年）、杭州来福士广场（2008年）、多哈地铁网络（2012年）、波恩贝多芬音乐厅（2014年）、芝加哥电影和摄影博物馆（2014年）、史基浦机场1号航站楼（2017年）等。

本·范·贝克尔的设计项目赢得了许多奖项，比如他的阿纳姆中央车站获得了城市发展和计划的"奥德堡集团奖"和2018年"德国城市空间和基础设施设计奖"；韩国天安市Galleria Centercity百货中心项目获得了2011年"英国皇家建筑师协会国际大奖"；上海189弄购物中心项目获得"亚洲国际房地产最佳零售发展金奖"；同时，多哈的Wafra Tower荣获绿色建筑委员会QGBC 2017年的"最佳住宅绿色建筑"的称号。

本·范·贝克尔还曾在世界各地的许多知名建筑院校讲学和授课，比如鹿特丹的贝尔拉格学院、伦敦建筑联盟学院、法兰克福国立美术学院，他还是哥伦比亚大学、普林斯顿大学和哈佛大学的客座教授。2011年，他被任命为哈佛大学设计学院Kenzo Tange教授。

除了项目获奖，贝克尔个人也获得了非常多的奖项，如"艾林·格雷奖"（1983年）、"英国议会奖学金"（1986年）、"夏洛特科勒奖"（1991年）、"德国风景园林师协会荣誉会员"（1997年）、"英国皇家建筑师协会Charles Jencks奖"（2007年）、AIA荣誉院士（2013年）以及"荷兰皇家建筑师协会Kubus奖"（2016年）。

Product Design　产品设计

Dutch Design is gaining widespread popularity all over the world, they are particularly strong in product design. In recent years, The Dutch design teams and individuals have started to focus on the cooperation and globalisation, especially the in-depth cooperation with Chinese brands.

In this area, there are projects that focus on the idea of a single designer, such as the works from Marcel Wanders, Studio Drift and Studio Henny van Nistelrooy. There are also cooperation's with SOHO China, fashion brand zuczug and design store HAY. Other areas of Dutch design are also gaining ground in China, for example the bicycle designers Van Moof sell their bikes at several specialist stores around the country.

The Netherlands is also strong in high-end design services, here you could think of design management which has also developed in the Netherlands.

※ Knotted Chair-Moooi-Marcel Wanders

The Knotted Chair is just a miniature, one of many works by Marcel Wanders, which makes Marcel Wanders known to many people in the industry.

Marcel Wanders is a Dutch designer, graduated cum laude from the Hogeschool voor de Kunsten Institute of the Arts Arnhem in 1988 after being expelled from the Design Academy Eindhoven.

In 2000 Marcel Wanders opened his studio in Amsterdam. In 2001 he co-founded the design label Moooi, of which he is a co-owner and art director. Since 2014 Wanders works as a product and interior designer and art director, he works in his Powerhouse studio with around 50 international design specialists. They have realised over 1,700+ projects for private clients and premium brands such as Bisazza, KLM, MAC Cosmetics, Flos, Swarovski, Puma, among others.

Marcel Wanders received various design prizes, including the Rotterdam Design Prize (he has been nominated several times) and the Kho Liang Ie Prize. He has lectured at the San Francisco Museum of Modern Art, Limn, the Design Academy, Nike, IDFA, FutureDesignDays and at many of the world's most prestigious design academies. In July 2002 *Business Week* selected Marcel Wanders as one of Europe's "25 leaders of change". Wanders is an Advisory Board member of THNK School of Creative Leadership.

Many of Marcel Wanders' designs have been selected for design collections and exhibitions, included in such significant museum collections as MoMA New York, The Stedelijk Museum, Amsterdam, and the V&A Museum, London. In 2006 he was elected International Designer of the Year by Elle Decoration, and he has further published numerous books and is extensively profiled in the global media, appearing in such publications as *the New York Times*, *Domus*, *The Financial Times* and *Wallpaper Magazine*.

49

※ Vitra (furniture) - Jongeriuslab ₁ Hella Jongerius

Hella Jongerius is a renowned Dutch designer known for her inventive approach to products. She graduated from Design Academy Eindhoven in 1993. She rose to prominence soon after graduating with a series of her designs being produced by the influential Dutch conceptual design collective, Droog Design. Jongerius started her own design company, Jongeriuslab, in 1993 in Rotterdam.

The designer Hella Jongerius has become known for the manner in which she fuses industry and craft, high-and-low-tech, traditional and contemporary. Her designs focuses on combining opposites; for example, new technology and handmade objects, industrial manufacturing and craftsmanship, and the traditional and the contemporary. Her works are often highly textural; for example, rough edged leather is rolled up to create wheels, paint is splashed on earthenware, ceramics are sewn onto cotton tablecloths, sinks are made of rubber.

Hella Jongerius has worked for many prestigious clients, including IKEA, KLM, Vitra, Maharam, Royal Tichelaar Makkum, and Nymphenburg. Her designs have been exhibited at galleries and museums such as the Cooper Hewitt National Design Museum in New York, Museum of Modern Art, Stedelijk Museum Amsterdam, Museum Boijmans Van Beuningen, the Design Museum London, Galerie kreo Paris and Moss gallery in New York,

Since 2008 Jongerius has worked as art director for colours, textiles and surfaces at Vitra (Basel, Switzerland). In 2012, Jongerius designed a new interior and seats for the business class cabin in KLM's Boeing 747. 2013 also saw her collaborating with fellow Dutch creative Rem Koolhaas on a new interior for the North Delegates' Lounge in the UN headquarters New York as well as being appointed as design director for Dutch rug firm Danskina.

※ Van Gogh Path -Studio Roosegaarde - Daan Roosegaarde

Daan Roosegaarde is a name strange to many people, but its projects are familiar to many, most notably his "Van Gogh Path" and his "SMOG FREE PROJECT ". The Van Gogh Path is located in Nuenen, North Brabant, in the Netherlands, less than 10 kilometers away from Eindhoven. This is the first luminous cycling path in the world, which runs through the province of North Brabant, where the famous artist Vincent van Gogh was born and raised. This luminous bike trail with a rotating starry night was inspired by Van Gogh's famous painting "Starry Night." This trail has now been rated as one of the most worthy places for Eindhoven by tourists.

The SMOG FREE PROJECT is another well-known project of Daan Roosegaarde. This project is a series of urban innovations led by Daan Roosegaarde to reduce pollution and provide an inspirational experience of a clean future.

Inspired by Daan Roosegaarde and his team who invented the SMOG FREE TOWER, Daan Roosegaarde once lived in a hotel in the CBD of Beijing but could not see the CCTV building in close proximity because of the large haze. This inspired him to design and instal the SMOG FREE TOWER in Jordan Park in Warsaw, Tianjin and Beijing. The SMOG FREE TOWER uses patented positive ionisation technology to produce smog free air in public space, allowing people to breathe and experience clean air for free.

The tower was installed in Beijing in 2016 and it sucks in surrounding air from the surrounding area, tests prove that the tower can capture up to 70% of the PM10 particles. The filtered air is released back in the surrounding area where it mixes with the dirty air and this results in a 45% reduction in PM10 pollution within 20 meters of the tower. The tower also reduces another form of pollution, known as PM2.5, it reduces this pollution by as much as 25%. (The results were obtained by Eindhoven University of Technology.)

In 2017, Roosegaarde presented a new addition to Smog Free Project: SMOG FREE BICYCLE. The concept draws its inspiration from the recent Smog Free workshop which featured artist Matt Hope and Prof. Yang from Tsinghua University and led to new creative output. The innovative bicycle inhales polluted air, cleans it, and releases clean air around the cyclist.

The projects developed by Studio Roosegaarde have always been attracting attention. Roosegaarde has always been committed to the combination of urban environment and technology, and at the same time, his projects must have some artistic appreciation.

He designed the Beyond, a 121 meters long lenticular print of cloud images, back-lit by LED lamps at Amsterdam's Schiphol Airport, which gives the illusion of depth into the image.

He worked with Leiden university to develop the Rainbow Station project, which illuminates the 125-year-old Amsterdam Central Station.

The work from his Studio Roosegaarde has been exhibited at the Rijksmuseum, Tate Modern, Tokyo National Museum, Victoria and Albert Museum, and the Design Museum in London. Roosegaarde won the London Design Innovation medal in 2016.

荷兰式设计在世界各地广受关注，尤其是在产品设计方面更为突出。近年来，荷兰设计团队和个人开始关注全球化的合作，特别是与中国品牌的深度合作。

在这一领域，有一些项目非常注重设计师的设计理念，比如来自于Marcel Wanders、Drift工作室和Henny van Nistelrooy工作室的作品。还有与SOHO中国、时尚品牌zuczug和HAY设计店的合作。荷兰设计的其他领域也在中国取得了进展，例如自行车设计师Van Moof所设计的自行车在中国的几家专卖店都能看到。

荷兰在高端设计服务方面也很强大，可以想象得到设计管理在荷兰已经得到了长足发展。

※ 打结的椅子（Moooi 马塞尔·万德斯）

《打结的椅子》只是马塞尔·万德斯许多作品中的一个，这是他在业内最广为人知的一个作品。

马塞尔·万德斯是一名荷兰设计师，在离开埃因霍温设计学院以后去了阿纳姆艺术学院，在1988年以优异的成绩从那里毕业。

2000年，马塞尔·万德斯在阿姆斯特丹开创了自己的工作室。2001年与他人共同创立了设计品牌Moooi，他是该公司的共同所有者和艺术总监。从2014年开始，万德斯担任他的Powerhouse工作室的产品和室内设计师和艺术总监，这是一个拥有大约50名国际设计师的团队。他们合作的私人客户和高端品牌已经超过了1 700个，诸如装饰品牌Bisazza、荷兰皇家航空、专业彩妆品牌MAC、灯具品牌Flos、施华洛世奇、彪马等。

马塞尔·万德斯获得的各种设计奖项也名目繁多，包括被多次提名的"鹿特丹设计奖"和"Kho Liang Ie设计奖"。他还在旧金山现代艺术博物馆、Limn、耐克、阿姆斯特丹国际纪录片电影节、Future Design Days以及世界上许多鼎鼎大名的设计学院举行讲座和授课。在2002年7月的《商业周刊》中，马塞尔·万德斯被选为"欧洲25位变革领导人"之一。他也是THNK创意领导学院的顾问委员会成员。

马塞尔·万德斯的许多设计作品都被收藏在世界各大博物馆和展厅，像纽约现代艺术博物馆、阿姆斯特丹市立博物馆和伦敦维多利亚和阿尔伯特博物馆 (V&A) 这些重量级的博物馆。2006年，他被ELLE杂志评选为"年度国际设计师"，甚至还出版了大量书籍，在全球媒体上广泛报道，出现在《纽约时报》、Domus、《金融时报》和Wallpaper杂志等刊物上。

※ Vitra家具（Jongeriuslab工作室海拉·容格里乌斯）

海拉·容格里乌斯是一位著名的荷兰设计师，以其创新的产品设计方法而闻名。她于1993年毕业于艾恩霍芬设计学院。毕业后，她因为荷兰颇具影响力的概念设计集团Droog Design的一系列设计而迅速崛起。容格里乌斯于1993年在鹿特丹创立了自己的设计公司Jongeriuslab。

设计师海拉·容格里乌斯以她融合工业和工艺、高科技和基础科技、传统和现代的方式而被众人知晓。她的设计侧重于对立组合，例如新技术和手工制品、工业制造和工艺以及传统和现代手法。她的作品往往具有高度的质感，比如把粗糙的边角皮革卷成卷做成椅子的轮子、用油漆颜料装饰到陶器上、把陶瓷和棉质桌布缝合在一起、用橡胶制作水槽。

海拉·容格里乌斯曾为许多知名客户效力，包括宜家、荷兰皇家航空、Vitra家具、家居品牌maharam、荷兰Makkum皇家陶瓷、德国Nymphenburg皇家瓷器。她的设计已经被纽约Cooper Hewitt国家设计博物馆、现代艺术博物馆、阿姆斯特丹市立博物馆、阿姆斯特丹博物馆、鹿特丹范·博宁恩博物馆、伦敦设计博物馆、巴黎Galerie kreo画廊和纽约Moss画廊等展出与收藏。

自2008年起，容格里乌斯一直在瑞士巴塞尔Vitra家具品牌担任颜色、纺织和外观艺术总监。2012年的时候，她为荷兰皇家航空公司波音747的商务舱设计了一全新的内饰和座椅。2013年，她还与极富创意的荷兰设计师库哈斯为纽约联合国总部设计了全新的代表大厅North Delegates' Lounge，并被任命为荷兰地毯公司Danskina的设计总监。

※ 梵高夜光自行车道（Roosegaarde工作室丹·罗斯加德）

丹·罗斯加德这个名字对很多人来说都很陌生，但它的项目对很多人来说都很熟悉，尤其是他的"Van Gogh Path"——很多人都知道的一条夜间发光的自行车小道，和他的"无霾项目"。"梵高小路"（Van Gogh Path）位于荷兰北布拉班特的纽南，距离艾恩霍芬不到10公里的距离。这是世界上第一条发光的自行车道，贯穿北布拉班特省，那里是著名的艺术家文森特·梵高出生并长大的地方。这条夜间会发出光亮的自行车道是受到梵高的著名画作《星夜》的启发，现在已经成了艾恩霍芬最值得去的地方之一。

"无霾项目"是丹·罗斯加德的另一个知名项目。该项目是由罗斯加德领导的一系列城市创新项目之一，旨在减少污染，并为清洁的未来提供鼓舞人心的经验。

罗斯加德与其团队开发"雾霾净化塔"还是因为受到了北京空气质量的启发，当时罗斯加德住

52

在北京CBD的一家酒店里，但由于雾霾太大，就连近在咫尺的CCTV大楼都几乎看不到。这件事给了他启迪，设计了雾霾净化塔并安装在了华沙的乔丹公园、天津和北京。雾霾净化塔运用了专利的离子技术在公共场所创造出一个无霾空间，使人们无须消费即可享受清新空气。

该塔于2016年在北京安装，它从周围吸入有霾空气，测试证明该塔可以捕捉并收集高达70%的PM10雾霾颗粒。过滤后的清新空气会再被释放到周围的空气中，与污浊空气混合，这样可以在塔内20米的范围内减少45%的PM10的污染。该塔还对PM2.5的污染有减少作用，可以将其降低25%。——该结果由艾恩霍芬科技大学研究获得。

在2017年，罗斯加德又提出了一个新的雾霾项目，"无霾自行车"。这个概念的灵感源自最近由艺术家Matt Hope和清华大学杨教授共同参与主持的减霾论坛。这种革新性的自行车会吸入被污染的空气然后进行清洁，再释放到骑车人的周围。

罗斯加德工作室开发的项目一向都备受瞩目。他们一直致力于城市环境与技术的结合，同时项目也要具备一定的艺术欣赏力。

在阿姆斯特丹史基浦机场，罗斯加德设计了一幅长达121米的透视云图像，由LED灯背光照明，让人对图像有深度的错觉。

他与莱顿大学合作开发了彩虹站项目，该项目照亮了有着125年历史的阿姆斯特丹中央车站。

罗斯加德工作室的作品在荷兰国立博物馆、伦敦Tate现代美术馆、东京国立博物馆、维多利亚和阿尔伯特博物馆和伦敦的设计博物馆都有展出。罗斯加德还在2016年赢得了"伦敦设计创新奖"。

Art and Culture　艺术和文化

When thinking about Dutch art and culture, the first thing that comes to mind are the famous painters, architects and sculptors from the 17th century: the so called Dutch Golden age. During the Dutch Golden age a large number of giants of painting, architecture and sculpture emerged. When thinking about painters famous names such as Rembrandt van Rijn, Johannes Vermeer, Jacob Isaakszoon van Ruisdael come to mind; architects as Jacob van Campen, Pieter Jansz Pos have left their traces and sculpture such as Hendrick De Keyser, Artus Quellinus are known to many.

What many don't realize is that current Dutch performing arts are just as famous around the world as the famous painters in the Golden age.

Dutch performing artists are in demand around the world. The Netherlands is also a popular destination for international artists. Dutch audiences are always in for something new and the country has good venues. Dutch dance companies are internationally renowned, from large established ones like the NDT to smaller troupes. The Royal Concertgebouw Orchestra also has a solid international reputation.

※ Nederlands Dans Theater

Nederlands Dans Theater (NDT), a Dutch contemporary dance company is one of the top dance companies in the world. Nederlands Dans Theater is headquartered at the Lucent Danstheater in The Hague. In addition to the Lucent Danstheater, NDT performs at other venues in the Netherlands, including Amsterdam's Het Muziektheater and Nijmegen's Stadsschouwburg.

NDT was founded in 1959 by Benjamin Harkarvy, Aart Verstegen and Carel Birnie together with a group of 18 members of the Dutch National Ballet (which was directed by Sonia Gaskell). Their intention was to break away from the more traditionally oriented Dutch National Ballet, NDT focused onto new ideas and experimentation with the exploration of new forms and techniques of dance.

In 1961 the Nederlands Dans Theater got subsidy from the city of The Hague and from the government. In the 1960s the NDT's repertoire comprised classical dance with a strong influence by American modern dance. The NDT got unprecedented recognition and success with the guidance of different persons like Hans van Manen and Jiří Kylián as artistic directors.

Nederlands Dans Theater is one of the most productive dance companies in the Netherlands, if not in the world. With six programs and nine world premieres in season 2015/2016 alone, NDT shows an unprecedented number of new ballets.

The Nederlands Dans Theater, the choreographers, the dancers and the groups have won several awards. Both Hans van Manen and Jiří Kylián are crowned as Officers in the Order of Orange Nassau by Queen Beatrix. In the Netherlands itself, the Nederlands Dans Theater has received the VSCD award (Vereniging van Schouwburgen en Concertgebouwdirecties) twelve times. The Zwaan awards for "most impressive dance production 2009" and for "most impressive dance performance 2009" have been handed to the Nederlands Dans Theater. In foreign countries the NDT has also won several awards, including the Nijinsky Awards. The choreographers Hans van Manen and Jiří Kylián have won awards on the prestigious Edinburgh International Festival.

※ Royal Concertgebouw Orchestra

The Concertgebouw opened on April 11 1888. The Concertgebouw Orchestra was established several months later, and gave its first concert in the Concertgebouw on November 3 1888, conducted by the orchestra's first chief conductor, Willem Kes.

The Royal Concertgebouw Orchestra (RCO) is considered as one of the world's leading orchestras. Time and time again, critics have lauded its unique sound, which clearly stands out among thousands of others. The RCO's string section has been called "velvety", the sound of the brass 'golden', the timbre of the woodwinds "distinctly personal" and the percussion have an international reputation. In 1988, Queen Beatrix conferred the "Royal" title upon the orchestra.

RCO Amsterdam is made up of 120 players hailing from over 20 countries. Despite its size, the orchestra actually functions more like a chamber orchestra in terms of the sensitivity with which its members listen to, and work in tandem with, one another. Indeed, this requires both a high individual calibre and a great sense of mutual trust and confidence. This is a very high requirement for chief conductors.

Daniele Gatti is the seventh chief conductor since The Royal Concertgebouw Orchestra was founded in 1888, everyone has made a great contribution to the orchestra.

Willem Mengelberg (1895–1945) laid the foundation for the orchestra's acclaimed Mahler tradition.

Bernard Haitink (1963–1988) refined the orchestra sound and broadened the repertoire.

Under the direction of Mariss Jansons(2004-2015), the orchestra consistently focused on composers such as Bruckner, Mahler, Strauss and Brahms, as well as important twentieth-century composers like Shostakovich and Messiaen, to whom large-scale thematic projects have been devoted.

Daniele Gatti enriches the symphonic tradition of the orchestra with French repertoire, the Second Viennese School and contemporary music.

In addition to some eighty concerts performed at the Concertgebouw in Amsterdam, the Royal Concertgebouw Orchestra gives forty concerts at leading concert halls throughout the world each year. The orchestra reaches some 250,000 concert-goers a year. Thanks to regular radio and television broadcasts in collaboration with its media partners, the Dutch broadcasting network AVROTROS, and increasingly with Mezzo TV and Unitel Classica, that exposure is further increased. The orchestra has made over 1,100 LP, CD and DVD recordings to date, many of which have won international distinctions. Since 2004, the orchestra boasts its own in-house label, RCO Live.

※ Royal Theatre Carré

The Koninklijk Theater Carré is a Neo-Renaissance theatre in Amsterdam, located near the river Amstel. When the theatre was founded in 1887, it was originally meant as a permanent circus building. Currently, it is mainly used for musicals, cabaret performances and pop concerts.

German circus director Oscar Carré, looking for a location for circus performances in the winter, opened Circus Carré on December 3 1887. In the beginning, it was just a wooden building with a stone façade. In the first years, it was only in use in the winter, but from 1893 on, Dutch theatre producer Frits van Haarlem brought vaudeville shows in the summer months. The shows became very successful, thus changing the circus building to a theatre for all forms of popular entertainment. In 1920, it changed its name to Theater Carré.

In 1956, Carré introduced musical theatre to the Netherlands with Porgy and Bess. The one-man show followed in 1963, when Toon Hermans gave his first solo cabaret show. At the end of the 1960s, the theatre was in danger of being demolished. After protests from artists, the municipality of Amsterdam finally refused permission for demolition. In 1977 the municipality bought the building. In 1987, at the centenary, the Royal Predicate was granted and the name was changed to Koninklijk Theater Carré. In 2004, the theatre was completely renovated. The historic façade and interior design have been retained.

130 years later Carré has a lot more to offer besides the famous World Christmas Circus. From cabaret to concerts and from opera to musicals, the Koninklijk Theater Carré has something for everyone. National and international stars from the world of circus, variety theatre and music have celebrated their greatest triumphs in Carré. Carré is consequently in the top three of famous cultural brands.

当我们想到荷兰的艺术和文化时，首先想到的是17世纪著名的画家、建筑师和雕塑家，也就是所谓的荷兰"黄金时代"。在荷兰黄金时代，大量绘画、建筑和雕塑的巨匠涌现出来。一提到画家，伦勃朗、维米尔、雅各布·范·雷斯达尔这些大师的名字立刻出现在脑海；建筑师雅各布·范·坎彭、皮特·扬森·博斯也都留下了他们的痕迹；还有雕塑家比如亨德里克·德·凯瑟和阿图斯·奎林努斯。

许多人没有意识到的是，当前荷兰的表演艺术和黄金时代的著名画家一样在世界各地都很出名。

荷兰的表演艺术家在世界各地都有需求。荷兰也是国际艺术家探索和表现的热门目的地。荷兰的观众总是喜欢新事物，而这里还有着很好的场地设施。荷兰舞蹈公司在国际上享有盛誉，既有着像NDT这样的大型舞蹈团，也有小型歌舞团。荷兰皇家交响乐团也有良好的国际声誉。

※ 荷兰舞蹈剧场

荷兰舞蹈剧场（NDT）汇集着世界顶级的舞者，舞团非常热衷于打破传统不断创新。

荷兰舞蹈剧场（NDT）是荷兰的一个现代舞公司，是世界顶级的舞蹈公司之一。荷兰舞蹈剧场总部设在海牙的路圣特舞蹈剧院。除了路圣特，荷兰舞蹈剧场还在荷兰的其他场所演出，包括阿姆斯特丹的歌剧音乐剧院和奈梅亨的城市剧院。

荷兰舞蹈剧场于1959年由本杰明·哈卡维、阿尔特·范斯特根、长雷尔·伯尼以及18个来自荷兰国家芭蕾舞团的成员（由索尼亚·加斯克尔指导）共同创立，他们的目的是打破荷兰国家芭蕾舞团的旧的传统。荷兰舞蹈剧场在探索舞蹈的新形式和新技术的过程中，聚焦于新的思想和尝试。

1961年，荷兰舞蹈剧场得到了来自海牙市和政府的补贴。在20世纪60年代，他们的剧目包括受美国现代舞强烈影响的古典舞。在荷兰舞蹈大师汉斯·范·曼恩和扬名世界的编舞家季利安等艺术总监的指导下，荷兰舞蹈剧场获得了前所未有的认可和成功。

荷兰舞蹈剧场是荷兰最具生产力的舞蹈团之一。仅在2015和2016赛季，就有6个曲目和9场世界首次公演，荷兰舞蹈剧场展现了空前数量的新芭蕾曲目。

荷兰舞蹈剧场、舞蹈指导、舞蹈演员和团体多次获得重要奖项。汉斯·范·曼恩和季利安双双被贝娅特丽克丝女王加冕为"奥伦治拿骚勋章"官员。仅仅在荷兰，荷兰舞蹈剧场就已经12次获得荷兰舞蹈界最高奖项VSCD奖。"天鹅奖"把"2009年最令人印象深刻的舞蹈制作"和"2009年最令人印象深刻的舞蹈表演"授予了荷兰舞蹈剧场NDT。在国外，NDT照样频繁获奖，包括"Nijinsky奖"。舞蹈指导汉斯·范·曼恩和季利安还在著名的爱丁堡国际艺术节上获得了奖项。

※ 皇家管弦乐团

皇家音乐厅在1888年4月11日开幕。几个月后，管弦乐团成立，并于1888年11月3日在音乐厅举行了第一次音乐会，由乐队的第一指挥威廉·克斯指挥。

荷兰皇家管弦乐团（简称RCO）被认为是世界上最著名的管弦乐团之一。评论家们一次又一次地赞扬了其独特的声音，这种赞美之声声声入耳。荷兰皇家管弦乐团的弦乐被盛赞为那"天鹅绒般的弦乐"、发出"金质"般声音的铜管、"非常私人"的木管乐器的音色以及名副其实的国际水准的打击乐。1988年，贝娅特丽克斯女王授予乐团"皇家"的称号。

荷兰皇家管弦乐团的120多名音乐家来自20多个国家。尽管规模庞大，但乐团实际上更像是一个室内管弦乐团，所有的成员都要相互感知、紧密配合。确实如此，这需要高水平的个人能力和相互间高度的信任和自信心。这对首席指挥来说是一个非常高的要求。

丹尼尔·加蒂是自1888年皇家管弦乐团成立以来的第七任首席指挥，每个人都为乐团做出了巨大贡献。

威廉姆·门格伯格（1895～1945年）奠定了乐团著名的马勒曲目的基础传统。

伯纳德·海特克（1963～1988年）改进了管弦乐队的演奏，并扩大了演奏曲目。

在马里斯·扬颂斯（2004～2015年）的指导下，管弦乐团一直专注于布鲁克纳、马勒、施特劳斯和勃拉姆斯等作曲家，以及像肖斯塔科维奇和梅西安这样的20世纪重要作曲家的大型主题曲目。

丹尼尔·加蒂以法国曲目、第二维也纳学派和当代音乐，丰富了管弦乐团的交响乐传统。

除了在阿姆斯特丹的皇家音乐厅定期举办的大约八十场音乐会之外，荷兰皇家管弦乐团每年还在世界各地的主要音乐厅举行四十场音乐会。乐团每年接待大约25万名音乐会观众。由于与荷兰AVROTROS广电公司定期的广播和电视媒体的合作，以及与Mezzo TV和Unitel Classica逐渐频繁的合作，乐团的曝光度进一步增加。迄今为止，皇家管弦乐团已制作了1100多张黑胶唱片、CD和DVD，其中许多已经赢得了国际声望。从2004年起，乐团还拥有了自己的品牌RCO Live。

※ 卡雷皇家剧院

卡雷皇家剧院是阿姆斯特丹的新文艺复兴剧院，位于阿姆斯特尔河畔。剧院始建立于1887年，原本是要当作一个固定性的马戏团建筑，现在主要用于音乐剧、歌舞表演和流行音乐会。

德国马戏团总监奥斯卡·卡雷为了给马戏团在冬季表演的时候找场地，于是在1887年12月3日开设了卡雷马戏团。起初，这只是一座带石头外立面的木制建筑。头几年，这里只在冬天的时候启用，但从1893年起，荷兰戏剧制作人弗里斯·范·哈勒姆在夏天的几个月里也推出了杂耍表演。因为演出非常成功，因此把马戏团的建筑改成了各种形式的大众娱乐的剧场。1920年，这里改名为"卡雷剧院"。

卡雷皇家剧院坐落在阿姆斯特尔河畔，景色雅致，曾面临被拆除的境地。

1956年，卡雷把音乐剧波吉与贝丝引入到荷兰。1963年，荷兰著名的喜剧演员董·海曼斯在这里举行了他的第一场单独卡巴莱表演，独角戏形式的表演也就开始吸收进来。20世纪60年代末，剧院面临被拆除的处境，在艺术家们的抗议之后，阿姆斯特丹市政府终于撤销了拆除剧院的决定。1977年，这栋大楼被市政府买下。1987年，在百年纪念期间，剧院被授予皇家的至尊称号，名字改为"卡雷皇家剧院"。2004年，剧院进行了彻底翻修，历史悠久的建筑外立面和室内装饰被保留下来。

在130年之后，除了著名的世界圣诞马戏团演出，卡雷皇家剧院还有非常多形式的演出。从法国卡巴莱喜剧形式到音乐会、从歌剧到音乐剧，剧院的演出适合每一个人观看。来自马戏团界、综艺剧院和音乐界的国内和国际明星都在卡雷倾情演出欢聚一堂，因此卡雷也是著名的文化品牌的前三甲。

Television, Film and Entertainment Industries
电视电影和娱乐产业

Cinema in the Netherlands refers to the film industry based in Netherlands. Because the Dutch film industry is relatively small, and there is little or no international market for Dutch films, almost all films rely on state funding. This funding can be achieved through several sources, for instance through the Netherlands Film Fund or the public broadcast networks. But one thing the Dutch are proud of is that the Dutch Documentary films have received worldwide acclaim. The International Documentary Film Festival Amsterdam, held annually in November, is considered one of the largest documentary film festivals in the world. The most prominent Dutch directors, especially those who started their careers before World War II, came from a documentary background, for instance Joris Ivens and Bert Haanstra. Since the early 1970s, however, documentary production aimed at a theatrical release has declined, perhaps due to a shift towards television documentary. Television program production in the Netherlands is even better. It is the world's third largest television exporter. In addition, the Netherlands is one of the world's top ten record markets and one of the fastest growing music streaming services. More than 15,000 people live on radio and television.

※ Television

"The Voice of China" a show familiar to many in China, but if you tell them that it a product from the Netherlands them you are often met with looks of disbelieve, it is hard for many to think that a small European country known for tulips, windmills and wooden shoes ranks third in the world in terms of entertainment output, behind only Britain and the United States.

The Dutch television shows are among the best in the world. The reason why the Netherlands has become the cradle of creative ideas for television programs around the world cannot be separated from the support of hardware and software production all over the country. "Dutch Valley" is undoubtedly the brain and organisation in these production lines. The "Dutch Valley", located southeast of Amsterdam, was built in the 1960s, surrounded by trees and beautifully landscaped. Unlike the large number of artificial landscaping sites in the western studios, "Dutch Valley" is more like an industrial park, which can be used for creative, photographic recording and post-production activities by major broadcasters and media companies. In the 1960s, there was only one broadcaster in the Dutch Valley. Later, many radio and television companies moved in order to save costs and form a cluster effect. Now, there are more than 200 top-notch TV institutions in the "Dutch Valley", with top-notch equipment and powerful influence that has attracted television talent from all over Europe. Every day, creative people from different companies get together to brainstorm.

World famous programs such as "The Voice", "Sing It", "Celebrity Big Brother" and "1 vs 100" are all produced here. The Netherlands version of "Celebrity Big Brother" is more so the originator of the world's reality show, which was watched by about two-thirds of the Dutch when it premiered. Although the content of "Celebrity Big Brother" has been attacked by many people, it is still very popular. Some countries such as Germany, Spain and the United States have successively launched local versions. Subsequently, other countries have begun to launch a variety of reality shows, such as "Survivor" "Temptation Island" "Loft Story".

There is one person and two companies that we have to mention when talking about Dutch television, these are John de Mol and program production company Endemol and Talpa Network.

In 1997-1999 John de Mol developed the highly popular reality television series Big Brother with his eponymous production company, John de Mol Produkties. In 1994 his company merged with Joop van den Ende TV-Producties into Endemol, but it still functioned on its own. He also produced "Fear Factor", "Love Letters", "1 vs 100" and "Deal or No Deal" for Endemol. De Mol sold his share of Endemol in 2000 to Telefónica, but continued to serve as creative director until 2004.

Talpa Network is the company in which John de Mol Jr. has transferred all of its media activities. The program "The Voice" is from Talpa Network.The Talpa Network's official website lists nearly 50 countries with "The Voice" copyright, and countries with similar programming models are far more than that. However, "The Voice" is just one of the Talpa Network's many programs, only in China, there are "We 15", "I Love China", "Men VS Women", "Dating in the Dark" and other programs are from this company. So far, Talpa Network has launched more than 60 programming models and sold the rights to hundreds of countries.

※ Film

Although the Dutch film industry is relatively small, there have been several active periods in which Dutch filmmaking thrived. The first boom came during the First World War when the Netherlands was one of the neutral states. Studios like Hollandia produced an impressive cycle of feature films. A second wave followed in the 1930s, as talking pictures led to a call for Dutch-spoken films, which resulted in a boom in production: between 1934 and 1940, 37 feature films were released. The first Dutch film was the slapstick comedy *Gestoorde hengelaar* (1896) by M.H. Laddé. Willy Mullens who was one of the influential pioneers of Dutch cinema in the early 1900s. His slapstick comedy film *The Misadventure of a French Gentleman Without Pants* at the Zandvoort Beach is the oldest surviving Dutch film.

59

Until the World War II, the private Dutch film industry came to a near halt. In the years directly following the war, most effort was given to the reconstruction of the country; film was not a priority. In the late 1950s the Dutch film industry professionalized. The Nederlands Film Fund was established in 1957, the Nederlandse Filmacademie in 1958. Documentary filmer Bert Haanstra made his first fiction film, *Fanfare*, in 1958. Even though the film was a big success, this success was only incidental. Dutch cinema did temporarily provide a sound of its own in this period, in the form of what is now considered to be the "Dutch documentary tradition" or "Dutch documentary school". Headed by Haanstra, who won an Academy Award for Documentary Short Subject with 1959's *Glass* and also won prizes in Berlin and Cannes, the movement also included Herman van der Horst, who won a Golden Bear for Best Documentary and John Fernhout, whose *Sky Over Holland* won a Golden Palm at the Cannes Film Festival and was nominated for an Academy Award for Documentary Short Subject in 1968. Famous documentary directors include also Joris Ivens, Johan van der Keuken and Jos de Putter. Ivens won a César Award and a Golden Lion, as well as a career achievement award at the Venice Film Festival.

Below are some recommended by Dutch filmmakers, directors and films:

Rutger Hauer, Dutch actor/Valerian and *The City of a Thousand Planets* (2017), *Batman Begins* (2005), *Blade Runner* (1982).

Jeroen Krabbé, Dutch actor/*The Discovery of Heaven* (2001), *Left Luggage* (1998).

Famke Janssen, Dutch actress/*X-Men*, *Taken*.

Carice van Houten, Dutch actress/*Game of Thrones* (2012), *BlackBook* (2006).

Paul Verhoeven, Dutch director/*BlackBook* (2006), *Starship Troopers* (1997), *Basic Instinct* (1992).

Menno Meyjes, Dutch director/*Martian Child* (2007), *Indiana Jones and the Last Crusade* (1989).

Marleen Gorris, Dutch director/*Mrs Dalloway* (1997), *Antonia* (1995).

※ Entertainment industries

In this section we mainly talk about the music industry in the Netherlands. The Netherlands has a very well-developed music industry and market. The huge number of important music festivals in the country, the pop music and jazz developed in the country play a decisive role in the world of music. Another area in the world of music that is strongly influenced by the Dutch is that of dance of music. Dutch DJs play a very important and decisive role in this part of the music Industry.

In the early 1990s, Dutch DJ's developed a style of electronic dance music called Gabber. The style was developed in reaction to the commercialisation of house music and was heavily influenced by early hardcore from Frankfurt and New York City. The DJs stripped the music of what they perceived as excess sounds, songs were reduced to a high-speed monotonous beat, of

sometimes over 260 beats per minute. The first ever record to be labeled Gabber was 'Amsterdam waar lech dat dan?' by Rotterdam-based 'the Euromasters' as a reaction to the media always focusing on Amsterdam. It has to be said that Amsterdam-based D-Shake was probably to be the first to use the term Gabber in a 1990 Dutch TV program.

The Netherlands has also spawned many Eurodance acts, such as 2 Unlimited, Alice Deejay, the Venga Boys, the Two Brothers on the 4th Floor and Twenty Four Seven. Many of the world's top trance DJs are Dutch, such as Armin van Buuren, Ferry Corsten and DJ Tiësto. The DJ Magazine Top 10 has been dominated by the Dutch for many years. In 2012 five of the 10 DJs were Dutch. In 2016 it was more so, six of the top 10 DJs in the ranking are Dutch. Even also, twenty-year-old Martin Garrix has become the youngest ever winner of DJ Mag's top 100 DJs poll. DJ Tiesto has been awarded best DJ for three times in a row by *DJ Magazine* and is still present in the top 10. Many foreign DJs live in and operate from the Netherlands. Drum and bass is also popular in the Netherlands, artists including Noisia and Black Sun Empire. The Netherlands is home to many of the largest trance events on earth, including Sensation and Trance Energy.

荷兰电影是指荷兰的电影工业。由于荷兰电影业规模较小，荷兰电影几乎或者说没有国际市场，差不多所有的电影都依靠国家资助。这种资助可以通过几个来源实现，例如通过荷兰电影基金或公共广播网络。但有一件事是荷兰人引以为豪的，那就是荷兰的纪录片在全世界都广受赞誉。每年11月举行的阿姆斯特丹国际纪录片电影节，被认为是世界上最大的纪录片电影节之一。荷兰最著名的导演，尤其是那些在"二战"前开始职业生涯的荷兰导演，都有纪录片的相关背景，比如尤里斯·伊文思和柏特·汉斯卓。然而，自20世纪70年代初以来，旨在出场上映的纪录片的产量下降了，或许是由于转向了电视纪录片。荷兰的电视节目制作则要好得多。荷兰是世界第三大电视节目制作出口国。此外，荷兰是全球十大唱片市场之一，也是发展最快的音乐流媒体服务之一。超过15 000人以广播和电视作为谋生之道。

※ 电视

"中国好声音"是很多中国人都非常熟悉的节目，但是如果你告诉他们这是一个来自荷兰的选秀节目，会经常让人怀疑。因为对许多人来说，这个以郁金香、风车和木鞋知名的欧洲小国在世界娱乐产业输出上竟然排名第三，仅次于英国和美国，着实令人难以置信。

荷兰的电视节目是世界上最好的节目之一。荷兰之所以成为世界各地电视节目创意的摇篮，这与全国各地的硬件和软件产出的支持大为相关。"Dutch Valley"，可以称之为"荷兰谷"，或者就叫"Dutch Valley"无疑是这条娱乐生产线上大脑组织。位于阿姆斯特丹东南的"Dutch Valley"建于20世纪60年代，周围树木环绕，风景优美。与西方电影公司的大量人工景观场地不同，"Dutch Valley"更像是一个工业园区，可以用于一些重要的广播公司和媒体公司的创意、摄影记录和后期制作活动。在20世纪60年代，"Dutch Valley"只有一家广播公司。后来，许多电台和电视公司为了节约成本形成集群效应。现在，"Dutch Valley"驻扎着200多家顶级的电视机构，拥有一流的设备和强大的影响力，吸引了来自欧洲各地的电视人才。每天，来自不同公司的创意人才都会聚在一起集思广益。

世界上一些著名的节目如"好声音（The Voice）""我心唱响（Sing It）""名人老大哥（Celebrity Big Brother）"和"1 vs 100"都是在这里制作的。而荷兰版的"名人老大哥"更是世界上真人秀节目的鼻祖，该节目在荷兰首播时，有大约三分之二的荷兰观众都收看了该节目。虽然"名人老大哥"的内容受到很多人的攻击，但仍然挡不住人们对它的喜爱。德国、西班牙和美国等一些国家相继推出了本地版本。随后，其他国家也开始推出各种真人秀节目，如"幸存者（Survivor）""诱惑岛（Temptation Island）""阁楼故事（Loft Story）"。

好声音在中国的纠纷让人唏嘘，但这个由荷兰原创的节目已经输出至上百个国家。

在谈到荷兰的电视制作时，有一个人和两家公司不得不提到，他们就是约翰·德莫尔，节目制作公司Endemol和Talpa Network。

1997年至1999年，约翰·德莫尔与他的同名制作公司John de Mol Produkties共同开发了非常受欢迎的真人秀系列"老大哥"。1994年，他的公司与Joop van den Ende TV-Producties合并成立了Endemol，但它仍可独立运营。他还为Endemol制作了"冒险极限（Fear Factor）""情书（Love Letters）""以一敌百（1vs100）"和"成交不成交（Deal or No Deal）"。德莫尔在2000年将他的Endemol份额出售给了西班牙电话公司Telefónica，但在2004年之前仍然担任创意总监。

Talpa Network是德莫尔将其所有的媒体活动转接的公司。"好声音"节目就是来自Talpa Network。Talpa Network的官方网站列出了近50个拥有"好声音"版权的国家，而节目类型相似的国家则远不止这些。但是，"好声音"只是Talpa Network开发的众多节目之一，仅仅在中国引进的就有"我们15个""我爱我的祖国""男左女右""完美暗恋"等。到目前为止，Talpa Network已经推出了60多个节目类型，并将这些版权出售给了数百个国家。

※ 电影

尽管荷兰电影产业相对较小，但荷兰的电影制作也经过了几个蓬勃发展时期。第一次的繁荣时期是在第一次世界大战期间，当时荷兰是中立国家之一，像Hollandia这样的电影公司制作了一系列令人印象深刻的故事片。20世纪30年代出现了第二波电影制作浪潮，因为有声电影催生了对荷兰语电影的需求，从而产生了电影业的繁荣：在1934年到1940年间，发行的故事片达到了37部。第一部荷兰电影是由M.H. Ladde在1896年制作的喜剧片《被惊扰的垂钓者》。威利·穆伦斯是20世纪早期荷兰电影的先驱之一，他的喜剧电影《没穿裤子的法国绅士》是现存最老的荷兰电影。

直到第二次世界大战之前，荷兰的私营电影产业几乎停滞不前。在战争之后的几年里，整个国家全身心地投入到战后重新建设当中，电影不是重点。20世纪50年代后期，荷兰电影工业趋向专业化。1957年成立了荷兰国家电影基金会，1958年成立了荷兰电影公司。1958年，纪录片制片人伯特·哈恩斯特制作了他的第一部故事片《大张旗鼓》。尽管这部电影取得了巨大的成功，但它的成功只是偶然的。这一时期的荷兰电影公司在业内开始短暂发声，现在被认为是"荷兰纪录片传统"或"荷兰纪录片学校"。以哈恩斯特为首，他的影片《玻璃》获得1959年奥斯卡最佳纪录片奖，同时也在柏林和戛纳赢得了奖项；还有海尔曼·范德·豪斯特赢得了最佳纪录片金熊奖；约翰·菲恩豪特的《荷兰的天空》获得了戛纳电影节金棕榈奖，并获得1968年奥斯卡最佳纪录片提名。荷兰著名的纪录片导演还有Joris Ivens、Johan van der Keuken和Jos de Putter。在威尼斯电影节上，Ivens获得了凯撒奖和金狮奖，并获得了终身成就奖。

下面推荐几位荷兰电影制片人、导演及其部分影片（包括其导演、制作、参演）：

荷兰的电影产业虽没有电视强劲，但仍有杰出的影人，如保罗·范霍文，电影《黑皮书》和《本能》都出自他手。

鲁特格尔·哈尔，演员，《星际特工：千星之城》（2017年）、《蝙蝠侠》（2005年）、《银翼杀手》（1982年）；

杰罗恩·克拉比，导演、演员，《发现天堂》（2001年），《失落的行李》（1998年）；

法米克·詹森，演员、导演，《X战警》系列，《飓风营救》；

卡里斯·范·侯登，演员，《权力的游戏》（2012年），《黑皮书》（2006年）；

保罗·范霍文，导演、编剧，《黑皮书》（2006年），《星河战队》（1997年），《本能》（1992年）；

曼诺·迈依杰斯，导演、编剧，《火星的孩子》（2007年），《夺宝奇兵》（1989年）；

玛琳·格里斯，导演，《黛洛维夫人》（1997年），《安东尼娅家族》（1995年）。

※ 娱乐产业

在这一节，我们主要讨论荷兰的音乐产业。荷兰拥有非常发达的音乐产业和市场。荷兰国内有着众多的音乐娱乐活动，荷兰的流行音乐和爵士乐在全球音乐界都有着非常重要的影响力。另一个受到荷兰人强烈影响的音乐领域是舞蹈音乐，荷兰的DJ在音乐产业中扮演着非常重要和决定性的角色。

20世纪90年代早期，荷兰DJ创造了一种叫作Gabber的电子舞曲。这种风格是在对家庭音乐商业化的反应中发展起来的，并深受法兰克福和纽约早期的Hardcore的影响。DJ们把他们认为是多余的音乐去掉了，歌曲被简化成一个高速单调的节拍，有时甚至每分钟超过260次。有史以来第一个被称为Gabber的记录是驻守在鹿特丹的"The Euromasters"乐队的"Amsterdam waar lech dat dan"——意为"阿姆斯特丹在哪里"——借由这首曲子透过媒体表达他们对阿姆斯特丹的态度（这里有一个背景，"二战"后鹿特丹进入重建时期，这里生活着大多数都是低收入者和农民群体，而在80年代，阿姆斯特丹兴起house音乐，浮华的优越感和朴素的鹿特丹格格不入，让鹿特丹人觉得他们装腔作势，于是鹿特丹的音乐青年决定玩儿点儿狠的）。但不得不说，阿姆斯特丹的D-Shake乐队可能是第一个在1990年的荷兰电视节目中使用Gabber这个词的。

荷兰也催生出了许多欧陆舞蹈表演，如舞曲组合2 Unlimited、电子乐队Alice Deejay、锐舞组合Venga Boys、2 Brothers on the 4th Floor组合和Twenty 4 Seven组合。世界上许多顶级的DJ都是荷兰人，比如Armin van Buuren、Ferry Corsten和DJ Tiesto。《DJ》杂志的前10名多年来一直由荷兰人主宰。2012年，10名DJ中有5位是荷兰人。在2016年更甚，排名前十的DJ中有6个都是荷兰人。即使如此竞争激烈，20岁的Martin Garrix还是成为《DJ》前100名DJ中最年轻的得主。Tiesto连续三次被《DJ》杂志评为最佳DJ，目前仍在前十名之中。许多来自国外的DJ都选择到荷兰居住和发展。鼓和贝斯在荷兰也很流行，著名的艺术家有Noisia和Black Sun Empire。荷兰还是全球最大的传思（Trance，也称迷幻舞曲）派对的发源地，像Sensation和Trance Energy。

Tijd voor Nederlands 荷兰语时间

● 单词+短语

荷 beroep	荷 kantoor	荷 kunst
英 career	英 office	英 art
译 职业	译 办公室	译 艺术
荷 stijl	荷 brug	荷 universiteit
英 style	英 bridge	英 university
译 风格	译 桥梁	译 大学
荷 gebouw	荷 ontwerper	荷 ontwerpen
英 building	英 designer	英 design
译 建筑	译 设计师	译 设计
荷 studeren	荷 werk	
英 study	英 work	
译 学习	译 工作	

● 例句

荷 Wat voor werk doet u?	荷 Mijn beroep is ont werper.
英 What kind of work do you do?	英 My profession is a designer.
译 你是做什么工作的？	译 我的职业是设计师。
荷 Ik hou erg van kunst.	荷 Ik hou echt van deze stijl.
英 I like art very much.	英 I really like this design style.
译 我非常喜欢艺术。	译 我很喜欢这个设计风格。
荷 Ik studeer kunst aan de universiteit en nu heb ik mijn eigen kantoor	荷 Dit gebouw is ontworpen door Nederlanders.
	英 This building was designed by the Dutch.
英 I studied art at university and now I have my own office.	译 这栋建筑是由荷兰人设计的。
译 我在大学学习艺术，现在我有自己的办公室。	
荷 De Chinezen hebben vele bruggen ontworpen en gebouwd.	
英 The Chinese designed and built many bridges.	
译 中国人设计和建造了很多桥梁。	

3. 荷兰品牌
Dutch Brand

In the eyes of many people, the Netherlands is not a traditional "name-brand" country, but still many Dutch brands are known to all, even without realising it. Such as the famous electronics company Philips, famous beer brand Heineken, designer clothing brand Viktor & Rolf, trendy denim brand G-Star, fast fashion brand C&A and WE, mints brand Mentos, as well as world-renowned baby food brands Friso, Nutrilon, Dumex, Hipp and so on. However, in addition to these brands, leading brands in many fields are from the Netherlands, especially in the fields of energy, chemicals, finance and insurance.

在许多人看来，荷兰并不是一个传统的"名牌"国家，但仍有许多品牌众所周知，只是人们并没有意识到它们实际上来自荷兰。比如非常有名的品牌如电子产品公司飞利浦、著名啤酒品牌喜力、设计师服装品牌Viktor & Rolf、时尚牛仔品牌G-Star、快时尚品牌C&A和WE、薄荷糖品牌曼妥思（Mentos），以及世界知名的婴儿食品品牌美素佳儿（Friso）、牛栏/诺优能（Nutrilon）、多美滋（Dumex）、喜宝（Hipp）等。然而，除了这些品牌之外，还有很多其他领域的领先品牌都来自荷兰，尤其是在能源、化工、金融和保险领域。

65

Energy and Chemicals 能源和化工

※ Shell (Royal Dutch Shell)

Royal Dutch Shell ranks among the largest oil companies in the world for years, with it ranking the second in the list of the largest oil companies announced by *Forbes* magazine in 2017.

Royal Dutch Shell, commonly known as Shell, formed in 1907 through the amalgamation of the Royal Dutch Petroleum Company of the Netherlands and the "Shell" Transport and Trading Company of the United Kingdom. The history of both companies can be traced back to the late 19th century. The Royal Dutch Petroleum Company was a Dutch company founded in 1890 to develop an oilfield in Pangkalan Brandan, North Sumatra, and initially led by August Kessler, Hugo Loudon, and Henri Deterding. The "Shell" Transport and Trading Company was a British company, founded in 1897 by Marcus Samuel, 1st Viscount Bearsted, and his brother Samuel. It is the sixth-largest company in the world measured by 2016 revenues, and the largest based in Europe. Shell was first in the 2013 *Fortune* Global 500 list of the world's largest companies; In that year its revenues were equivalent to 84% of the Netherlands' $556 billion GDP.

Shell is active in every area of the oil and gas industry, including exploration and production, refining, transport, distribution and marketing, petrochemicals, power generation and trading. It also has renewable energy activities, including in biofuels, wind and hydrogen. Shell has operations in over 70 countries, produces around 3.7 million barrels of oil equivalent per day and has 44,000 service stations worldwide.

Shell's logo, known as the "pecten", is one of the most familiar commercial symbols in the world.

※ Akzo Nobel

Akzo Nobel is a global fortune 500 company, based in the Netherlands, is the leading large-scale industrial company and one of the largest decorative paint companies in the world, has activities in more than 80 countries and and employs approximately 46,000 people. In China alone, Akzo Nobel has already set up more than 30 production bases, one innovation center, one service center and sales offices all over the country, with nearly 7,600 employees. Akzo Nobel has a very wide range of products, including industrial coatings, ships and protective coatings, packaging coatings, pulp and paper chemicals, etc. The brands we are familiar with, such as DuoLeShi, Levis, International, Eka, Cuprinol, Sikkens, etc, are all from Akzo Nobel.

Akzo Nobel has a long history of mergers and divestments. Parts of the current company can be traced back to 17th century companies. The milestone mergers and divestments are the formation of AKZO in 1969, the merger with Nobel Industries in 1994 forming Akzo Nobel, and the divestment of its pharmaceutical business and the merger with ICI in 2007/2008 resulting in current day Akzo Nobel.

※ 荷兰皇家壳牌

2017年，荷兰皇家壳牌石油公司跻身全球最大的石油公司之列，它在《福布斯》杂志2017年宣布的最大的石油公司名单中名列第二。

荷兰皇家壳牌公司俗称"壳牌"，于1907年通过荷兰皇家石油公司和英国的"Shell"运输和贸易公司合并而成立。两家公司的历史可以追溯到19世纪末。荷兰皇家石油公司是一家成立于1890年的荷兰公司，目的是为了开发北苏门答腊Pangkalan Brandan的油田，最初由August Kessler、Hugo Loudon和Henri Deterding领导。"Shell"运输和贸易公司是一家成立于1897年的英国公司，由英国皇商马库斯·塞缪尔，封贝尔斯泰德庄一代子爵和他的兄弟塞缪尔创立。以2016年的收入计算，荷兰皇家壳牌是全球第六大公司，也是欧洲最大的公司。壳牌在2013年《财富》全球500强企业榜单上排名第一。在那一年，它的收入相当于荷兰5 560亿美元GDP的84%。

壳牌在石油和天然气工业的各个领域都很活跃，包括勘探和生产、提炼、运输、分销和销售、石化、发电和贸易。它在可再生能源领域也有涉猎，包括生物燃料、风能和氢气。壳牌在超过70个国家开展了业务，每天生产约370万桶石油当量，在全球拥有44 000个加油站。

壳牌的标志被称为"扇贝"，是世界上最被人熟知的商业标志之一。

※ 阿克苏诺贝尔

阿克苏诺贝尔公司（Akzo Nobel）是全球财富500强企业，总部设在荷兰，是全球领先的大型工业企业，也是全球最大的装饰涂料公司之一，在80多个国家都开展有业务，并雇用了大约46 000名员工。仅在中国，阿克苏诺贝尔就已在全国各地建立了30多个生产基地，一个创新中心，一个服务中心和销售办事处，拥有近7 600名员工。阿克苏诺贝尔公司拥有非常广泛的产品系列，包括工

业涂料、船舶和防护涂料、包装涂料、纸浆和造纸化学品等。我们熟悉的品牌包括多乐士、来威、International、Eka、Cuprinol、Sikkens等，都来自阿克苏诺贝尔公司。

阿克苏诺贝尔公司合并和拆分有着比较长的历史，目前公司的一部分可以追溯到17世纪。1969年AKZO公司的形成是一次里程碑式的合并和拆分。1994年，AKZO又与Nobel Industries合并形成了阿克苏诺贝尔公司，公司于2007/2008年剥离了其制药业务，并与ICI合并，这才形成当前的阿克苏诺贝尔。

Finance and Insurance 金融和保险

※ ING Group

ING is a short term for Internationale Nederlanden Groep, an international financial services company. Its primary businesses are retail banking, direct banking, commercial banking, investment banking, asset management, and insurance services. ING Bank was included in a list of global systemically important banks in 2012. It served over 48 million individual and institutional clients in more than 40 countries, with a worldwide workforce exceeding 51,000. Orange is the colour of the royal Dutch family, the orange lion on ING's logo alludes to the Group's Dutch origins under the House of Orange-Nassau.

ING was founded in 1991 by a merger between Nationale-Nederlanden and NMB Postbank Group. Since 1991, ING has developed from a Dutch company with some international business to a multinational with Dutch roots. This was achieved through a mixture of organic growth, such as the creation of ING Direct from scratch, as well as various large acquisitions. The first large acquisition took place in 1995, when ING took over Barings Bank. This acquisition increased the brand recognition of ING around the world and strengthened its wholesale banking presence in the emerging markets. The other acquisitions including Belgian bank Banque Bruxelles Lambert (BBL) in 1998, US-based insurance company Equitable of Iowa and the commercial bank Furman Selz. It also acquired Frankfurt based BHF-Bank in 1999, although disposed of this later.

On March 25 2005, the company announced the acquisition of a 19.9% stake in the Bank of Beijing and the deal was worth about 1.7 billion *yuan*, or $200 million. As of 2017, ING is still the largest shareholder of Bank of Beijing. Meanwhile, ING ranks among the top foreign insurers in China, the only foreign company in China that has two Life insurance licences—Pacific Antna Life and BOB—Cardif Life.

In addition, ING real estate established a representative office in Beijing as early as 1996. In 2003, it established a real estate investment management company in Shanghai and real estate projects in Beijing, Shanghai and other cities.

※ Aegon

Aegon, founded in 1983, is one of the largest listed life insurance groups in the world and headquartered in The Hague, the Netherlands. But Aegon's roots stretch back more than 160 years. At that time, Aegon provided modest funds in the Netherlands for people to arrange burials for their family members and other loved ones. The oldest of these original companies was Algemeene Friesche, created by two civil servants in the northern Dutch province of Friesland in 1844.

In 1968, three insurers—Algemeene Friesche, Groot Noordhollandsche and Olveh—joined forces to create a new company called AGO. The next many years, AGO acquired large insurers in the United States, Spain, Scotland, Hungary, and set up a greenfield operation in China Taiwan in 1993. Over the next few years, the company strengthened its position in China Taiwan, which played a significant role in helping Aegon expand into Asia. In 2002, Aegon and CNOOC (China National Offshore Oil Corporation) respectively formed AEGON-CNOOC Life Insurance Company with a 50% contribution. In 2014, Tsinghua Tongfang bought 50% of the shares and AEGON-CNOOC changed its name to AEGON-THTF Life Insurance Company in 2015.

※ 荷兰国际集团

荷兰国际集团（ING）是一家国际金融服务公司。它的主要业务是零售银行业务、直接银行业务、商业银行业务、投资银行业务、资产管理和保险业务。2012年，ING银行被列入全球系统重要的银行名单。ING在全世界40多个国家为超过4 800多万个人和机构提供服务，它的全球员工超过了51 000人。橙色是荷兰皇室的颜色，ING徽标上的橙色狮子暗指集团的奥伦治——拿骚家族血统。

ING国际集团是荷兰最大的金融集团之一，标志性的橙色狮子让人印象深刻，是北京银行的最大股东。

ING成立于1991年，是由保险公司Nationale-Nederlanden和邮政银行集团合并而成。自1991年以来，ING已从一家荷兰公司发展成为一家具有荷兰根基的跨国公司。这是通过不断的合并和组建实现的，比如从ING Direct创建到各种大型收购。第一次大型收购发生在1995年，当时ING接管了巴林银行，此次收购提高了ING在全球的知名度，并加强了其在新兴市场的批发银行业务。其他收购包括1998年的比利时布鲁塞尔银行、美国爱荷华保险公司和商业银行Furman Selz。1999年ING还收购了总部位于法兰克福的私人银行BHF，不过后来又脱手卖掉了。

2005年3月25日，ING宣布收购北京银行19.9%的股份，该交易价值约17亿元人民币，约合2亿美元。截至2017年，ING仍是北京银行的最大股东。同时，ING还是中国最大的外资保险公司之一，是中国唯一一家拥有两份人寿保险牌照的外资公司——太平洋安泰人寿和中荷人寿。

此外，ING房地产公司早在1996年就在北京设立了代表处。2003年，ING在上海成立了房地产投资管理公司，并在北京、上海等城市建立了房地产项目。

※ 荷兰全球保险集团

荷兰全球保险集团（Aegon）成立于1983年，是世界上最大的上市人寿保险集团之一，总部设在荷兰海牙，但荷兰全球保险的创业史却可以追溯到160多年以前。当时，荷兰全球人寿保险公司为人们提供适当的资金用于安葬他们的家人和其他亲人。最早期的公司叫Algemeene Friesche，是由荷兰北部弗里斯兰省的两个公务员在1844年创立的。

1968年，三家保险公司——Algemeene Friesche、 Groot Noordhollandsche和Olveh，联手组建了一家名为AGO的新公司。在接下来的许多年里，AGO在美国、西班牙、苏格兰、匈牙利并购了一系列大型保险公司，并于1993年在我国台湾开展了一项绿地业务。在接下来的几年里，该公司在我国台湾的地位得到加强和巩固，对其在亚洲地区业务的扩展发挥了重要作用。2002年，荷兰全球保险集团和中国海洋石油集团（CNOOC）各自出资50%组建了海康人寿保险公司。2014年，清华同方收购了该公司50%的股份，并于2015年更名为同方全球人寿。

Biology and Medicine 生物和医药

※ DSM

DSM is an international nutrition health care products, chemical raw materials and pharmaceutical group, headquartered in the Netherlands, in Europe. It has more than 200 institutions in Asia, north and South America, more than 20,000 employees worldwide. At the end of 2016 DSM employed 20,786 people in around 50 countries and posted net sales of €8 billion. DSM is a world leader in many areas, has five main divisions: nutrition, pharmaceuticals, performance materials, polymer intermediates, basic chemistry and materials.

DSM's name comes from the acronym of its original English translation. DSM's Dutch name is "De Nederlandse Staatsmijnen", translated into English is "Dutch State Mines (DSM)", meaning the Dutch state-owned coal mining company. In 1902. DSM was formed by the Dutch State to mine coal reserves in southern Limburg and although the company had diversified into commodity chemicals and petrochemicals by 1973 when the last mine closed. DSM retains a link to its origins by continuing to use the initials of the original 'Nederlandse Staatsmijnen' (Dutch State Mines) to this day.

The DSM began to trade with China in 1963 and established its first sales representative office and the first production site in China in the early 1990s. In 2005, DSM established DSM China R&D Centre in Shanghai. In 2011, DSM China R & D Centre was established as the main innovation base of DSM in China

※ Organon

Before 2007, Organon was the human health care business unit of Akzo Nobel. In November 2007, Schering-Plough Corporation, based in New Jersey, USA, acquired Organon from Akzo Nobel. Now, Organon is a pharmaceutical company based in Oss, the Netherlands, and Roseland, New Jersey, USA.

Organon was founded by Dr. Saal van Zwanenberg in Oss, the Netherlands, in 1923 as Zwanenberg-Organon. Its first product was insulin in 1923. In the thirties it manufactured estrogens. In 1948, Organon acquired the Newhouse research site in Scotland, United Kingdom. The production of cortisone was initiated in 1953. In 1962 it bought the stock of the Nederlandsche Cocaine factory. Organon now mainly involved in areas includes: reproductive medicine, contraception, mental class, hormone replacement therapy and anaesthesia. These include several leading products, such as the treatment of infertility Puregon, muscle relaxant Remeron, antidepressant Mirtazapine and contraceptive products NuvaRing, Marvelon. Marvelon, the first modern oral contraceptives in the world, has now become the most widely used oral contraceptive brand.

Organon has branches in more than 60 countries and has production lines in 15 countries. The main production of Organon is based in the Netherlands, and marketing is also the main function of the European headquarters. In addition to the Netherlands, the UK and Germany, the other three major production lines are located in China, the United States and Japan.

※ 帝斯曼

帝斯曼是一家国际营养保健品、化工原料和制药集团，总部位于荷兰。集团在亚洲和南北美洲设有200多个机构，全球超过20 000名员工。到2016年底，DSM在50个国家雇用了20 786名雇员，净销售额达到80亿欧元。帝斯曼在许多领域都处于世界领先地位，主要分为五大部门：营养、制药、性能材料、聚合物中间体、基础化学和材料。

DSM的名字来源于它最初的英文翻译的缩写。DSM的荷兰名字是"De Nederlandse Staatsmijnen"，翻译成英语是"Dutch State Mines(DSM)"，意思是荷兰国有煤矿公司。1902年，帝斯曼由荷兰政府在林堡南部开采煤矿而成立，尽管公司在1973年最后一座矿山关闭时已经实现商品化学品和石化产品的多元化，但帝斯曼通过继续使用原来的名字"Dutch State Mines"的首字母的缩写来保留其与起源的联系。

帝斯曼在1963年开始与中国进行贸易往来，并于20世纪90年代初在中国建立了第一个销售代表处和第一个生产基地。2005年，帝斯曼在上海成立了DSM中国研发中心。2011年，DSM中国研发中心成为帝斯曼在中国的主要创新基地。

※ 欧加农

2007年之前，欧加农是阿克苏诺贝尔公司的人体健康护理业务部门。2007年11月，总部位于美国新泽西州的先灵葆雅公司从阿克苏诺贝尔手中收购了欧加农。现在，欧加农是一家制药公司，总部设在荷兰的奥斯和美国新泽西州的Roseland。

欧加农是由茨瓦纳柏格博士于1923年在荷兰奥斯创立的，当时是茨瓦纳柏格-欧加农。它的第一个产品是1923年的胰岛素，在20世纪30年代，它制造了雌激素。1948年，Organon收购了英国苏格兰的Newhouse研究所。1953年，欧加农开始生产可的松。1962年，它又买下了荷兰可卡因工厂的股票。目前，欧加农主要涉及的领域包括：生殖医学、避孕、精神类、激素替代疗法和麻醉。这其中包括几种主导产品，如治疗不孕不孕症的普丽康、肌肉松弛剂瑞美隆、抗抑郁药物米氮平和避孕产品避孕环NuvaRing以及避孕药妈富隆。妈富隆是世界上第一个现代口服避孕药，现在已经成为最广泛使用的口服避孕药品牌。

欧加农在全球60多个国家设有分支机构，在15个国家设有生产线。荷兰是欧加农的主要生产基地，也承担着欧洲总部的主要市场职能。除荷兰、英国和德国外，其他三大生产线分别位于中国、美国和日本。

Communication and Multimedia 通信和多媒体

※ Philips

Philips should be one of our most familiar Dutch brands. It was founded in Eindhoven in

1891, by Gerard Philips and his father Frederik.

In 1891, the Philips Company was founded in Zaltbommel. Gerard Philips and his father Frederik, a Jewish banker based in Zaltbommel, financed the purchase and setup of an empty factory building in Eindhoven, where the company started the production of carbon-filament lamps and other electro-technical products in 1892. In the 1920s, the company started to manufacture other products, such as vacuum tubes. In 1939, they introduced their electric razor, the Philishave. In the USA, it was called the "Norelco", which remains a part of their product lines today.

Philips is a great brand. Its greatness lies in changing people's lives. Philips has invented and created many new things. In 1949, the company began selling television sets. In 1950, it formed Philips Records, which eventually formed part of PolyGram. In 1963, Philips introduced the first combination portable radio and cassette recorder, which was marketed as the "radiorecorder", and is now better known as the boom box. In 1972, Philips launched the world's first home video cassette recorder, in the UK, the N1500. In 1982, Philips teamed with Sony to launch the Compact Disc; this format evolved into the CD-R, CD-RW, DVD and later Blu-ray, which Philips launched with Sony in 1997 and 2006 respectively. These, we mentioned earlier in this chapter.

In the 1990s, Philips implemented a major restructuring plan to simplify the company's architecture and streamline its business. In the 21st century, the company began to plan a new blueprint, showing the technical strength in the field of Philips Consumer Lifestyle, Philips Healthcare and Philips Lighting. This is also the current three main divisions.

※ TomTom

TomTom is a Dutch company that produces traffic, navigation and mapping products. It also makes action cameras, GPS sport watches, fleet management systems, and location-based products. As of 2015 TomTom's business has four business units: Consumer, Automotive, Licensing and Telematics.

TomTom began with software development for B2B mobile applications and personal digital assistants (PDAs) for consumers in 1991. Soon after, TomTom became the market leader in PDA software with navigation applications such as RoutePlanner and Citymaps. In 2004 TomTom launched the first personal navigation device (PND), creating a new consumer electronics category.

Especially after entering the age of intelligence, TomTom has been very active in innovation and business cooperation. In 2011, TomTom teamed up with Nike to create a fitness watch. Since then, TomTom has introduced their own smart bracelet TOMTOM TOUCH, the running watch TOMTOM RUNNER, the outdoor sports watch TOMTOM ADVENTURER GPS, and the TOMTOM TOUCH also won the ISPO 2017 award. On April 29 2015, TomTom announced their latest innovation, the TomTom Bandit action camera. It is TomTom's first try in the action camera segment.

TomTom did well in his partnership with Apple, and it has been a major mapping data provider for Apple maps since 2012 when Apple launched its Maps app trying to compete with Google.

※ 飞利浦

飞利浦应该是我们最为熟悉的荷兰品牌之一，它由杰拉德·飞利浦和他的父亲弗雷德里克于1891年在艾恩霍芬创立。

飞利浦是个伟大的品牌，它开创了很多个第一，改变了现代人的生活。图为飞利浦早期的海报。

1891年，飞利浦公司在扎尔特博默尔成立，杰拉德·飞利浦和他的父亲弗雷德里克——扎尔特博默尔的一名银行家，出资购买了艾恩霍芬的一个空厂房，公司在1892年开始生产碳丝灯和其他电子技术产品。20世纪20年代，该公司开始制造生产其他产品，如真空管。1939年，他们推出了电动剃须刀Philishave。在美国，它被称为"Norelco"，这款剃须产品今天仍然是飞利浦产品线的一部分。

飞利浦是一个伟大的品牌，它的伟大之处在于改变了人们的生活。飞利浦发明并创造了许多新事物。1949年，飞利浦公司开始销售电视机。1950年，公司成立了飞利浦唱片，后来成了宝丽金的一部分。1963年，飞利浦公司推出了第一款组合便携式收音机和盒式磁带录音机，它被称为"无线电收音机"，就是现在人们习惯于称的"音响"。1972年，飞利浦公司在英国推出了世界上第一台家用录像机N1500。1982年，飞利浦与索尼合作推出光盘，这一格式后来演变成1997年和2006年两家合作推出的CD-R、CD-RW、DVD和后来的蓝光。我们在本章的前面已经提到过。

20世纪90年代，飞利浦实施了一项重大重组计划，以简化公司架构，精简业务。在21世纪，公司开始规划新的蓝图，展现了其在飞利浦消费者生活方式、飞利浦医疗健康和飞利浦照明领域的技术力量。这也是目前的三个主要部门。

※ TomTom公司

TomTom是一家生产交通、导航和测绘产品的荷兰公司。它还生产研发运动相机、GPS运动手表、车队管理系统和基于位置服务的产品系列。截止到2015年，TomTom公司业务涵盖消费电子、汽车、地图授权和远程信息技术四大板块。

TomTom在1991年开始为B2B移动应用程序和个人数字助理开发软件。不久之后，TomTom成为带有导航应用程序（如RoutePlanner和Citymaps）的PDA软件的市场领导者。2004年，TomTom推出了第一款个人导航设备（PND），创造了一种新的消费类电子产品。

特别是在进入智能时代之后，TomTom在创新和商业合作方面一直非常活跃。2011年，TomTom和耐克联手打造了一款健身手表。从那以后，TomTom推出了自己的智能手环TomTom TOUCH、跑步手表TomTom RUNNER、户外运动手表TOMTOM ADVENTURER GPS，智能手环TomTom TOUCH还获得了ISPO2017年度大奖。2015年4月29日，TomTom发布了他们最新的创新产品，TomTom Bandit运动相机。这是TomTom在运动相机领域里的首次尝试。

TomTom在与苹果公司的合作中取得了不错的成绩，自2012年苹果地图应用程序试图与Google竞争以来，它一直是苹果地图的主要地图数据提供商。

Life Service Industry 生活服务

※ Unilever

Unilever is another well-known Dutch enterprise. It is now a British-Dutch transnational company. Because of the outfall from Brexit, the company is from 2018 only headquartered in Rotterdam, Netherlands, whereas before it also had a headquarter in London.

In 1872, Antoon Jurgens, founded the first margarine factory in the world in Oss, Netherlands. Then, in 1888, Samuel van den Bergh, also from Oss, opened his margarine factory in Kleve. These two companies merged in 1927 to form Margarine Unie. In 1930, Unilever was founded by Unie and the British soapmaker Lever Brothers.

Early in the 20th century, Unilever began its market expansion in Africa, the America and Asia. Meanwhile, under the influence of World War Ⅱ, Unilever has gained huge business promotion in the UK and the USA and carried out a series of m&a activities. By the mid-1960s, laundry soap and edible fats still contributed around half of Unilever's corporate profits. However, a stagnant market for yellow fats and increasing competition in detergents and soaps from Procter & Gamble forced Unilever to diversify. In this period, Unilever acquired the British-based Lipton Ltd from Allied Suppliers. In the 1980s, Pond's, Vaseline, Calvin Klein Cosmetics and Elizabeth Arden were acquired. More than 400 brands under Unilever are now sold in more than 170 countries around the world, with a turnover in 2017 of over 53 billion euros, and a dozen brands with sales of over one billion euros: Dove, Lux, Magnum, Knorr, Lipton, Rexona, Sunsilk, etc.

Unilever entered the Chinese market in the 1930s and opened a factory to produce "lux" soap in Shanghai. So far, Unilever has opened dozens of factories in China. It opened six R&D centers in the UK, the Netherlands, the United States, India and China and has nearly 300 production bases on six continents. In the Chinese market, we are familiar with the care brands such as Dove, Lux, Clear, Sunsilk; detergent brand Comfort, Omo; ice cream brand Wall's, Ben & Jerry's; condiment Knorr, tea brand Lipton, etc these are all from Unilever.

※ Booking.com

In recent years, China's outbound travel has grown exponentially, no matter if you are traveling abroad or when you are on a domestic business trip, you must be familiar with Booking. com. But chances are you don't even know that this is a native Dutch company. Booking.com is a website that helps you book accommodation around the world online. It lists more than 1.8 million accommodations in more than 120, 000 destinations across 226 countries and regions and books 1,200,000 room nights per day. The site offers reservations for 43 languages, making it a great convenience for people from all over the world.

Booking.com was formed when bookings.nl, founded in 1996 by Geert-Jan Bruinsma, merged in 2,000 with Bookings Online. In July 2005, the company was acquired by The Priceline Group for USD133 million.

Since 2010, Booking.com has launched the accommodation booking app for iPad, Android, iPhone and Windows 8 platform. A continuous growth in Booking.com's mobile bookings has been shown, its mobile bookings grew 160% in 2013.

Given the huge demand of Chinese users, Booking.com and Ctrip, the largest online travel company of China, formed a partnership with a commercial agreement in August 2012. This allows Ctrip to access Booking.com's global portfolio. In 2013, Booking.com Shanghai Customer Service Center was established to provide Chinese users with service support in Mandarin, Cantonese, English, and Asian and European languages.

※ Randstad

Randstad is a Dutch multinational human resource consulting firm headquartered in Diemen,

Netherlands. Randstad is the world's second-largest HR service provider after Adecco.

Randstad was founded in 1960 by Frits Goldschmeding and Ger Daleboudt, who were both studying economics at the time at VU University Amsterdam. At that time, the agency was called 'Uitzendbureau Amstelveen'. In the first years, Uitzendbureau Amstelveen mainly provided personnel for the insurance industry, banks and the health-care sector. In 1963, the agency also opened branches in Leiden and Rotterdam and changed its name from 'Uitzendbureau Amstelveen' to 'Randstad Uitzendbureau'. At that time, "Randstad" also meant the area covered by Amsterdam, Utrecht, The Hague and Rotterdam.

From 1965, Randstad opened a branch in Brussels, in 1967 in London and in 1968 in Düsseldorf, Germany, France followed in 1973. Between 1990 and 2000, Randstad gave more focus to internationalisation, established company in the USA, became a sponsor in Atlanta of the 1996 Olympic Games, greatly increasing its name recognition. Today, Randstad operates in more than 40 countries. The first branch in China began in 2005. In early 2006, it established Talent Shanghai and Shanghai Dispatch Talent with Shanghai Human Resources and Social Security Bureau. Now the branch has spread all over east China, north China and most of south China.

※ 联合利华

联合利华 (Unilever) 是另一家知名的荷兰企业，它是一家英荷跨国消费品公司，因为英国脱欧问题的影响，该公司从2018年起将单一总部设在了荷兰鹿特丹，而此前伦敦也同为总部。

联合利华的产品渗透了人们日常生活的方方面面，是荷兰知名度最高的公司之一。

1872年，安东·约更斯在荷兰的奥斯创立了世界上第一个人造黄油工厂。然后在1888年，同样来自奥斯的塞缪尔·范·登博格在克莱沃开了他的人造黄油工厂。这两家公司于1927年合并成为Margarine Unie。1930年，Unie和英国的肥皂制造商Lever Brothers合并成立了Unilever，即联合利华。

早在20世纪，联合利华就开始在非洲、美洲和亚洲进行业务拓展。同时，在第二次世界大战的影响下，联合利华在英国和美国的商业推广得到巨大发展，并开展了一系列的并购活动。到20世纪60年代中期，洗衣皂和可食用脂肪仍占联合利华公司利润的一半左右。然而，由于黄油市场停滞不前，以及来自宝洁公司的洗涤剂和肥皂的竞争日益加剧迫使联合利华实现多元化。在此期间，联合利华从Allied Suppliers手里收购了英国茶品牌立顿。20世纪80年代，联合利华又收购了旁氏、凡士林、卡尔文·克莱恩 (CK) 化妆品和伊丽莎白·雅顿。目前，联合利华旗下的400多个品牌在全球170多个国家销售，2017年营业额超过530亿欧元，销售额超过10亿欧元的十多个品牌有多芬、力士、Sunsilk、梦龙、家乐、立顿、舒耐等。

20世纪30年代联合利华就进入了中国市场，当时在上海开了一家生产"力士"香皂的工厂。到目前为止，联合利华已经在中国开设了几十家工厂，在英国、荷兰、美国、印度和中国开设了6个研发中心，在6个大洲拥有近300个生产基地。在中国市场，我们所熟悉的护理品牌多芬、力士、清扬、Sunsilk；洗涤剂品牌奥妙、金纺；冰激凌品牌和路雪、Ben & Jerry's；调味品牌家乐、茶叶品牌立顿等均来自联合利华。

※ 缤客网

近年来，中国出境游呈指数级增长，无论你是出国旅游还是国内出差，你对缤客网（Booking.com）一定不会陌生。但你可能不知道，这是一家荷兰本土公司。Booking.com是一个网站，可帮助你在线预订世界各地的酒店住宿。缤客网在线包含来自226个国家和地区的12万多个目的地的超过1 800万个住宿设施，每天有1 200 000个房间被预订。缤客网提供43种语言的预订服务，为来自世界各地的人们提供了极大的便利。

Booking.com是由Geert-Jan Bruinsma于1996年创立的bookings.nl与Bookings Online在2000年合并成立的。2005年7月，该公司被Priceline集团以1.33亿美元收购。

自2010年以来，缤客网陆续推出了iPad、Android、iPhone和Windows8平台的住宿预订应用程序。缤客网的移动预订量持续增长，2013年移动设备预订量增长了160%。

鉴于中国用户的巨大需求，缤客网和中国最大的在线旅游公司携程于2012年8月达成商业合作伙伴关系，这使得携程进入到缤客全球性投资组合当中去。2013年，缤客网成立了上海客户服务中心，为中国用户提供普通话、粤语、英语和亚洲及欧洲语言的服务支持。

※ 任仕达

任仕达是一家总部位于荷兰迪门的跨国人力资源咨询公司，是继Adecco之后全球第二大人力资源服务提供商。

任仕达于1960年由Frits Goldschmeding和Ger Daleboudt创立，他们当时都在阿姆斯特丹自由大学学习经济学。成立之初，这是一家称为"Uitzendbureau Amstelveen"的机构，意思是阿姆斯特芬职业介绍所。在最初的几年里，Uitzendbureau Amstelveen主要为保险业、银行和医疗保健部门提供人员介绍。1963年，该机构还在莱顿和鹿特丹开设了分支机构，并将其名称从"Uitzendbureau Amstelveen"改为"Randstad Uitzendbureau"（任仕达职业介绍所）。那时，"Randstad"泛指阿姆斯特丹、乌得勒支、海牙和鹿特丹覆盖的地区。

从1965年开始，任仕达在布鲁塞尔开设了分支机构，1967年在伦敦开设分支机构，1968年在德国杜塞尔多夫开设分支机构，紧随其后的是1973年的法国分支机构。1990年至2000年期间，任仕达更加注重国际化的发展方向，于是在美国成立公司，成为1996年亚特兰大奥运会的赞助商，大大提高了知名度。今天，任仕达的业务遍及40多个国家。中国的第一家分公司成立于2005年。2006年初，任仕达与上海市人力资源和社会保障局合作成立了上海人才有限公司和上海派遣人才有限公司。目前，其分公司已经遍及华东、华北和华南大部分地区。

Tijd voor Nederlands 荷兰语时间

● 单词+短语

荷 merk	荷 dingen	荷 multinationaal bedrijf
英 brand	英 things	英 multinational company
译 品牌	译 东西	译 跨国公司

荷 wereld	荷 kwaliteit	荷 melkpoeder
英 world	英 quality	英 milk powder
译 世界	译 质量	译 奶粉
荷 beroemd	荷 produceren	荷 gebruiken
英 famous	英 produce	英 use
译 知名的	译 生产	译 使用
荷 beginnen		
英 begin		
译 开始		

● 例句

荷 Dit is een zeer beroemd merk	荷 Veel dingen in Nederland worden in China geproduceerd.
英 This is a very famous brand.	英 Many things in the Netherlands are produced in China.
译 这是一个非常有名的品牌。	译 荷兰的很多东西都是中国生产的。
荷 Ons bedrijf staat in de top 500 van de wereld.	荷 De kwaliteit van dit melkpoeder merk is goed.
英 Our company is the world's top 500.	英 This brand of milk powder is of good quality.
译 我们公司是全球五百强。	译 这个牌子的奶粉品质很好。
荷 Unilever is een multinationaal bedrijf en ik heb hun producten gebruikt.	荷 Ik ken veel Nederlandse merken, zoals Philips, Shell en Heineken.
英 Unilever is a multinational company and I have used their products.	英 I know many Dutch brands, such as Philips, Shell and Heineken.
译 联合利华是一家跨国公司，我使用过他们的产品。	译 我知道很多荷兰的品牌，比如飞利浦、壳牌和喜力。
荷 We zullen samenwerken aan het project met dat Nederlandse bedrijf.	荷 We willen een nieuw bedrijf beginnen in Nederland.
英 We will cooperate on the project with that Dutch company.	英 We want to open a new company in the Netherlands.
译 我们想要就这个项目和那家荷兰公司达成合作。	译 我们想在荷兰开设一家新公司。

荷兰文化遗产

A Taste of Dutch Cultural Heritage

The Netherlands is a country with one of the highest museum density in the world with almost 1200 museums. Besides the well-known museums such as the Rijksmuseum and the Van Gogh Museum, there are hundreds of mostly smaller museums all over the Netherlands, Many of these started as private collections, for example the Museum of Bags and Purses, the Perfume Bottles Museum and the Bottle-ship Museum. Visiting a museum is a favourite pastime in the Netherlands.

荷兰全国有近1 200家博物馆，是世界上博物馆密度最高的国家之一。除了像国家博物馆和梵高博物馆这样著名的博物馆之外，荷兰还有数百家中小型博物馆。这些博物馆中很多都是私人收藏，比如箱包和手袋博物馆、香水瓶博物馆和瓶中船博物馆。参观博物馆是荷兰人最喜爱的消遣方式。

1. 阿姆斯特丹的博物馆
Museums in Amsterdam

The museums of Amsterdam are one of the city's main tourist attractions. Het Rijksmuseum (the Netherlands' National Museum, which harbours nearly 1 million works of art–including Rembrandt's famous Night watch), Het Van Gogh Museum, Het Anne Frank House and Het Stedelijk Museum (literally, Municipal Museum, but it is in fact the National Museum of Modern Art) are one of the most popular choices, but there are also many interesting small museums. There are about 90 museums in the city of Amsterdam and they attract almost seven million visitors every year. Alongside the impressive wealth of majestic Golden Age paintings, you'll find exciting modern art, press, film, theatre and photography museums and some unique Dutch treats like the Heineken Experience, Ajax Arena Tours and the Houseboat Museum.

All but seven museums in Amsterdam are privately owned, and nearly all charge an entrance fee.

In a time of dwindling government subsidies, many museums have developed commercial activities: they are attracting non-tourist visitors with temporary exhibits, or have accepted financial aid from sponsors.

All museums are closed on Mondays with the exception of the Rijksmuseum, the Van Gogh Museum and the Stedelijk Museum.

阿姆斯特丹的博物馆是这座城市主要的旅游景点之一。 Rijksmuseum博物馆（这是荷兰的国家博物馆，收藏了近100万件艺术作品，包括伦勃朗著名的作品《夜巡》、梵高博物馆、安妮故居和阿姆斯特丹市立博物馆（Stedelijk Museum，字面上的意思是城市博物馆，但它实际上是国家现代艺术博物馆），这些是非常受游客欢迎的博物馆，但阿姆斯特丹还有许多有趣的小博物馆。阿姆斯特丹大约有90个博物馆，每年吸引着近700万游客参观游览。除了宏伟壮丽的黄金时代画作，你还会发现令人兴奋的现代艺术、新闻、电影、戏剧和摄影等的博物馆，还有一些非常独特的，比如喜力博物馆、阿贾克斯竞技场和游艇博物馆。

阿姆斯特丹只有七家博物馆是非私人所有，其他所有博物馆均为私人所拥有，差不多所有的博物馆都收取门票。

在政府补贴不断减少的时期，许多博物馆开展了一些商业活动，以临时性展览吸引了一批批非游客前来参观，或者接受赞助商的资助。

除了国立博物馆、梵高博物馆和阿姆斯特丹市立博物馆外，所有的博物馆在周一都会关闭。

※ Rijksmuseum

The Rijksmuseum is among the world's finest art museums, packing works by local heroes Rembrandt, Vermeer and Van Gogh as well as 7,500 other masterpieces over 1.5km of galleries.

It is in 1800, that The Amsterdam Rijksmuseum first opened its collection to the public as the Nationale Kunstgallerij (National Art Gallery). Since then, it moved several times before being established in Amsterdam (1808) by the decree of the King of the Netherlands Louis Bonaparte, brother of the French emperor Napoleon Bonaparte. It was named the Royal Museum, but in 1815 received from the Dutch King Willem I its present name. In 1885 the Rijksmuseum moved to its beautiful building, designed by the Dutch architect Petrus J.H. Cuypers. It has been built in the then fashionable Dutch neo-Renaissance style, using historical neo-Gothic elements in its form and decoration.

- **Unique status**

The Rijksmuseum in Amsterdam has throughout its existence gained an unique status in the Netherlands and in the world, not only because of the possession of many masterpiece paintings of Dutch but also because of its sublime collection of world art. Along with the masterworks like Rembrandt's Night watch, several paintings by Vermeer, Anthony van Dyck and Jan Steen, the museum has truly exceptional collection of the antique objects that reflect Dutch culture. It also possesses a vast collection of prints, drawings and the classic photography.

- **All aspects of Dutch history**

As said above, visitors to the Rijksmuseum in Amsterdam can expect much more than just paintings by Dutch Masters from the Golden Age. The museum's expansive, evocative collection also includes Delftware, sculptures, archaeological artefacts, clothing, Asian art, prints, items from Dutch maritime history and many other culturally significant objects, all combining to vividly present 800 years of Dutch history within a global context. And naturally, the collection isn't frozen in time—new items arrive to represent modern times, too, such as a Mondrian-inspired dress by Yves Saint Laurent dating from 1965.

- **A monumental building**

The construction of this beautiful building began in 1876 and it finally opened in 1885 as the largest museum in the Netherlands. Following 10 years of extensive restoration and renovation, the Rijksmuseum reopened in April 2013 to worldwide acclaim. And in 2014 the museum expanded further with the opening of the redeveloped Philips Wing, ensuring that the Rijksmuseum is one of the most modern 'old' museums in the world.

Tickets: Adults: €17.5

Youth aged 18 and under, Museumkaart holders, members of ICOM, ICOMOS, the Rembrandt Association, KOG, Vrienden van de Aziatische Kunst, Vrienden van het Rijksmuseum, BankGiro Lottery VIP-KAART: free admission

Holders of CJP, Stadspas or EYCA: 50% reduction on regular ticket price

Hours: Daily 9am–5pm

Address: Museumstraat 1,1071 XX AMSTERDAM

Contact: 020-6747000

http://www.rijksmuseum.nl

※ Van Gogh Museum

Het Van Gogh Museum in Amsterdam is situated at the Museumplein in Amsterdam-Zuid, on the Paulus Potterstraat 7, between the Stedelijk Museum and the Rijksmuseum. The museum maintains the world's largest collection of the works of the world's most popular artist—Vincent

van Gogh (1853-1890)—more than 200 paintings, 500 drawings and 700 of his letters, completed with the art of his contemporaries. Each year, 1.6 million visitors come to the Van Gogh Museum, making it one of the 25 most popular museums in the world.

The design for Het Van Gogh Museum was commissioned by the Dutch government in 1963 to Dutch architect and furniture designer Gerrit Rietveld. Rietveld died a year later, and the building was not completed until 1973, when the museum opened its doors. In 1998 and 1999, the building was renovated by the Dutch architect Martien van Goor and an exhibition wing by the Japanese modernist architect Kisho Kurokawa was added. In 2015 the museum opened a new entrance directly on the Museumplein, providing a modern and attractive entry point that better caters to the large number of visitors.

For both locals and far-travelling visitors, visiting the Van Gogh Museum is a unique and inspirational experience. Alongside the legacy of Vincent van Gogh's instantly recognisable impressionist works, such as his landscapes, self-portraits and still lifes—especially "Sunflowers"—the museum provides opportunities to track the artist's development and compare his paintings to works by other artists from the 19th century—those who inspired him and those who drew inspiration from him.

Tickets:	Adults: €18
	Children under 18 years, Museumkaart holders, Stadspas, ICOM members, FREE
Hours:	Daily 9am–5pm, Friday 9am–9pm
Address:	Museumplein 6, 1071 DJ Amsterdam
Contact:	020-5705200
	http://www.vangoghmuseum.nl

※ Rembrandt House Museum

Not far from the Chinese quarter of Amsterdam, in a direct proximity of the Waterlooplein, stands the house in which the famous Dutch painter Rembrandt once lived in. The Rembrandt House Museum (Dutch: Museum Het Rembrandthuis) is a historic house and art museum in Amsterdam in the Netherlands. Painter Rembrandt lived and worked in this house between 1639 and 1658.

The large house dates back to 1607. Rembrandt himself moved in in 1639 after purchasing the building for 13,000 guilders which at the time was considerable sum of money. Rembrandt stayed in the house for 19 years, producing some of his most famous and finest works including the NightWatch which can be seen at the Rijksmuseum.

In 1658 after paying off his debts Rembrandt was declared bankrupt–a detailed inventory of his possessions was made on behalf of his creditors–and Rembrandt moved to a smaller house on the Rozengracht (Amsterdam) where he remained until his death.

For around the next 250 years the house had a number of different occupants before being bought by the city council who turned it over to a foundation–it was finally opened as a museum dedicated to the artist in 1911. In the 1990s a modern new wing was added and the house was restored carefully. The bankruptcy inventory was vital in helping create an authentic recreation of the home.

Today the house gives us a good feel of how and where Rembrandt lived and worked, it also gives us a glimpse into the life in the 17th century. Check out the small box-beds in which people of those days slept in semi-upright positions, they slept in such a manor because of the fear of too much blood rushing to their heads. The largest room in the house is Rembrandt's original studio where he painted his masterpieces.

Rembrandt also had a bizarre collection of rarities from all over the world including busts of Roman emperors, spears, shells and butterflies—these can be seen in the Cabinet Room.

Tickets: Adults pay €13, children 6-17 pay €4, FREE for children 0-5

CJP, Stadspas, Students and ISIC, €10

Free entry for members of ICOM and the Rembrandt Association, Museumkaart and I Amsterdam City Card holders

Note, special exhibitions can attract a small supplement.

Hours: Daily 10am–6pm

Address: Jodenbreestraat 4, 1011 NK Amsterdam

Contact: 020-5200400

http://www.rembrandthuis.nl

※ EYE Film Museum EYE

EYE is the only museum in the Netherlands that is exclusively dedicated to film and the moving image. EYE exhibits film as art, entertainment, cultural heritage, and a conveyer of information. It offers exhibitions and corresponding film programs with a keen eye for current, historical and artistic developments, paying particular attention to young people as well.

EYE is located in the Overhoeks neighbourhood of Amsterdam on the northern side of the waterfront, directly across from Amsterdam's Central Station. It includes a cinematography museum formerly called Filmmuseum, founded in 1952. Its predecessor was the Dutch Historical Film Archive, founded in 1946. The Filmmuseum was situated in the Vondelparkpaviljoen since 1975, but in 2009, plans were announced for a new home on the north bank of Amsterdam's waterfront. It was officially opened on April 4, 2012 by Queen Beatrix. The EYE filmmuseum collection includes 37,000 film titles, 60,000 posters, 700,000 photographs and 20,000 books. The earliest materials date from the start of the film industry in the Netherlands in 1895.

The Vienna-based firm Delugan Meissl Associated Architects designed a striking complex that houses four screens, 640 seats, and 1,200 square meters of exhibition space.

Tickets: Tickets are different for films and exhibition:

Film, regular €10.5, children for 11years old and under €8, I Amsterdam-city card €8.4

Exhibition, regular €10, children from 11 to 18 years old €5, FREE for children for 11years old and under, I Amsterdam City Card and Museum card holders; Combiticket exhibition & film €16

Hours: Daily 10am–7pm

Address:　　IJpromenade 1, 1031 KT Amsterdam

Contact:　　020-5891400

　　　　　　　http://www.eyefilm.nl/en

※ The National Maritime Museum

The National Maritime Museum (Het Scheepvaartmuseum) is the national maritime museum and is located on the eastern docklands area of Amsterdam. The museum building dates from 1656, it was designed by Daniël Stalpaert and at the time it was an architectural wonder. To construct it on the artificial island created in the Amsterdam harbour, 1800 wooden piles had to be sunk deep into the muddy ground. It remained a navy building until 1973 when it was converted to the country's national maritime museum.

During the recent renovation, a vast space of the building inner courtyard has been covered by a glass roofing, creating a pleasant space for the visitors. In the evening hundred of tiny LED lights placed between shields of glass give an impression of the starry sky.

The replica of the three-masted "Amsterdam", a large vessel of the Dutch East India Company, which when on its maiden journey to Batavia sank in a storm in the English Channel in the winter of 1749, stands high above the waters of IJ Bay, directly at the Amsterdam maritime museum quay. The wreck of the ship has been discovered off the English coast in 1969, and the museum replica has been completed in 1990. Visiting the ship, you can experience how small and primitive the spaces were that were used to house 350 people during the ship's journey, with more comfortable but equally minute quarters for the ship's captain and officers.

Het Scheepvaartmuseum has a rich and colourful collection of maritime artefacts and it takes hours just to walk through its show. The collection has been divided into several smaller exhibits with many diverse themes. Just to list the most important one's–"see You in the Golden Age", "Port 24/7", "Voyage at Sea", "the Ship Decorations", "the Navigational Instruments" and the themes that focus on kids from age of 6–"the Tale of the Whale", "My Expo" and "Sal and Yori and Circus Sea".

Tickets:　　Adults €16, children 4-17 €8, FREE entry to children 0-3

Hours:　　Daily 9am–5pm

Address:　　Kattenburgerplein 1, 1018 KK AMSTERDAM

Contact:　　020-5232222

　　　　　　　http://www.hetscheepvaartmuseum.nl/

※ NEMO Science Museum NEMO

NEMO Science Museum is the largest science centre in the Netherlands.

The museum has its origins in 1923, when the Museum of Labour was opened by the artist Herman Heijenbrock on the Rozengracht in Amsterdam. In 1997 the name was changed to New Metropolis. The name Science Center Nemo was introduced in 2000. In 2016, the name was changed to NEMO Science Museum. It attracts annually over 500,000 visitors, which makes it the fifth most visited museum in the Netherlands.

The museum contains five floors of hands-on science exhibitions. The main concepts on the first floor are DNA and chain reactions which include a room with giant dominoes with contraptions like a giant bell and a flying car. Also on the first floor is a show on the half-hour, which features a large chain reaction circuit.

On the second floor is a ball factory where small plastic balls are sent on a circuit where participants are to group them in weight, size and colour and then send them to a packing facility where the balls go into a small metal box. There are five stations at which the people stick magnetic barcodes on the boxes and send them off to start the circuit again. On the second level there is also a small caféteria and a movie and performance hall where various acts and movies about science are shown.

The third floor has a giant science lab in which people can do science experiments such as testing vitamin C in certain substances and looking at DNA. There is also a small section on money and business.

On the fourth floor is a section about the human mind, it has such experiments as memory tests, mind problems and sense testers. The fourth floor is quite dark which adds to the eeriness of the surroundings.

The fifth floor or upper deck has a caféteria, a children's play area and a great view of the city surroundings.

Tickets:	Regular for adults and children over 4 years old €16.50; FREE for I Amsterdam City Card, Museum card holder.
Hours:	Daily 10am–5:30pm, Monday closed
Address:	Oosterdok 2, 1011 VX Amsterdam
Contact:	020-5313233 http://www.nemosciencemuseum.nl/en

※ Stedelijk Museum Amsterdam

Het Stedelijk Museum Amsterdam was established as the municipal museum in 1895, but only became a state museum in 1938. Its interests were divided in many disciplines, such as art, objects documenting the history of Amsterdam which are now in the collection of Amsterdam Museum as well as specific subjects like history of medicine. It was only in the beginning of the 1970's that Het Stedelijk Museum became solely a modern art museum.

Het Stedelijk Museum's design collection also documents the history of design from the turn of the last century to the present, showcasing furniture, ceramics, posters, jewellery and other objects.

Today the Stedelijk Museum in Amsterdam has one of the richest modern art collections in the world. Along with all important names of modern painting movements as Impressionists, Fauvism, Cubism, Expressionism, it has a unique collection of 29 paintings by Kazimir Malevich, an equally exceptional collection of De Stijl and Cobra movement, a superb Dutch photography collection, a very good collection of Dutch design and furniture and a interesting collection of European and American trends in art since 1950 as works of Matisse, Picasso, Newman, Rauschenberg and Warhol completed with Italian Arte Povera and German modern painting.

Tickets:	For adults the price is €17.5, for children under 18 is FREE

Hours:　　　Daily 10am–6pm, Friday 10am–10pm

Address:　　Museumplein 10, 1071 DJ Amsterdam

Contact:　　020-5732911
　　　　　　　http://www.stedelijk.nl/

※ Amsterdam Museum

Amsterdam, the capital of the Netherlands is a 1000-year-old trading city that has a special relationship with water and a strong focus on entrepreneurship, creativity, citizenship and free-thinking. In the monumental Amsterdam Museum building you will discover the story of Amsterdam through a large number of masterpieces, such as an aerial map from the Middle Ages and Breitner's "The Dam". In this museum you can see, read about, hear and experience how the city has developed into the Amsterdam we know today.

The Amsterdam Museum, till was 2011 called the Amsterdams Historisch Museum, and is a museum about the history of Amsterdam. Since 1975 the Amsterdam Museum has been located in a spectacular building on the Kalverstraat, where in the Middle Ages the Saint Lucien's Monastery was situated and in 1578 the City Orphanage (Burgerweeshuis) was established. The orphanage was home to thousands of children between 1580 and 1960, many of whom had lost their parents due to the plague. The children also received an education here: the older boys attended school elsewhere in the city, while the girls received instruction within the orphanage and were trained in domestic skills. In memory of the time of the orphanage, the Regents' Room (Regentenkamer) and orphans' cupboards in the inner courtyard have been left intact and The Small Orphanage (Het Kleine Weeshuis), a family presentation where you can find out all about the world of Amsterdam's orphans, was established. The boys' and girls' inner courtyards, where boys and girls played separately, also originate from that time.

The Amsterdam Gallery, a covered street leading from Begijnensteeg to the museum, is one of the few freely accessible 'museum streets' in the world. Original group portraits, made between 1530 and 2007 by artists such as Bartholomeus van der Helst and Erwin Olaf, hang in the gallery. Even Goliath can be found here: our world famous 350-year-old wooden giant.

The Amsterdam Museum is a meeting place for anyone who wants to learn more about the city.

Tickets:　　Adults €13.5, FREE for children under18
　　　　　　　Free entry for members of ICOM and the Rembrandt Association, Museumkaart
　　　　　　　and I Amsterdam City Card holders

Hours:　　　Daily 10am–5pm

Address:　　Kalverstraat 92, 1012 PH Amsterdam

Contact:　　020-5231822
　　　　　　　http://www.amsterdammuseum.nl/

※ Hash Marihuana & Hemp Museum

These are in fact two small museums, for the price of one. Both are located in a short walking distance one from another at Oudezijds Achterburgwal, one of the canals of the Red Light District.

First exhibit, called the Museum covers different uses of the hemp plant and some of its varieties used for recreational purposes and usually called cannabis. The hemp plant is one of the oldest crops known to man, which has been used for thousands of years as a material to make textiles (similar to linen), ropes and even paper. Hemp has been also a source of oil–which while eatable, has been produced mainly to impregnate textiles, as a fuel for oil lamps, as a medicine and to make paints and soap. Today, the hemp plant is seen as an important alternative of cotton, because the cultivation of cotton asks for a lot of water and pesticides and its harvest is labour consuming, but the hemp plant is a strong, undemanding, versatile crop, harvesting of which may be easily mechanised.

Second exhibit called Hemp Gallery, puts an accent on civilised use of cannabis, its history and tradition in arts, again repeating the arguments for the wider use of hemp. A small art gallery where individual shows of painters and photographers take place, is located at the back of the exhibit.

Tickets:	Admission is €9.0 per person. Admission is FREE for children under 13 years when accompanied by adults
Hours:	Daily 10am–10pm
Address:	Oudezijds Achterburgwal 148, 1012 DV Amsterdam
Contact:	020-6248926
	http://hashmuseum.com

※ Sex Museum Amsterdam

It's a serious, interesting museum that circumvents the bluntness of pornography. It's the 4th most visited museum of Amsterdam, after the Van Gogh Museum, Rijksmuseum and Anne Frank House.

The museum aims to reveal and illustrate the attitude people had towards sex from Classical Antiquity until the Victorian period. And indeed, if you think today's morals are loose, take a look at how revealing the ancient Greeks and Romans could be.

Among the items on display one can find paintings, cartoons, photographs, statues and recordings. The large collection is displayed in several rooms bearing the name of personalities who are said to have influenced the history of sex and eroticism, such as the Marquise de Pompadour, Marquis de Sade, Mata Hari, and so on.

The Amsterdam Sex Museum is sillier and more fun than other erotic museums in the Red Light District. Minimum age for entry is 16. It is located within walking distance from Central Station, at Damrak 18, one of the busiest streets of the city.

Tickets:	16 years and older: €4.0
Hours:	Daily 9:30am–11:30pm
Address:	Damrak 18, 1012 LH Amsterdam
Contact:	020–6228376
	http://www.sexmuseumamsterdam.nl

※ 阿姆斯特丹国立博物馆

阿姆斯特丹国立博物馆或国家博物馆是世界上最好的艺术博物馆之一，包括当地备受崇拜的伦勃朗·维米尔和梵高的作品以及珍藏了7 500件杰作，长度超过1.5公里的画廊。正是在1800年，阿姆斯特丹国立博物馆以国家美术馆的身份首次向公众展出其收藏作品。从那时起，一直到1808年阿姆斯特丹被法兰西皇帝拿破仑·波拿巴的弟弟路易·波拿巴接管之前它搬迁了好几次。它曾经名为皇家博物馆，但在1815年，荷兰国王威廉一世赐予了博物馆它现在的名字。1885年，国立博物馆搬到了一座由荷兰建筑师佩特鲁斯·库伯斯 (Petrus J. H. Cuypers) 所设计的漂亮的建筑里面。这座建筑采用荷兰新文艺复兴风格建造而成，使用新哥特式元素加以装饰。

阿姆斯特丹国家博物馆是世界上最好的艺术博物馆之一，也是荷兰最大最重要的博物馆，珍藏着诸多世界知名画作，大家非常熟悉的《夜巡》也是其臻品之一。

● 独特的地位

阿姆斯特丹国立博物馆自建造以来在荷兰和整个世界中都有着举足轻重的地位，这并不仅是因为这里所收藏的荷兰著名画家的绘画作品，还因为它蕴藏着世界艺术的瑰宝。像伦勃朗的《夜巡》这样的杰作，还有维米尔、安东尼·范·戴克和扬·斯特恩的数幅画作，以及收藏了反映荷兰文化的古董文物。博物馆还拥有大量的印刷、素描和经典摄影作品。

● 多面的荷兰史

就像前面说的，到阿姆斯特丹国立博物馆的游览参观值得期待的不仅仅是来自黄金时代荷兰大师的画作。博物馆的展品包罗万象，包括代尔夫特蓝陶、雕塑作品、考古文物、服装、亚洲艺术、出版印刷、荷兰海事发展史的展品以及其他许多有着重大文化意义的物品，所以这些来自不同领域的展品结合在一起，生动地讲述了荷兰在全球范围内的800年的发展史。当然，这些藏品也不是一成不变的——这里还有一些近现代的新展品，比如伊夫圣罗兰 (Yves Saint Laurent) 1965年创作的一件蒙德里安风格 (Mondrian-inspired) 的连衣裙。

● 不朽的建筑

国立博物馆所在的这栋美丽的建筑始建于1876年，最终在1885年作为荷兰最大的博物馆建成完工。在历经10年大面积的修复和翻新后，2013年4月，国立博物馆在全世界一片赞誉声中重新开放。2014年，随着重建的飞利浦翼楼的开幕，博物馆进一步扩展，确保了阿姆斯特丹国立博物馆成为了世界上最现代的"旧"博物馆之一。

门票： 成年人每人17.5欧元

18岁及以下以及博物馆卡持有者、国际博物馆协会 (ICOM) 成员、国际古迹遗址理事会 (ICOMOS) 成员、伦勃朗协会 (Rembrandt Association) 成员、皇家考古学会 (KOG) 成员、 亚洲艺术之友 (VVAK) 成员、博物馆协作人士、BankGiro Lottery 基金会VIP持卡人，免费入内

青年卡 (CJP) 持有者、城市直通卡 (Stadspas) 持有者或欧洲青年旅行证 (EYCA) 的持有者，门票五折

开放时间：　　每天早上9点至下午5点

地址：　　　　阿姆斯特丹，博物馆街1号

联系方式：　　020-6747000

　　　　　　　http://www.rijksmuseum.nl

※ 梵高博物馆

　　阿姆斯特丹梵高博物馆位于南阿姆斯特丹区的博物馆广场，在保罗斯·波特街7号，位于市立博物馆和国立博物馆之间。梵高博物馆收藏了世界上最受欢迎的艺术家文森特·梵高的200多幅油画、500幅素描和700幅他的书信，以及与他同时代的艺术作品。每年来梵高博物馆参观的游客有160万，使它成为世界上25个最受欢迎的博物馆之一。

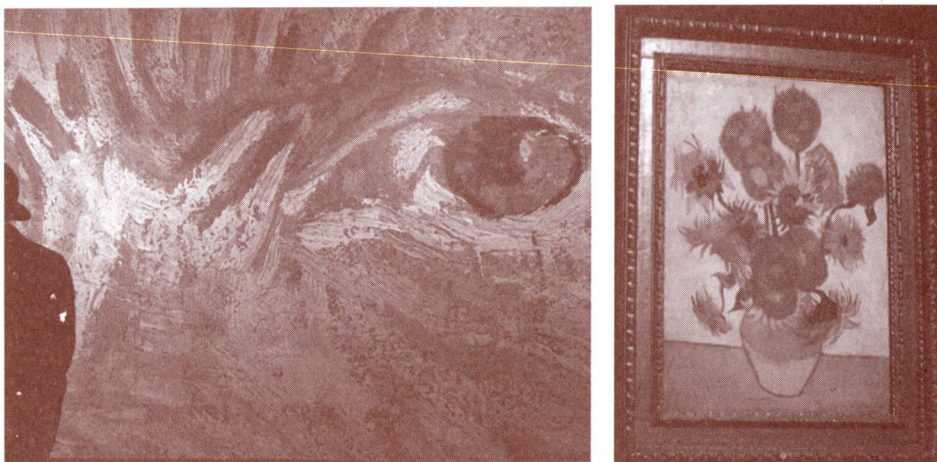

梵高博物馆位于阿姆斯特丹博物馆广场，是受访者最多的荷兰博物馆之一，鉴于其丰富的臻品收藏，很难被游客忽略。
左图为追寻梵高足迹的艺术家的作品。右图为梵高著名画作《向日葵》。

　　1963年，荷兰建筑师和家具设计师格里特·里特维尔德受荷兰政府的委托设计了梵高博物馆。但是里特维尔德一年后就去世了，直到1973年博物馆才完工对外开放。1998年和1999年，荷兰建筑师马丁·范·格尔对建筑进行了翻新，并增添了由日本现代派建筑师黑川纪章所设计的展览翼楼。2015年，梵高博物馆直接在博物馆广场的位置开设了一个新的入口，这个现代化的、漂亮的入口更好地迎合了广大游客。

　　对于当地人以及远道而来的游客来说，参观梵高博物馆是一个独特的、鼓舞人心的经历。站在这些遗产的旁边，人们一眼就能认出梵高的印象派作品，如他的风景画、自画像、静物画，尤其是他的画作《向日葵》——博物馆还提供了一个平台，可以来追寻艺术家作品风格的变迁，并将19世纪其他艺术家的作品与他的画作相比较——那些启发了他的人和从他那里汲取了灵感的人。

门票：　　　　成人每人18欧元；18岁以下及持博物馆卡、城市直通卡、国际博物馆协会
　　　　　　　（ICOM）成员等免费

开放时间：　　每天上午9点至下午5点，周五上午9点至晚上9点

地址：　　　　阿姆斯特丹，博物馆广场6号

联系方式：　　020-5705200

　　　　　　　http://www.vangoghmuseum.nl

※ 伦勃朗故居博物馆

距离阿姆斯特丹唐人街不远的地方，在红灯区的后面，滑铁卢广场的附近，矗立着著名的荷兰画家伦勃朗曾经住过的那间房子。伦勃朗故居博物馆是荷兰阿姆斯特丹的历史故居和艺术博物馆。伦勃朗在1639年到1658年期间曾在这所房子里生活。

这座大房子可以追溯到1607年。伦勃朗在1639年花了13 000个荷兰盾将房子买下来，这在当时可是相当可观的一笔数目。伦勃朗在这所房子里住了19年，创作了一些他最著名和最出色的作品，包括《夜巡》，这幅最知名的画作收藏在阿姆斯特丹国立博物馆内。

在这所房子里，伦勃朗创造了最知名的作品，这里的工作室极大地还原了伦勃朗工作的场景。

1658年，在偿清债务之后伦勃朗破产——他的财产详细清单是由他的债权人所列出的，于是伦勃朗就搬到了玫瑰运河的一所小房子里，直到去世。

在接下来的250年里，这座房子迎来了许多不同的主人，后来被市议会买下并将其移交给了一个基金会，终于在1911年，这座房子成了一个博物馆，用于纪念伦勃朗。在20世纪90年代，房子增添了一个侧楼，并进行了精心的修复。清算的财产遗物对于重现伦勃朗在此生活的情景起到了至关重要的作用。

今天，这所房子让我们深切体会到当初伦勃朗是如何在这里生活和工作的，也给我们展示了17世纪的社会生活场景一瞥。看看那些半直立着的小盒子，因为害怕头部充血太多，当时的人们就睡在这样的床上。房子里最大的房间是伦勃朗原来的工作室，他便是在那里进行创作的。

伦勃朗还收集了来自世界各地的奇异珍品，包括罗马皇帝的半身像、长矛、贝壳和蝴蝶，这些都可以在陈列室看到。

门票：　　　　成人13欧元；6～17岁4欧元；5岁以下免费
　　　　　　　青年卡（CJP）持有者、城市直通卡（Stadspas）持有者10欧元
　　　　　　　博物馆卡持有者、国际博物馆协会（ICOM）成员、伦勃朗协会成员及阿姆斯特丹城市卡持有者免费
　　　　　　　注意，特殊临时展览可能需要补充额外少许费用。

开放时间：　　每天上午10点至下午6点

地址：　　　　阿姆斯特丹，犹太人宽街4号

联系方式：　　020-5200400

　　　　　　　http://www.rembrandthuis.nl

※ 电影博物馆

EYE是荷兰唯一一个专门致力于电影和移动影像的博物馆。EYE将电影展示为艺术、娱乐、文化遗产和信息传递者。EYE电影博物馆以它敏锐的目光和洞察力对于当前的、历史的和艺术的发展提供展览展示，也同时做相关影片的展映，以及关注于年轻人群体。

EYE位于阿姆斯特丹北部的Overhoeks区，在滨水区的北面，正对着阿姆斯特丹的中央车站。EYE包括一个以前称为电影博物馆的电影摄制艺术博物馆，在1952年成立。博物馆的前身是荷兰历史电影资料馆，成立于1946年。从1975年开始，电影博物馆就坐落在冯德尔公园内的Vondelparkpaviljoen建筑内，但在2009年博物馆决定搬迁至阿姆斯特丹滨水区北部的新地址。2012年4月4日，贝娅特丽克丝女王启动了博物馆的新址。现在的EYE电影博物馆内收藏了3.7万部影片、6万张海报、70万张照片和2万本书。最早的资料来源于1895年荷兰电影工业刚开始的时期。

这个引人注目的综合体建筑由总部位于维也纳的DMAA事务所所设计，内部有四块屏幕，640个座位和1 200平方米的展览空间。

门票：　　　博物馆的电影票和展览门票是不可通用的

电影票10.5欧元，11岁以下儿童8欧元，阿姆斯特丹城市卡8.4欧元

展览门票10欧元，11~18岁的未成年5欧元，11岁以下儿童免费，I Amsterdam-city 卡及博物馆卡免费；电影和展览门票通票16欧元

开放时间：　每天上午10点至晚上7点

地址：　　　阿姆斯特丹，IJpromenade 1号

联系方式：　020-5891400

http://www.eyefilm.nl/en

※ 荷兰国家海事博物馆

荷兰国家海事博物馆位于阿姆斯特丹东部港区。这座博物馆建于1656年，由丹尼尔·斯塔帕特设计，这在当时可是一个建筑奇迹。为了在阿姆斯特丹港口的人工岛上建造它，必须将1 800根木桩深深地打到淤泥里。在1973年被改造为国家海事博物馆之前，这里一直是栋海军建筑。

在最近的改造中，建筑内部一个巨大的庭院被玻璃屋顶覆盖起来，为游客创造了一个极为舒适的空间。华灯初上的夜晚，数百盏LED灯在玻璃之间的防护板上点亮，给人一种漫天星辰的假象。

"阿姆斯特丹"号的复刻版自20世纪就停泊在海事博物馆的码头，煞是引人注目。

站在"阿姆斯特丹"号上，远眺停泊在水上的船只与游艇。

海事博物馆的码头，荷兰东印度公司的一艘大型三桅"阿姆斯特丹"号的复制品——原"阿姆斯特丹"号在1749年前往巴达维亚的处女航行中在风暴中沉入英吉利海峡——高高耸立在IJ Bay水面之上。原失事船只的残骸是1969年在英国海岸被发现的，博物馆的复制品在1990年完成。参观这艘船的过程中，你会体验到它在航行中容纳了350人共同使用是多么狭小和简陋，船长和官员们的空间虽说要舒适一些，但也同样窄小。

荷兰国家海事博物馆收藏了丰富多彩的海事艺术品，参观完全部要花上好几个小时。这些收藏品被分成了几个较小的展厅，主题各异。这里只列几个比较重要的主题展厅："See You in the Golden Age（黄金时代见）""Port 24/7（港口24/7）""Voyage at Sea（横渡海洋）""The Ship Decorations（船舶装饰）""The Navigational Instruments（导航仪）"和针对6岁以上的孩子们的"The Tale of the Whale（鲸鱼传说）""My Expo（我的世博）"和"Sal and Yori and Circus Sea（萨尔、尤瑞和马戏海洋）"。

门票：　　　成年人16欧元，4～17岁的未成年人每人8欧元，4岁以下的儿童免费入场

开放时间：　每天早上9点至下午5点

地址：　　　阿姆斯特丹，Kattenburgerplein 1号

联系方式：　020-5232222
　　　　　　http://www.hetscheepvaartmuseum.nl/

※ 科学博物馆

NEMO科学博物馆是荷兰最大的科学中心。

NEMO科学博物馆起源于1923年，当时是由艺术家赫尔曼·海恩布鲁克在阿姆斯特丹的玫瑰运河所开设的劳动博物馆。1997年，原博物馆更名为新都市中心，而科学中心这个名字则是在2000年推出的。2016年，中心正式更名为NEMO科学博物馆。这个博物馆每年吸引超过50万的游客，成为荷兰第五大最受游客欢迎的博物馆。

NEMO科学博物馆坐落在中央车站左侧的湖面上，图为一艘游船从博物馆附近驶过。

NEMO科学博物馆有五层的实践科学展厅。第一层的主要概念是DNA和链式反应，其中包括一个巨大的多米诺骨牌的房间，像一个巨大的铃铛和一辆飞车。还有一个半小时演示也在一楼，展示了一个大型连锁反应电路。

二楼有一个球形工厂，小塑料球被放置到电路中，参与者要把它们按重量、大小和颜色进行分组，然后把它们输送到一个包装设施里，在那里塑料球被放入一个小的金属盒子里。然后共有5个环节，在每个环节人们要在箱子上贴上磁性条形码，然后再把它们输送出去以便启动电路。二楼还有一个小餐厅、一个小影院和表演厅，里面展示了各种各样的科学演示和电影。

三楼有一个巨大的科学实验室，人们可以在里面做一些科学实验，比如在某些物质中检测维生素C和观察DNA。还有一小部分是有关货币和商业的。

四楼是关于人类大脑的一个区域，里面有关于记忆测试、心理问题和感觉测试的实验。四楼光线很暗，使周围的环境看起来很诡异。

再往上的五层有一个自助餐厅、一个儿童游戏场和一个视野极好的观景区。

门票：　　　成年人及4岁以上未成年人，均一票价16.5欧元

阿姆斯特丹城市卡、博物馆卡持有者免费入内

开放时间：　周二至周日，每天上午10点至下午5点半；周一不开放

地址：　　　阿姆斯特丹，Oosterdok 2号

联系方式：　020-5313233

http://www.nemosciencemuseum.nl/en

※ 阿姆斯特丹市立博物馆

阿姆斯特丹市立博物馆是在1895年被确立为城市博物馆的，1938年，当时的Stedelijk即城市博物馆成为国家的博物馆，按其兴趣范畴被划分为诸多学科，如艺术，如今收藏在阿姆斯特丹博物馆的有记载了城市历史的文物以及有关医学历史的特殊藏品。直到20世纪70年代初，城市博物馆才成为现代艺术博物馆。

阿姆斯特丹市立博物馆的设计收藏展现了从20世纪末到现在的设计历史，展示了家具、陶瓷、海报、珠宝和其他物品。

今天，阿姆斯特丹市立博物馆有着世界上丰富的现代艺术藏品之一。除了所有重要的现代绘画流派，像印象派、野兽派、立体主义、表现主义，它还收藏了29幅由卡兹米尔·马列维奇绘制的合集，同样出彩的风格派和眼镜蛇派的作品，一流的荷兰摄影作品，荷兰设计和家具的典藏，自1950年以来欧洲和美国艺术趋势的作品收藏，如来自马蒂斯、毕加索、纽曼、劳森伯格和沃霍尔的作品和意大利"贫穷艺术"及德国现代绘画的完整收藏。

门票：　　　成年人17.5欧元；18岁及以下的儿童免费

开放时间：　每天上午10点至下午6点，周五上午10点至晚上10点

地址：　　　阿姆斯特丹，博物馆广场10号

联系方式：　020-5732911

http://www.stedelijk.nl/

※ 阿姆斯特丹博物馆

荷兰首都阿姆斯特丹是一个拥有千年历史的贸易城市，它与水有着特殊的关系，非常注重企业家精神、创新能力、公民意识和自由思考。在极具纪念意义的阿姆斯特丹博物馆大楼里，你会通过大量的杰作深度了解阿姆斯特丹的故事，比如中世纪的空中地图和布莱特纳的作品《大坝》。在这个博物馆里，你可以观看、阅读、聆听和体验这座城市是如何发展成如今我们所看见的阿姆斯特丹的。

在2011年之前，阿姆斯特丹博物馆一直被称为阿姆斯特丹历史博物馆，它是一个有关阿姆斯特丹发展史的博物馆。阿姆斯特丹博物馆从1975年起就坐落在卡弗街一座壮观的建筑内，这里在中世纪的时候是圣·卢西恩修道院，1578年城市孤儿院又在此成立。在1580到1960年间，成千上万的孩子们的父母在瘟疫中丧命，孤儿院成了孩子们的家园。孩子们在孤儿院也接受了教育——大一些的男孩在城里的其他地方上学，而女孩们则在孤儿院接受教导，并掌握了家庭技能。为了纪念孤儿院的那段时期，内院的摄政室和孤儿的橱柜都保存完好，小孤儿院是一个家庭展示的地方，你可以在那里了解到阿姆斯特丹孤儿的世界。男孩和女孩的内部庭院是男孩和女孩分开玩耍嬉戏的地方，也是起源于那个时代。

阿姆斯特丹博物馆是了解阿姆斯特丹非常重要的一处信息来源，博物馆的两个入口很容易被错过。

阿姆斯特丹画廊是世界上为数不多的免费的"博物馆街"之一，它是由贝居安巷通往博物馆的一条加了屋顶盖的街道。由艺术家如巴塞洛缪斯·赫尔斯特和埃文·奥拉夫在1530年到2007年之间创作的原始团体肖像画悬挂在画廊里。在这里，甚至还能看到已经有着350岁高龄的著名的木头巨人——歌利亚。

阿姆斯特丹博物馆是任何想了解更多关于这个城市的人的聚会场所。

门票：　　　成年人每人13.5欧元；18岁以下免费
　　　　　　博物馆卡持有者、国际博物馆协会（ICOM）成员、伦勃朗协会成员、阿姆斯特丹城市卡及城市直通卡持有者免费
开放时间：　每天上午10点至下午5点
地址：　　　阿姆斯特丹卡弗街92号
联系方式：　020-5231822
　　　　　　http://www.amsterdammuseum.nl/

※ 大麻博物馆

这实际上是两个小博物馆，但只需买一张票。这两处都位于红灯区的Oudezijds Achterburgwal运河，相距不远。

第一个展馆称为博物馆，展示涵盖了大麻植物的不同用途和一些用于消遣娱乐方面的多样性品种，通常称为cannabis，即大麻。大麻植物是人类已知的最古老的作物之一，它被用来制造纺织品（类似于亚麻）已经达上千年的时间，还用来结绳索甚至制造纸张。大麻也是制造油类的一种来源，尽管大麻油是可食用的，但人们主要用它来作油灯的燃料，也会当作药品以及用来制作颜料和肥皂。今天，大麻成为棉的重要替代品，棉花的种植要求充沛的水供应和使用杀虫剂，并且其收割极度耗费人力，而大麻是一种坚韧、种植要求低、适应性非常强的作物，大麻的收割也可以完全依靠机械实现。

第二个展馆是大麻画廊，重点介绍了大麻的使用文明，其历史演变和艺术传统，重申了广泛使用大麻的论点。在展馆的后面有一个小型的艺术画廊，里面有一些画家和摄影师的作品展览。

门票：	每人9欧元；13岁以下儿童免费入场，但需要有成人陪同
开放时间：	每天上午10点至晚上10点
地址：	阿姆斯特丹，Oudezijds Achterburgwal 148号
联系方式：	020-6248926
	http://hashmuseum.com

※ 阿姆斯特丹性博物馆

这是一个正经严肃而有趣的博物馆，绝非仅是赤裸裸的色情作品展览。阿姆斯特丹性博物馆是阿姆斯特丹第四受欢迎的博物馆，仅次于梵高博物馆、国立博物馆和安妮故居。

博物馆的目的是揭示和说明人们对性的态度，一直从古典时期延续到维多利亚时期。事实上，如果你认为今天的道德是宽松的，那么看看古希腊人和罗马人就会发现他们把这个问题看得有多透彻。

博物馆展出的物品包括油画、漫画、照片、雕像和录制品。大型展品陈列在几个承载着一些名人名字的房间内，据说这些人对性和色情的发展产生了很大影响，比如蓬帕杜夫人、萨德侯爵、玛塔·哈里等。

阿姆斯特丹性博物馆比红灯区的其他情色博物馆更迷人，也更有趣。博物馆位于离中央车站不远的最繁忙的达姆拉克大街18号，博物馆只允许16岁及以上的人员参观。

门票：	16岁及以上，每人4欧元
开放时间：	每天上午9点半至晚上11点半
地址：	阿姆斯特丹，达姆拉克大街18号
联系方式：	020-6228376
	http://www.sexmuseumamsterdam.nl/

Tijd voor Nederlands 荷兰语时间

● 单词+短语

荷 schilder	荷 schilderij	荷 toegangskaartje
英 painter	英 painting	英 ticket
译 画家	译 绘画	译 门票
荷 toerist	荷 tentoonstelling	荷 openingstijden
英 tourist	英 exhibition	英 opening time
译 游客	译 展览	译 营业时间

续表

荷 maandag/dinsdag/ woensdag/donderdag/ vrijdag/zaterdag/zondag 英 Monday/Tuesday/Wednesday/ Thursday/Friday/Saturday/ Sunday 译 星期一/星期二/星期三/ 星期四/星期五/星期六/ 星期日	荷 eeuw 英 century 译 世纪	荷 bezoeken 英 visit 译 参观
荷 reserveren 英 book 译 预定	荷 luid 英 loudly 译 大声地	荷 gesloten/open 英 closed/open 译 关的/开的

● 例句

荷 Nederland heeft veel beroemde schilders, bijvoorbeeld Van Gogh, Rembrandt, Vermeer, etc. 英 The Netherlands has many famous painters. For example, Van Gogh, Rembrandt, Vermeer, etc. 译 荷兰有很多有名的画家，比如梵高、伦勃朗、维米尔等。	荷 Dit schilderij is een werk uit de zestiende eeuw. 英 This painting is a work of the sixteenth century. 译 这幅绘画是十六世纪的作品。
荷 Wat zijn de openingstijden van het museum? 英 What is the opening time of the museum? 译 博物馆的营业时间是几点?	荷 Vandaag is het maandag, het museum is gesloten. 英 Today is Monday, the museum is closed. 译 今天是星期一，博物馆关门。
荷 Er zijn veel toeristen in het museum. U moet uw toegangskaartje online reserveren. 英 There are many tourists in the museum. You must reserve your tickets online. 译 博物馆的游客非常多，你必须从网上订票。	荷 Er is vandaag een speciale tentoonstelling in het museum. 英 There is a special exhibition in the museum today. 译 博物馆里今天有一个特别的展览。
荷 Het is interessant om het museum te bezoeken. 英 It is interesting to visit the museum. 译 参观博物馆是一件有意思的事。	荷 Spreek niet te luid in het museum. 英 Do not speak loudly in the museum. 译 不要在博物馆内大声说话。

95

2. 鹿特丹的博物馆
Museums in Rotterdam

Compared with Amsterdam, the number of museums in Rotterdam is a little less. But this is the Netherlands, which, as said has the highest density of museums in the world so Rotterdam also offers a wide variety of museums and permanent exhibitions. Some museums in Rotterdam are internationally renowned, but there are also lesser known specialised museums that are certainly worth a visit!

与阿姆斯特丹相比，鹿特丹博物馆的数量要少一些。但别忘了这里可是荷兰，这里拥有世界上最高的博物馆密度，所以在鹿特丹也有各种各样的博物馆和永久展览。鹿特丹有一些博物馆在国际上享誉盛名，但也有一些不太知名的专业博物馆值得参观！

※ Museum Boijmans van Beuningen

If you are going to visit museums in Rotterdam, Museum Boijmans Van Beuningen must be your first choice. It is the biggest museum in Rotterdam.

The Museum Boijmans Van Beuningen was founded in 1849, when the lawyer and art collector Frans Jacob Otto Boijmans left his collection to the City of Rotterdam. Just over a hundred years later, the famous collection by industrialist Daniël George van Beuningen was added. The museum was opened in 1935. The Building was designed especially to house the Boijmans collection and remains a Rotterdam landmark. Its distinctive tower is a familiar feature of the city's skyline to this day.

Unlike many other museums that specialise in specific periods of time, among Europe's finest museums, the Museum Boijmans van Beuningen has a permanent collection spanning all eras of Dutch and European art, including superb old masters. Among the highlights are The Wedding Feast at Cana by Hieronymus Bosch, the Three Maries at the Open Sepulchre by Van Eyck, the minutely detailed Tower of Babel by Pieter Brueghel the Elder, and Portrait of Titus and Man in a Red Cap by Rembrandt.

Paintings and sculpture from the mid-19th century are another strength. There are many Monets and other French Impressionists; Van Gogh and Gauguin can also be found here; and there are statues by Degas. The museum Boijmans van Beuningen rightly prides itself on its collection by a group it calls 'the other surrealists', including Marcel Duchamp, René Magritte and Man Ray. Salvador Dalí got a special room in the recent expansion and the collection is one of the largest of his work outside Spain and France.

There's also a good café and a pleasant sculpture garden (featuring Claes Oldenburg's famous Bent Screw, among others).

Tickets:　　Admission adult €20; Admission students €10; FREE for admission children up to 18 years

Hours:　　Daily 11am–5pm, Monday closed

Address:　Museumpark 18, 3015 CX Rotterdam

Contact:　010-4419400

　　　　　　http://www.boijmans.nl

※ Kunsthal Rotterdam

The world-famous architect Rem Koolhaas designed the Kunsthal in 1988-1989 in conjunction with the project architect Fuminori Hoshino from the Rotterdam firm of architects OMA (Office for Metropolitan Architecture). The work immediately attracted wide international attention for its features as for its innovative use of material. This new building used not only expensive, classic materials such as marble and parquet for the Kunsthal, but also cheap, "common" materials such as corrugated plastic, bare concrete, galvanised steel gratings and rough tree trunks. Each exhibition space has its own character and atmosphere, use of material and format. The Kunsthal was officially opened on 1 November 1992. The robust building houses seven exhibition spaces, a characteristic auditorium, and a café with an ambience of its own.

Equally as impressive as the building is the Kunsthal's rich variety of exhibitions. Without having its own private art collection, the museum has the freedom to host more than 20 exhibitions each year. The art on display at any one time can vary from photography and sculpture to fashion and film, celebrating the art history canon alongside emerging artists. One of the Kunsthal's most successful exhibitions to date is "the fashion world of Jean Paul Gaultier: from the sidewalk to the catwalk" in 2013, which attracted unprecedented international interest.

After an intense renovation lasting seven months, the Kunsthal reopened on 1 February 2014. The result of the renovation supervised by OMA is a sustainable building that is easier to access and to run. The main entrance has been moved to the Museumpark. The inviting entrance area includes the Kunsthal café, the shop and the ticket office. The splendid auditorium with a seating capacity of more than 300 is used by the Kunsthal for programme activities, but it can now also be rented separately as a location for events.

Tickets:　　€16.5 for adults; FREE for children up to 17 years

Hours:　　Daily 10am–5pm, Sunday 11am–5pm，Monday closed

Address:　Westzeedijk 341, 3015 AA Rotterdam

Contact:　010-4400300

　　　　　　http://www.kunsthal.nl

※ Maritime Museum Rotterdam

The Maritime Museum is situated in the Netherlands' oldest and largest open-air harbour museum. The building, designed by Dutch architect Wim Quist, was opened in 1986 right in the heart of the city's Leuvehaven.

A part of the Maritime Museum Rotterdam dates back to 1852, when the Model Room for the Royal Dutch Yachting Club was created. This Model Room was the basis for a public municipal museum created in 1874, which makes the Maritime Museum Rotterdam the oldest maritime museum of the Netherlands. The important collection of ship models spans seven centuries and contains a large part of the ship types which were used in the Netherlands for hundreds of years. One of the top pieces of the Maritime Museum Rotterdam is the Mataró that dates back to early 15th century and which is the oldest ship model in Western Europe.

Next to the Maritime Museum lies the open-air Maritime Museum Harbour, or Museumhaven Rotterdam in dutch, which merged with the Maritime Museum in 2014.The collection of the museum consisted in 1874 of about 300 items: ship models, technical models, a small library of prints, drawings and cards. Since 1998, the number of maritime objects in the collection has grown to half a million, divided into categories like ship models, paintings, prints, drawings, nautical charts and globes, ship plans, photos, films, videos, navigation instruments, nautical instruments, ship furniture and other numerous personal objects, such as documents and clothes.

Besides the indoor collection, The Maritime Museum Rotterdam also displays many ships of the former Harbour Museum outside. At Leuvehaven you'll find historic ships as well as cranes, a tugboat, a lighthouse, a steam powered grain elevator and a locomotor.

Tickets: Adults: €12.5; Children from 4 to 15: €9,0; FREE for under 4 years old

Hours: Daily 10am–5pm; Sunday 11am–5pm; Monday closed

Address: Leuvehaven 1, 3011 EA Rotterdam

Contact: 010-4132680

http://www.maritiemmuseum.nl/

※ Wereldmuseum

The Wereldmuseum located in an elegant 19th-century building on the River Maas, it is a window to the world in the heart of Rotterdam. The museum opened its doors in 1885 in response to increasing demand created by Dutch trade relations abroad, growing colonialism, increased missionary activity, and the newly emerging science of ethnology. The new Wereldmuseum– then known as the Museum for Geography and Ethnology–provided Rotterdam's citizens with a rare glimpse into other, rarely seen cultures through its dazzling showcase of priceless objects spanning 2,000 years of global history.

The Wereldmuseum is the home to some of Rotterdam's most important historical treasures. Some 1800 objects are on display in the museum, reflecting 160 years of Rotterdam's colonial exploration. Collected from the five continents of the globe and a vast variety of civilisations both

ancient and modern, each artefact has a unique story to tell about the people that produced it, and Rotterdam's relationship with that culture. From Asian across Oceana, Africa and the Americas, the museum showcases all aspects of life in different cultures around the world, from clothing to cooking utensils, weaponry, transport and priceless art. Visitors can take a fascinating journey through distant civilisations and see the world through the eyes of Rotterdam's maritime merchants and explorers.

Tickets:	Adults: €15; Free for children under 13
Hours:	Daily 10am–5pm; Monday closed
Address:	Willemskade 25, 3016 DM Rotterdam
Contact:	010-2707172
	http://www.wereldmuseum.nl

※ Nederlands Fotomuseum

The Netherlands Photo Museum (Nederlands Fotomuseum) was founded in 1989, under the name Nederlands Foto Archief. And was subsidised by the Dutch government. In 2003, it was reborn, through an endowment from Hein Wertheimer, a wealthy Dutch lawyer, and renamed to Nederlands Fotomuseum.

Each year the Nederlands Fotomuseum mounts around ten exhibitions. These alternate between historical and present-day photography and between Dutch and international work. Over recent years, there have been major exhibitions of work by such world-famous photographers as Henri Cartier-Bresson, Nan Goldin, Lewis Hine, Alfredo Jaar, Josef Koudelka and Viviane Sassen. In addition, the Nederlands Fotomuseum concerns itself with young, emerging photographers. Its annual Steenbergen Stipendium awards and Quickscan NL exhibition series are evidence of this interest.

The Nederlands Fotomuseum is the only museum in the Netherlands to possess an in-house conservation studio for photography. The studio not only conserves the museum's own collection, but also works on the photographic collections of other museums, private individuals, archives and companies. This makes the Nederlands Fotomuseum one of the most important museums of photography in Europe in terms of its expertise concerning the preservation and conservation of photographic materials.

For photography enthusiasts, this is a museum that is unlikely to be missed.

Tickets:	Adults 26 and over: €14; Age 18 to 25 €7; FREE for children and under 18
Hours:	Daily 10am–5pm; Monday closed
Address:	Wilhelminakade 332, 3072 AR Rotterdam

Contact:　010-2030405
http://www.nederlandsfotomuseum.nl

※ 博曼斯·范·博宁恩美术馆

如果你打算在鹿特丹逛博物馆，那么博曼斯·范·博宁恩美术馆一定是你的首选。它是鹿特丹最大的博物馆。

博曼斯·范·博宁恩美术馆成立于1849年，当时的律师和艺术品收藏家弗兰斯·雅各布·奥托·博曼斯把他的收藏品献给了鹿特丹市政府。就在一百多年后，著名工业家丹尼尔·乔治·范·博宁恩的私人收藏也被增添到博物馆藏品之列。该博物馆于1935年对外开放，这座建筑是专门为博伊曼的收藏所设计的，是鹿特丹的地标建筑。直到今天，它独特的塔尖仍然是这座城市天际线的一个熟悉的特征。

博曼斯·范·博宁恩美术馆是鹿特丹最重要的博物馆，博物馆名称来源于早期的艺术品收藏家和工业家的合称。

与其他许多专注于特定时期的博物馆不同，在欧洲最优秀的博物馆中，博曼斯·范·博宁恩美术馆或博物馆有一个永久的收藏，涵盖了荷兰和欧洲艺术的各个时代，包括杰出的古代大师的作品。这些大作中最引人注目的是由耶罗尼米斯·博斯所创作的《迦南的婚宴》、范·艾克所创作的《空墓前的三圣女》、彼得·勃鲁盖尔所精心创作的《巴别塔》，还有伦勃朗的《提图斯》和《戴红帽的男人》。

19世纪中叶的绘画和雕塑是另一种力量。这一时期出现了许多犹如莫奈般的画家和其他法国印象派画家，这里也有梵高和高更的作品，以及埃德加·德加的雕像。博曼斯·范·博宁恩美术馆以其所谓的"其他超现实主义者"的作品收藏而自豪，包括马塞尔·杜尚、雷尼·马格利特和曼·雷的作品。在最近的一次扩建中，有一个特别的房间是专门为萨尔瓦多·达利准备的，除了西班牙和法国，这里是收藏了他最多作品的博物馆之一。

彼得·勃鲁盖尔的作品《巴别塔》，又叫《通天塔》是博曼斯·范·博宁恩美术馆的重要藏品之一。

博物馆内还有一个不错的咖啡馆和一个令人悦目的雕塑花园，以克莱斯·奥登伯格著名的"弯曲的螺丝"为特色。

门票：　　　成人20欧元；学生10欧元；18岁以下免费

开放时间：　周二至周日，每天上午11点至下午5点；周一不开放

地址：　　　鹿特丹，博物馆公园18号

联系方式：　010-4419400

http://www.boijmans.nl

※ 昆莎美术馆

　　世界著名的建筑师雷姆·库哈斯在1988至1989年与来自鹿特丹大都会建筑事务所OMA的项目建筑师星野纪文共同设计了昆莎，这个项目因其创新材料的使用立即引起了广泛的国际关注。这座新建筑不仅使用了如大理石、镶木地板这样昂贵的一流材料，另外还使用了诸如瓦楞塑料、裸露混凝土、镀锌钢铬栅板和粗糙的树干这种普通甚至廉价的材料，每个展览空间都运用材料和空间结构创造出独有的特点和氛围。昆莎美术馆于1992年11月1日正式开放。这栋坚固的建筑包含了七个展览空间、一个特色礼堂和一个氛围别具一格的咖啡馆。

雷姆·库哈斯设计了昆莎美术馆，他的作品还包括北京中央电视台新址.

咖啡馆前绿地上的大耳朵兔子是非常多人拍照留影的园内标志铜像，更深受孩子们的喜爱。

　　昆莎美术馆内丰富多样的展览活动同样给人留下了深刻的印象。在没有内部收藏展览的时候，美术馆内每年还会举办20多个临时性展览。这些不定期的临时展览领域涵盖广泛，从摄影和雕塑到时装和电影，与新兴的艺术家们一起研讨艺术的发展、行业的规范。迄今为止，昆莎最成功的一次临时展览是2013年让·保罗·高缇耶的时尚展"From the sidewalk to the catwalk"（从人行道到时装T台），吸引了前所未有的国际关注。

　　经过7个月的紧张翻新后，昆莎美术馆于2014年2月1日重新开放。由OMA监督的翻修工程是一个可持续性和更加人性化的建筑，使进入馆内更加便捷，展馆的运行也更加通畅。翻修后的展馆主入口被移到了博物馆公园，新入口区域包括昆莎咖啡馆、礼品商店和售票处。拥有300多个座位的富丽堂皇的礼堂被用作美术馆的项目活动场地，现在也可以作为活动场地单独对外出租。

门票：　　　成人16.5欧元；17岁以下免费

开放时间：　周二到周六，每天上午10点至下午5点；周日上午11点至下午5点；周一不开放

地址：　　　鹿特丹，Westzeedijk 341号

联系方式：　010-4400300

http://www.kunsthal.nl

※ 鹿特丹海事博物馆

鹿特丹海事博物馆位于荷兰历史最悠久、规模最大的露天海港博物馆，是由荷兰建筑师维姆·奎斯特所设计的，于1986年在鹿特丹的勒弗港中心落成。

鹿特丹海事博物馆其中的一部分可以追溯到1852年，当时是皇家荷兰游艇俱乐部的模型室。这个模型室成了一个建于1874年的公共市政博物馆的基础，它使鹿特丹海事博物馆成为荷兰最古老的海事博物馆。这个博物馆内所收藏的重要的船舶模型跨越了7个世纪，其中包含了许多在荷兰使用了几百年的船型。馆中有一件顶级的作品是马塔罗号，它可以追溯到15世纪早期，是西欧最古老的船模。

在海事博物馆旁边的是露天海事博物馆海港，于2014年与海事博物馆合并。

在海事博物馆旁边的是露天海事博物馆海港，或者叫鹿特丹海港博物馆，它于2014年与海事博物馆合并。海港博物馆的藏品包括来源于1874年的大约300件物品，有船模、技术模型、一个小型的图书馆、手绘和卡片。自1998年以来，收藏的海事物品数量已增加到50万件，门类众多，有船模、油画、印刷品、素描、海图和地球仪、航行规划、照片、电影、视频、导航仪、航海仪、船舶家具等，还有众多个人物品，如文件、服装等。

除了室内收藏，鹿特丹海事博物馆还展示了海港博物馆许多以前的船只。在勒弗港，你还会发现历史悠久的船只，还有起重机、拖船、灯塔、蒸汽动力的谷物升降机和移动设备。

门票：　　　成人12.5欧元；4～15岁的未成年人9欧元；4岁以下的儿童免费

开放时间：　周二到周六，每天上午10点至下午5点；周日上午11点至下午5点；周一不开放

地址：　　　鹿特丹，勒弗港1号

联系方式：　010-4132680

http://www.maritiemmuseum.nl/

※ 世界艺术博物馆

世界艺术博物馆坐落在马斯河一座19世纪的优雅的建筑中，它是鹿特丹市中心开向世界的一扇窗户。1885年，随着荷兰贸易关系的不断扩大，殖民主义的发展，传教士活动的增加，以及新兴的民族学科学的兴起，博物馆的大门也随之敞开。新的世界艺术博物馆彼时被称作地理与民族学博物馆——通过令人眼花缭乱的跨越2 000年全球历史的无价物品展示，为鹿特丹公民提供了其他罕见文化的视角。

世界艺术博物馆是鹿特丹一些最重要的历史宝藏的藏身之所。博物馆展出了大约1 800件展品，反映了鹿特丹160年的殖民探索。从世界五大洲和古代、现代的各种文明中，每一个人工制品

都有一个独特的故事来讲述生产和制造它的人，以及鹿特丹与此文化的关联。从亚洲横穿大洋到非洲和美洲，博物馆展示了世界各地不同文化生活的方方面面，从服装到烹饪用具、武器、交通工具和无价的艺术品。游客们可以通过鹿特丹的海上商人和探险者的眼睛进行眺望，在遥远的文明中畅游一番。

门票：	成人15欧元；13岁以下儿童免费
开放时间：	周二到周日，每天上午10点至下午5点；周一不开放
地址：	鹿特丹，Willemskade 25号
联系方式：	010-2707172
	http://www.wereldmuseum.nl

※ 荷兰摄影博物馆

荷兰摄影博物馆在1989年以荷兰照片档案馆的名字成立，并得到了荷兰政府的资助。2003年，一位来自荷兰的富有律师海因·沃瑟梅尔对档案馆进行了资助，档案馆重获新生，并更名为荷兰摄影博物馆。

每一年，荷兰摄影博物馆都会举办大约10场展览，这些展览在历史摄影和现代摄影、荷兰国内与国际摄影间轮番交替。近年来，有很多世界著名的摄影师，如亨利·卡蒂埃-布列松、南·戈尔丁、刘易斯·海恩、阿尔弗雷德·加尔、约瑟夫·库德尔卡和薇薇安·萨森等都在这里举办了大型展览。此

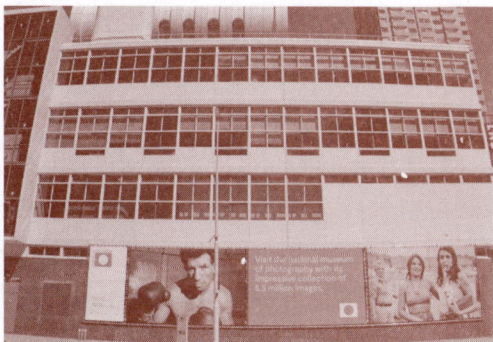

就摄影材料的保存保护方面的专业知识而言，荷兰摄影博物馆成为欧洲最重要的摄影博物馆之一。

外，荷兰摄影博物馆也关注年轻新兴摄影师的发展，它所承办的年度"斯滕贝亨奖"和"快速扫描"摄影展有效地佐证了这一点。

荷兰摄影博物馆是荷兰唯一一家拥有室内摄影保护工作室的博物馆。该工作室不仅保存了博物馆自己的藏品，还收藏了其他博物馆、个人、档案馆和公司的摄影藏品。这使得荷兰摄影博物馆就摄影材料的保存保护方面的专业知识而言，成为欧洲最重要的摄影博物馆之一。

对于摄影爱好者来说，这是一个不太可能被错过的博物馆。

门票：	26岁及以上的成人14欧元；18～25岁7欧元；18岁以下免费
开放时间：	周二到周日，每天上午10点至下午5点；周一不开放
地址：	鹿特丹，Wilhelminakade 332号
联系方式：	010-2030405
	http://www.nederlandsfotomuseum.nl

3. 海牙的博物馆
Museums in The Hague

※ Mauritshuis Museum

If The Peace Palace is the first tourist attraction in The Hague, the Mauritshuis must be the first must-visit museum.

The Mauritshuis was built as a home between 1636 and 1641, during John Maurice's governorship of Dutch Brazil. The Dutch Classicist building was designed by the Dutch architects Jacob van Campen and Pieter Post. The two-storey building is strictly symmetrical and contained four apartments and a great hall. Each apartment was designed with an antechamber, a chamber, a cabinet, and a cloakroom. Originally, the building had a cupola, which was destroyed in a fire in 1704.

The Mauritshuis was privatised in 1995. This building, which is the property of the state, is rented by the museum. In 2007, the museum announced its desire to expand. The renovation started in 2012 and finished in 2014. During the renovation, about 100 of the museum's paintings were displayed in the Gemeentemuseum in the Highlights Mauritshuis exhibition. About 50 other paintings, including the Girl With the Pearl Earring, were on loan to exhibitions in the United States and Japan. The museum was reopened on 27 June, 2014 by His Royal Highness King Willem-Alexander.

The museum houses the Royal Cabinet of Paintings which consists of 841 objects, mostly Dutch Golden Age paintings. The collections contains works by Johannes Vermeer, Rembrandt van Rijn, Jan Steen, Paulus Potter, Frans Hals, Jacob van Ruisdael, Hans Holbein the Younger, and others. Originally, in the 17th century the building was the residence of count John Maurice of Nassau. It is now the property of the government of the Netherlands and is listed in the top 100 Dutch heritage sites.

Tickets:	Adults €15.5; Children (up and until 18) FREE
Hours:	Monday 1pm–6pm
	Thursday 10am–8pm
	Tuesday to Sunday 10am–6pm
Address:	Plein 29, 2511 CS Den Haag
Contact:	070-3023456
	http://www.mauritshuis.nl

※ Museum Escher in het Paleis

Maurits Cornelis Escher (1898-1972), who was born in Leeuwarden, was a genius at drawing impossible situations. He is one of the world's most famous graphic artists. His art is enjoyed by millions of people all over the world, as can be seen on the many web sites on the internet.

M.C. Escher, during his lifetime, made 448 lithographs, woodcuts and wood engravings and over 2000 drawings and sketches. Like some of his famous predecessors, - Michelangelo, Leonardo da Vinci, Dürer and Holbein-, M.C. Escher was left-handed.

Apart from being a graphic artist, M.C. Escher illustrated books, designed tapestries, postage stamps and murals. He is most famous for his so-called impossible constructions, such as Ascending and Descending, Relativity, his Transformation Prints, such as Metamorphosis I, Metamorphosis II and Metamorphosis III, Sky & Water I or Reptiles.

The museum features a permanent display of a large number of woodcuts and lithographs by M.C. Escher, among them the world-famous prints,

Air and Water (birds become fish); Belvedere (the inside out of a Folly); Waterfall (where water seems to flow upwards); Drawing (two hands drawing each other). Escher in Het Paleis shows the early lovely Italian landscapes, the many mirror prints and a choice from the tessellation drawings, also the three versions of the Metamorphosis, from the first small one, to the third, of 7 meters. This one is shown in a circle. It underlines the new vision of the museum on the work of M.C. Escher.

Tickets:	Adults €9.5; Children 7–15 year €6.5; Children until 6 year FREE
Hours:	Daily 11am–5pm; Monday closed
Address:	Lange Voorhout 74, 2514 EH Den Haag
Contact:	070-4277730
	http://www.escherinhetpaleis.nl

※ Gemeentemuseum Den Haag

The Gemeentemuseum is a modern palace of the arts. With 150,000 works of art, and it is one of Europe's biggest art museums too. With Mondrian, Monet, Kandinsky, Van Gogh, Picasso, Dumas, Constant, Francis Bacon and Louise Bourgeois and many others under one roof, the museum is an art lover's fantasy. If you want to see it all, you can easily spend a whole day at the museum.

Some figures about the museum :

The Gemeentemuseum Den Haag has the world's biggest collection of works by Piet

Mondriaan, the highlight being his last abstract work Victory Boogie Woogie.

The Gemeentemuseum Den Haag has an excellent collection of modern art works by Monet, Picasso, Egon Schiele, Wassily Kandinsky, Louise Bourgeois, Francis Bacon and many others.

The Gemeentemuseum Den Haag also has a wide variety of Delft pottery, rare Hague silverware, a stunning dolls' house and seven period rooms.

The museum is a stunning Art Deco building designed by architect H.P. Berlage, known as the Dutch Frank Lloyd Wright. In the Wonderkamers you will find a whole new world, the collection is presented in an entirely novel way, involving colour, atmosphere and interaction.

In The Gemeentemuseum Den Haag many public art exhibitions are held throughout the year, making it one of those art museums that you must have visited at least once in your life.

Tickets: Adults €15; Children (up and until 18) FREE

Hours: Daily 10am–5pm; Monday closed

Address: Stadhouderslaan 41, 2517 HV Den Haag

Contact: 070-3381111

https://www.gemeentemuseum.nl

106

※ Historical Museum of The Hague

The Historical Museum of The Hague (Haags Historisch Museum) is located in the historical heart of The Hague. The museum is housed in the former archery house of St. Sebastian's Guild and dates from 1636. It is built on the spot of a gatehouse that was used by the civic guard. Since the late 18th century, after the dissolution of the civic guard guild the building has been used as a hotel, court house and museum. Since 1986 the Historical Museum of The Hague resides in the St. Sebastiaansdoelen.

The Hague is unlike other Dutch cities, it is the centre of government, a Royal Residence, an international city of peace and justice but also the home of the Beatstad music festival, the ADO football team and the stork in The Hague town arms. The Hague is diverse, and the diversity of the city is well presented in the museum.

In The Hague Historical Museum you will see in the paintings of Jan van Ravesteyn, P.C. la Fargue and Jan Steen how the city has developed over time and how people experienced life in the city. A series of townscapes from different periods show how life was lived in olden times, revealing the city's long history as the political and administrative centre of the Netherlands.

In addition, the museum has some unusual collections: the carefully arranged doll's houses by Lita de Ranitz, also the tongue and finger of the De Witt brothers, curiously preserved.

Tickets:	Adults €10; Children (6-17years) €2.75; Children under 6 FREE
Hours:	Monday Closed
	Tuesday to Friday 10am–5pm
	Saturday & Sunday 12am–5pm
Address:	Korte Vijverberg 7, 2513 AB Den Haag
Contact:	070-3646940
	http://www.haagshistorischmuseum.nl

※ Panorama Mesdag

Panorama Mesdag is a panorama by Hendrik Willem Mesdag, housed in a purpose-built museum in The Hague, It is the largest circular canvas in Europe.

As an example of the typical 19th century 'instruction and entertainment' idea, Panorama Mesdag is unique in being the last vestige of the maritime panorama in the Netherlands. The painting is important as a product of The Hague School, not only because of its size, brushstrokes and theme employed, but also as a result of the collaborating artists of The Hague School.

Panorama Mesdag grandly and gloriously sets forth the effect of illusion in a manner unsurpassed. The transition from the artificial dune to the painting is achieved with phenomenal artistic skills and strongly suggests to visitors that they are outside. However, this was the real appearance of the sea, the beaches and the village of Scheveningen in the late 19th century.

Panorama is a cylindrical painting more than 14 metres high and about 40 metres in diameter, the surface area is about 1 680 m^2. It was painted by the painter H.W. Mesdag in four months, supported by several fellow artists, including Breitner. Mesdag was a notable marine painter of The Hague School. The entire work, which comprises the structure and panorama, was completed between 1880 and 1881.

Tickets:	Adults €10; Children(4-11years) €5; Students €8.5
Hours:	Daily 10am–5pm; Sunday 11am–5pm
Address:	Zeestraat 65, 2518 AA Den Haag
Contact:	070-3106665
	http://www.panorama-mesdag.nl

※ Prison Gate Museum

The Prison Gate Museum tells the thrilling tale of crime and punishment in days gone by. Since 1882, the mediaeval prison has operated as a museum. It lies on the Hofvijver, close to the Binnenhof in The Hague.

107

From 1420 until 1828, the prison was used for housing people who had committed serious crimes while they awaited sentencing. Its most famous prisoner was Cornelis de Witt, who was held on the charge of plotting the murder of the stadtholder. He was lynched together with his brother Johan on 20 August 1672 on the square in front of the building called groene zoodje. When public executions went out of fashion the area was used to build the "Witte Society", a literature club that still exists today, but had to move when the street was built in 1923.

In 1882, the Prison Gate became a prison museum. The "gate" function was lost in 1923 when the houses adjoining the Hofvijver were taken down to build the street that now allows busy traffic to run by it.

Tickets:	Adults €10; Children under 12 years €6
Hours:	Monday Closed
	Tuesday to Friday 10am–5pm
	Saturday & Sunday 12am–5pm
Address:	Buitenhof 33, 2513 AH, The Hague
Contact:	070-3460861
	http://www.gevangenpoort.nl

※ 莫瑞泰斯皇家美术馆

如果说和平宫是海牙的第一个旅游景点，那么莫瑞泰斯皇家美术馆一定是第一个必须参观的博物馆。

莫瑞泰斯皇家美术馆就位于二院旁边，在海牙最中心位置，建于17世纪，是一栋严格对称的独栋建筑。

莫瑞泰斯皇家美术馆是在1636年至1641年间约翰·莫里斯任荷兰巴西州长期间所建造的住宅房屋。这栋荷兰古典主义风格建筑是由荷兰建筑师雅各布·范·坎彭和彼得·波斯特设计的。这栋两层的建筑是严格对称的，有四套公寓和一个大厅。每个公寓都有一个前厅、一个房间、一个储藏柜和一个衣帽间。这座建筑起初还有一个圆顶，但是在1704年的一场大火中被烧毁。

莫瑞泰斯皇家美术馆在1995年被私有化。因为这栋建筑是国家的财产，因此这里只是美术馆租借的场地。2007年，美术馆对外宣布了扩建的意愿。2012年，美术馆开始新一次的整修，并于两年后的2014年竣工。在翻修期间，莫瑞泰斯皇家美术馆的大约100幅画作都被转移到海牙市立博物馆作为莫瑞泰斯皇家美术馆的特别展览。还有大约50幅其他画作，包括《戴珍珠耳环的女孩》，被租借到美国和日本的博物馆进行展出。2014年6月27日由威廉·亚历山大国王重新开放了美术馆。

　　莫瑞泰斯收藏有由841件物品组成的皇家油画陈列柜，其中大部分是荷兰黄金时代的绘画作品。这些收藏品包括维米尔、伦勃朗、扬·斯特恩、保罗斯·波特、弗兰斯·哈尔斯、雅各布·范·雷斯达尔、小汉斯·荷尔拜因等人的作品。最初在17世纪，建筑属于约翰·莫里茨伯爵的住所，但现在它是荷兰政府的财产，被列入荷兰文化遗产前100名之列。

门票：	成年人15.5欧元；18岁以下免费
开放时间：	周一，下午1点至下午6点；周四，上午10点至晚上8点 周二到周日，上午10点至下午6点
地址：	海牙，海牙广场29号
联系方式：	070-3023456 http://www.mauritshuis.nl

※ 埃舍尔博物馆

　　莫里茨·科奈里斯·埃舍尔出生在吕伐登，他是一个描绘现实非存在画作的天才。他是世界上最著名的图形艺术家之一，他的艺术被全世界数以百万计的人所喜爱，就像我们在互联网上的许多网站上看到的一样。

　　埃舍尔在一生中制作了448张石版画、木刻和木雕和2 000多幅素描和速写。像一些著名的前辈如米开朗琪罗、达·芬奇、丢勒和荷尔拜因一样，埃舍尔也是个左撇子。

　　除了是一名平面艺术家，埃舍尔还绘有画册，设计了挂毯、邮票和壁画。他最著名的创作是他所谓的不可能的结构，如《上升和下降》《相对性》，他的转换画作，如《变形Ⅰ》《变形Ⅱ》《变形Ⅲ》《天与水Ⅰ》《蜥蜴》。

埃舍尔最著名的创作是他所谓的不可能的结构，上既是下，让人感觉匪夷所思。

　　博物馆的一大特色是永久性地展示了埃舍尔大量的木刻版画和石版画，其中有世界闻名的《空气和水》——鸟变成鱼、《观景楼》——荒唐的内部结构、《瀑布》——仿佛向上的水流、《画手》——互绘的双手。埃舍尔博物馆展示了很多早期漂亮的意大利风景画，许多镜像图案和镶嵌图画，还有三个版本的《变形》，从第一个小的到长度达7米的第三个大作，这些被展示在一个环形结构里，充分强调了博物馆对埃舍尔作品的新愿景。

门票：　　　成年人9.5欧元；7～15岁6.5欧元；6岁以下免费

开放时间：　周二到周日，上午11点至下午5点；周一不开放

地址：　　　海牙，Lange Voorhout 74号

联系方式：　070-4277730

　　　　　　http://www.escherinhetpaleis.nl

※ 海牙市立博物馆

　　海牙市立博物馆是现代艺术的殿堂，这里拥有15万件艺术品藏品，也是欧洲最大的艺术博物馆之一。皮特·蒙德里安、莫奈、康定斯基、梵高、毕加索、杜马斯、康斯登、弗朗西斯·培根、路易斯·布尔乔亚以及其他许多艺术家的巨作都在同一个屋檐下被展出，这个博物馆是一个艺术爱好者的幻想成真的地方。如果你想全部都参观一遍，博物馆里随随便便就得花上一整天的时间。

海牙市立博物馆拥有世界上最大量的皮特·蒙德里安的作品收藏，是欧洲最大的艺术博物馆之一。图为馆内展现蒙德里安作品的一处展室。

　　这里是一些与本博物馆相关的数据：

　　海牙市立博物馆拥有世界上最大量的皮特·蒙德里安的作品收藏，最著名的非他最后一部抽象作品《胜利之舞》莫属。

　　该博物馆收藏了许多来自莫奈、毕加索、埃贡·席勒、瓦西里·康定斯基、布尔乔亚、培根等人的现代艺术珍品。此外，海牙市立博物馆也藏有各种各样的代尔夫特陶器、稀有的海牙银器，精美绝伦的惊人的"玩偶之家"和七间时代展室。

　　这座博物馆是一幢令人叹为观止的装饰艺术建筑，是由被称为荷兰的弗兰克·劳埃德·赖特的建筑师贝拉吉所设计的。在神奇房间内，你会发现一个全新的世界，它以一种全新的方式呈现，包括色彩、氛围和互动。

　　海牙市立博物馆全年都会举办众多的公共艺术展，因此这是一个值得你一生至少要参观一次的博物馆。

门票：　　　成年人15欧元；18岁及以下免费

开放时间：　周二到周日，上午10点至下午5点；周一不开放

地址：　　　海牙，Stadhouderslaan 41号

联系方式：　070-3381111

　　　　　　https://www.gemeentemuseum.nl

※ 海牙历史博物馆

海牙历史博物馆位于海牙市中心。这栋建筑始建于1636年，位于圣·塞巴斯蒂安工会的前射箭馆，建在了公民卫队的据点。从18世纪后期公民卫队解散后，这座建筑被用作酒店、法院和博物馆。从1986年起，海牙历史博物馆便把家安置在这里。

跟其他的荷兰城市不同，海牙是政府的中心、皇室居所所在地、一个和平公正的国际城市，同时也是Beatstad音乐节、ADO海牙足球俱乐部和海牙城市市标里面鹳的家园。海牙是多样化的，城市的多样性在博物馆中得到了完美的呈现。

在海牙历史博物馆里，你会在艺术家扬·范·拉维斯蒂恩、拉法格和扬·斯特恩的画中看到这座城市是如何随着时间变化而发展的，以及人们又如何在这座城市中生存生活的。一系列来自不同时期的城市景观展示了古时候人们的生活，揭示了这座城市作为荷兰政治和行政中心的悠久历史。

此外，博物馆还收藏了一些不同寻常的藏品：由利塔·德·拉尼茨精心布置的玩偶房间，还有德威特兄弟的舌头和手指，都保存完好。

门票：　　　成年人10欧元；6～17岁2.75欧元；6岁以下儿童免费

开放时间：　周一不开放

　　　　　　周二至周五，上午10点至下午5点

　　　　　　周六、周日，上午12点至下午5点

地址：　　　海牙，Korte Vijverberg 7号

联系方式：　070-3646940

　　　　　　http://www.haagshistorischmuseum.nl

※ 梅斯达格全景美术馆

梅斯达格全景美术馆内的全景图是亨德里克·威廉姆·梅斯达格创造的，位于海牙的一个专门建造的博物馆里，它是欧洲最大的圆形画布。

作为19世纪"教学和娱乐"理念的典型范例，梅斯达格全景图是荷兰海事全景的最后一抹痕迹。这幅画作为海牙学校的一部分显得尤为重要，不仅是因为它的尺寸大、手法和主题独特，更因为它是海牙学校的艺术家们合作的成果。

壮观的全景图极大地展现了一种无与伦比的错觉效果。从人工沙丘过渡到绘画

梅斯达格全景美术馆并不大，但来这里参观的游客都是奔着这幅席凡宁根的全景图而来，这就是19世纪末席凡宁根海岸的真实景象。

的过程，是通过非凡的艺术技巧实现的，并强烈地给游客们一种身处外面的错觉。然而，画布上所展现的却是19世纪末席凡宁根的大海、沙滩、村庄的真实面貌。

全景图是一幅高度超过14米、直径约40米的圆柱形绘画，表面面积约为1 680平方米。这幅画是画家梅斯达格在4个月里完成的，并得到了包括布莱特纳在内的几位艺术家的支持。梅斯达格是海牙学校著名的海洋画家。整个作品，包括结构和全景全部在1880年到1881年间完成。

门票：　　　成人10欧元；12～18岁8.5欧元；4～11岁5欧元；4岁以下免费

开放时间：　周一到周六，上午10点至下午5点；周日，上午11点至下午5点

地址：　　　海牙，Zeestraat 65号

联系方式：　070-3106665

　　　　　　http://www.panorama-mesdag.nl

※ 监狱门博物馆

监狱门博物馆讲述了在过去的日子里犯罪和惩罚的惊险故事。这座中世纪监狱从1882年以来就一直是一个博物馆。它靠近海牙国会大厦，就在廷池的旁边。

从1420年到1828年，这座监狱被用来关押那些在等待判决时犯下严重罪行的人。最著名的囚犯是康尼利斯·德·威特，他被指控策划谋杀总督。1672年8月20日，康尼利斯和他的弟弟约翰在名为"绿色养科"的建筑前的广场上一起被处死。当公开行刑

监狱门博物馆的参观让人毛骨悚然，图为一位行人从博物馆旁走过。

逐渐取缔以后，这个地区被用来建造了一个"白色社会"，这是一个至今仍存在的文学俱乐部，但在1923年因为要修建这条街道，俱乐部迫不得已挪至它处。

1882年，Prison Gate（字面意思为"囚犯的大门"）变成了监狱博物馆。1923年，连接廷池的房屋被拆除，用来修建那条现在被交通和行人挤满的道路，"门"的功能也自然就消失了。

门票：　　　成人10欧元；12岁以下儿童6欧元

开放时间：　周二到周五，上午10点至下午5点；周六周日，上午12点至下午5点；周一不开放

地址：　　　海牙，Buitenhof 33号

联系方式：　070-3460861

　　　　　　http://www.gevangenpoort.nl

4. 乌特勒支的博物馆
Museums in Utrecht

※ Railway Museum

The Railway Museum is the Dutch national railway museum located in Utrecht. The museum was founded in 1927, but the museum has been housed in the former Maliebaan railway station since 1954. When the museum first opened to the public, its modest collection consisted of documents, a few objects and pictures. During the 1930s, railway equipment of historical significance was conserved with the intention of putting them on display in the museum. Unfortunately, a large portion of the collection was destroyed during World War II.

Railway museum can offer much more than watching trains.

Railway Museum–Utrecht–The Big Discovery Tour through an old English mining village and view a model of the famous steam locomotive The Rocket designed by Michael Longdridge in 1829. Stop for a moment and admire the first Dutch steam locomotive, "De Arend". Continue your museum visit in "Dream Journeys". In an oriental auditorium, actors play scenes about the well-known Orient Express.

In the Workshop exhibit, visitors can explore the different parts of locomotives and learn how they work. A collection of model trains can also be found as well as a restaurant.

Here, visitors will be taken on a journey through two centuries of railway history. The museum also features an extensive outdoor area for visitors to explore. An entire trip through the museum takes an average of 3.5 hours to complete.

Tickets:	Tickets €17.5; Children under 4 years FREE
Hours:	Daily 10am–5pm; Monday closed
Address:	Maliebaanstation 16, 3581 XW Utrecht
Contact:	030-2306206
	http://www.spoorwegmuseum.nl

※ Centraal Museum Utrecht

The Centraal Museum is the oldest municipal museum in the Netherlands. The museum officially opened to the public on 5 September 1838. Over the years, the building has been renovated, expanded and redesigned on several occasions. The last major renovation took place in 1999.

The Centraal Museum started in 1830 in four rooms on the top floor of the Utrecht town hall, initially consisting mostly of antiquities. In 1921 the collection merged with various private collections in the new "centralised museum" (hence the name "Centraal museum", centraal being the Dutch word for central) located in the former medieval monastery at the Nicolaaskerkhof. Currently, the museum has a wide-ranging collection, comprises pre-1850 art, modern art, applied

113

art, fashion and the city history of Utrecht.

The collection of the paintings by the Northern Mannerist Joachim Wtewael is by a long way the largest anywhere in the world. Other highlights are many significant paintings by the Utrecht Caravaggisti.

Since 2006, the museum also runs the Miffy Museum, a museum across the street dedicated to Dick Bruna and his rabbit character Miffy. It also runs the Rietveld Schröder House, a famous Modernist house built in 1924 by the Dutch architect Gerrit Rietveld for Mrs. Truus Schröder-Schräder and her three children, which is now owned by the museum and open to the public.

Tickets: Adults €13.5; Children (13–17 years) €5.5; Children under 13 FREE

Hours: Daily 11am–5pm; Monday closed

Address: Agnietenstraat 1, 3512 XA Utrecht

Contact: 030-2362362

http://centraalmuseum.nl/

※ Museum Speelklok

Museum Speelklok is a museum in Utrecht, The Netherlands. It has a collection of automatically playing musical instruments, most of which still work and therefore still can play their music. The history of these instruments started back in 16th century in the Netherlands with the use of church carillons. Over the centuries, the general desire of people to be surrounded by music, led to the invention of all sorts of self-playing musical instruments: musical clocks, musical boxes, orchestrions (self-playing orchestras) and the traditional Dutch street organs. All of these instruments, including the famous street organ named Arabier and the so-called 8th world wonder the Violina, can be admired and heard during the lively museum tour.

The museum had its origins in an exhibition of mechanical organs and other musical automata in Utrecht in the summer of 1956. The great success of this led to the creation of a permanent national museum dedicated to mechanical musical instruments. In 1984 the museum's present housing in the central medieval Buurkerk (citizens' church) was officially opened by Queen Beatrix.

Tickets: Adults €13; Children 4–17 years €7; Under 4 years FREE

Hours: Daily 10am–5pm; Monday closed

Address: Steenweg 6, 3511 JP Utrecht

Contact: 030-2312789

http://www.museumspeelklok.nl/

※ Rietveld Schröder House

The Rietveld Schröder House in Utrecht was built in 1924 by Dutch architect Gerrit Rietveld for Mrs. Truus Schröder-Schräder and her three children.

She commissioned the house to be designed preferably without walls. Rietveld worked side by side with Schröder-Schräder to create the house. He sketched the first possible design for the building; Schröder-Schrader was not pleased. She envisioned a house that was free from association and could create a connection between the inside and outside. The house is one of the best known examples of De Stijl-architecture and arguably the only true De Stijl building. Mrs. Schröder lived in the house until her death in 1985. The house was restored by Bertus Mulder and now is a museum open for visits, run by the Centraal Museum. It is a listed monument since 1976 and UNESCO World Heritage Site since 2000.

Tickets:	Adults€16.5; Children13–17 years €8.5; Children under 13 €3
Hours:	Daily11am–5pm; Monday closed
Address:	Prins Hendriklaan 50, 3583 EP Utrecht
Contact:	030-2362310
	www.centraalmuseum.nl/Rietveld

※ Miffy Museum

Miffy is the main character in 32 of the 124 little picture books published by Dick Bruna (Utrecht, 1927). In the stories, Miffy, in Dutch called Nijntje, actively explores the world around her, often together with her family and friends. Dick Bruna deliberately creates a world that children can fill with their own imagination. This is a key part of the philosophy behind the Miffy Museum.

The Miffy Museum is a series of miniature worlds. Children immediately relate to the characters created by Dick Bruna and the adventures they go on. Ten rooms, each dedicated to a different subject, invite young children to discover the world around them step by step. The miniature worlds created in these rooms include Miffy's house and familiar everyday experiences such as going to the doctor and going to the zoo.

Miffy Museum has three floors. You can crawl and climb through the house and explore all of the rooms. At Miffy's house you can bake a cake in the kitchen, mow the lawn in the back garden and put Miffy to bed. Especially for children, The Miffy Museum will be their first step in exploring a museum.

Tickets:	family ticket (valid for 2 adults and 2 children), €22.5; Children 2–12 years €9; Over 12 years €5
Hours:	Daily 10am–5pm; Monday closed
Address:	Agnietenstraat 2, 3512 XB Utrecht
Contact:	030-2362399
	https://nijntjemuseum.nl

※ Sonnenborgh Observatory

Sonnenborgh Observatory was originally located on Smeetoren, one of the largest and oldest fortifications of Utrecht. It was there that Utrecht University's first observatory was established in 1642.

By the middle of the 19th century, the building was in such a poor state of repair that physicist Buys Ballot proposed building a new observatory and meteorological office on top of the Sonnenborgh bastion. Utrecht's observatory has five telescopes and the oldest telescope is more than 150 years old.

One of the most spectacular attractions here in this museum is the meteorite which was found in a city near Utrecht. It is composed of significantly 5 meteorites and was kept in the safe where there is one significant thing that happens in this museum which is related to this meteorite.

In 2014 a safe with meteorites was stolen from the observatory. Fortunately, the thieves did not take the meteorite, and they were dumped in the bushes, but unfortunately, when the meteorites were found, they were broken.To celebrated the return of the meteorites a new exhibition was held in Sonnenborgh museum & observatory.

Tickets: Adults € 7.5; Children 4–17 years €4.5; Children under 4 FREE

Hours: Daily 11am–5pm; Sunday 1pm–5pm; Monday & Saturday closed

Address: Zonnenburg 2, 3512 NL Utrecht

Contact: 030-8201420

http://www.sonnenborgh.nl/

※ 铁路博物馆

位于乌特勒支的铁路博物馆是荷兰国家铁路博物馆。博物馆成立于1927年，但自1954年起博物馆被设立在原来的马利班火车站。博物馆第一次向公众开放时，仅藏有一些简朴的文件、物品和图片。在20世纪30年代，一些具有历史意义的铁路设备被存放到博物馆里展出，但不幸的是，大部分藏品在第二次世界大战期间被毁掉了。

铁路博物馆里的参观游览可不只是看看火车这么简单。

在乌特勒支，在铁路博物馆，开启一个大型探索之旅——游览一个古老的英国采矿村，仔细端详由迈克尔·朗德里奇于1829年设计的著名的蒸汽机车"火箭"号的模型。驻足片刻再观摩一下荷兰的第一个蒸汽机车"De Arend"。在"梦幻之旅"中继续参观博物馆。在一个东方大礼堂里，演员们正在表演着著名的"东方快车"里的场景。

无论是对于成人还是孩子，乌特勒支的铁路博物馆都是极受欢迎的，从蒸汽火车到荷兰铁路公司的现代火车，从怀旧的老车站和候车室到现代的4D体验，铁路博物馆的游览让人非常愉快。

在车间展区，游客可以探索机车的不同部分，并了解它们是如何运转的。在一列藏品展车里还有一家餐馆。

游客们在铁路博物馆将经历两个世纪的铁路历史之旅。博物馆还设有一个宽敞的户外区域供游客探索，整个博物馆的探索之旅平均需要3.5小时才能完成。

门票：　　　　4岁及以上，每人17.5欧元；4岁以下免费

开放时间：　　周二到周日，上午10点至下午5点；周一不开放

地址：　　　　乌特勒支，马利班火车站16号

联系方式：　　030-2306206

　　　　　　　http://www.spoorwegmuseum.nl/

※ 乌特勒支中央博物馆

乌特勒支中央博物馆是荷兰最古老的市政博物馆，开放于1838年。图为刚刚参观完博物馆的游客。

乌特勒支中央博物馆是荷兰最古老的市政博物馆，该博物馆在1838年9月5日正式对外开放。多年以来，这栋建筑经过了多次翻修、扩建和重新设计。上一次重大翻修是在1999年。

乌特勒支中央博物馆于1830年设置在乌特勒支市政厅顶层的四间房间里，最初主要由古物组成。1921年，这些藏品与位于尼古拉斯教堂中世纪修道院的新中央博物馆的各种私人藏品集中整合在一起。现在的中央博物馆馆藏极其广泛，包括1850年之前的艺术、现代艺术、应用艺术、时尚以及乌特勒支的城市发展史。

其中一幅由北方的风格派画家约阿希姆·维特威尔所创作的绘画作品是世界上最大的画作。来自乌特勒支的卡拉瓦乔主义者众多有影响力的作品也是博物馆珍藏的一大亮点。

从2006年起，中央博物馆开始对米菲博物馆进行管理，后者就在街道的对面，是一个专门为迪克·布鲁纳和他所创造的米菲兔建造的博物馆。另外，著名的施罗德住宅也是由中央博物馆所运营管理的，这是一个由荷兰建筑师格里特·里特维尔德在1924年为图卢斯·施罗德–施雷德夫人和她的三个孩子建造的一所现代主义建筑，现在作为博物馆面向公众开放。

门票：　　　　成人13.5欧元；13～17岁5.5欧元；13岁以下的儿童免费

开放时间：　　周二到周日，上午11点至下午5点；周一不开放

地址：　　　　乌特勒支，Agnietenstraat 1号

联系方式：　　030-2362362

　　　　　　　http://centraalmuseum.nl/

※ 音乐盒博物馆

音乐盒博物馆位于荷兰乌特勒支。这里是一个自动播放乐器设备的大集合，其中所展出的大部分音乐设备仍然能正常演奏。这些乐器的历史可以追溯到16世纪的荷兰，不过当时使用的是教堂的钟琴。几个世纪以来，人们很渴望被音乐所萦绕的那种氛围，于是发明了各种各样自动演奏的乐器：音乐钟、音乐盒、自动管弦乐团和传统的荷兰街头风琴。所有这些乐器，包括珍贵的"Arabier（自动管弦乐团）"和被誉为"世界第八大奇观"的"Violina（自动小提琴）"，都能在这一生动立体的参观过程中欣赏到。

音乐盒博物馆是一个特色鲜明的博物馆，展示的大多数音乐盒、自动播放乐器都如常工作，同时受到成人和孩子们的欢迎。

这个博物馆起源于1956年夏天在乌特勒支举办的机械风琴和其他音乐自动播放设备的展览，这次展览的巨大成功直接促成了致力于机械乐器的永久性国家博物馆的建立。于是，1984年由贝娅特丽克丝女王在中世纪的教区教堂正式主持了音乐盒博物馆的揭幕仪式。

门票：　　　　成人13欧元；4～17岁7欧元；4岁以下免费

开放时间：　　周二到周日，上午10点至下午5点；周一不开放

地址：　　　　乌特勒支，Steenweg 6号

联系方式：　　030-2312789

http://www.museumspeelklok.nl/

※ 施罗德住宅

乌特勒支的里特维尔德·施罗德住宅建于1924年，由荷兰建筑师格里特·里特维尔德为图卢斯·施罗德—施罗德夫人和三个孩子设计建造。

施罗德—施罗德夫人希望建造一所没有墙壁的房子，因此与格里特·里特维尔德并肩工作，创造了这所住宅。里特维尔德最初先构造了一张设计草图，但是施罗德—施罗德夫人并不满意。她所设想的房子最好与周围的房子保持独立，内部要做到空间上的互通连接。该住宅是"荷兰风格派运动"最为知名的建筑样例之一，大概也是唯一正宗的荷兰风格派运动建筑物。施罗德—施罗德夫人一直住在这栋房子里，直到1985年去世。后来，这座房子由伯图斯·穆德进行了修复，现在作为博物馆向游人开放，由乌特勒支中央博物馆负责运营管理。施罗德住宅从1976年就被列为纪念遗址，从2000年起被联合国教科文组织列为"世界文化遗产"。

门票：　　　　成人16.5欧元；13～17岁8.5欧元；13岁以下3欧元

开放时间：　　周二到周日，上午11点至下午5点；周一不开放

地址：　　　　乌特勒支，亨德里克王子路50号

联系方式：　　030-2362310

www.centraalmuseum.nl/Rietveld

※ 米菲之家

米菲是迪克·布鲁纳所出版的124本图书中的32部的主角。在创作的这些故事中，米菲经常和她的家人、朋友一起积极地探索周围的世界。迪克·布鲁纳给孩子们创造了一个充满无限想象力的世界，这正是米菲博物馆建立背后的一个重要理念。

米菲博物馆是一系列微型世界。孩子们立即就会联想到迪克·布鲁纳笔下的人物和他们所经历的冒险行为。博物馆一共有十个房间，每一个房间都有一个不同的主题，引导孩子们一步一步地发现周围的世界。这些房间里构造

米菲博物馆是孩子们探索博物馆的第一步，位于中央博物馆对面，统一由乌特勒支中央博物馆管理运营。

出了图书中米菲所经历的日常生活中的趣事，比如米菲去看医生和米菲逛动物园。

米菲博物馆有三层，你可以慢慢地探索所有的房间。在米菲博物馆，你还可以在厨房里烤蛋糕，要不就去后院的草坪上割草，或者把米菲乖乖地放到床上去。尤其是对于孩子们来说，米菲博物馆将是他们探索博物馆的第一步。

门票：   家庭票（2个成人和2个孩子）22.5欧元；2～12岁9欧元；12岁以上5欧元

开放时间：   周二到周日，上午10点至下午5点；周一不开放

地址：   乌特勒支，Agnietenstraat 2号

联系方式：   030-2362399
            https://nijntjemuseum.nl

※ 索南伯格天文博物馆

索南伯格天文博物馆/观测台最初位于斯密托仑，它是乌特勒支最大、最古老的防御堡垒之一。1642年，乌特勒支大学第一个天文台成立。到了19世纪中叶，斯密托仑建筑急需要修复，物理学家白贝罗提议在索南伯格堡垒的顶部建造一个天文台和气象台。现在，乌特勒支天文台拥有5台天文望远镜，其中最古老的望远镜已经有150多年的历史了。

这个博物馆最引人注目的是在乌得勒支附近的一个城市发现的陨石，这5块陨石存放在保险箱里，关于这个保险箱还曾发生过一件趣事。

2014年，天文台装有陨石的保险箱被偷走。所幸窃贼并没有带走陨石，而是将它们丢弃在了灌木丛中，但遗憾的是，陨石被找到的时候已经破损了。为了庆祝陨石的失而复得，索南伯格天文博物馆又举办了一次新的展览。

门票：   成人7.5欧元；4～17岁4.5欧元；4岁以下儿童免费

开放时间：   周二到周五，上午11点至下午5点；周日，下午1点至下午5点；周一和周六不
            开放

地址：   乌特勒支，Zonenburg 2号

联系方式：   030-8201420
            http://www.sonnenborgh.nl/

119

5. 其他重要的博物馆
Other important museums

※ The Netherlands Open Air Museum

The Netherlands Open Air Museum, which can be found near Arnhem, is an open air museum/park with antique houses, farms and factories from different parts and times of the Netherlands. It is a national museum that focuses on culture associated with everyday lives of ordinary people. The museum is also possible to visit when it's raining, there are around forty historic buildings that you can enter and see from the inside and there is also a historic tram that can transport you through the park.

Inside, visitors enter a spacious, light entrance foyer that houses the café and museum shop, with stepped split-levels that adapt to the rolling landscape. A long glass facade interspersed with staggered timber frames overlooks the open-air museum. On the lowest level, where the exhibition halls are located, a tunnel leads to the HollandRama panorama theatre inside the boulder.

The park was founded in 1912 with 44 hectares in area. In 1987, the Dutch government was primed to shut down the museum, but in a demonstration of solidarity for the historic museum, Dutch crowds flooded the museum's doors, hoping to view the exhibits before they closed. The museum was allowed to remain open due to its unprecedented success during this time and was given greater autonomy over its organisation. The museum also has a collection of historical clothing and jewellery. New indoor exhibition space was built in 1999–2000. The museum won the European Museum of the Year Award in 2005.

Tickets: Adults from 13 year € 12.5; Children from 4 to 12 years €9.5
FREE for under 4 years and Museum card holder

Hours: Daily 10am–5pm

Address: Hoeferlaan 4, 6816 SG Arnhem

Contact: 026-3576111
http://www.openluchtmuseum.nl/en

※ Naturalis Biodiversity Center

The Naturalis Biodiversity Centre is the most visited museum in Leiden. Naturalis Biodiversity Centre is a national museum of natural history and a research centre on biodiversity in Leiden, Netherlands. Although its current name and organisation is relatively recent, its history can be traced back to the early 1800s.

The beginnings of Naturalis go back to the creation of the National Museum of Natural History by King William I on August 9, 1820. In 1878, the geological and mineralogical collections of the museum separated into two institutions. These remained distinct until the merger of the Rijksmuseum van Natuurlijke Historie and the Rijksmuseum van Geologie en Mineralogie in 1984, as the Nationaal Natuurhistorisch Museum or National Museum of Natural History.

As of 2010, the National Museum of Natural History further combined with the Zoological Museum Amsterdam of the University of Amsterdam, and the Dutch National Herbaria at the universities of Leiden, Amsterdam and Wageningen, to form the Nederlands Centrum voor Biodiversiteit. The combined institute was formally opened as part of the "International Year of Biodiversity 2010" by Ronald Plasterk and Gerda Verburg. As of 2012 the name became the Naturalis Biodiversity Center.

The current museum is known for the numerous objects in its collections. Prior to the merger with the Zoölogisch Museum Amsterdam and National Herbarium of the Netherlands, there were approximately 10 million zoological and geological specimens in the Naturalis collection. Following the merger with the collections of the Zoölogisch Museum Amsterdam and National Herbarium of the Netherlands in 2010-12, there are now approximately 37 million specimens: it is one of the largest natural history collections in the world.

Tickets:　Adults €12, children from 4 to 17 years € 9; free for children under 4 years and Museum card holder

Hours:　Daily 10am–5pm; Thursdays 10am–8pm

Address:　Pesthuislaan 7, 2333 BA Leiden

Contact:　071-7519600

http://www.naturalis.nl/en/

※ Kröller-Müller Museum

The Kröller-Müller Museum is one of the must-see museums especially as it houses the "second-largest collection of paintings by Vincent van Gogh".

The Kröller-Müller Museum is a national art museum and sculpture garden, located in the Hoge Veluwe National Park in Otterlo in the Netherlands. The museum was founded by Helene Kröller-Müller, an avid art collector who, being advised by H.P. Bremmer, was one of the first to recognise Vincent van Gogh's genius and collect his works. In 1935, she donated her whole collection to the state of the Netherlands. In 1938, the museum, which was designed by Henry van de Velde, opened to the public. The sculpture garden was added in 1961 and the new exhibition wing, designed by Wim Quist, opened in 1977.

Kröller-Müller Museum has a considerable collection of paintings by Vincent van Gogh, such as Café Terrace at Night, Sorrowing Old Man and a version of The Potato Eaters, making it the second-largest collection of Van Gogh paintings in the world (after the Van Gogh Museum in Amsterdam). Apart from the Van Gogh paintings other highlights include works by Piet Mondrian, Georges-Pierre Seurat, Odilon Redon, Georges Braque, Paul Gauguin, Lucas Cranach, James Ensor, Juan Gris, and Pablo Picasso.

Tickets:	Adults € 19; Children from 6 to 12 years € 9.5; FREE for under 6
Hours:	Daily 10am–5pm; Monday closed
Address:	Houtkampweg 6, 6731 AW Otterlo
Contact:	031-8591241
	http://krollermuller.nl

※ Groningen Museum

The radically modernist structures that form the Groninger Museum stand in a canal opposite the Groningen railway station. They consist of three main pavilions: a silver cylindrical building designed by Philippe Starck, a yellow tower by Alessandro Mendini, and a pale blue deconstructivist space by Coop Himmelb(l)au. A bridge that connects the museum to the train station is part of a cycling and walking path to the centre of the city.

It is the most high-profile museum in the Netherlands. This is due not only to its striking design by Italian architect Mendini, but also because of varying exhibitions, including works by Russian painter Repin, American photographer Andres Serrano, Dutch photographer Erwin Olaf and the collection of Chinese and Japanese porcelain.

The Groninger Museum is home to various exhibitions of local, national, and international works of art, most of them modern and abstract. Some have provoked controversy, such as the photo exhibition of Andres Serrano, but others are more conventional such as the exhibition of the works by Ilya Repin, the "Russian Rembrandt". While the exhibition "David Bowie is" took place at the museum at the very moment that the death of David Bowie was announced. The museum responded by opening a condolence register and opening its doors to visitors on Monday (while the museum is normally closed).

In 2017, the museum had more than 300,000 visitors. It is the most visited museum of the province of Groningen.

Tickets:	Adults € 15; FREE for 0 to 18 years
Hours:	Daily 10am–5pm; Monday closed
Address:	Museumeiland 1,9711 ME Groningen
Contact:	050-3666555
	http://www.groningermuseum.nl/en

※ Frans Hals Museum

Frans Hals is a very important portrait painter of the seventeenth century. Five times he was given the very important commission to paint the civic guard. He had an unrivalled ability to portray the members of the civic guard as a cohesive, animated group.

Until the nineteenth century, the work of Frans Hals was very influential as demonstrated by visits to Haarlem by impressionists such as Claude Monet, Gustave Courbet and Edouard Manet, who visited especially to admire the portraits of the Regents and Regentesses of the Old Men's Almshouse from 1664.

The Frans Hals Museum was established in 1862. In 1950, the museum was split in two locations when the collection of modern art was moved to the Museum De Hallen. The main collection, including its famous 17th-century Frans Hals paintings and a large number of paintings owned by the City of Haarlem, which includes over 100 artworks seized from Catholic churches in the 1580s after the Protestant Reformation, and Haarlem art rescued from demolished local buildings from the 15th century onwards. In addition, the museum also boasts numerous top pieces by other famous Haarlem artists such as Hendrik Goltzius, Ruisdael and Saenredam.

Tickets: Adults € 23; Museum card and I Amsterdam City Card holder € 8; FREE for 0 to 18 years

Hours: Daily 11am–5pm; Sunday 12am–5pm; Monday closed

Address: Groot Heiligland 62, 2011 ES Haarlem

Contact: 023-5115775

http://www.franshalsmuseum.nl/en/

※ 荷兰露天博物馆

位于阿纳姆附近的荷兰露天博物馆是一个露天博物馆/公园，里面有古老的房子、农场和来自荷兰不同地区和时代的工厂。这是一个国家博物馆，专注于与普通人日常生活点点滴滴相关的文化。即使在下雨天参观露天博物馆也没有问题，因为这里有大约40座历史建筑，下雨时可以在内部参观这些建筑，另外还可以乘坐一辆历史悠久的有轨电车从公园穿梭而过。

荷兰露天博物馆展现了不同区域、不同年代荷兰普通平民的传统和生活，面积庞大，身处绿树丛林之中，是游览和散心的胜地。

在建筑的内部，首先进入一个宽敞明亮的门厅，里面有咖啡厅和博物馆商店，错综起伏的台阶映出流动的风景图。一个长长的玻璃幕墙点缀着交错的木架，俯瞰着露天博物馆。在展览厅所在的最底层，一条隧道通向大圆石内部的荷兰全景剧院。

该公园建于1912年，占地44公顷。在1987年，荷兰政府本来是要准备关闭博物馆的，但为了

123

表示对博物馆的支持，很多人在博物馆关闭前参观。由于在此期间取得了空前的成功，博物馆才得以保持开放，并获得了更大的自治权。露天博物馆收藏了许多具有历史价值的服饰和珠宝，在1999年到2000年还兴建了新的室内展览空间。该博物馆于2005年获得欧洲博物馆年度奖。

门票：　　　13岁及以上12.5欧元；4～12岁9.5欧元；4岁以下及持有会员卡者免费

开放时间：　每天上午10点至下午5点

地址：　　　阿纳姆，Hoeferlaan 4号

联系方式：　026-3576111

　　　　　　http://www.openluchtmuseum.nl/en

※ 自然生物多样性中心

自然生物多样性中心藏馆的标本数量超过了3 000万，是世界上藏品数目最庞大的博物馆之一。

自然生物多样性中心是莱顿最受欢迎的博物馆。它位于荷兰莱顿，是国家自然历史博物馆和生物多样性研究中心。中心现在的名称表述和研究机构的职能较为贴切，其历史发展最早可以追溯到19世纪早期。

自然生物多样性中心起源于1820年8月9日威廉一世国王所创建的国家自然历史博物馆。1878年，该博物馆的地质和矿物学收藏分割成了两大机构。直到1984年，国家自然博物馆和国家地质矿物博物馆合并成为了国家自然历史博物馆。

斗转星移到2010年，国家自然历史博物馆又与阿姆斯特丹大学的动物学博物馆，莱顿、阿姆斯特丹和瓦格宁根的大学的国家植物标本馆进行了整合，从而形成了自然生物多样中心。2010年，合并后的机构由内政部长普拉斯特克和农业部长费尔堡共同负责，并成为"2010年国际生物多样性年"的一部分。到2012年，机构的名字便成为现在所称呼的"自然生物多样性中心"。

　　目前，这所博物馆以其藏品的庞大数量而闻名。在与阿姆斯特丹大学动物学博物馆和荷兰国家植物标本馆合并之前，这里所收藏的动物和地质标本的数量就已经达到了1 000万件。在2010至2012年，随着动物学博物馆和国家植物标本馆合并后，其收藏的标本数量已经达到了3 700万件，成为世界上藏品数目最庞大的博物馆之一。

门票：　　　成人12欧元；4～17岁9欧元；4岁以下免费

开放时间：　每天上午10点至下午5点；周四上午10点至晚上8点

地址：　　　莱顿，Pesthuislaan 7号

联系方式：　071-7519600

　　　　　　http://www.naturalis.nl/en/

※ 克勒勒－米勒博物馆

克勒勒－米勒博物馆是必看的博物馆之一，特别是它作为"收藏梵高作品第二多"的博物馆。

克勒勒－米勒博物馆包括一个国家艺术博物馆和一座雕塑花园，位于荷兰奥特洛的梵高国家森林公园。该博物馆由热心的艺术品收藏家海伦娜·克勒勒－米勒在最先认识到梵高的天赋并开始收藏其作品的H.P.布莱摩尔的建议下创立的。1935年，她把自己的全部藏品都捐献给了荷兰政府。1938年，由亨利·范·德·威尔德设计的博物馆向公众开放。1961年，博物馆增添了雕塑花园，由维姆·奎斯特设计的新展区也于1977年开放。

克勒勒－米勒博物馆收藏了大量的文森特·梵高的画作，比如《露台咖啡馆》《悲伤的老人》，以及《吃马铃薯的人》的一个版本，这使它成为世界上第二大梵高画作的收藏馆，紧随阿姆斯特丹的梵高博物馆之后。除了梵高的画作，克勒勒－米勒博物馆还收藏了诸多亮点作品，包括蒙德里安、乔治·秀拉、奥迪隆·雷东、乔治·布拉克、高更、卢卡斯·克拉纳赫、詹姆斯·恩索尔、胡安·格里斯和毕加索的作品。

《露台咖啡馆》这幅作品重复出现在《至爱梵高·星空之谜》这部动画电影中，其收藏在克勒勒－米勒博物馆，这是世界上收藏梵高作品第二多的博物馆。

门票：　　　成人19欧元；6～12岁9.5欧元；6岁以下免费

开放时间：　周二到周日，上午10点到下午5点；周一不开放

地址：　　　奥特洛，Houtkampweg 6号

联系方式：　031-8591241
　　　　　　http://krollermuller.nl

※ 格罗宁根博物馆

格罗宁根火车站对面的一条运河里，矗立着一栋激进现代主义建筑——格罗宁根博物馆。这栋建筑由三个主要的展馆组成：一栋由菲利普·斯塔克设计的银色圆柱形建筑，一个由亚历山德罗·门迪尼设计的黄色的塔，还有一个由奥地利著名的蓝天组所设计的淡蓝色的解构主义空间建筑。一座连接着博物馆和火车站的桥梁是通往市中心的自行车车道和步行的一部分。

格罗宁根博物馆是荷兰最引人注目的博物馆，不仅是因为意大利建筑师门迪尼的设计引来的目光，还因为这里有着非凡的作品展览，包括俄罗斯画家伊利亚·列宾的巨作、美国摄影师安德里斯·塞拉诺的作品、荷兰摄影师埃文·奥拉夫的摄影作品，以及弥足珍贵的来自中国和日本的瓷器。

格罗宁根博物馆是许多地方性、国家和国际艺术作品展览的所在地，其中大部分是现代和抽象的。有些展览一度引发人们的争论，比如安德里斯·塞拉诺的摄影作品展，但也有一些更为传统的，比如有着"俄罗斯的伦勃朗"之称的列宾的作品展。这里在大卫·鲍伊去世之后还举办了意义非凡的纪念性展览活动"David Bowie is"，为此，博物馆还特别在周一对游客开放（博物馆周一通常不开放），并对大卫·鲍伊的离开表达了缅怀之意。

2017年，格罗宁根博物馆的访客超过了30万人次，它是格罗宁根省参观人数最多的博物馆。

门票：　　　成人15欧元；18岁以下免费

开放时间：　周二到周日，上午10点至下午5点；周一不开放

地址：　　　格罗宁根，Museumeiland 1号

联系方式：　050-3666555

http://www.groningermuseum.nl/en

※ 弗朗斯·哈尔斯博物馆

弗朗斯·哈尔斯是17世纪一位非常重要的肖像画家，他曾经多达5次被委以重任为公民警卫队进行画像。他凭借非凡的绘画能力，将公民警卫队的成员们描绘成一个具有凝聚力的、有活力的群体。

弗朗斯·哈尔斯的作品直到19世纪才产生了巨大的影响力，尤其是印象派画家比如克劳德·莫奈、居斯塔夫·库尔贝和爱德华·马奈等人专门造访哈乐姆去欣赏哈尔斯于1644年所创作的《哈勒姆养老院的男管理员》和《哈勒姆养老院的女管理员》，其影响可见一斑。

弗朗斯·哈尔斯是荷兰非常有影响力的肖像画家。

哈尔斯博物馆建于1862年。1950年，现代艺术的藏品被转移到哈伦博物馆，于是哈尔斯博物馆被一分为二。这里主要的藏品包括17世纪弗朗斯·哈尔斯最出名的绘画作品和隶属于哈勒姆市的大量画作，这其中有1580年新教改革后从天主教教会攫取的100多件艺术品，以及从15世纪被拆毁的当地建筑物中所挽救出来的哈勒姆的艺术品。此外，博物馆还拥有众多来自哈乐姆的艺术家的顶级作品，如亨德里克·高侟斯、雷斯达尔、萨恩勒丹。

门票：　　　成人23欧元；18岁以下及持博物馆卡、城市卡者免费

开放时间：　周二到周六，上午11点至下午5点；周日上午12点至下午5点；周一不开放

地址：　　　哈乐姆，Groot Heiligland 62号

联系方式：　023-5115775

　　　　　　http://www.franshalsmuseum.nl/en/

Remarks:

○ Prices of museum tickets and business hours are only for a reference.

○ The opening hours of the museum may be affected by temporary exhibitions, season and holidays. Please check the official website before visiting.

○ Ticket prices may vary depending on online booking or counter purchase. Holding a museum card, I Amsterdam City Card, Stadspas, BankGiro Loterij VIP-KAART, student ID card, members of ICOM, ICOMOS, the Rembrandt Association and group booking, will also affect the price. Please check the official website before visiting.

○ Temporary exhibitions in some museums may also affect the price of tickets.

备注：

○ 博物馆的门票和营业时间仅供参考。

○ 博物馆的开放时间可能因临时展览、季节和假期的影响而更改，请在参观前查看官方网站。

○ 票价为图书编写之初的价格，仅供参考，还可能因网上预订或柜台购买不同的渠道有所差异。同时，荷兰博物馆卡、阿姆斯特丹城市卡、城市直通卡、青年卡、欧洲青年旅行证、BankGiro Lottery基金会VIP持卡人、学生证，以及国际博物馆协会成员、国际古迹遗址理事会成员、伦勃朗协会成员、皇家考古学会成员，持有以上卡种的人或团体订票，都会影响价格。请在参观前查看官方网站。

○ 一些博物馆的临时展览也会影响门票的价格。

Tijd voor Nederlands 荷兰语时间

● 单词+短语

荷 verdieping	荷 brief	荷 kunstenaar
英 floor	英 letter	英 artist
译 楼层	译 信函	译 艺术家

续表

荷 verhaal	荷 gids	荷 jaar
英 story	英 guide	英 year
译 故事	译 导游	译 年
荷 geleden	荷 huren	荷 opbergen
英 ago	英 rent	英 store
译 以前	译 租用	译 存放
荷 schrijven	荷 gebeuren	
英 write	英 to happen	
译 写	译 发生	

● 例句

荷 Ik ben een kunstenaar en ik hou van kunst.	荷 Ik ben een fotograaf, dus ik wil naar het Fotomuseum.
英 I am an artist and I love art.	英 I'm a photographer, so I want to go to the photo museum.
译 我是一名艺术家，我爱好艺术。	译 我是一名摄影师，所以我想去摄影博物馆。
荷 Het meest beroemde schilderij bevindt zich op de tweede verdieping van het museum.	荷 Deze brief is in 1880 door hem geschreven.
英 The most famous painting is located on the second floor of the museum.	英 This letter was written in 1880 by him.
译 最有名的那幅画位于博物馆的二层。	译 这封信是他在1880年写的。
荷 Het Dagboek van Anne Frank is een verhaal over een meisje.	荷 Dit verhaal gebeurde 50 jaar geleden.
英 *Annie's Diary* is a story about a girl.	英 This story happened 50 years ago.
译 《安妮日记》讲述了一个女孩的故事。	译 这个故事发生在五十年前。
荷 Ik wil een audioguide huren.	荷 U kunt uw tas niet meenemen, u moet hem even opbergen in een kluisje.
英 I want to rent an audioguide.	英 You can not take your bag with you, you have to store it.
译 我想租用一台语音导游系统。	译 您不能把包带进去，包需要寄存一下。

食在荷兰

Eating in the Netherlands

Unlike the French or the Italians, the Dutch are not generally known for their sophisticated cuisine. The Dutch diet is so simple that you could even call it plain. Dutch people are good at planning and calculation. They enjoy life more on a spiritual level than that they lavish themselves in material and culinary enjoyments. When preparing a meal, nutritional value is the focus point, and taste is only a good second.

As such, many Chinese who live in the Netherlands consider it nothing short of a culinary desert. Of course, this is not completely true. Chinese and western tastes are quite different from each other, and you should definitely try some Dutch local delicacies rather than move through this country and miss a chance to enjoy some interesting culinary experiences. You can take my word for it: it surely will be a surprise.

跟法国或意大利截然不同，荷兰没有因为其饮食文化声名在外，荷兰人的饮食很简单，甚至可以说是简朴。荷兰人擅长计划和计算，他们对生活的享受更多的是在精神层面，而不是单一的追求物质或者食物的享乐，在荷兰人的饮食理念中，营养搭配才是焦点，口味是次要的。

因此，对于许多居住在荷兰的中国人来说，荷兰简直就是美食界的荒漠。当然，事实绝非是这样的。中西方的口味大相径庭，身处荷兰，当地的传统食品还是要体验的，而不是人到了他乡，嘴巴却依然留在家中。相信吧！新鲜的尝试也将能带给你出其不意的惊喜。

1. 荷兰的饮食
Dutch Diet

The History of the Dutch Diet 饮食结构发展史

Traditionally, Dutch cuisine is simple and straightforward, it is nowhere as complex or exquisite as for example the French or Italian cuisine is. The Dutch diet contains many dairy products and is relatively high in carbohydrates and fat, reflecting the dietary needs of the labourers whose culture moulded the country. Without many refinements, it can best be described as rustic, reflecting a Calvinistic approach to life, though many holidays are celebrated with special foods.

There are very few dietary records and information about the Dutch diet before the fourteenth century. In the fourteenth and fifteenth century the Dutch fishing industry formed an important part of the economy of the Netherlands, the North Sea herring fishery became the backbone of the fishing industry, it became very advanced after the invention and streamlining of the preservation process of herring at sea. The herring would be preserved in salt and in this way it not only permitted the ships to stay at sea longer but herring could also be sold inland. The invention of preserving herring at sea kick-started a lucrative trade in the fish and this lead the Dutch to build more and better ships and to expand their fleet, which contributed to the rise of the Dutch as a strong seafaring nation which moved from mainly trading in herring to trade in spices and eventually colonising many countries around the world. Herring lies at base of the Dutch golden age and now is still a favourite snack of the Dutch.

During the 15th century haute cuisine began to emerge, largely limited to the aristocracy. Cookery books from this period were aimed at the upper class. Recipes for sauces, jam, jellies, pies, tarts, eggs, dairy products, candied quinces began to appear.

From the sixteenth to the seventeenth century，the expanded trading network of The United East-Indian Company, better known to the Dutch as "de VOC" enabled spices, sugar, and exotic fruits to be imported to the country. The United East India Company was the first to import coffee on a large scale to Europe and by the late 17th century, consumption of tea and coffee was increasing and became a part of everyday life.

The diet of the Dutch in the 19th century was frugal, consisting of bread, a great deal of potatoes and herring. Throughout 19th century many people suffered from some mild form of malnutrition.

The modest and plain look of what is nowadays considered the traditional Dutch cuisine, appears to be the result of fairly recent developments in the twentieth century. From the late 19th

131

century to the 20th century, many parents sent their daughters to a new kind of school called Huishoudschool (housekeeping school) where the girls were to study housework and cooking skills. Simple meals were a major part of the curriculum, often based on more traditional Dutch dishes, and leading to increased uniformity in the Dutch diet.

传统的荷兰式烹饪简单而直接，它不像法国菜或意大利菜那样复杂或精致。荷兰人的饮食中含有很多乳制品，其中的碳水化合物和脂肪的含量相对也较高，这也反映了塑造出整个国家的劳动者们的饮食需求。这是一种没有经过太多改进的饮食方式，可用简单质朴来描述，体现了加尔文简约主义的生活方式，不过荷兰节日众多，佳节之际仍旧会制作一些特殊的食物来进行庆祝。

荷兰离不开鲱鱼，荷兰人吃鲱鱼持续了几个世纪。图为最为典型的街头鲱鱼店铺。

在14世纪以前，有关荷兰饮食的记录和信息很少。在14～15世纪，渔业成为荷兰经济的重要组成部分，北海鲱鱼渔业成为支柱产业，尤其是在海上将鲱鱼经过处理之后从而可以达到食物保存的这一技术流程发明后，其渔业的发展变得更为先进。把鲱鱼用盐腌起来，这样不仅可以为船舶在海上的长时间航行提供保障，还可以把这些鲱鱼在陆地上卖出去。鲱鱼储存技术的发明开启了有利可图的渔业贸易，导致了荷兰建造更多、更好的船只并壮大了他们的船队，这促使荷兰崛起成为一个强大的航海国家，贸易范畴也从鲱鱼转向香料，也开始了在世界多国进行殖民的道路。鲱鱼产生在荷兰黄金时代后期，到现今仍旧是荷兰人最喜欢的小吃。

在15世纪，高级烹饪开始出现，但主要局限于高贵显赫之族。这一时期的烹饪书籍也都是针对上层阶级的。酱料、果酱、果冻、馅饼、蛋挞、鸡蛋、乳制品、蜜饯开始出现在餐桌之上。

16～17世纪，贸易网络扩大后的东印度公司（在荷兰以"de VOC"的名字更为人知）将香料、糖和异国的水果进口到荷兰。联合东印度公司还是第一家大规模向欧洲进口咖啡的公司，到了17世纪晚期，茶叶和咖啡的消费量逐渐上升，成为人们日常生活的一部分。

19世纪荷兰人的饮食都很节俭，包括面包、大量的土豆和鲱鱼。整个19世纪，许多人都患有轻度的营养不良。

简单朴素是现在最传统的荷兰菜给人的直观感觉，这似乎是顺应20世纪发展的结果。从19世纪后期到20世纪，很多家长把女儿送到"家政学校"，让女孩们在那里学习做家务和烹饪技能。课程最重要的部分就是学做简单的膳食，通常是做一些很传统的荷兰菜，这也使得荷兰饮食结构变得更加一致，或者叫单一。

Three Meals a Day 一日三餐

Dutch breakfast is relatively simple, mainly bread with a wide variety of cold cuts, cheeses and sweet toppings such as sprinkles, something you would normally put on a cake, they have many variations, for example chocolate, that they call "hagelslag", aniseed or fruit flavours, which they call muisjes (little mice). There are many other sweet toppings, jam, honey, hazelnut-chocolate spread and peanut butter. Beschuit, a round piece of toasted bread, with strawberries, buttered ontbijtkoek (a cake made with rye flour and spices like cloves, cinnamon, ginger, and nutmeg) and currant buns with cheese are also a favourite. For breakfast the Dutch also like to eat yoghurt or milk with muesli or oatmeal or Brinta (whole grain porridge). Of course a strong cup of coffee cannot be left out.

Bread with toppings or yoghurt with muesli is in itself a quite straightforward simple way of starting the day, the Dutch don't like to waste time on their breakfast, so no cooking, no pots and pans makes that breakfast is settled in less than 10 minutes.

lunch time at work is never more than half an hour, so to make sure that you finish your meal on time it also has to be simple. The vast majority of the Dutch bring their own pre-packed lunch to work, which they have prepared themselves at home. A typical Dutch lunch consists of a "broodje kaas" or cheese sandwich, most often it is whole grain as this is considered healthy, whereas white bread is considered unhealthy, some people like to top their sandwich with ham or chicken breast and vegetables or salad. The Dutch love to drink a nice glass of buttermilk with their lunch. If the company a Dutch person works for, has its own canteen he or she may also go for a "broodje bal" (a meatball on a soft white bun), a sausage roll, a tosti (usually a toasted sandwich with ham and cheese), a "broodje kroket" (a deep fried meat ragout croquette on a soft bun), soup or a salad, with a buttered roll and a boiled egg. In short, Dutch lunch is unlikely to be a nice cooked meal.

A traditional Dutch dinner is served early, with many families gathering around the table at about 5 or 6 o'clock in the afternoon. Dinner is simple and consists potatoes, one or two vegetables and meat. A very familiar side at the Dutch dining table is "stamppot", a potato vegetable mash with one or more kind of vegetables and served with gravy and sausage. The Dutch also like to serve vegetable stews with potatoes, for example red cabbage with apples, or beetroot. Regular spices used in stews of this kind may be bay leaves, juniper berries, cloves, and vinegar, although strong spices are generally used sparsely. Stews are often served with pickles, including gherkins or cocktail onions.

Some very traditional Dutch dishes are:

Hutspot, made with mashed potatoes, carrots, and onions served with meats like rookworst (smoked sausage), slow-cooked meat, or bacon.

Zuurkoolstamppot, sauerkraut mashed with potatoes. Served with fried bacon or a sausage.

Boerenkoolstamppot, curly kale mixed with potatoes, served with gravy, mustard, and rookworst sausage. It is one of the oldest and most popular Dutch dishes.

The final course is a sweet dessert, traditionally yogurt with some sugar or "vla"—a very common dessert which has the consistency of yoghurt and tastes sweet, it comes is all kind of flavours, from vanilla to chocolate and from strawberry to caramel.

荷兰的早餐相对简单，主要是面包，还有各种各样的冷切、奶酪，和一些通常撒在蛋糕上的甜的配料，不尽相同，比如巧克力，荷兰语里叫"hagelslag"，有茴香味的或水果味的，人们把这些东西叫作muisjes（小老鼠）。还有许多其他的甜味搭配，如果酱、蜂蜜、榛子巧克力酱和花生酱。加草莓的圆形吐司片，以及名为"ontijtkoek"的黄油蛋糕（由黑麦粉与丁香、桂皮、姜、肉豆蔻等香料做成），还有带奶酪的葡萄干面包也很受欢迎。荷兰人早餐也喜欢吃酸奶或牛奶加什锦麦片、燕麦片或Brinta（荷兰品牌，早餐重要食物全谷物粥的主要品牌）。当然，一杯浓咖啡更是不可或缺的。

在很多人看来，荷兰人的早餐简直是简朴，只有面包有可能是热的。

荷兰人的一天以简简单单的面包加配料或酸奶配麦片的早餐开始，他们不喜欢在早餐上浪费太长时间，所以不会有开火做饭这种事发生，早餐也不需要锅碗瓢盆这些东西，10分钟不到就可以解决吃饭问题。

荷兰人工作午餐的时间几乎不超过半个小时，所以你要确保自己能够在此时间内用餐完毕。绝大多数荷兰人会在家准备好午餐，然后带到公司和单位。典型的荷兰式午餐包括"面包加奶酪"或"奶酪三明治"，面包通常是全麦的，会健康些，而人们觉得白面包没有那么健康，有些人喜欢加上火腿、鸡胸肉、蔬菜或沙拉。荷兰人还喜欢在午餐时喝上一杯脱脂牛奶。要是上班的地方有自己的食堂的话，人们也会去吃上一份"broodje bal"（白面包加肉丸）、香肠肉卷、一个tosti（通常是烤面包片加火腿和奶酪），或者一份"broodje kroket"（圆面包加油炸肉类或油炸蔬菜棒）、汤或沙拉，再配上一个黄油面包和一个煮鸡蛋。总之，不要太期待荷兰式的午餐有多么精致美味。

传统的荷兰晚餐开始的时间比较早，很多家庭在下午五六点钟的时候就已经在餐桌旁围坐好了。晚餐朴素大方，包括土豆、一两道蔬菜和肉。荷兰的餐桌上有一道很常见的菜是"stamppot"，这是一道泥状的以土豆作为主料的菜，再配上一种或多种其他蔬菜，然后再淋上肉汁配上香肠。荷兰人还喜欢土豆炖菜，比如用紫甘蓝和苹果，或者甜菜根一起炖煮。辛辣的调料不是荷兰人常用的，人们会用月桂叶、杜松子、丁香和醋等一些常规的香料和佐料。通常情况下，炖菜还会配上泡菜，像小黄瓜或小洋葱这些。

这些是一些非常传统的荷兰菜：

Hutspot，用土豆、胡萝卜和洋葱做成泥状，佐以烤肉（熏香肠）、小火煨肉或熏肉。

Zuurkoolstamppot，用土豆加酸菜捣碎，配上炸培根或香肠。

Boerenkoolstamppot，一种用羽衣甘蓝加土豆、肉汁、芥末配熏香肠的餐食，它是荷兰最古老、最受欢迎的菜肴之一。

餐点的最后一道是甜品，传统的酸奶加糖或vla。vla是一种很常见的酸奶的衍生甜品，从香草味到巧克力味，从草莓味到焦糖味，口味非常多样。

2. 荷兰餐桌礼仪
Dutch Table Etiquettes

Dutch people have many specific etiquettes, many of which we will address in the section "Dutch social culture". Only table manners or eating etiquettes are discussed here.

荷兰人礼仪繁多而具体，我们将主要在"荷兰人的社交文化"这一部分进行讨论。本节讲述的只是关于荷兰人的餐桌礼仪或饮食礼仪。

Eating out with Dutch 与荷兰人外出就餐

"Going Dutch" is a saying that is familiar to a lot of people around the world and it is often used as an example of Dutch stinginess. Dutch people are practical and straightforward, to avoid awkwardness when ordering in a restaurant the Dutch normally go Dutch, in this way you can order what you like and you only have to take your own wallet in consideration. This also means that if a Dutch friend suggests that the two of you go for dinner you don't need to expect your friend to pick up the tab for you, if your friend has the intention to take you out and foot the bill he or she will make that clear to you.

Dutch women are very emancipated and going Dutch is not much of a problem when going out with your female colleague.

"Going Dutch"（AA制）的说法世人皆知，这常用来形容荷兰有多么的吝啬。荷兰人很实际，也很直截了当，为了避免不必要的尴尬，荷兰人在餐厅点餐时通常都是AA制，这样的话，点餐时你点自己喜欢的就好了，反正你的钱包支付的只会是自己的那部分。也就意味着，倘若一个荷兰朋友跟你说一块儿去吃饭的时候不要想当然地以为别人要请你吃饭或为你买单，如果你的朋友打算跟你出去且会做东的话他或她会非常明确地跟你说的。

荷兰女性思想开放，如果跟你的女同事外出约会，AA制也没什么大不了。

Be Guests in Dutch People 去荷兰人家做客

Have a home dinner with Dutch people, is something that will rarely occur unless you are very close friends or relatives, this is a result of the Dutch cherishing their privacy and time with their own family. If you are invited to have dinner at someone's home, it is polite to bring a bottle of wine along to thank them for the dinner and to show appreciation for the invitation. A bouquet or a bowl of flowers is also a very good and much appreciated gift, the lady of the house will often immediately prepare a vase, cut the stems of the flowers to appropriated length and place the vase with the flowers in prominent place in the house for everyone to admire.

When invited for a meal in someone's home, people are expected to eat all the food that is on their plate. So as to avoid being forced to eat too much of something you don't really like, or having to keep eating while already being full it is better to take multiple small portions of food than to take too much at once and not eat all of it (which is considered wasteful or a sign that the food was not to your liking, or worse the cook will take it as an affront to his or her cooking skills).

被荷兰人邀请做客一定要学会用荷兰语说 "LEKKER"，意思是好吃，因为这是主人一定会问你的。图片为冬季荷兰一种季节性家庭烹饪甜品——红酒梨。

除非你是他们非常亲密的朋友或亲戚，否则在荷兰人家里吃饭这种事不太可能发生，因为荷兰人很看重隐私，也很珍惜跟家人在一起的时间。倘若有幸被邀请到某人家里吃饭，那就带上一瓶酒来答谢他们的晚餐和诚挚的邀请吧！或者买一束花或者一盆花，这同样是一份很不错的礼物，女主人一般会立即准备一个花瓶，将长长短短的花束修剪一番，然后放到屋内的醒目位置以便大家能够抬头可见。

当被邀请到某人家里吃饭时，主人会很期待你把盘子里的食物都消灭殆尽。为了避免吃太多，或者吃到自己根本不喜欢的东西，又或者明明肚子里面已经装满但还是得做出好吃到停不下来的样子，最好少食多取，而不是一次取太多又眼大胃小吃不了（这会让别人觉得你浪费食物，或者认为你觉得东西不好吃，更糟糕的是这会让做饭的人觉得自己的厨艺受到了怀疑甚至侮辱）。

Table manners 饭桌礼仪

Wait with sitting down at the table until the host suggest that every gets seated for dinner. One should always wait before starting to eat until everyone has sat down at the able to eat, unless some dishes or dinner guests take longer to arrive and you are being told that it is all right if you want to start.

It is considered impolite to leave the table during dinner, even to go to the bathroom. During a long dinner, one may leave the table between courses to visit the bathroom. It is considered good manners to ask if one may be excused.

During the entire meal, the fork is always held in the left hand when used. Knife and spoon are held in the right hand. When eating you keep the knife in your right hand, even after cutting the meat. The spoon is only used for eating soup or dessert, and all other foods are eaten with fork and knife. Soup is eaten with the spoon and not drunk. Bread is allowed to be eaten by hand.

Also during the entire meal, it is good manners to keep your hands and elbows above the table at all times. Your hands may rest on the table, but your elbows may not.

Making noises while eating, like eating with one's mouth open (burp, slurp, snarf, crunch or making other eating noises) can be a cause of annoyance to your table companions and is considered extremely uncivilised, as is putting more food your mouth, or drinking and speaking while there is still food in your mouth.

When one does not wish to eat certain foods, or if you have an food allergy it is appreciated if the host is told in advance.

在主人没说可以用餐之前，你要坐在餐桌前稍候，主人建议吃饭时人们才能开始。要是还有人没有落座也需要等一下，直到每个人都落座后才能开吃，除非有的菜或者就餐的客人要花比较长的时间才能准备好或者才能到达，那主人会告诉你可以先开始，这时候是没有问题的。

吃饭期间离座被认为是不礼貌的举动，即使是去洗手间也是不礼貌的。在持续时间较长的晚餐中，期间是可以去洗手间的，但要对离席表示一下歉意。

在整个用餐过程中，总是左手持叉子，把餐刀和勺拿在右手。吃东西的时候也要将餐刀拿在右手，即便切完肉也不要放下。勺子仅可用来喝汤及吃甜点，其他食物都是用刀叉吃的。喝汤记得要用勺而不能够直接抱碗喝。面包可以用手直接拿来吃。

整个用餐过程中也要保持仪态，手和手肘置于餐桌以上是礼仪之举。手也可以放在桌子上，但手肘就不行了。

吃饭时制造响声，比方说张大嘴吃（打嗝、发出啧啧声、狼吞虎咽、嘎吱嘎吱地嚼食物，或发出其他一些吃东西时可能产生的声音）可能会让同在一个饭桌上的人感到很厌烦，并且觉得你是个粗鲁的人，还有不停地往嘴里塞满食物，或者嘴里满是食物的时候喝东西以及说话都不可取。

要是有你不喜欢的食物，或者对某些食物过敏时，事先告知主人是不会唐突的，反而会让人赞赏懂理。

3. 荷兰传统食物
Dutch Traditional Food

Dutch cuisine may not be as rich in flavours and have an expanded variety as the Chinese cuisine does, but there are still many Dutch specialties that are certainly worth trying, even if it is once. Some snacks and dessert are only eaten in the Netherlands and will raise an eyebrow with many a visitor from abroad.

荷兰菜的烹饪味道可能不像中餐那样丰富，但有许多荷兰特产值得一试，哪怕只有一次。有些只有在荷兰才能够吃到的零食和甜品会让很多外国游客颇感意外难以忘怀！

※ Cheese

Of course, the manufacture of cheese is not exclusive to the Netherlands, a variety of nomadic tribes from Europe, the Middle East and Central Asia are known to be making cheese from milk for thousands of years. In ancient times cheese was typically produced by storing fresh milk in flasks fashioned from pig or cow stomach, before leaving to ferment and being transform into cheese by bacteria.

Archaeological excavations reveal that cheese making is a practice in the Netherlands that has started as early as 800 BC. The Dutch provinces now known as Noord-Holland, Zuid-Holland and Friesland in particular, produced large quantities of cheese, arguably largely because of the conditions of the damp soil in these areas which made them rather suitable for rearing dairy cattle. Ancient writings also refer to the early cheese dairies located in what many call the Low Countries, including the book, "Commentarii de Bello Gallico", by famous Roman politician, general and writer, Gaius Julius Caesar.

These days most Dutch cheese is factory produced, but it is still possible to buy traditionally produced cheese directly from a farmer. This special type of Dutch cheese is known in the Netherlands as "boerenkaas" which means as much as farmhouse cheese and often is made from milk of the cows that are reared at farmers own from the farm's. The highly distinctive flavour of this kind of cheese is mostly thanks to its traditional preparation technique and unique ripening process. Fine examples of such a high quality Dutch farmhouse cheese include Beemster cheese and Boer 'n Trots. Even though most Dutch cheese is usually made from cow's milk, there are also quite a few varieties which are prepared from goat's milk, including the popular goat's cheese made by exclusive Dutch label, Landana.

The variety of cheese produced in the Netherlands is wide, mostly they are semi-hard or hard cheeses, like "Gouda" and "Edam" which are also the most popular cheeses produced in the Netherlands.

During the course of history dairy farmers sold their delicious homemade cheeses at Dutch cheese markets, including the celebrated cheese market in Alkmaar, this market was established in 1581, and till this day Alkmaar remains a showcase for some of the finest Dutch cheese and is an incredibly popular tourist attraction to boot. There are also other cheese markets operating in the Netherlands, besides Alkmaar there is also Gouda, Edam, Hoorn and Woerden, this last one is an modern working commercial cheese market while the other four are operated like traditional merchant cheese markets as it was in the post-medieval period, and are operating mostly during the summer months.

※ Dutch cheese factsn

- 10 litres of milk is required for the preparation of just 1 kilo of Gouda cheese.
- In addition to fat and protein, Dutch cheese contains calcium and vitamins A, B and D.
- Holland annually exports around 600 million kilos of cheese (predominantly Gouda and Edam). In 2016, the export of Dutch cheese exports reached $3.3 billion, ranking second in the world.
- The average Dutch person enjoys some 17 kilos of cheese per year.

※ Pannenkoeken

Pannenkoeken or Dutch crêpes are a style of pancakes which finds its origins in the Netherlands, The crêpes are made from flour, milk, salt, and eggs. They are usually larger and much thinner than their American or Scotch's counterparts, but not as thin as the French crêpes. They may incorporate slices of bacon, apples, cheese, or raisins. Plain ones are often eaten with treacle, appelstroop, molasses made of apple or powder sugar.

Pannenkoeken are usually eaten as a main course, most supermarkets have pre-prepared pannenkoeken, which can be heated directly in the microwave. They make a great treat for children's birthday parties.

And believe it or not, but the Dutch even made up a holiday as an excuse to eat their favourite treat, which is known as "Sint Pannekoek" (saint pancake). It is a Dutch pseudo holiday on the 29th of November. It was first introduced in 1986 in a Dutch comic called "Jan, Jans en de kinderen" (Jan, Jans and the kids). Grandpa and the kids didn't feel like eating veggies for dinner, so they made up a fake holiday called Saint Pancake, where the family bakes pancakes and put pancakes on their heads waiting for the father to come home and wishing him "a happy and blessed Saint Pancake".

Who said that the Dutch were a boring bunch?

※ Poffertjes

You can think of a poffertjes as a baby version of the pancake，but the two are slightly different, the poffertjes are much fluffier as pannenkoeken and are made with yeast and buckwheat flour and typically served with a lump of butter and powdered sugar.

Although poffertjes can be eaten in both summer and winter, they are more common and popular during winter. In the cold winter outdoors, the poffertjes stalls are always busy. They are sold on a small cardboard (sometimes plastic) plate and come with a small disposable fork the size of a pastry fork, this is the most common situation. Flipping poffertjes is considered a skill on its own.

※ Stroopwafel

Popular throughout the world, the 'stroopwafel' is undoubtedly the most famous and popular pastry from The Netherlands. This sweet snack is a waffle cookie, made from butter, flour, yeast, milk, brown sugar and eggs, with a sticky syrup filling in the middle.

Stroopwafels are particularly good with a cup of coffee or tea. The cookies come in various sizes, but the most common size fits perfectly as a lid on a cup of coffee, tea or hot chocolate.The warmth of your beverage will soften the cookie and melts the sweet syrup, making a delightful dessert or snack.

Almost all supermarkets sell Stroopwafel, and make a great souvenir for friends and relatives at home.

※ Drop

Drop (liquorice) is probably something Chinese scratch their heads to understand. Drop can be regarded as the Dutch national candy, you could say that every Dutch person loves drop, they even have friends and family posting it to them when they are on vacation or when they have immigrated to another country.

With more than 2 kilograms per year per person, the Dutch consumption of liquorice is the highest in the world. You will come across it everywhere: the supermarket, the pharmacy, at the market and gas stations. 'Drop' comes in different flavours and sizes, but basically there are two major differences: salty liquorice and sweet liquorice.

A word of warning, the Dutch think it is a funny game to try and feed expecting foreigners drop and watch their reaction.

※ Oliebol

An oliebol is a ball of dough which is deep-fried, it is traditional Dutch food. The dough is made from flour, eggs, yeast, some salt, milk, baking powder and usually sultanas, currants, raisins and sometimes zest or succade (candied fruit). Oliebollen are usually served with powdered sugar.

Oliebollen are a seasonal food sold only in the winter, there are special temporary booths where they are for sale. Interesting things: there is an national agency ranking the taste of oliebollen at different stalls, and the results are published in the newspapers at the end of the year.

※ Kroket

The "kroket" is a deep fried roll with meat ragout inside, covered in breadcrumbs. The original Dutch "kroket" is made from beef or veal, but there are many different flavours like chicken satay, shrimps, goulash or even a vegetarian "kroket". You can eat a "kroket" as a snack, but most of the time they are served on sliced white bread or hamburger buns with mustard on the side.

You can buy 'kroket' almost everywhere in the Netherlands: regular snack bars, cafés, restaurants, even McDonald's. But if you want to keep up appearance then you will buy your kroket at Dungelmann, close to the Royal Palace at hoogstraat in The Hague.

※ Kibbeling

A very familiar smell floating through the streets in the Netherlands, it is the smell of fried fish.

"Lekkerbekje" and "Kibbeling" are the two main types of fried fish, both from the North Sea. The only difference between these two is that "kibbeling" is cut into chunks, while "lekkerbekje" is not. "Kibbeling" is served with dipping sauces like a mayonnaise-based remoulade sauce or garlic sauce. These days also fried scrimps and salmon are served. Do be aware that eating your kibbeling in the open air is at your own risk, the seagulls in the Netherlands are real daredevils and before you know it they will have picked you piece of kibbeling from your fork, plate or even out of your mouth.

※ 奶酪

奶酪的制造当然并不仅出现在荷兰，其在欧洲、中东和中亚的多个游牧部落中已经延续了几千年的历史。在古代，人们把新鲜的牛奶存放在猪或者牛的胃里，牛奶开始发酵，变成奶酪霉菌，最后制成奶酪取出来。

考古挖掘表明，奶酪制作是荷兰的一种做法，早在公元前800年就已经开始了。荷兰省，即现在的北荷兰省、南荷兰省和弗里斯兰省，可能是由于这些地区潮湿的土壤条件更加适合饲养奶牛，于是制成了大量的奶酪。古代的著作还提到早期的奶酪场，大多位于所谓的低地国家的这些地区，这些著作中便包括著名的罗马政治家、将军兼作家伽尤斯·尤利乌斯·恺撒的著作《高卢战记》一书。

如今，大多数荷兰奶酪都产自工厂，但仍有一部分传统的奶酪可以直接从农民手中购买。这种特殊的荷兰奶酪在荷兰被称为"boerenkaas"，中文为"农民奶酪"，意思为农场奶酪，通常是由农场饲养的奶牛产的牛奶制成的。这种独特风味的奶酪主要归功于其传统的制备工艺和独特的成熟过程。这种高质量的荷兰农家干酪如Beemster奶酪和Boer'n Trots。尽管大多数荷兰奶酪通常是由牛奶制成，但也有相当一部分品种是由羊奶制成的，如荷兰独家品牌Landana生产的深受欢迎的山羊奶酪。

荷兰产的奶酪种类繁多，主要是半硬或硬奶酪，比如荷兰产的豪达（Gouda）和艾登（Edam），这也是最受欢迎的奶酪。

在过去的历史中，奶农们在荷兰的奶酪市场上出售美味的自制奶酪，还在1581年建立了著名的阿尔克马尔奶酪市场，直到今天，阿尔克马尔仍然留存着专门给荷兰最好的奶酪用作展示的陈列柜，如今这里也已然成为一个非常受欢迎的旅游景点。除了阿尔克马尔奶酪市场，荷兰还有其他奶酪市场同时在运营，像豪达、艾登，霍恩和武尔登，最后一个是一个现代经营商业性质的奶酪市场，而其他四个更像是后中世纪传统商业运作的奶酪市场，并且一般只在夏天开放运行。

荷兰的奶酪生产和奶酪消耗都居世界前列，荷兰人的生活很难有一天离得开奶酪。图为市场上排队买奶酪的民众。

关于荷兰奶酪的一些小知识：

● 生产一公斤的豪达奶酪需要10升的牛奶。

● 除了脂肪和蛋白质外，荷兰奶酪还含有丰富的钙、维生素A、维生素B和维生素D。

● 荷兰每年出口约6亿公斤的奶酪（主要是豪达和艾登）。 2016年，荷兰奶酪出口创汇达到33亿美元，位居世界第二。

● 荷兰人平均每人每年消耗17公斤的奶酪。

※ 荷兰煎饼

Pannenkoeken或叫Dutch crepes是一种薄煎饼，它起源于荷兰，由面粉、牛奶、盐和鸡蛋制成。这种煎饼通常比美国或苏格兰的同类产品更大、更薄，但不像法国薄饼那么薄。有时可能会加一些培根、苹果、奶酪或葡萄干在里面。一般的吃法是抹上糖浆、苹果酱、苹果制成的慕斯或者撒上糖霜粉。

人们通常把荷兰煎饼当作主食吃，大多数超市都卖有荷兰煎饼的成品，直接在微波炉中加热就可以吃了。如果恰逢孩子们生日聚会，荷兰煎饼常用来招待这些小客人，这是很受欢迎的。

信不信由你，荷兰人甚至假借节日之名就为了满足一下肚子里的馋虫，而这只是为了吃到他们最爱的东西——圣饼，这是一个荷兰的节日，在每年的11月29日。1986年，这一节日第一次被画进荷兰漫画中，名为"Jan, Jans en de kinderen"。因为爷爷和孩子们不喜欢吃蔬菜，所以他们造了一个假的节日，叫作圣饼节，一家人围在一起烤饼，还把煎饼放在头顶上等着父亲回家，并祝愿他"圣饼节快乐"。

所以，这么好玩儿的事，怎么能说荷兰人很无聊呢！

※ 荷兰小松饼

你可以把荷兰小松饼看作是缩小版的荷兰煎饼，但是这两个又略有不同，荷兰小松饼由酵母和荞麦面粉做成，通常再搭配一块黄油和糖霜粉食用，小松饼的口感要比荷兰煎饼蓬松很多。

夏天和冬天都能够吃到荷兰小松饼，但在冬天更常见也更受欢迎一些。在寒冬的户外，荷兰小松饼的摊位总是生意忙碌。每份小松饼都用一块小的硬纸板（有时是塑料）做的小盘子盛放着，还有一个一次性的小叉子，一般情况下都是这样。做小松饼的人，将每一个小松饼翻个可以看作是一项技能。

※ 华夫饼

风靡全球的华夫饼无疑是荷兰最著名、最受欢迎的点心。这是一种华夫饼干，由黄油、面粉、酵母、牛奶、红糖和鸡蛋制成，中间夹有一层黏稠的焦糖糖浆。

华夫饼和咖啡或茶简直是绝配。这种饼干大小不一，但最常见的大小整好和一杯咖啡、茶或热巧克力的盖子大小相当，可当作盖子盖到上面。热饮的蒸汽和热度会将华夫饼软化，里面的糖浆也融化，让人心情舒畅，回味无穷。

几乎所有的超市都可以买到华夫饼，买给亲朋好友是个很好的礼品。

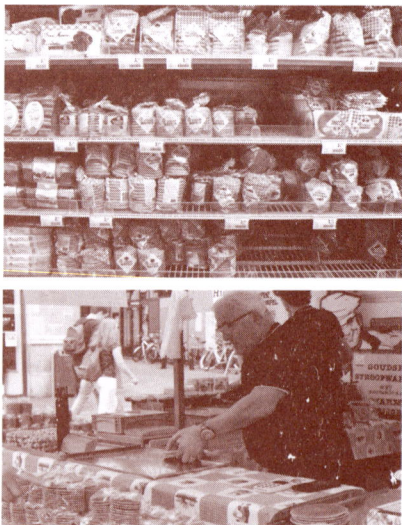

如果购买特色实物当礼品，那最不应该错过的应该就是华夫饼，基本在所有的大小商店都可以买到。图一为超市货架上的华夫饼。图二为摊位上新鲜热乎的华夫饼。

※ 甘草糖

甘草糖（drop）大概是最让中国人一言难尽的一种食物。但甘草糖却可以看作是荷兰的国民糖果，说人尽皆爱绝无夸大，甚至更夸张的是，有人的朋友和家人在外国度假或移民到其他国家时，他们都要把甘草糖专门寄过去。

荷兰人甘草糖的消费量每人每年超过了2公斤，是世界上最高的。甘草糖无处不在，在超市里、药店里、市场上和加油站，处处可寻到甘草糖的踪迹。甘草糖的口味和大小并不都是一样的，但最大不同就是有咸甘草糖和甜甘草糖之分。

小小的提示，荷兰人觉得给外国人吃甘草糖然后观察他们的反应是件非常好玩儿的事情。

※ 油炸面团

油炸面团是一种深炸过的生面团，是一种传统的荷兰食物。面团由面粉、鸡蛋、酵母、盐、牛奶、发酵粉混合制成，也常常搭配着白的或紫的葡萄干、黑加仑干、有时还会加一些橘皮或水果蜜饯。食用的时候一般撒上糖霜粉。

油炸面团是一种只在冬季出售的季节性食品，有专门的临时摊位出售。有一个有趣的事：每年都会有专门的机构对所有售卖油炸面团的摊位进行口味上的排名，结果会在当年年底刊登在报纸上。

海牙中心街头一家售卖油炸面团的摊位，这是种仅在岁末才有的季节性食品。

※ 可乐饼

可乐饼是一种里面是碎肉，外面裹以面包屑在油里面深炸过的肉卷。最初的荷兰可乐饼是由牛肉或小牛牛肉制成的，但也有很多不同的口味，比如鸡肉沙爹、虾、炖牛肉，甚至是素的可乐饼。你可以把可乐饼当作零食，但大多数情况下，人们都把可乐饼夹在白吐司面包片或汉堡面包里面，再浇上芥末酱食用。

你可以在荷兰的任何地方买到可乐饼。普通的小吃店、咖啡馆、餐馆，甚至麦当劳。但如果你想要原汁原味的可乐饼，那就去海牙皇宫附近的胡格街的Dungelmann去买最正宗的吧。

※ 炸鱼

荷兰人爱吃炸鱼，搭配酱料后并不觉油腻，鱼肉厚实鲜嫩。

荷兰的街头经常飘着一缕熟悉的香气，那是炸鱼的味道。"Lekkerbekje"和"Kibbeling"是市面上两种主要的炸鱼，这两种鱼都产自于北海。两者之间唯一的区别是，"Kibbeling"被分切成大块，而"lekkerbekje"则不是。炸鱼的酱料多种，蘸蛋黄酱是主流，或者蘸蒜酱食用。现在还开发出了炸小虾和三文鱼。要是在露天吃炸鱼的话你可得注意风险了，荷兰的海鸥鲁莽大胆，经常趁人们不注意直接把食物从叉子上、盘子里甚至是从食客的嘴里夺走并逃之夭夭。

Tijd voor Nederlands 荷兰语时间

● 单词+短语

荷 toetje 英 dessert 译 饭后甜点	荷 brood 英 bread 译 面包	荷 aardappel 英 potato 译 土豆
荷 haring 英 herring 译 鲱鱼	荷 ontbijt/lunch/avondeten 英 breakfast/lunch/supper 译 早餐/午餐/晚餐	荷 maaltijd 英 meal 译 餐食
荷 wijn 英 wine 译 酒	荷 gewoonte 英 habit 译 习惯	荷 traditioneel 英 traditional 译 传统的
荷 eten/drinken 英 eat/drink 译 吃/喝	荷 uitnodigen 英 invite 译 邀请	

● 例句

荷 Nederlanders eten altijd een toetje na het avondeten. 英 Dutch people always eat dessert after dinner. 译 荷兰人在饭后总是会吃甜点。	荷 De meeste Nederlanders eten brood voor de lunch. 英 Most Dutch people eat bread for lunch. 译 大部分荷兰人午餐都吃面包。
荷 Aardappels zijn traditioneel Nederlands voedsel. 英 Potato is a traditional Dutch food. 译 土豆是荷兰人的传统食物。	荷 Nederlanders houden van haring, ik heb het ook gegeten. 英 The Dutch like to eat herring, I have already eaten it. 译 荷兰人热爱鲱鱼，我也已经吃过了。
荷 Nederlanders hebben niet de gewoonte om 's middags warme maaltijden te eten. 英 The Dutch don't have the habit of eating hot meals at noon. 译 荷兰人没有中午吃热餐的习惯。	荷 Mijn vriend nodigde me uit voor een diner bij hem thuis. 英 My friend invited me to dinner at his house. 译 我的朋友邀请我去他家吃晚餐。
荷 Ik dronk een wijntje na het avondeten. 英 I drank a little wine after dinner. 译 我在晚餐后喝了一点儿酒。	

行在荷兰

Transportation in the Netherlands

The Netherlands is both a very densely populated and a highly developed country, in which transport is one of the main key factors of the economy, because of this the Netherlands also has a very dense and modern infrastructure, facilitating transport with road, rail, air and water networks. In this chapter we will mainly focus on traveling by rail.

荷兰既是人口非常稠密又是高度发达的国家，其中交通运输是经济发展的关键因素之一，因此荷兰也拥有非常密集和现代化的基础设施，极其便利的公路、铁路、航空运输和水上交通网络。在本章节中，我们将主要介绍一下相关的铁路旅行。

1. 出行在荷兰
Getting around in the Netherlands

In the Netherlands mobility is considerable. Road mobility has grown continuously since the 1950s and now exceeds 200 billion km travelled per year. Transport by car is responsible about 75% of this number. Daily leisure and business trips conducted through different means of transportation around half of these are made by car, 25% by bicycle, 20% walking, and 5% by public transport.

Rail is the most used form of public transport in the Netherlands. The Netherlands, like many other European countries, has a dense and busy railway network, totalling about 7,000 kilometres of rail track which connects virtually all major towns and cities. The Nederlandse Spoorwegen (NS) (Dutch Railways) is the main public rail transport provider, besides the NS there are also some minor providers such as Arriva, Syntus, Connexxion, Breng, DB Regio, NMBS, Veolia and DB Regionalbahn Westfalen. During week days all railway stations are serviced at least twice an hour in each direction or more.

Cycling is a very common and comfortable mode of transport in the Netherlands, with 36% of the people listing their bicycle as their most preferred and frequent used mode of transport. In cities, the proportion of people who travel by bike is extremely high, in Amsterdam, for example, 36% of the inhabitants travel by bike, while in smaller cities this is even higher, as in Zwolle, up to 46% of the people go out by bike. This high frequency of bicycle travel is enabled by excellent cycling infrastructure such as cycle paths, cycle tracks, protected intersections, ample bicycle parking and by making cycling routes shorter, quicker and more direct than car routes. China is known as a big bicycle country because we have a huge population and a lot of bikes. But the Netherlands has far more bikes per capita than we do. The Netherlands has 110 bicycles per 100 people, which means that the Netherlands has more bicycles than people.

The Dutch bicycle is mainly a practical mode of transport, and the bicycles come in all shapes and sizes, some of them are eye-openers, try a cargo bike to bike with your little ones, or a romantic family tandem to go on outings together.

Cycling with one child in front and one on the back, having your dog running next to you on a lead, while pulling a trailer with your weekly shopping and talking to a friend on the phone - is that allowed in Holland? Yes. It might not be safe, but it isn't illegal. If you go cycling in Holland, it's important that you're aware of the legal requirements for your bicycle and the traffic regulations for cyclists.

A bicycle bell is compulsory on every bike. Other traffic users have to be able to hear it at a distance of 25 metres. You're not likely to be fined if your bicycle bell does not meet the requirements, but a good bell does make it easier to pass other traffic on narrow and busy roads.

As soon as you're out on your bicycle in the dark or when visibility is bad, bicycle lights and reflectors are compulsory. The rules are very strict. If your bike doesn't meet the requirements, you risk a fine—or worse, a car driver might not see you in time.

Tips: it is also compulsory to indicate with hand signals which direction you want to turn.

147

Turn right-extend your right arm straight out to the right horizontally.

Turn left-extend your left arm straight out to the left horizontally.

Remember to look over your shoulder to check if any other traffic is coming from behind.

在荷兰，公路产生的人口流动性增长巨大。自20世纪50年代以来，道路交通一直在持续增长，现在每年的道路运行公里数超过2 000亿公里，汽车交通占了这个数字的75%。日常的休闲和商务旅行凭借各种不同的交通工具来实现，其中一半是汽车、25%是自行车、20%是步行、5%是公共交通工具。

铁路是荷兰最常用的公共交通工具。和许多其他欧洲国家一样，荷兰有着密集而繁忙的铁路网络，总长约7 000公里，几乎连接了所有主要的城镇和城市。荷兰铁路公司（人们通常称NS）是主要的公共铁路运输承运商，除了NS，荷兰还有一些小型的供应商，如Arriva、Syntus、Connexxion、Breng、NMBS、Veolia和德国DB铁路运输公司。在工作日里，所有的火车站在每个方向的列车至少每个小时两班或更多。

在荷兰，骑自行车是一种非常普遍和舒适的交通出行方式，有36%的人把自行车列为他们最喜欢和经常使用的交通工具。在城市里，骑自行车出行的人比例极高，比如在阿姆斯特丹，有36%的居民骑自行车出行。而在小城市，这一比例就更高了，如兹沃勒，有高达46%的人出行靠骑自行车。这种高频率的自行车出行是全依仗于荷兰完善的自行车基础设施，如供自行车使用的路径、专用自行车道、交叉口的自行车优先权、宽敞的自行车存放处，并且自行车路线也会比汽车路线更加简短、快捷和直接。中国被称为自行车大国，那是因为我们有庞大的人口基数和庞大的自行车数量。但论人均自行车数量，荷兰远远超过我们。荷兰每100人平均拥有110辆自行车，意思就是说荷兰的自行车数量比国家人口数还要多。

荷兰的自行车数量已经远超其国家人口，无关车辆价值，人们都喜欢装扮自己的车并使其物尽其用。图为停靠在社区街道的一辆旧自行车。

荷兰自行车的主要功能是它作为一种交通工具的实用性，各式各样形状和大小的自行车都有，有些类型的自行车一定让你大开眼界，比如有一种专门载重的自行车（cargo bike），可以把孩子们安顿在开放式的车厢里一起出行，或者全家出动，来一个浪漫的自行车外出。

载着一周的生活必备，前后还驮着两个孩子，爱犬在前面屁颠屁颠地欢快地奔跑着，又要忙着跟朋友煲电话粥，这在荷兰都可以？是的，没错，可能存在安全隐患，但这并不违法。如果你要在荷兰骑自行车的话，有很重要的一点你得需要了解，那就是法律对骑自行车的有关规定和骑车的人必须要遵守的交通规则。

每辆自行车都必须安装自行车铃铛，还要保证其他的路上行人能够在25米的距离内听到铃铛的响声。自行车铃声不符合要求，被罚款的事一般不会发生，但铃声响彻入耳能让你在狭窄繁忙的道路上骑行更顺畅一些，不是吗？

但你若是在黑暗或者能见度不好的时候骑车，那么一定要保证自行车车灯和反光设备正常使用，这是强制性的，必须严格遵守规定。如果你的自行车不符合要求，那就极有可能被罚款了——或者更糟的是，汽车司机可能不能及时注意到你。

小贴士：骑车时若要转弯，请必须做出手势以便后面的人看到：

右转弯——伸出右手臂，水平指向右方。

左转弯——伸出左手臂，水平指向左方。

伸出手臂时请观察一下是否有其他骑行车辆从后面赶上。

2. 在荷兰出入境
Entry and Exit

The first stop to reach the Netherlands and the last stop to leave the Netherlands is basically Schiphol Airport. Of course, if you take a train to the surrounding countries or from neighbouring countries by train to the Netherlands, it should be the corresponding train station.

● From Schiphol to Amsterdam city centre or other cities

Schiphol's train station is located directly underneath the airport and trains run 24 hours a day. From 06:00 to 00:00 trains depart several times an hour. During the night, from midnight to 06:00, there's only one train per hour. If you'd like a more detailed overview of your train journey, you can always check the timetables at the official website of the NS.

You can buy train tickets at the yellow ticket machines on the platforms at Schiphol Plaza, the main hall at Schiphol or at the NS offices near the Meeting Point, which is a large square cube, at the same Plaza Schiphol. People who live in the Netherlands normally have a public transport card that they can top up at these machines.

Schiphol is an important traveling hub in the Dutch rail network. It's very easy to get from there to anywhere across the country or even travel to other European countries.

The tracks can be found underneath the main hall, they can be reached via escalators or elevators which are clearly indicated when you walk towards the exit of the main hall. Trains to Amsterdam usually leave from track 3. Trains to and from Amsterdam Central Station run 8x an hour—so once every 7.5 minutes. Signs above the escalators will show you when the next few trains depart, and where they are headed. Signs near the yellow ticket machines list trains that will depart within the next half hour or so.

Notes:

- The Dutch trains are divided into Sprinter, Intercity and Intercity direct. The Sprinter is relatively slow and stops at all the smaller stations, Intercity usually stops at bigger stations and the Intercity Direct only at a few larger stations.

- The ticket machines are easy to use (English language option available) and accept standard international credit cards. If you need assistance, visit the ticket counter instead.

- You must activate your ticket (a chip card) at one of the card readers near or at the top of the escalators, or next to the elevators.

- Do not buy return trip tickets, unless you plan on returning to the airport on the same day. Round-trip tickets are valid for same-day travel only.

● Arrival Schiphol for Departure

The same information applies to departures of the Netherlands. Below are the train frequency and time to reach Schiphol in several major cities:

- **Den Haag Centraal-Schiphol**

Peak departure time, on average, every six or seven minutes nonstop train, including sprinters and Intercity. Sprinters and Intercity run for 50 minutes and 29 minutes respectively.

- **Den Haag HS-Schiphol**

A direct Intercity train departs about every half hour and takes about half an hour to get to Schiphol.

- **Rotterdam Central-Schiphol**

A direct Intercity train departs about every half hour and takes about 50 minutes. Also Intercity direct takes 24 minutes.

- **Utrecht Centraal-Schiphol**

A train departs every 14 minutes on average, and takes about 30-35 minutes.

Delays and annulments of train journeys by the NS are common. You are advised to check your journey online or in the NS App, which are relatively easy to use. Make sure you reserve ample of time for your retour journey to Schiphol, we advise you to do like the Dutch and take one train early to avoid missing your plane because of a train delay.

抵达荷兰的第一站和离开荷兰的最后一站是史基浦机场。当然，如果你乘火车去周边的国家或从邻国乘火车来荷兰，那对应的就是火车站了。

- **从史基浦到阿姆斯特丹市中心或其他城市**

史基浦机场的火车站位于机场地下，火车每天24小时不间断运行。每天从早上6点到夜间零点，每小时的列车有数次。在夜间，从午夜到凌晨到6点，每小时只有一列火车。如果你想要更详细地了解列车的行程，那么还是要随时查看荷兰铁路官方网站（https://www.ns.nl/en）的列车时间表。

黄蓝是荷兰铁路公司列车的颜色，自动售票机采取了同样配色，在机场和车站甚是显眼，提供多语言选择。图为NS售票机。

你可以直接在史基浦机场广场、正厅，或者NS的售票处购买火车票，那附近有一个很大的方形隔间，名为"Meeting Point"，同在机场广场上。常住荷兰的人一般都有一张公共交通卡OV-chipkaart，可以在黄色的售票机上充值。

史基浦站是荷兰铁路网的重要旅游枢纽。从这里到全国各地，甚至到其他欧洲国家旅行都很容易。

站台在主厅的地下，可以通过自动扶梯或电梯到达，从到达处出口出来后很容易找到。通往阿姆斯特丹的火车通常从3号站台出发。

往返于阿姆斯特丹中央车站和机场的列车每小时可运行8次，也就是大概每7.5分钟就有一班车。自动扶梯上方有显示屏，会清晰地告诉你下面几个班次的火车分别出发的时间以及目的地。黄色售票机附近也有显示屏，能看到未来半小时左右出发的所有列车的信息。

- 注意：

- 荷兰火车有短程车或者叫慢车（Sprinter）、城际列车（Intercity）和城际直通车（Intercity direct）之分。慢车在一些较小的车站也停靠，相对慢一些；城际列车只停靠在较大的车站；而城际直通车通常只在少数大站停靠或直达。

- 售票机的使用比较简单，可以选择英文，机器接受标准国际信用卡。如果你不明白或需要帮助，也可以到售票处去询问或购票。

- 乘车前，请务必在自动扶梯旁边或直梯旁边的读卡器上刷卡激活。

- 如果你当天不返回机场，那只买单程票就好了，往返机票只适用于当日旅行。

- 前往史基浦机场出发离境

上面的相关信息也适用于从荷兰离境。以下是在荷兰几个主要城市的列车频次和到达史基浦机场所需要的大概时间：

- 海牙中央车站—史基浦

包括慢车和城际列车，平均每6～7分钟一班车。慢车和城际列车的路程时间分别为50分钟和29分钟。

- 海牙老火车站—史基浦

直达城际列车大约每半小时一班车，大约半小时就能到达史基浦机场。

- 鹿特丹中央车站—史基浦

直达城际列车大约每半小时开一班，大约50分钟。同时也有城际直通车，用时24分钟。

- 乌特勒支中央车站—史基浦

平均每14分钟就有一列火车出发，大约需要30～35分钟。

NS的火车延迟甚至取消也是会经常发生的，建议你使用NS的官方APP随时在线查询相关的列车信息，这是一个荷兰人使用非常频繁的手机应用小程序。并且请你一定要预留足够的返程时间至史基浦机场，我们也建议你像荷兰人一样尽量乘坐早一班火车，以免因为列车晚点错过飞机。

3. 在荷兰境内旅游
Travel in the Netherlands

Railway travel is a truly convenient means of transportation in the Netherlands. The country boasts an extensive railway network, and the trains are modern and perfectly comfortable. Since Holland is a relatively small country, you can travel from Amsterdam to Utrecht in just 30 minutes and from the Hague to Amsterdam Central Station in just 50 minutes. And even traveling all the way up north (Groningen) and down south (Maastricht) takes just 2 hours from Amsterdam Central. In other words, travelling by train is a perfect way to discover many beautiful places in Holland!

※ Holland Travel Ticket

Holland Travel Ticket is One ticket for all public transport. If you would like to travel to a city by train and visit different places by bus or metro, Holland Travel Ticket is a good choice. You can buy the Holland Travel Ticket at the NS Ticket & Service desk at most train stations or the NS ticket machines. It's important to note, when starting your journey, use the ticket to check in at the gates in the station. Please note that your ticket will be valid only after you check in. When you get off at your destination, use the ticket to check out at the gates and leave the station. And you must also check out and in when you switch from one railway company to another.

There are two different tickets. The off-peak ticket costs €39 and is not valid during morning peak hours from Monday to Friday after 06:30 and before 09:00 and valid all day at weekends. If you want to travel within this time window, buy a full day ticket for €59.

The Netherlands boasts a very comprehensive public transport network, and the Holland Travel Ticket will take you wherever you want to go in Holland.

※ OV-chipkaart

You can use a single-use chipcard or an OV-chipkaart (smart card) to travel by train in Holland. The single-use chipcard is perfect for incidental travellers. You can buy it at an NS ticketing machine or service desk. Single-use chipcards always cost 1 euro more per trip. You don't have to charge credit to the card but you do have to check in and out.

If you plan to use the train more often while staying in Holland, we recommend buying an "anonymous OV-chipkaart". You can buy them at NS ticketing machines or the service desk. There is a one-time fee of EUR 7.50 for an anonymous OV-chipkaart (which can also be used on buses, trams, metros and ferries). If you want to travel by train, you need at least 20 euros worth of credit on your OV-chipkaart! You must check in prior to every trip and check out at the end. Look for the OV-chipkaart pillars on the station.

Do note that there is no refund of the one-time fee.

※ Class

Virtually every NS train offers 1st and 2nd class travel (classes are marked inside and outside the trains). If you buy an anonymous OV-chipkaart, you will normally travel in 2nd class. If you wish to have more comfort and space, you can opt for travelling 1st class, in which case you will have to pay extra.

※ Night trains

If you want to travel home by train after a night on the town, you can sometimes take a night train. These service several routes and run after the last regular train that day until early in the morning. They usually run every hour and tickets are available at the regular price. Please note that night trains are available nightly in the Randstad area, but are generally available on weekends only in other regions. Night trains are also often available to Amsterdam Airport Schiphol and Eindhoven Airport.

※ Train stations

The Netherlands boasts some 400 stations. There are historic stations like Haarlem, small stations like Soestdijk, and big stations like Amsterdam and Utrecht. Station facilities vary, but every station has an NS ticketing machine to buy your ticket. Bigger stations also have a service desk and an information desk, which can answer any questions and offer advice. Service desks also sell tickets. Bigger stations usually also contain a range of food shops as well as shops for buying flowers, books, perfumes and clothes.Therefore, it is a good idea to go to the train stations shops at the time of the transfer. But generally speaking, the transfer time of the Dutch train won't be long, unless you want to wait for a later train.

153

在荷兰，铁路旅行是一种真正便利的交通出行方式。这个国家拥有庞大的铁路网络，现代化的列车也非常舒适。荷兰是一个相对较小的国家，从阿姆斯特丹到乌特勒支只需30分钟，从海牙到阿姆斯特丹中央车站只需50分钟。即使是一路北上到格罗宁根和南下马斯特里赫特，从阿姆斯特丹中心出发也不过需要2个小时。换句话说，乘火车旅行是发现荷兰更多美丽风景的最佳方式！

荷兰铁路是人们最重要的出行方式，各个方向的列车发车频次每小时都有数班。图为鹿特丹中央车站站台的NS列车。

※ 荷兰旅行票

荷兰旅行票是适用于所有公共交通工具的一种票据。如果你想坐火车去荷兰其他城市，或者乘坐公共汽车或地铁前往不同的地方，旅行票是一个不错的选择。在大多数火车站的NS售票机上或者NS售票处都能买到旅行票。特别需要注意的，当你开始使用旅行票搭火车时，请一定要在车站的刷卡机上刷上，只有刷卡后的车票才算有效车票。当你到达目的地以后，请再次在刷卡机上刷出，然后离站。要是你所乘坐的列车隶属不同的铁路公司，必须要先在本次列车刷出，然后再在下一个铁路公司的刷卡机上刷入。

荷兰旅行票有两种。票价39欧元的非高峰票，在早上6点半以后到上午9点这个高峰时间段不能使用，周末全天无时间限制。如果你想要在高峰时间段内坐车的话，那么你需要购买59欧元的全天票。

荷兰拥有非常完善的公共交通网络，凭借荷兰旅行票，你就可以去往荷兰的任何地方了。

※ 公共交通卡

在荷兰，你也可以使用单次交通卡或者智能芯片卡，即OV-chipkaart来乘坐火车旅行。单次磁卡对于偶尔坐车的游客来说是个好选择，可以在NS售票机上或服务台购买。单次磁卡每趟行程会多付1欧元，相当于工本费。卡内也不需要储值，但乘车时也必须刷进刷出才算有效车票。

如果你在荷兰逗留期间会频繁乘坐火车，那么我们建议你买一张不记名的OV-chipkaart，也可以在NS售票机或服务台买到。这种不记名OV-chipkaart收取工本费7.5欧元，也可用于公共汽车、电车、地铁和渡轮。如果你想坐火车，那卡里至少需要充值20欧元。每段行程也必须要刷进刷出，刷卡机就是火车站或者站台的黄色小柱子。

请注意，不记名OV-chipkaart的工本费是不退还的。

※ 车厢等级

事实上，NS的每一列火车都分一等车厢和二等车厢（列车的车身内外都有标记）。如果你买的是不记名的OV-chipkaart，通常只能在二等车厢就坐。如果你想空间更大更舒适些，也可以选择一等车厢，这样的话你就需要多付费了。

※ 夜间列车

在夜里想从城里乘火车回住处，有时也能坐夜班车的。夜间列车有好几条路线，从白天的最后一班火车开始一直运营到凌晨时分。夜间列车通常每小时有一个车次，而且票价是固定的。请注意，夜间列车在Randstad地区（就是阿姆斯特丹、鹿特丹、海牙、乌特勒支四大城市及周边）一般每晚都运行，但在其他地区通常只有周末才有。在阿姆斯特丹史基浦机场和埃因霍温机场中间也通常有夜间列车。

※ 火车站

荷兰大约有400个火车站。有像哈乐姆这样充满历史气息的车站、像莎士迪克这样的小车站，还有像阿姆斯特丹和乌得勒支这样的大型车站。车站设施各不相同，但每一个车站都会有NS售票机可供购票。较大的车站还有服务台和问询处，可以回答任何旅行问题并提供建议。服务台也出售车票。更大的车站还有一系列的食品店，以及商店可购买鲜花、书籍、香水，还有服装店。所以，在换乘的时候去火车站商店逛逛也是不错的。不过话说回来，荷兰火车的换乘时间都不会太长，除非你要等晚几班的火车。

荷兰的火车站数量约有400个，通往全国任何一个小城，其车站功能性也非常强。图为小城哈乐姆火车站。

154

4. 荷兰和其他申根国家
The Netherlands and Other Schengen Countries

The Netherlands is a small country. It is part of the Benelux, European union, and the Schengen area. This means that if you have ample of time at your disposal you could opt to travel a bit around in Europe. You can have a try especially if you have a Schengen visa. This visa will allow you to travel to all the countries who have signed the Schengen agreement. The complete list of countries in the Schengen area is as followed (by the end of 2017): Belgium, Denmark (excluding the Faroe Isles and Greenland), Germany (excluding Heligoland), Estonia, Finland, France (excluding French Guiana, Guadeloupe, Martinique, Mayotte and La Reunion), Greece, Hungary, Italy, Latvia, Liechtenstein, Lithuania, Luxembourg, Malta, the Netherlands, Norway (excluding Spitsbergen), Austria, Poland, Portugal (including the Azores and Madeira), Slovenia, Slovakia, Spain (including the Balearic Islands and the Canary Islands), Czech Republic, Iceland, Sweden, Switzerland.

As said, if you have a Schengen visa or a Schengen residence permit, you can travel to other Schengen countries without another visa. Do be aware that although one is eligible to travel within the whole Schengen area being that the visa Schengen bureaucracy is the same in every Schengen country, however, there are some predetermined rules and regulations concerning at which embassy or consulate the applicant most apply in order to get a Schengen visa and be able travel hassle free to their desired Schengen destination.

- In cases where the applicant will be travelling to one and only one Schengen country, the applicant has to apply at the appropriate embassy/consulate of the certain country.

- If the applicant is planning to visit two or more Schengen countries, it is highly recommended to be applying for the visa in the embassy/consulate of the country you will be residing in for most of the travelling days, referred to as the main destination.

- In case there is no main destination but just a random visit to several Schengen countries, the applicant has to apply for the visa in the embassy/consulate on the first Schengen country he/she will enter according to the itinerary.

Failing to do so can result into a rejection of entry at the border, Dutch customs can be very strict in this.

The Netherlands is a very important destination and transit hub Europe. Traveling from the Netherlands to other Schengen countries is very convenient and fast, you can take the train, enjoy the beautiful scenery along the way, but you can also take the plane, fast and affordable.

※ Air travel

Amsterdam Airport Schiphol is Europe's fourth largest airport, behind London's Heathrow Airport, Paris-Charles de Gaulle Airport and Frankfurt International Airport. From Schiphol Airport you can fly to over 170 destinations, if your next destination is not a country in the Schengen area you still have 130 destinations to choose from.

Many people abroad are familiar with Schiphol airport, but besides this Schiphol the Netherlands has three other main airports: Eindhoven Airport, Rotterdam The Hague Airport and Groningen Airport, located respectively in the southern, central and the northern parts of the Netherlands. Flights from these airports include the popular destinations in the Schengen area, such as London, Paris, Barcelona, Rome, Prague, Vienna and many more.

When travelling through a Schengen airport, flights are separated into Schengen and non-Schengen flights, similar to domestic and international flights elsewhere. This means if your flight originates from a non-Schengen country but are connecting via a Schengen airport to another Schengen country (or vice-versa), you must clear passport control at the first (or last) airport you travel through within the Schengen area.

If you are a non-EU/EFTA national (even if you are visa-exempt, unless you are Andorran, Monégasque or San Marinese), make sure that your passport is clearly stamped both when you enter and leave the Schengen Area with all the pertinent dates visible. Without an entry stamp, you may be treated as an overstayer when you try to leave the Schengen area; without an exit stamp, you may be refused entry the next time you seek to enter the Schengen area as you may be deemed to have overstayed on your previous visit too. For those who need another visa in the future, the application may be refused or the processing of your application may experience further prolonged processing. If you cannot obtain a passport stamp or the ink is not too visible, make sure that you retain documents such as boarding passes, stamps of passports from other countries, transport tickets, financial documents, attendance records at work/school, which may help to convince border inspection staff that you have stayed in the Schengen area legally.

※ Train travel through Europe

In the Schengen countries, traveling by train to surrounding countries is a very comfortable and enjoyable thing. Trains maybe are not as quick as planes, but traveling by train in Europe is also an interesting thing. You can travel freely from country to country, experiencing every city along the way, and Europe has its fair share of cities and places that are worth while visiting.

A popular destination is Paris, starting from Amsterdam you will be traveling via Rotterdam, Antwerp, Brussels to the terminal is Paris-Nord. The whole journey will take only a little over three hours.

The routes from Amsterdam to Berlin and Frankfurt are also very popular, it takes about 4 and 6 hours respectively. From Frankfurt you can easily travel to Munich, Vienna and Zurich, as well as Bern.

If you have obtained a visa for the UK then you can also travel to London by train, you will need to transfer in Brussels, but the train from Brussels who passes through the channel tunnel under the English Channel (yes you are traveling under the bottom of the sea) will bring you to the Centre of London, helping you to avoid a lot of airport hassle.

If you choose to take a multi-country tour by train, you can buy a Eurail Pass from Eurail. com. This is the official online sales channel for Eurail Passes, based in the Netherlands. They have offices operating from the USA, Ireland and Singapore.

Eurail Passes includes a variety of packages such as Global Pass or an One Country Pass, you can choose according to your own requirements, for example you can select two or three countries and then choose the number of days you want to travel. There are passes for seven days of travel within a month, or 15 consecutive days. Eurail.com also regularly offers discounted tickets, and the site offers multilingual services, including Chinese. For more information please check their official website: https://www.eurail.com/cn.

荷兰是一个小国，它是比荷卢经济联盟的一员，同时也是欧盟和申根地区的一部分，这意味着如果你时间充裕，可以选择在欧洲境内旅行，尤其是你有申根签证的情况下更应该一试。凭申根签证可前往所有签署申根协议的国家。申根地区国家的完整名单如下（截至2017年年底）：比利时、丹麦（不包括法罗群岛和格陵兰岛）、德国（赫尔戈兰岛除外）、爱沙尼亚、芬兰、法国（不包括法属圭亚那、瓜德罗普、马提尼克、马约特和留尼汪）、希腊、匈牙利、意大利、拉脱维亚、列支敦士登、立陶宛、卢森堡、马耳他、荷兰、挪威（不包括斯匹次卑尔根）、奥地利、波兰、葡萄牙（包括亚速尔群岛和马德拉群岛）、斯洛文尼亚、斯洛伐克、西班牙（包括巴利阿里群岛和加那利群岛）、捷克共和国、冰岛、瑞典、瑞士。

如上所述，如果你持有申根签证或申根居留许可，你可以在没有其他签证的情况下前往其他申根国家。请注意，虽然申根国家的申根签证机构在每个申根国家都是一样的，凭此签证也可以在整个申根地区畅通无阻，但是有一些确定的规则和法规需要明确，这关系到你需要在具体哪个国家的大使馆或者领事馆申请申根签证，才可以轻轻松松地前往你渴望的申根目的地。

如果申请人将前往一个或只有一个申根国家，申请人必须在相关国家的大使馆/领事馆申请；

如果申请人计划访问两个或两个以上的申根国家，强烈建议在你旅程中停留时间最多的国家或

主要停留目的地国家的大使馆/领事馆申请签证;

如果没有主要的目的地,只是在几个申根国家随意旅行,申请人必须在行程当中的第一个申根国家的大使馆/领事馆申请签证;

如果不遵循申根签证规定,可能会遇到在边境被拒绝入境的情况,荷兰海关在这方面非常严格。

荷兰是欧洲非常重要的目的地和中转枢纽。从荷兰到其他申根国家旅游非常方便快捷,你可以乘坐火车,沿途的美丽景色尽收眼底,但你也可以乘坐飞机,快捷且实惠。

※ 飞机旅行

阿姆斯特丹史基浦机场是欧洲第四大机场,仅次于伦敦希思罗机场、巴黎戴高乐机场和法兰克福国际机场。从史基浦机场出发,可以飞抵全球170多个目的地,如果你的下一个目的地不是在申根地区的国家,那还有130个目的地可供选择。

许多外国人对史基浦机场很熟悉,但是除了史基浦机场之外,荷兰还有另外三个主要的机场:埃因霍温机场、鹿特丹海牙机场和格罗宁根机场,分别位于荷兰南部、中部和北部。从这些机场飞出的航班前往包括伦敦、巴黎、巴塞罗那、罗马、布拉格、维也纳等众多的申根区。

在旅程中,申根机场航班被分为申根和非申根航班,类似于其他地方的国内和国际航班。这意味着,如果你的航班来自一个非申根国家,而需要通过申根机场前往另一个申根国家(反之亦然),你必须在申根地区的第一个(或最后一个)机场办理护照通关手续。

如果你持非欧盟/EFTA国家护照(即使你是免签证的,除非你有安道尔、摩纳哥或圣马力诺护照),请一定要确保你的护照在你进入和离开申根区时都明确地盖过章,并且所有相关的日期都清晰可见。如果没有入境印章,当你试图离开申根区时可能会被当作逾期停留。如果没有出境印章,在下一次进入申根区时可能会被拒绝入境,因为你会被认为之前的停留超出签证允许的范围。对于那些在未来需要另外签证的人来说,申请可能会被拒绝,或者处理申请的时间会加长。如果你没能盖取印戳或印戳墨渍不清晰,请确保保存好如登机牌、在其他国家加盖的护照印章、交通票据、财务文件、在工作/学校的出勤记录等有效证明文件,这可能有助于你说服边境检查人员你在申根地区的合法停留。

※ 在欧洲乘火车旅行

在申根国家,乘火车到周边国家旅行是一件非常惬意和愉悦的事情。火车可能不像飞机那么快,但乘火车在欧洲穿行却别有乐趣。你可以自由地从一个国家穿行到另一个国家,体验沿途的每一个城市,欧洲有相当一部分城市和地区都值得专程前往。

一个很受欢迎的目的地便是巴黎,从阿姆斯特丹出发,途经鹿特丹、安特卫普、布鲁塞尔到终点站巴黎北站。整个旅程只需要3个小时多一点儿。

从阿姆斯特丹出发，途经鹿特丹、安特卫普、布鲁塞尔，到巴黎的线路是热门线路，沿途都是名城。图为刚抵达安特卫普中央车站的旅客。

从阿姆斯特丹到柏林和法兰克福的路线也很受欢迎，分别需要4个小时和6个小时即可到达。再从法兰克福，轻轻松松地就能到慕尼黑、维也纳和苏黎世，还有伯尔尼。

如果你有英国签证，那么你也可以乘火车去伦敦旅行，需要在布鲁塞尔转车（从鹿特丹的直达伦敦的列车已经提上日程），但是火车从布鲁塞尔出发穿过英吉利海峡下面的海底隧道（没错，这部分的旅程位于海底）便直接把你带到伦敦市中心了，帮你避免了很多乘坐飞机带来的旅途烦恼。

如果你选择乘火车去多国旅行，你可以从Eurail购买一张欧洲铁路通票。这是欧铁通票的官方在线销售渠道，总部设在荷兰。他们在美国、爱尔兰和新加坡均设有办事处。

欧铁通票有全球通票或单国通票等各种票务组合方式，你可以根据自己的要求选择，例如你可以选择两个或三个国家，然后选择你想要旅行的天数。比方说在一个月内任意的7天行程，或连续15天的行程。Eurail也定期提供折扣票，网站还提供多种语言服务，包括中文。有关的更多信息请查询他们的官方网站：https://www.eurail.com/cn。

Tijd voor Nederlands 荷兰语时间

● 单词+短语

荷 trein	荷 kaartje/vervoersbewijs	荷 klas
英 train	英 ticket	英 class
译 火车	译 车票	译 舱位
荷 spoor	荷 retourtje	荷 instappen/uitstappen/ overstappen
英 platform	英 return	英 get in/get out/transfer
译 站台	译 往返	译 上车/下车/转车

续表

荷 wanneer/wat/waar/welk/wie/hoe 英 when/what/where/which/who/how 译 什么时候/什么/哪里/哪个/谁/怎样	荷 aankomen 英 arrive 译 到达	荷 vertrekken 英 depart 译 出发
荷 richting 英 direction 译 方向	荷 vertraging 英 delay 译 延迟	荷 volgend 英 next 译 下一（个）

● 例句

荷 Mag ik een retourtje naar Amsterdam? 英 May I have a return ticket to Amsterdam? 译 能给我一张去阿姆斯特丹的往返票吗？	荷 Kan ik alleen in de tweede klas zitten met mijn kaartje? 英 Can I only sit in second class with my ticket? 译 我的车票是只能坐在二等座吗？
荷 Gaat deze trein naar Amsterdam? 英 Will this train go to Amsterdam? 译 这辆火车是去阿姆斯特丹的吗？	荷 De trein richting Rotterdam vertrekt vanaf spoor 4. 英 The train to Rotterdam departs from Platform 4. 译 去往鹿特丹方向的火车从4号站台出发。
荷 De trein komt eraan. U kunt hier instappen en uitstappen in Den Haag. 英 The train is coming. You could get in here and get off in The Hague. 译 火车来了，你可以在这里上车，然后在海牙下车。	荷 De trein naar de luchthaven heeft vertraging. 英 The train to the airport is delayed. 译 去机场的火车延迟了。
荷 Deze trein gaat niet naar de luchthaven, u moet in Leiden overstappen. 英 This train will not go to the airport, you have to transfer in Leiden. 译 这列车不去机场，你必须在莱顿转车。	荷 Wanneer gaat de volgende trein naar Berlijn? 英 When will the next train go to Berlin? 译 下一趟去柏林的车是什么时候？

第六章
Chapter 6

城市和景点
Cities and Sights

*V*isitors to the Netherlands flock to Amsterdam, home to some of the world's densest art collections and a splendid nightlife, and not to forget, many great places to go sightseeing. Amsterdam's cityscape is absolutely unique.

However unique the city is, it cannot represent the whole country. The development of the Netherlands is balanced, but there are significant differences between different areas, which leaves a lot to discover for you as a tourist. The Hague and Rotterdam are also some big cities, which don't deserve to be neglected. This chapter will introduce some other interesting cities and regions that are most definitely worth a visit if you are willing to look beyond a tourist's view of the Netherlands.

来荷兰的游客大多涌向了阿姆斯特丹，这里拥有世界上密度最高的艺术收藏馆以及让人眼花缭乱的灯红酒绿，阿姆斯特丹的城市景致也绝对是独一无二的，还有一些标签也唯独在这里可以被寻见。

但这座城市可不能完全代表荷兰。荷兰发展均衡，但旅游业的发展差异显著，海牙和鹿特丹等依旧是大城市，值得被纷至沓来。这一章就会介绍其他的城市和地区，如果不只是走马观花，想越过游客的视野看荷兰，这些地方绝对值得一游。

1. 行政区域和主要城市
Administrative Division and Important Cities

The twelve administrative regions that make up the Netherlands are called provinces, each is under a Governor, who is called in Dutch Commissaris van de Koningin (Commissioner of the Queen), with the exception for the province Limburg where the commissioner is called Gouverneur (Governor).

These provinces are divided into municipalities (gemeenten), 388 in total (as of 2017). Besides being divided into provinces and municipalities the country is also subdivided in water districts, which are governed by a water board (waterschap or hoogheemraadschap), each having authority in matters concerning water management. As of 2017 there are 22 of these water districts. The water boards have developed over the long history of the struggle against the water in the Netherlands and actually pre-dates that of the nation itself, the first appearing in 1196. The Dutch water boards are among the oldest democratic entities in the world still in existence.

※ North Holland

The province of North Holland is part of the Dutch mainland but also consists of the islands of Texel and Noorderhaaks, which are themselves part of the Frisian archipelago. The green landscape of North Holland is flat, dotted with patches of blue water which are often torn by the strong winds coming from the North Sea. Amsterdam being the capital of the country is the biggest town of the North Holland province, but although it is the capital of the country it is not at the same time the provincial capital, which is Haarlem. Several old towns as Hoorn, Edam, Alkmaar, Naarden and traditional villages as Monnickendam, Marken, Volendam, and Zaanse Schaans are well worth a visit.

※ Friesland

The province of Friesland is part of the Dutch mainland but also includes additionally the West Frisian Islands, called "Waddeneilanden" in Dutch. Leeuwarden is the capital of the province. Friesland is a region where people speak the official recognised Frisian language and many old traditions and traditional ways of life are preserved. Beautifully preserved nature is been cut by canals indicating human activity. Friesland is home to the famous 'Elfstedentocht' or the Eleven Cities Tour it is the world's longest skating competition, and its course winds 200km along frozen lakes, rivers and canals and past eleven historic Frisian towns.

※ Groningen

This northern province is also part of the Dutch mainland and includes a few small islands in the Frisian archipelago (Rottumerplaat, Rottumeroog, Zuiderstrand, and Simonszand) with the big city Groningen as its capital. The contrasts between the modern way of life and Dutch traditional life are nowhere more visible in the country than in the province of Groningen province. Groningen harbours several natural parks and areas for water sports.

※ Drenthe

Drenthe is an agricultural province, and in the Middle Ages it was a free republic of farmers. Today it also harbours its fair share of impressive forests and many of them are protected as natural parks. The capital of Drenthe is Assen. In Drenthe you'll find a region where there are fifty-two mysterious Neolithic monuments called ´hunebedden´ (dolmens) which can be visited, these hunebedden are even older than Stonehenge or the Egyptian pyramids.

※ Overijssel

Overijssel is another province and lies to the south of Drenthe. The provincial capital is Zwolle. The province grew very rich in the Middle Ages and as a result of this Overijssel has quite a lot interesting historical monuments which can be seen to this day. Many of them can be found in the old city of Kampen located at the IJssel river, which gave the province its name as the name Overijssel translates to "on the other bank of the IJssel". A small village well known all over the world and especially in China is Giethoorn. It is a quintessence of the Dutch rural life. It was established in 1230 and built at the side of a lake called Giethoorn, it can be visited by boat and is one of several tourist attractions in Overijssel.

※ Flevoland

A new province only created in 1986, when the southern and eastern Flevopolders were merged into one province. Almost all of the land belonging to the province was reclaimed from the Zuiderzee, later called IJsselmeer. Flevoland was named after Lacus Flevo, a name recorded in Roman sources and indicated a large inland lake which later-formed the Zuiderzee, an inland sea that the crafty Dutch turned into a lake again, which is now called IJsselmeer. Flevoland is a very flat, agricultural region of the Netherlands.

※ Utrecht

With the old city of Utrecht as its capital the province Utrecht is the central mainland province of the Netherlands. It is densely populated and forms since thousands of years a vibrant commercial active centre of the Netherlands, the province of Utrecht has many interesting historical monuments, old castles and several nature reserve parks, which attracts a lot of visitors all year round.

※ South Holland

The province of South Holland was created in 1840, at this time constitutional amendments were introduced and it was decided to split the province Holland into two provinces called "South Holland" and "North Holland". It includes a mainland part and the islands of Goeree-Overflakkee, Voorne-Putten, Beijerland-Hoekse Waard, IJsselmonde. The provincial capital is The Hague (Dutch: Den Haag) which is also the seat of the Dutch parliament and government, the city has been an important center of the Dutch political life since the Middle Ages. Several interesting old cities as Delft, Leiden, Gouda, and good sea resorts with sandy beaches with Scheveningen as the best known surround the city.

※ Gelderland

The east central mainland province, south of Overijssel, the province of Gelderland is the least populated and the biggest of the Dutch regions. Gelderland has several big national parks as well as some industrial areas. Its capital Arnhem is known for the World War II battle with Nazi Germany. An interesting modern art museum-The Kröller-Müller Museum which was built in the forest near Otterloo, draws thousands of cycling visitors every year.

165

※ Zeeland

Zeeland takes its name from the sea (in English: Sea land) and nowhere in the Netherlands the water makes its presence felt as in this province. Zeeland includes a mainland part and the islands of Schouwen Duiveland, Tholen, Noord-Beveland and Sint Philipsland and centuries of keeping the sea at bay has had a great impact on the local traditions, ways of life and even the language. Its capital Middelburg is a lovely laid back city which has witnessed many wars throughout its history but till today most of its important monuments are still there for us to admire.

※ North Brabant

The southern province of North Brabant is busy with activities, crowded with traffic and businesses, but it is also an interesting place for a visit. Its capital 's-Hertogenbosch (or shorter Den Bosch) is an old town with an interesting city centre, it contains several historical monuments within its borders. Another big city Eindhoven is an important industrial centre with factories of Philips (electronics) and DAF (trucks). Several smaller towns are worthy a visit, because of their interesting old architecture.

※ Limburg

Limburg is a province in the southeast of the Netherlands, the province borders Germany and Belgium. Its capital Maastricht is a nice city, known recently for the European Treaty signed there. Limburg is one of the most interesting regions to visit. It has a varied landscape, with woods, a big river—Maas, beautiful natural parks, and very special in the Netherlands, it has a region of hills or Heuvelland as they call it in Dutch. There are several interesting small towns, castles, good museums not to mention some small wineries.

※ Overseas territories of the Netherlands

Tropical islands Aruba and Netherlands Antilles are overseas dependencies (Dutch: landen en gebiedsdelen overzee) of the Netherlands, nominally the same as that of the provinces. Today, an attractive destination of people escaping to the sun from Europe and from the United States.

荷兰由12个行政区域组成，每个行政区称为省，省长在荷兰语里被称为"女王的专员"，对每一个省进行管理，但有一个例外，林堡省的专员被称为"总督"。

这些省份又被划分为"基础政权或市镇"，截至2017年，市镇的数量为388个。除了划分为省和市镇之外，荷兰还有水域的划分，这些地区由水利委员会（Waterschap或Hoogheemraadschap）管理，在水资源管理方面各有权威。到2017年，一共拥有水域22个。这些水域是在荷兰与水不断斗争的漫长历史中发展形成的，实际上比国家本身的形成还要早，第一次出现在1196年。荷兰水利委员会是世界上现存最古老的民主实体之一。

※ 北荷兰

北荷兰省就是阿姆斯特丹所在的地区，这是游客相对到访较多的地区，有很多古城小镇美丽非凡。图为雨后的小城霍恩市中心广场。

北荷兰省是荷兰本土的一部分，但也包括了德塞尔岛和诺德哈克斯岛，这些岛屿本身就是弗里西亚群岛的一部分。北荷兰绿色的景观一马平川，点缀着被北海凛冽的强风撕扯着的一片片蓝汪汪的水域。阿姆斯特丹是该国的首都，是北荷兰省最大的城镇，然而它是这个国家的首都，却并非为本省的省会，北荷兰的省会是哈勒姆。北荷兰省有几个古老的城镇，如霍恩、艾登、阿尔克马尔、纳尔登和一些传统村落，如蒙尼肯丹、马尔肯、沃伦丹和桑斯安斯，都是值得一游的地方。

※ 弗里斯兰

弗里斯兰省也是荷兰本土的一部分，另外还包括荷兰的西弗里斯兰群岛，荷兰语里称为"瓦德尼兰"，吕伐登是这个省的首府。弗里斯兰省是一个官方所认可的弗里斯兰语地区，许多古老的传统和传统的生活方式在这里被传承和保存了下来。标示着人类活动的运河在受到保护的美丽自然景观里横穿而过。弗里斯兰是著名的"Elfstedentocht"或"十一城之旅"的所在地，它是世界上最长的滑冰比赛场所，沿着冰冻的湖泊、河流、运河和11个历史悠久的弗里西亚城镇蜿蜒200公里。

※ 格罗宁根

这个北部省份也是荷兰本土的一部分，包括弗里斯兰群岛（Rottumerplaat、Rottumeroog、Zuiderstrand和Simonszand）的几个小岛，其中的大城市格罗宁根是省会所在地。没有一个地方能比格罗宁根更能体现出现代生活方式与荷兰传统生活之间的巨大差异了。格罗宁根有几个天然公园和水上运动区。

※ 德伦特

德伦特是一个农业省，在中世纪，它是一个自由的农民共和国。如今，德伦特拥有令人印象深刻的森林区，多片森林区被保护为天然公园。德伦特的省会是阿森。在德伦特你会发现一个新石器时代的遗迹——巨石群，石群由52块石头组成，其年代甚至比巨石阵和埃及金字塔还古老，可以前往参观。

167

※ 上艾瑟尔

上艾瑟尔是位于德伦特省南边的另一个省，省会是兹沃勒。在中世纪，上艾瑟尔省非常富有，因此，直到今天在这里仍然可以见到很多有趣的历史遗迹。在艾瑟尔河岸的古老城市坎彭可以见到这些遗迹，这也是上艾瑟尔省名字的起源，意思是艾瑟尔河的另一岸边。另有一个世界闻名的小村庄，尤其是在中国更是人尽皆知，那便是羊角村。这是荷兰乡村生活的精髓。羊角村建于1230年，建在一个叫做Giethoorn的湖的一侧，可以乘船游览，是上艾瑟尔的几个旅游景点之一。

※ 弗里福兰

这是一个成立于1986年的新的省份，当时南部和东部的弗莱福圩田合并成一个省。这个省几乎所有的土地均是从南海争取来的，后者后来被称为艾瑟尔湖。弗里福兰的名字来源于Lacus Flevo，这是一个罗马人名，意思是指"一个巨大的内陆湖"，后来这里形成了南海，一个内陆海，荷兰人又把它改造成了湖泊，这个湖便是现在所称的"艾瑟尔湖"。弗里福兰是荷兰一个非常广阔平坦的农业地区。

※ 乌特勒支

乌特勒支省是荷兰的中部省份，它的省会是乌特勒支。乌特勒支人口稠密，几千年来一直是荷兰活跃的商业中心，乌特勒支省有许多有趣的历史古迹，古老的城堡和一些自然保护区公园，每年吸引了大量的游客。

※ 南荷兰

南荷兰省形成于1840年，当时宪法修正案被引进，并决定将荷兰省划分成两个省，称为"南荷兰"和"北荷兰"。南荷兰省包括了大陆地区，以及Goeree-Overflakkee、Voorne-Putten、Beijerland-Hoekse Waard、Ijsselmonde几个岛屿。省会城市是海牙（荷兰语：Den Haag，英语：The Hague），这也是荷兰议会和政府的所在地，自中世纪以来，这座城市一直是荷兰政治生活的重要中心。环绕着海牙还有几个有趣的古老城市，有代尔夫特、莱顿、豪达，以及著名的海滩度假胜地席凡宁根。

※ 海尔德兰

海尔德兰是荷兰本土东部靠中间的省份，在上艾瑟尔省的南部，是人口最少、面积最大的省份。海尔德兰有几个大型的国家公园和一些工业区。它的省会是阿纳姆，一个因"二战"期间与纳粹德国战争而闻名的城市。一个有趣的现代艺术博物馆——在奥特洛附近的森林里建造的克勒勒-米勒博物馆，每年吸引了成千上万的自行车游客前往参观。

※ 泽兰

泽兰的名字来自于海，在荷兰，没有任何地方可以像在这里这样让人深切地感受到水的存在。泽兰省包括了一部分大陆地区，和Schouwen Duiveland、Tholen、Noord-Beveland和Sint Philipsland几个岛屿，几个世纪以来为维持海洋的平静持续做着斗争，已经对当地的传统、生活方式乃至语言都产生了巨大的影响。它的省会米德尔堡是一个美丽的城市，见证了许多战争的历史，直到今天，大部分重要的纪念碑仍然矗立在那里供人们瞻仰。

※ 北布拉班特

南部的北布拉班特是一个繁忙、充满活力、交通拥挤和商业繁荣的省份，同时也是一个有趣的游览地。它的省会斯海尔托亨博斯（'s- Hertogenbosch或Den Bosch）是一个有着一个有趣的市中心的古老城市，市内有几处历史遗迹。另一个大城市是埃因霍温，是一个重要的工业中心，拥有飞利浦电子和DAF卡车工厂。有几个较小的城镇，建筑古老而有趣，值得参观。

※ 林堡

林堡是荷兰东南部的一个省，与德国和比利时接壤。它的省会马斯特里赫特是一个美丽的城市，以近代在此签署的一系列欧洲条约而为人所知。林堡是最有趣的参观游览地区之一。它有着多样的自然景观，有树林、有大河——马斯河、有美丽的自然公园和荷兰极为特别的一处丘陵地带，在荷兰语里称为Heuvelland，意为山地。那里还有几个有趣的小镇、城堡和有趣的博物馆，当然还有一些小酒厂。

※ 荷兰海外领地

热带岛屿阿鲁巴和荷属安的列斯群岛是荷兰的海外属地，在名义上与各省份相同。现今它们是欧洲和美国人趋之若鹜的阳光度假胜地，备受青睐。

2. 阿姆斯特丹
Amsterdam

With 175 nationalities Amsterdam is truly the most multicultural city in the world. It is a crazy, colourful and inclusive city. Its appeal lies in the fact that it is a metropolis but yet at the same time it doesn't seem bigger than a big village, full of little wonders to explore.

From its humble beginnings as a 13th-century fishing village on a river bed next to the Amstel river to its current role as a major hub for business, tourism and culture, Amsterdam has long had and still has a strong tradition as a centre of culture and commerce.

With 100 kilo metres of canals and nearly 7,000 buildings dating from the 18th century or earlier, Amsterdam is one of Europe's best preserved cities. Rembrandt would not have any difficulty finding its way back home in the Amsterdam of today.

The ancient canals and charming buildings are not the only ones in Amsterdam. From the top of the art hall to the red light district near the canals, Amsterdam is an ambivalent but harmonious city.

Amsterdam is surrounded by many clichés, the red light district, its openness to alternative life styles and condoning that what in other countries and cities would not be condoned. We would advise you to leave these labels behind you and explore the city in your own pace, there is certainly something that will appeal to you, in the dictionary of Amsterdam you will definitely not find the word "impossible".

阿姆斯特丹这里生活着175个民族，是世界上最多元化的城市。这是一个疯狂、多彩、包容的城市。它的魅力在于它是一个大都市，但同时它似乎并不比大村庄更大，一个充满了小奇观的地方。

从13世纪在阿姆斯特尔河旁边的河床上兴起的渔村开始，到现在作为商业、旅游和文化的主要枢纽，阿姆斯特丹作为一个文化和贸易的中心已经并且仍然拥有强大的传统。

阿姆斯特丹拥有100公里的运河和近7 000座建造于18世纪或者更早的建筑，是欧洲保存最完好的城市之一，如果伦勃朗还建在，即使生活在今天也会轻而易举的找到回家的旧街巷。

古老的运河和迷人的建筑并不是阿姆斯特丹的唯一。从顶级的艺术到散落在运河附近的红灯区，阿姆斯特丹充满矛盾，却又无比和谐。

阿姆斯特丹周围是许多陈词滥调、红灯区，以及在其他国家和城市将不被容忍的开放、另类的生活方式，我们建议你抛开这些刻板印象，用自己的步履探索这座城市，会有很多东西将你深深吸引，在阿姆斯特丹的字典里，就没有"不可能"这个词！

Sights and Landmarks 景点和地标性建筑

※ Dam Square

Dam Square lies in the historical centre of Amsterdam, approximately 750 meters south of its main transportation hub "Centraal Station". The square is located at the original location of a dam in the river Amstel, therefor the name Amsterdam, or dam in the river Amstel. It is roughly

169

rectangular in shape, stretching about 200 meters from west to east and about 100 meters from north to south.

On the west end of the square is the neoclassical Royal Palace, which served as the city hall from 1655 until its conversion to a royal residence in 1808. Beside it are the 15th-century Gothic Nieuwe Kerk (New Church) and the Madame Tussaud's Wax Museum. The National Monument, a white stone pillar designed by J.J.P. Oud (Jacobus Johannes Pieter Oud) and erected in 1956 to memorialise the victims of World War II, dominates the opposite side of the square. Also overlooking the plaza are the NH Grand Hotel Krasnapolsky and the upscale department store De Bijenkorf.

Like many famous squares in the world, several times a year the square is the site of a funfair. From time to time there are other events as well, such as concerts, sports events or a used-book market. At the dam square, you can do nothing, of course, you can also do a lot of things if you would like, you can watch people come and go, just like in the rest of Amsterdam the whole world passing by in front of your eyes. Stand still in the middle of the square or find a corner for yourself and watch the people come by, so you will find that Amsterdam belongs to everyone.

Sit at that monument, just like the hippies in the late sixties when Amsterdam was their Mecca. They held their love-ins at the Vondelpark, where many also spent the night. The Dam was another popular meeting point, and many hippies slept there overnight—the so-called "Damslapers" (Dam sleepers). A new city ordinance brought an end to this practice in August 1970, this largely due to the nuisance the hippies caused. Over time sitting at the monument became accepted as a reflection of the freedom Amsterdam represents.

※ The Royal Palace Amsterdam

The Royal Palace was built in the seventeenth century as the Town Hall of Amsterdam, after a design by Jacob van Campen. Its paintings and sculptures were made by some of the most distinguished artists of the time and allude to the city's influence and prosperity in the Golden Age of the Netherlands. In 1808 Louis Napoleon, the brother of the French Emperor Napoleon Bonaparte, became King of Holland and converted the Town Hall into its Palace. The superb collection of Empire furniture, clocks and chandeliers date from that period and is one of the best preserved in the country.

In 1813, Prince William of Orange, later King William I, returned the palace to the city of Amsterdam but maintained the right to use it as a royal residence and hosting space when in the capital.

Today, the Royal Palace is used for state visits, the Dutch Royal House's New Year receptions and other official functions, including the annual presentations of the Erasmus Prize, the Royal Awards for Painting, the Silver Carnation Awards and the Prince Claus Prize. When not in use by the King or members of the Royal House, the palace is open to the public and features exhibitions through out the year.

※ Red Light District Amsterdam

Amsterdam's infamous Red Light District is a carnival of vice, but is will not be to everyone's taste.

If you choose to satisfy your curiosity with a wander around the area, keep your wits about you and watch out for pickpockets. Most importantly, remember that there's more to the Red Light

District than its salaciousness and much more to this multifaceted city than the Red Light District.

The Red Light District-a warren of medieval alleyways making up the inner-city area locally known as De Wallen—is just southeast of Centraal Station, on and around the parallel neon-lit canals Oudezijds Voorburgwal and Oudezijds Achterburgwal; Warmoesstraat is home to the district's main gay clubs.

- **Amsterdam Red Light District history**

A major trading harbour since the Middle Ages made Amsterdam a magnet for the "world's oldest profession". As early as the 1300s, women carrying red lanterns (due to their flattering light) met sailors near the port, and bars.

Since 2007, city officials have taken measures to clean up the district by reducing the number of red-light windows in an effort to eliminate pimps, human traffickers and money launderers (all of which are illegal). Project 1012, named for the area's postal code, encourages fashion studios, art galleries, cafés and other creative enterprises to set up here.

- **Choose the right time to experience the real Amsterdam**

Well, if curiosity does get the better of you, come down at night when the district really comes to life. During the day, the district is less lively and even less attractive as the more sordid aspects reveal themselves in natural daylight. Although there are women forever tapping on the windows even during the light hours, most of the action takes place around 11pm, when the district is swarming with crowds and the red neon lights illuminate the inky canals. The atmosphere pretty much thrives until around 2 or 3am when the crowds die down and businesses shut up shop.

171

※ Centraal Station

The building that houses Amsterdam's Central Station was built between 1881 and 1889, at the time when several important public buildings in Amsterdam such as the Rijksmuseum (National Museum), Concertgebouw (Amsterdam Philharmonics), Stadsschouwburg (City Theatre), Central Post Office (now a shopping mall Magna Plaza) were constructed. All these fine-looking buildings were built in Neo-Gothic or Neo-Renaissance styles. Central Station was designed by Petrus J.H. Cuypers—one of the biggest Dutch architects, assisted by Adolf L. Gendt, who was also responsible for the structure of the Station's building and its immense platform halls. Cuypers received Golden Medal in 1897 from the Queen for designing the Central Station building.

Amsterdam Central Station is the real heart of the city: central not only by the name, but also as the biggest public transport transfer spot, serving not only visitors to Amsterdam, but also the city inhabitants. Every day 250,000 people go through Amsterdam Central Station.

Final stops of several lines of city trams and buses are here, as well as waterfront stations of the city ferry lines which take cars and passengers to Amsterdam North (Amsterdam Noord).

※ Anne Frank House

One of Amsterdam's most popular museums is the Anne Frank House, often referred to as the Anne Frank Museum.

You will find the museum on the Prinsengracht canal in the centre of Amsterdam. It contains the secret annexe where the young girl Anne Frank and seven others hid from the Nazis during the German occupation of the Netherlands during World War II. It was here that she wrote her world-famous *Diary*.

The Anne Frank house originally opened back on the 3th of May 1960 and has been receiving visitors ever since. The museum underwent a major expansion in 1999, being reopened by her majesty Queen Beatrix, who has since then abdicated in favour of her son.

The museum is divided as follows: the original house (263 Prinsengracht) includes the canal-side part which was her father Otto Frank's office where the family's helpers worked. All the rooms in the house have been preserved to their original style and decor during the hiding period. There are films to watch as well as various objects, photos and documents which help illustrate the hiding and subsequent deportation.

The Secret Annexe at the back of the house is accessed via a concealed entrance through a bookcase. This part of the house contains no furniture-houses of deported Jews were stripped down with items taken away to Germany. You will see Anne's room with photos of movie stars and royalty glued on the wall. There are various salvaged documents and objects on display that belonged to the eight people who hid here.

The next-door building (at 265 Prinsengracht) is the renovated section of the museum-here you will find the Diary Room which shows Anne's original red and green checked diary plus some of her other manuscripts. There is also a temporary exhibition space which changes every 6 months. The museum has a bookshop and small café as well.

● About Anne Frank

Anne Frank was born in Frankfurt, Germany in 1929. She and the rest of the Frank family moved to Amsterdam in 1933. When World War II broke out in 1939, the Netherlands found itself under occupation of Nazi Germany, during the occupation the Jewish population experiencing increasing persecution. In July 1942 the Frank family went into hiding in the concealed rooms (the secret annexe) at Prinsengracht 263-the building where her father Otto Frank worked. It was here where Anne wrote her diary giving the reader a unique and touching perspective of wartime Amsterdam through the eyes of a teenage girl.

After 2 years the family was betrayed and the secret annexe was discovered by the Nazis. In September 1944 Anne and her sister Margot were taken to Auschwitz-Birkenau and then a few weeks later they were relocated to the Bergen-Belsen concentration camp. They died there of typhus in March 1945.

● Anne Frank's Diary

Otto Frank survived the war and returned to Amsterdam. Due to his efforts Anne's diary was being published in Dutch as Het Achterhuis in 1947 and 1950 it was translated into French and German and in 1952 came the first English edition entitled *The Diary of a Young Girl*. It has since been translated into many other languages and the diary has been portrayed in theatre plays and films around the world.

In 1957 the Anne Frank Stichting organisation came into being in order to save the Prinsengracht building which was due for demolition and set up a place where the Anne Frank's story and message could be preserved.

※ Zaanse Schans

In its 18th and 19th century heyday, the Zaan region was a rather important industrial area

hundreds of windmills were dotted around and they produced a whole range of products like linseed oil, paint, snuff, mustard, paper and other products. Till this day many of the Zaanse Schans' characteristic village houses still exist and are now museums, gift shops or workshops while others are still used as private residences. Some of the Zaanse Schans' remaining windmills are also open to the public.

• Windmills

During the 17th century, over 600 windmills were built in the area around the Zaanse Schans, creating the world's first industrial zone. Most of these windmills were used, among others, to make oil, grind spices, produce pigments for paints and of course saw wood. A number of these windmills still exist and often can be visited. You can see how these wind-powered machines work, inside and out.

• Museums

There are various museums you can visit at the Zaanse Schans. There is the Museumwinkel, for example: a grocer's from the past, as they existed before the emergence of large supermarkets. In the Bakkerijmuseum (Bakery Museum), you can discover the old craft of baking, and the Honig Breethuis presents the home of a 19th-century merchant family. The Museum Zaanse Tijd shows a collection of unique clocks, most of which still work. The Zaans Museum has a special collection of utensils, clothing and paintings from the area. You can also visit the Verkade Experience here, where you find yourself in a 20th-century chocolate factory. The original machines there are still at work to produce the very best chocolate and cookies.

※ Amsterdam Canals

173

Amsterdam was founded around 1250 with the building of the Dam that gave it its name. "Aeme Stelle Redamme" is Medieval Dutch for "Dam in a Watery Area". The first canals were dug for water management and defence. During the Middle Ages the city expanded and successive defence moats ended up inside the city walls, which caused them to lose their original function but they ended up acquiring a new and important one: transport of merchandise.

The Dam is still there as the heart of the city. But today this former barrier between the River Amstel and the "Southern Sea" is one of the few places in the centre of town that you cannot sail a boat to. The last part of the river leading to the dam fell victim to land-traffic in 1922. The street that came in its place is still called 'Damrak', which is Dutch for "Last section of the river, leading to the Dam". Today, a subway line is being built in the old riverbed.

• Middle Ages

During the 14th, but especially the 15th century, Amsterdam underwent a rapid development, which laid the foundation for the Golden Age. Only very few medieval buildings survive today. Some examples: the Old and New Churches and the Houten Huis (Wooden House) at the Begijnhof. Warehouses were built along the old defence moats and could store enormous quantities of trading goods that could be pipelined through those moat-canals to a harbour full of ships that sailed all over the known world in those days.

• Golden Age

Trade exploded in the 17th century and became Amsterdam's Golden Age. In one very ambitious expansion project that took 50 years, the 3 main canals of the city were dug and the houses around them were built. Completed around 1660, it made the city grow to 4 times its size and gave it the most intricate and efficient system of navigable waterways in the world. A maze of connecting canals brought merchandise from all over the world to the doorstep of every canal side merchant.

A fleet of thousands of small barges carried the goods from the big ships in the harbour to every corner of the city. More than a thousand warehouses on the canal-sides were supplied by these man-powered barges. On top of that, 9 specialised floating markets catered to the daily needs of 17th century Amsterdammers.

In those days, more goods were moved on barges in the canals by human power, than would even be possible today with trucks along the canal side.

● Amsterdam canals today

Almost half of the original waterways in Amsterdam was lost to landfills, but a full 25 percent of the city's surface still consists of navigable waterways. With 65 miles of ancient canals, Amsterdam is still the most watery city in the world.

Besides providing a stunning backdrop to the city's historical centre, floating down Amsterdam's canals is one of the most memorable ways to discover the city's sights and attractions. Whether you're a first-time or frequent visitor, everything in Amsterdam seems a bit more magical when viewed from a boat.

Most canal cruises take around an hour, in which you'll explore Amsterdam's UNESCO protected canal ring and discover plenty of interesting facts about the city along the way. As well as the excellent one-hour options, other types of canal cruises available include practical hop-on-hop-off services, romantic candle-lit tours, child-friendly adventures and intimate guided boat tours for smaller groups.

※ Damrak

The Damrak is an avenue and was originally a canal which now is lost to landfills. It is at the centre of Amsterdam, running between Amsterdam Central Station in the north and Dam Square in the south. It is the main street where people arriving at the station enter the centre of Amsterdam. When Damrak still formed a part of the Amstel, ships were loaded and unloaded over the entire width of what is now the street. Because of the construction of the Central Station, in the nineteenth century Damrak was filled in. The railway station was to be Amsterdam's new city gateway and Damrak was the logical route to the city centre. Filling in Damrak would create a spacious avenue from the station to the city centre, as in many nineteenth-century European cities. This space was soon reduced, however, due to the construction of Zochers exchange building on the Dam demolished in 1903 and later Berlages Exchange and the Bijenkorf department store on the east side of the street.

※ Nieuwe Kerk

When the Oude Kerk ("Old Church") grew too small for the expanding population of Amsterdam, the bishop of Utrecht in 1408 gave permission to build a second parish church, this would be called Nieuwe Kerk ("New Church"). This new church was to be consecrated to St. Mary and St. Catharine.

The church was damaged by the city fires of 1421 and 1452 and burned down almost entirely in 1645, after which it was rebuilt in Gothic style. It underwent major renovation in 1892–1914, which added many neo-Gothic details, and was again renovated in 1959–1980. The second renovation proved expensive for the Dutch Reformed Church, forcing the church to be closed most of the time in order to save money on maintenance. To keep the church open, ownership was transferred in 1979 to a newly formed cultural foundation called the Nationale Stichting De Nieuwe Kerk.

The church is used for Dutch royal investiture ceremonies (as per Article 32 of the Dutch Constitution) most recently that of King Willem-Alexander in 2013, as well as royal weddings, most recently the wedding of Willem-Alexander to Máxima in 2002. The investitures of the Queens Wilhelmina, Juliana and Beatrix also took place there.

The Nieuwe Kerk is no longer used for church services but is used as an exhibition space and it is also used for organ recitals.

※ Oude Kerk

The Oude Kerk in Amsterdam's Red Light District is the city's oldest building and one of the city's youngest art institutions. In the seven or so centuries since it was founded, the church has evolved into one of the most imposing Gothic ecclesiastical buildings in northern Europe.

Oude Kerk began as a wooden chapel in 1213. The original structure stood in the same place as the present day Oude Kerk stands. A stone church would replace the wooden chapel in 1306 and finally become consecrated that same year. Throughout history, the church has experienced a number of renovations through 15 generations of Amsterdam citizens. The first renovations took place only 50 years after the church was constructed. During this time, the aisles were extended to wrap around the choir area and provide support for the structure. Transepts were added at the turn of the 15th century.

Oude Kerk was originally Roman Catholic, but was taken over by the Calvinist Dutch Reformed Church. During the 16th century, the church was vandalised and looted a number of times. A mob destroyed the church's decorations during the Beeldenstorm of 1566. Among the destroyed fittings was an altarpiece painted by Jan van Scorel and Maarten van Heemskerck.

After the Reformation, the church became a registry of marriages and was also used to house the city archives. Important documents were locked inside of an iron plated chest inside of the church.

Among the church's most famous patrons was Rembrandt and his children. In fact, all of his children were christened here. Among all of the city's buildings, Oude Kerk is the only one that still remains in the same state as it did when Rembrandt walked its halls.

※ Begijnhof

The Begijnhof is an inner courtyard of Amsterdam and a quiet spot away from the city hustle and bustle. Originally a sanctuary for the "Beguines" sisterhood, today its houses are occupied by older single women.

The Beguinage was established somewhere probably in the 14th century to house the Begijnen. These women lived like nuns but were more independent and had more freedom. The Catholic faith was banned in the 16th century. The Begijnhof was the only Catholic institution that continued to exist because the houses were the private property of the women. They did have to give up the chapel. A new, so-called 'hidden church' was later built behind the facades of several residences.

The main feature is the 15th century English Church (Engelse kerk) located at the south side which is one of the oldest buildings in the city. It contains stained glass depictions of the Pilgrim fathers who probably worshiped at the church before leaving for the New World.

In February 2007 a special 400th anniversary church service was held attended by Queen Elizabeth and Queen Beatrix of Netherlands.

Opposite the church there is the smaller Begijnhof chapel where Catholics and Beguines attended in secret up until 1795.

The picturesque courtyard contains a garden area surrounded by traditional houses built from the 16th century onwards. The Wooden House (het Houten Huis) at number 34 is the oldest house in Amsterdam dating from 1420. There are also a number of interesting plaques and statues throughout the court.

The Begijnhof is located in the center of Amsterdam. The easiest way to get there is via Spuiplein. You will see a row of white houses with a brown house in between. This is where you will find the gate that gives onto the Begijnhof.

※ Rembrandtplein

At the centre of Amsterdam is a square called Rembrandtplein. It was built in 1668 from the remnants of a city port, the Rembrandtplein or Botermarkt (butter market) began as a quiet dairy market and the site of occasional local fairs. By the early 20th century as Amsterdam's urban population surged, the market evolved into a popular gathering spot, frequented by artists, labourers and young people.

The Rembrandtplein is named after the famous painter Rembrandt van Rijn who owned a house nearby from 1639 to 1658. This house is nowadays known as The Rembrandt House Museum. The Rembrandt House owns almost the complete and world famous collection of Rembrandt's etchings, and part of this collection is permanently shown in the exhibition gallery. In addition, there are frequent temporary exhibitions showing works of predecessors and contemporaries, and modern and current works of art in the modern wing of the museum. Rembrandt van Rijn is the creator of the famous painting *The Night Watch*. *The Night Watch* is one of the most famous paintings in the world.

※ Vondelpark

The Vondelpark is Amsterdam's most popular park, attracting thousands of tourists, residents and everyone in between every day. It is centrally placed south of Leidseplein and near Rijksmuseum, Stedelijk Museum and Van Gogh Museum, it is the largest city park in Amsterdam, and certainly the most famous park in the Netherlands.

The park was opened to public in 1865 as a horseback riding and strolling park named

Nieuwe Park. The name Vondelpark was adopted in 1867 when a statue of Dutch poet Joost van den Vondel was situated into the park. The committee soon raised money to enlarge the park and by 1877, it reached its current space of 45 hectares. At that time, its site was on the edge of Amsterdam, since then it has become central in the city.

The park that exists now for almost 150 years has many old plane trees, horse chestnut, Dutch red chestnut, catalpas and different sorts of birch trees. Numerous bushes and herbs complete the park's landscape. Vondelpark is also a home to many birds—wild ducks, blue herons and many smaller birds.

Theatre, dance performance and music is played during June, July and August. The open-air theater (Dutch: Open Lucht Theater) takes place in Vondelpark, near the entrance from Eeghenstraat. Admission is free, but some performances are so popular that we advise you to make an on-line reservation via their website.

※ Madame Tussauds Amsterdam

Madame Tousauds Figurines Madame Tussaud was a real person, Anna Maria Grosholtz. Born in Strasbourg, France, she moved to Switzerland, where she served as a housekeeper to a physician in Bern. Making a wax mask of dead person or casting a model of celebrity's hand was at the time one of the few ways of preserving the person's image for future generations and it has been a physician's job. Taught by her master and skilled herself in waxworks, the young woman moved to Paris, married François Tussaud and witnessed the violence of the French Revolution of years 1789-1799. The story goes, that she made hundreds of death masks and head sculptures of executed aristocrats, often pulling more interesting heads from the pile of hundreds decapitated bodies.

Tussaud lived later in London and when she died, her collection counted 400 figures. The first Tussaud's cabinet of wax figures opened in London at Baker Street in 1835. It included the "Chamber of Horrors" showing figures of victims of the French Revolution and famous criminals, already caught and hanged. Seriously damaged by fires of 1921 and 1941, during the Blitz–World War Ⅱ German bombings of London, when many valuable figures at the Tussauds just melted, the collection has been rebuilt and today is owned by British amusement parks operator Merlin Entertainment. Madame Tussauds exhibits exist in several major world cities.

Madame Tussauds Amsterdam Founded in 1970, it was the first Madame Tussauds that was opened in mainland Europe as well as being the first foreign branch of the British institution. The collection of Madame Tussauds Amsterdam consists of a collection of wax figures of famous celebrities in different categories such as the Golden Age of Dutch history, music, sport & movie.

※ Museumplein

Nestled south of Leidseplein is the plush 19th century Museumplein. Unashamedly, Museumplein is the pinnacle of sophistication and home to the three major and most important museums in Amsterdam, the Rijksmuseum, the Stedelijk Museum of Modern Art and the Van Gogh Museum which makes this an art lover's paradise par excellence.

The square was reconstructed in 1999 by the Swedish landscape architect Sven-Ingvar Andersson. It is used for events such as festivals, celebrations, and demonstrations. It includes underground parking spaces and an underground supermarket. In the winter, the pond is being transformed into an artificial ice skating area.

177

※ Leidseplein

Leidseplein is a busy square at the southern end of Amsterdam's central canal ring, almost facing the popular Vondelpark. Leidseplein is translated roughly as Leiden Square, as it sits at the end of Leidsestraat which, throughout much of the history of the square, was the main road to the town of Leiden.

This well-connected area started in the 17th century as a parking place for farmers' horses and carts. Today the area around Leidseplein and the streets nearby, offers you much of Amsterdam's nightlife. You'll find a broad assortment of cuisines to choose from: Argentinian and Greek to Italian and Indonesian. Try the rice table at Puri Mas or visit De Blauwe Hollander for traditional Dutch dishes.

Leidseplein is home to world famous live music venues, such as Paradiso and Melkweg, and intimate dance clubs like Jimmy Woo and Chicago Social Club. Cinemas, discos, theaters and a casino are located right on the square or within easy walking distance. If you want to go clubbing or feel like a nice meal, this is the place to be.

※ Beurs van Berlage

The Beurs van Berlage is the hundred years old former building of the Stock Exchange in Amsterdam and it is an important monument of the modern Dutch architecture. It was built between 1898 and 1903 by the prominent Dutch architect of the 20th century Hendrik Petrus Berlage.

The building is constructed of red brick, with an iron and glass roof and stone piers, lintels and corbels. It broke with the tradition of trying to imitate gothic or renaissance style which many important city buildings in Amsterdam erected at the end of the 19th century (just to name Rijksmuseum, Stedelijk Museum, Central Station, Stadsschouwburg) did, but established its own, new style.

The Beurs van Berlage building is simple. Its main decoration is a big clock placed high on the tower. On the corners of the Beurs stand three sculpture figures, that of Gijsbrecht van Aemstel, a legendary hero but not without controversy, celebrated in literature founder of Amsterdam, Jan Pieterszoon Coen, a hero officer of Dutch East India Company from its beginnings in the 17th century, and Hugo de Groot, a humanist, writer, philosopher and lawyer of international importance.

The Beurs van Berlage has the unique and well preserved interiors. The roof, made of double glass panes gives a lot of natural light inside the building. Several sorts of profiled and glazed bricks, as well as stone, wood and iron were used in a harmonious way.

The Main Hall used originally as a trading floor for commodities strikes with its simplicity but at the same time with the craftsmanship of its decorations.

Beurs van Berlage has been at the time of its construction, in an innovative building, which brought an international recognition to its creator and influenced other architects in the Netherlands, especially from the Amsterdam School movement.

※ Portuguese Synagogue

The Portuguese Jewish community, is the oldest Jewish community in the Netherlands. The community was established in 1639 by Spanish and Portuguese Jews who were forced to leave Antwerp after that city came under Spanish rules. They had previously fled Spain and Portugal to escape the Spanish Inquisition. These Sefardim found a safe haven in the tolerant city of Amsterdam. Until World War II there were Portuguese communities in Den Haag, Naarden, Rotterdam and Middelburg.

In 1665, the Jewish community decided to build a new synagogue. The new synagogue was to be the biggest in the world. Architects Elias Bouwman and Daniel Stalpaert were commissioned to build the synagogue. They started building in 1671 and in 1675 the Portuguese Synagogue was ready. It had cost the community not less than 186,000 florins. Minor restorations have been made but the synagogue still looks pretty much the same as 340 years ago.

The building is free-standing and rests on wooden poles; the foundation vaults can be viewed by boat from the canal water underneath the synagogue. It was the largest synagogue of its time and one of the biggest buildings of Amsterdam. A model of the Temple of Salomon in Jerusalem inspired the architects. The entrance to the main synagogue is off a small courtyard enclosed by low buildings housing the Winter Synagogue, offices and archives, homes of various officials, the rabbinate, a mortuary, and Etz Hayim library, one of the oldest Jewish libraries in the world, that holds valuable collections of Sephardic manuscripts.

179

※ 水坝广场

水坝广场位于阿姆斯特丹的历史中心，南边大约750米就是主要的交通枢纽中央火车站，广场位于阿姆斯特尔河畔一座大坝最初的位置，那里以阿姆斯特丹或阿姆斯特尔河大坝为名。它大致呈长方形，从西向东延伸约200米，从北到南约100米。

广场的西侧是新古典主义风格的皇家宫殿，从1655年起一直作为市政厅，直到1808年被改建为皇家官邸。旁边是15世纪的哥德式新教堂和杜莎夫人蜡像馆。一座建于1956年由Jacobus Johannes Pieter Oud设计的纪念碑用来纪念"二战"中的死难者，在广场的另一侧占据了主导位置。俯瞰广场的还有克拉斯波尔斯基NH大酒店和高档百货公司女王店。

阿姆斯特丹王宫如今用来招待国事到访要员，也可以入内参观。图片右侧即为王宫，左侧建筑为杜莎夫人蜡像馆和P&C百货。

像世界上许多著名的广场一样，水坝广场每年都会举办几次广场游乐活动。有时还会有其他的活动，比如音乐会、体育活动或二手书市场。

在大坝广场，你可以什么都不做，当然，你也可以做很多事情，如果你愿意，哪怕只是看看这世界一角的行色匆匆或悠闲面孔，就像在阿姆斯特丹的其他地方一样，整个世界都在你眼前一晃而过。站在广场中央，或者为自己找个角落，看着来来往往的人，你会发现阿姆斯特丹是属于每一个人的。

20世纪60年代，水坝广场西侧的纪念碑在这里见证了诸多嬉皮士们的爱情，这里也曾是他们集会的场所。

坐在纪念碑前，就像六十年代末的嬉皮士们一样，当时阿姆斯特丹是嬉皮士的圣地。他们会在冯德尔公园邂逅和见证自己的爱情，许多人也在那里度过整个夜晚。水坝便是另一个很受欢迎的集会地点，许多嬉皮士在此过夜——所谓的"大坝睡眠者"。但在1970年8月，一项新的城市条例终结了这种做法，这主要是由于嬉皮士造成的滋扰。随着时间的推移，在纪念碑前就坐成了阿姆斯特丹倡导自由的一种象征。

※ 阿姆斯特丹王宫

王宫建于17世纪，当时是阿姆斯特丹的市政厅，由雅各布·范·坎彭设计。它的绘画和雕塑是由当时最杰出的艺术家们创作的，暗示了这座城市在荷兰黄金时代的影响和繁荣。1808年，法国皇帝拿破仑·波拿巴的兄弟路易斯·拿破仑成为荷兰国王，并将市政厅改造为宫殿。华丽的帝国家具、钟表和枝形吊灯的珍藏便始于那个时期，是全国保存最好的。

1813年，威廉·奥兰治亲王，也就是后来的威廉一世，将宫殿归还给了阿姆斯特丹市，但保留了在首都使用其作为皇室住所和托管空间的权利。

今天，皇家王宫被用来进行国事访问，荷兰皇家学院的新年招待会和其他官方活动，包括一年一度的伊拉斯谟奖、皇家绘画奖、银色康乃馨奖和克劳斯亲王奖的颁奖活动。在国王或王室成员没占用王宫之际，王宫会对公众进行全年开放展览。

※ 阿姆斯特丹红灯区

阿姆斯特丹臭名昭著的红灯区是一场邪恶的狂欢，但这不是每个人的口味。

如果你来此闲逛来满足自己的好奇心，请保持警惕，小心扒手。最重要的是，请记住，红灯区拥有的并非仅是人们所认为的淫秽低俗，阿姆斯特丹这个多元的大熔炉拥有的也并不仅仅是红灯区。

红灯区，错综的中世纪街道和小巷组成的当地人称为德瓦伦的中心城区，位于中央火车站的东南方向，在两条霓虹闪烁的平行运河Oudezijds Voorburgwal和Oudezijds Achterburgwal的周围，Warmoesstraat街是该区同性恋者的主要家园。

● 阿姆斯特丹红灯区历史

中世纪主要的港口贸易促使阿姆斯特丹成为了吸引"世界上最古老的职业"的人们的一块磁铁。早在13世纪，妇女们就打着红灯笼在港口附近和酒吧与水手们相会。

从2007年以来，政府官员已经采取措施，通过减少红灯窗口的数量来清理该地区，以消除皮条客、人贩子和洗钱者（所有这些都是非法的）。以该地区的邮政编码命名的1012项目，鼓励时尚工作室、艺术画廊、咖啡馆和其他创意企业进驻这里。

● 选择合适的时间去体验真正的阿姆斯特丹

好吧，如果好奇心真的能让你得到满足，那就在这个地区真正苏醒之际的晚上过来一趟。白天，这个地区少了些喧闹和吸引力，更多的是暴露在自然日光下的脏乱和卑劣的外表。即使在白天，也会有女性工作者不停地敲打着窗户，但大部分还是在晚上11点左右，届时这里会挤满了人群，红色的霓虹灯照亮了漆黑的运河。喧嚣的气氛直到凌晨2点或3点才开始褪散，人群慢慢消失，商业和交易也相继终止。

※ 中央火车站

阿姆斯特丹中央火车站的建筑建造于1881年至1889年之间，当时阿姆斯特丹的一些其他重要公共建筑，如国立博物馆、皇家音乐厅、城市剧院、中央邮局（现在是麦格纳Magna Plaza购物中心）都已建成了。所有这些漂亮的建筑都是用新哥特式或新文艺复兴风格建造的。阿姆斯特丹中央车站由荷兰最大的建筑师之一佩特鲁斯·库伯斯设计，由阿道夫·L.根特协助，他还负责了车站建筑的结构和巨大的站台大厅的设计。1897年，库伯斯荣获当时荷兰女王所颁发的金奖以表彰设计中央车站做出的贡献。

阿姆斯特丹中央车站是这座城市真正的中心：中心不仅仅体现在名字上，它也是最大的公共交通中转枢纽，不仅服务于阿姆斯特丹的四方游客，同时也为城市居民提供了便捷的服务。每天有25万人要穿梭在阿姆斯特丹中央车站。

市内的几条有轨电车和公共汽车的线路终点站也设在这里，还有城市渡轮线的滨水站，它们将车辆和乘客们输送到阿姆斯特丹北部。

阿姆斯特丹中央车站由佩特鲁斯·库伯斯设计，因此被当时女王表彰。这是荷兰最大的中央车站，阿姆斯特丹的所有交通网络均汇集于此。

181

※ 安妮之家

阿姆斯特丹最受欢迎的博物馆之一是安妮之家，通常被称为安妮·弗兰克博物馆。

你会在阿姆斯特丹市中心的王子运河边发现这家博物馆。博物馆还囊括了一处隐秘建筑物，它是在"二战"德国占领荷兰期间，年轻的女孩安妮·弗兰克和纳粹集中营其他7人的藏身之处。正是在此，安妮·弗兰克写了她举世闻名的《安妮日记》。

安妮之家最初于1960年5月3日开放，此后一直接待游客。博物馆在1999年的时候进行了一次大规模的扩建，由贝娅特丽克丝女王重启开放，她后来退位由长子继任。

博物馆分为以下几个部分：初期的房子（王子运河263号），其中包括运河一侧的部分，这部分是她父亲奥托·弗兰克的办公室，家里的帮手们也在这里协助打点事务。这所房子里的所有房间都保留了安妮等人藏身之时的风格和装饰。还有一些影片可以观看，以及各种各样的物品、照片和文件，这些都有助于还原当时躲藏和之后遭受的驱逐等情景。

房子后面的隐秘空间由书柜的隐蔽入口进入。这部分的房子里没有家具，遭到驱逐的犹太人房子里的物品都被掠夺至德国。你会看到安妮房间的墙上挂着电影明星和皇室成员的照片。这里有各种各样的留存文件和物品，它们都属于曾经藏匿在这里的八个人。

隔壁王子运河265号的建筑是博物馆的翻新部分，在这里有一个日记室，你可以在里面看到安妮的红绿格子的日记，还有一些其他的手稿。这里还有一个每六个月轮换一次的临时展厅，博物馆内还有一个书店和小咖啡馆。

● 关于安妮·弗兰克

1929年，安妮·弗兰克出生于德国的法兰克福。1933年，她随弗兰克家庭成员搬到了阿姆斯特丹。1939年第二次世界大战爆发时，荷兰被纳粹德国占领，犹太人在荷兰被占领期间遭到迫害。1942年7月，弗兰克一家躲到了王子运河263号房子隐秘的那个空间，也就是她父亲奥托·弗兰克工作的那个房间。正是在这里，安妮写了她的日记，通过一个十几岁的女孩的眼睛，以一个独特而生动的视角给读者还原了战时阿姆斯特丹。

两年后，弗兰克家族被出卖，纳粹发现了建筑的隐秘空间。1944年9月，安妮和她的姐姐玛戈特被带到奥斯维辛集中营，几周后，她们又被转移到贝尔根－贝尔森集中营。1945年3月，她们死于斑疹伤寒。

安妮·弗兰克生于德国，1933年搬到阿姆斯特丹。图为安妮·弗兰克，图片翻拍自历史资料。

● 安妮·弗兰克的日记

奥托·弗兰克在战争中幸存下来，并回到了阿姆斯特丹。经过他的努力，安妮日记于1947年在荷兰出版，1950年被翻译成法语和德语，1952年出版了第一本英文版本，名为《一个年轻女孩的日记》。自那以后，它被翻译成许多其他语言，日记也在世界各地的戏剧和电影中被描绘出来。

1957年，安妮·弗兰克基金会成立，目的是为了拯救即将被拆迁的王子运河公寓大楼，并建立起一个安妮·弗兰克的故事和信息得以保存的地方。

※ 桑斯安斯风车村

在18世纪和19世纪的鼎盛时期，桑河地区是一个相当重要的工业区，数百架风车遍布其间，用于生产一系列的产品，如亚麻籽油、油漆、鼻烟、芥末、纸张和其他产品。直到今天，桑斯安斯的许多特色村舍仍然存在，现在用于博物馆、礼品店或者作坊，而其他的仍被用作私人住宅。还有一些桑斯安斯的余留的风车也向公众开放。

● 风车

在17世纪，桑斯安斯周围的地区建造了600多座风车，创造了世界上第一个工业区。大多数风车被用来炼油、研磨香料、生产绘画颜料，当然还会锯木。许多风车仍然保存完好，而且可以频繁地接待游客进行参观。你可以看一下这些风力机器内内外外是如何运转和工作的。

桑斯安斯的风车有些仍在使用，风车村可供参观的项目不少，如生产颜料和食用油的车间，还有博物馆和木鞋作坊。

● 博物馆

在桑斯安斯风车村有各种各样的博物馆可供参观。例如有一个博物馆商店，这过去是一家杂货商的，在他们形成大型连锁超市之前便是那个样子。在烘焙博物馆你还可以发现他们在用古老的工艺进行烘焙，而在蜂巢则展示了一个19世纪的商人的家庭住所。桑斯古董钟表博物馆展示了一系列独特的时钟，其中大部分仍在工作。桑斯博物馆专门收藏了该地区的器皿、服饰和绘画。你也可以到这里的维卡特体验中心，在那里你将发现自己置身于20世纪的巧克力工厂。那里最早的原始机器仍然在生产着最好的巧克力和曲奇饼干。

※ 阿姆斯特丹运河带

阿姆斯特丹大约在1250年建成，其修建的大坝同时也赋予城市的名字。"Aeme Stelle Redamme"的意思是"在水里的大坝"，这是中世纪的荷兰语。第一条运河是为治水和防御而挖掘的。在中世纪，城市得以扩张，连续的防御护城河在城墙内消失了，开凿期初原有的功能也丧失了，但是最终获得了一个新的重要的功能——货物运输。

期初的大坝仍然是这座城市的中心。但是今天，在阿姆斯特尔河和南海之间的这道原来的屏障是城市中心少数几个不能行船的地方之一。在1922年，通往大坝的河流的最后一段因为陆地交通的修建成了牺牲品，占据了它原来位置上的一条街道仍然被称为达姆拉克，在荷兰语里的意思是"河流的末端，通向大坝"。现在，旧河床上正在修建一条地铁线。

● 中世纪

在14世纪，尤其是15世纪，阿姆斯特丹经历了快速发展，为黄金时代奠定了基础。如今只有很少的中世纪建筑得以幸存下来。比如这些：旧教堂和新教堂、贝居安会院的木屋。古老的护城河边上还建造大型仓库，这样可以方便储存大量的商品和货物，然后将这些货物通过护城河输送到泊满船只的港口，那些船只从港口扬帆启航通往当时已知世界的各个角落。

● 黄金时代

17世纪贸易活动迸发，这一时期成为阿姆斯特丹的黄金时代。在一个耗时五十年的雄心勃勃的扩张计划中，这座城市的三条主要的运河被挖掘出来，周围此起彼伏地建造了很多房屋。城市扩张计划约在1660年完成，这座城市的规模扩大到原来的四倍，使其城内运河成为了世界上最错综复杂、最高效的通航水道系统。迷宫般接连的运河将商品从世界各地带到每一个运河边商人的家门口。

成千上万的小驳船从港口的大船上把货物载运到城市的每个角落。运河边的一千多个仓库的补充物资都是由这些人工驳船实现的。除了这些，还有九个特殊的水上市场为17世纪的阿姆斯特丹市民们的日常需求提供保障。

在那时期，大宗的货物完全依靠人力在运河的驳船上搬上搬下，而今天，即使靠运河边行驶的卡车来输送都不及当时的效率。

183

图为在运河上划船休闲的游人。

图为桥上的行人和咖啡吧休憩的人们。

● 今天的阿姆斯特丹运河

阿姆斯特丹起初水域的近一半都成了垃圾填埋场，但是整座城市25%的地表仍然是由通航的水道组成的。阿姆斯特丹有105公里长的古老运河，仍然是世界上最潮湿的城市。

除了为这座城市增添了一笔令人赞叹的历史时代背景之外，在阿姆斯特丹运河上漂流还是让人们探索这座城市的名胜和景点最令人难忘的方式之一。无论你是初次造访还是再次踏足，从船上观望，阿姆斯特丹的一切似乎都更加奇妙和迷人。

大多数运河巡游大概需要一个小时，你将探索的是阿姆斯特丹的联合国教科文组织（UNESCO）保护运河环，沿途你会发现许多关于这座城市的有趣事物。除了美妙的一小时运河巡游，还有其他类型的运河游览船可供选择，包括方便实用的随时靠岸游览船、浪漫的烛光船、儿童冒险活动游船以及为小团体提供的私人游船。

※ 达姆拉克街

达姆拉克大街异常好认，出中央车站正对着即是，路两侧分布着重要的购物街区和建筑。

达姆拉克大街的位置原本是一条运河，现在已经被填埋成了一条大道，它位于阿姆斯特丹中心，北起阿姆斯特丹中央火车站南接水坝广场。它是人们到达车站后去往阿姆斯特丹中心的主干街道。在达姆拉克尚属于阿姆斯特尔河一段的时期，船只停在与现在街道同等宽度的河面等待着装配和卸载。在19世纪，因为要修建中央车站，达姆拉克被填埋了。火车站是阿姆斯特丹新的城市门户，达姆拉克大街是通往市中心的必经之路。像许多19世纪的欧洲城市一样，把达姆拉克填好就可以创造出一条从车站到市中心的宽阔大道。然而，由于在1903年对大坝的股市交易大楼进行拆除，后来还在马路的东侧建造了证券交易所和女王百货商店，所以达姆拉克大街的空间很快就给缩减了。

※ 新教堂

老教堂对日益增长的阿姆斯特丹人口来说实在太小了，于是乌特勒支主教在1408年允许建造第二教区教堂，这座新的教堂便称为新教堂。这座新教堂用以呈奉给圣玛丽和圣凯瑟琳。

新教堂在1421年和1452年的城市大火中被毁坏，而后在1645年又几乎全部烧毁殆尽，之后以哥特式风格进行了重建。1892～1914年间教堂进行了重大的翻修，增添了新哥特式的许多细节部分，1959～1980年翻修再一次进行。第二次翻修的昂贵费用给荷兰归正会教带来巨大压力，为了节省维修费用，教堂不得已在大部分时间选择了关闭。为了能够保持教堂仍旧开放，其所有权在1979年被转移到了国家新教堂基金会，一个新成立的文化基金会。

新教堂现在已经不再用于教会服务，而是为一些展览展出提供空间，也会用于管风琴演奏会。

根据荷兰宪法第32条，新教堂现用于荷兰皇家授勋仪式，最近一次是2013年威廉·亚历山大国王的宣誓登基仪式，此外还进行皇室婚礼的承办，上一次是2002年威廉·亚历山大和王后马克西玛的结婚典礼。前女王威廉敏娜、朱莉安娜和贝娅特丽克丝的宣誓登基仪式也是在这里举行的。

※ 老教堂

阿姆斯特丹红灯区的老教堂是这座城市最古老的建筑，又是该市最年轻的艺术机构之一。在它成立以来的7个世纪里，这座教堂已经成为北欧最雄伟的哥特式教堂建筑之一。

老教堂是由1213年的一个木结构小教堂演变成现在的样子的。原来的木质结构和现在的老教堂矗立在同一个地方。1306年，人们决定建造一座石头教堂取代木结构小教堂，最终新的神圣的教堂落成。纵观历史，这座教堂经历了15代阿姆斯特丹市民的翻修。教堂建成的50年内便进行了第一次翻修。这一次的翻修对教堂的走道进行了加宽和延长，一直到唱诗班的区域，同时还对教堂的结构做了加固。15世纪初，又增加了耳堂的部分。

老教堂原本是罗马天主教堂，但后来被加尔文主义的荷兰归正会接管。在16世纪，教堂数次遭到肆意破坏和掠夺。1566年，一群暴徒在"圣像破坏运动"中摧毁了教堂的装饰。在被毁坏的配件中，包括一幅由扬·范·斯科尔和马尔滕·范·海姆斯凯尔克绘制的作品。

宗教改革后，教堂成了婚姻登记处，也被用来存放城市档案。重要的文件都被锁在教堂内部的铁柜子里。

教堂最著名的资助人是伦勃朗和他的子女。事实上，伦勃朗所有的孩子都是在这里接受洗礼的。在城市的所有建筑中，老教堂是唯一一个仍然保持着当初伦勃朗在其大厅时的状态的。

※ 贝居安会院

贝津修道院或贝居安会院是阿姆斯特丹的一个内部庭院，是远离城市喧嚣的一个安静的地方。最初，这里是贝居安妇女团体的避难所，如今房子都由年长的单身女性占用。

早在14世纪，贝居安会院就已经在某处被建立起来，用来安置那些贝居安士。这些妇女过着修女一般的生活，但更独立、更自由。16世纪天主教信仰被全面禁止，贝居安会院是唯一一个继续存在的天主教机构，因为这些房子是妇女们的私人财产，但他们不得不放弃附属的小教堂。后来，一座新的叫做"隐藏着的教堂"的教堂在几所住宅正门的后面被修建起来。

位于南侧的15世纪的英国教堂是贝居安会院的主要特色，它是这座城市最古老的建筑之一。它包含了对清教徒祖先的彩色玻璃描绘，他们可能在离开之前还在教堂做礼拜。

2007年2月，英国女王伊丽莎白和荷兰女王贝娅特丽克丝举行了一项特殊的仪式以纪念教堂建立四百周年。

在教堂对面，有一个较小的教堂，在那里天主教徒和贝居安士们一直隐秘地使用至1795年。

风景如画的庭院里还有一个花园，四周环绕着16世纪以来建造的传统房屋。34号的木屋是阿姆斯特丹最古老的房子，始建于1420年。整座院落里还有许多有趣的牌匾和雕像。

贝居安会院位于阿姆斯特丹市中心。最容易抵达的方法就是从Spuiplein广场过去。你会看到一排白色的房子中间夹着一栋棕色的房子，这里就是通往贝居安会院里面的大门了。

※ 伦勃朗广场

阿姆斯特丹的市中心有一个广场叫做伦勃朗广场。伦勃朗广场建于1668年，由一个城市港口的遗迹改造而成，伦勃朗或者黄油市场最初是一个安静的奶制品市场，偶尔也会有当地的露天集市。到20世纪初，随着阿姆斯特丹的城市人口激增，市场逐渐发展成为一个流行的聚集地，受到艺术家、工人们和年轻人的频繁惠顾。

这是《夜巡》的立体版，人物的表情和物理格局都遵循了原作，是广场上的焦点。

伦勃朗广场是以著名画家伦勃朗伦·范·莱因的名字命名的，他在1639年到1658年间在附近拥有一座房子，这所房子现在是伦勃朗故居博物馆。伦勃朗故居博物馆里几乎收藏了完整的世界著名的伦勃朗蚀刻版画作品，其中的一部分永久陈列在展览馆中。此外，这里还经常举办展览，展出和伦勃朗同时代人的作品，现代馆中还展出现代和当代艺术作品。伦勃朗是著名的绘画作品《夜巡》的创作者。它是世界上最有名的画作之一。

※ 冯德尔公园

冯德尔公园是阿姆斯特丹最受欢迎的公园，每天都吸引着成千上万的游客、居民其他所有人。公园位于莱顿广场南边，靠近荷兰国家博物馆、市立博物馆和梵高博物馆，它是阿姆斯特丹最大的城市公园，当然也是荷兰最著名的公园。

这个公园于1865年开放，开放的起初主要用于骑马和散步，名为新公园。在1867年，荷兰诗人约斯特·范·登·冯德尔的雕像被放置在公园里，于是冯德尔公园这个名字就被采用下来。委员会很快筹集到资金来扩建公园，到1877年，它的占地面积已经达到了45公顷。那时，公园的地盘就在阿姆斯特丹市的边缘，自此也就成了这个城市的中心。

冯德尔公园现在已经有150年的历史了，公园内栽种着许多古老的梧桐树、马栗树、荷兰红栗树、梓树和不同种类的桦树。茂密的灌木和花草植被形成了公园的美丽景观。冯德尔公园也是鸟类的家园，栖息着野鸭、蓝鹭和许多小型鸟类。

公园内的戏剧、舞蹈和音乐演出贯穿了每年的六月、七月和八月。著名的露天剧场就在冯德尔公园内，靠近Eeghenstraat路的入口处。门票是免费的，但是有些表演非常受欢迎，我们建议你通过他们的网站进行预订。

※ 阿姆斯特丹杜莎夫人蜡像馆

杜莎夫人蜡像馆中的杜莎夫人确有其人，安娜·玛利亚·格罗夫茨。她出生在法国斯特拉斯堡，后来搬到了瑞士，在伯尔尼的一名内科医生家里当女管家。当时，给一个死去的人做蜡膜，或者给一个名人做手模型，是将人们的形象留给后代的为数不多的方法之一，这是医生的一项工作。安娜在医生的教导下学会了娴熟的蜡像技术，后来她搬到巴黎与弗朗索瓦·杜莎结婚，目睹了1789年至1799年法国大革命的暴力。也正因此，她制作了数百个死去的人的蜡膜以及被处决的贵族的雕刻头像，还经常从数百具尸体堆里发现一些有趣的头颅。

杜莎夫人后来开始在伦敦生活，到她去世时，她已经收藏多达四百个蜡制头像。1835年，第一个杜莎蜡像馆在伦敦贝克街开业。第一间蜡像馆包括一个"恐怖屋"，展示了法国大革命被逮捕和被绞死的受害者和著名罪犯的蜡像。伦敦贝克街蜡像馆在1921年和1941年火灾中受到了严重损坏，"二战"期间德国对伦敦闪电战的轰炸导致许多有价值的蜡像都融化了，后来这些藏品都得到了重塑，如今属英国游乐管理公司默林娱乐集团所拥有。杜莎夫人蜡像馆在世界上主要的一些城市都有展出。

阿姆斯特丹杜莎夫人蜡像馆建于1970年，是在欧洲大陆开放的第一个杜莎夫人蜡像馆，也是英国机构的第一个国外分支机构。阿姆斯特丹杜莎夫人蜡像馆是由一系列各领域的名人蜡像组成，包括荷兰历史上的黄金时代、音乐、体育和电影。

※ 博物馆广场

位于莱顿广场南边的是华丽的19世纪的博物馆广场。毫无疑问，博物馆广场是高雅的巅峰之所，是阿姆斯特丹三大最重要的博物馆的所在地，阿姆斯特丹国家博物馆、现代艺术/市立博物馆和梵高博物馆，使其成为卓越的艺术爱好者们的天堂。

阿姆斯特丹博物馆广场在1999年由瑞典景观设计师斯文·英格瓦·安德森进行了设计重建。广场用于节日、庆典和游行等活动。地下还有停车场和超市。冬天的时候，广场上的池塘就成了一个人造滑冰场所。

※ 莱顿广场

莱顿广场是位于阿姆斯特丹中央运河环南端的一个繁忙的广场，差不多与广受喜爱的冯德尔公园面对面。Leidseplein的英文翻译大致是Leiden Square，即莱顿广场，它在莱顿街的尽头，在这个广场的大部分历史中，都源于它是通往莱顿重镇的主要道路。

这是阿姆斯特丹夜生活集中的一个地区，周围遍布的都是餐馆、酒吧和剧场，白天同样是个热闹的地方。

这一要塞区域始于17世纪用来给农民拴马匹和停放马车的场地。今天，在莱顿广场附近和周边的街道上，体会到的是异常丰富多彩的阿姆斯特丹的夜生活。在这里还有经营各式各样菜肴的饭馆供你选择，从阿根廷菜和希腊菜到意大利餐和印尼餐。去Puri Mas尝尝他们的亚洲菜和米饭，或者去De Blauwe Hollander尝试一下传统的荷兰菜肴。

莱顿广场是世界著名的现场音乐会的所在地，如Paradiso和Melkweg，还有像Jimmy Woo和Chicago Social Club这样的亲密舞蹈俱乐部。电影院、迪斯科舞厅、剧院和赌场都坐落在广场上，或在几步之遥的范围内。如果你想去夜店狂欢或者想要一顿饕餮美食，这就是你要去的地方。

※ 阿姆斯特丹股票交易所

阿姆斯特丹股票交易所是阿姆斯特丹证券交易的百年旧址，是现代荷兰建筑的重要地标。它建于1898年至1903年，由20世纪著名的荷兰建筑师亨德里克·佩特鲁斯·贝拉赫设计。

这座建筑是用红砖建造而成，有钢铁、玻璃屋顶和石墩、装饰以门楣和檐口。它打破了单一模仿哥特式或文艺复兴风格的传统，在19世纪末，阿姆斯特丹兴建了许多重要的城市建筑（像是国家博物馆、阿姆斯特丹市立博物馆、中央车站、城市剧院都在这期间完成），但所有的建筑都树立了自己新的风格。

阿姆斯特丹股票交易所大楼简约朴素，它最主要的装饰是一座悬挂在塔楼上的大钟。大楼的拐角处竖立着三座人物雕塑，争议性的传奇英雄、著名的阿姆斯特丹文学的创始人海斯布莱赫特·范·阿姆斯特尔，17世纪开创荷兰东印度公司的英雄官员扬·皮特斯佐恩·科恩，以及霍·德赫罗特，一位国际人道主义者、作家、哲学家和国际性的重要律师。

阿姆斯特丹股票交易所的内部装饰独特且保存完好。屋顶由双层玻璃制成，可以将充足的自然光引入到建筑内部。各种不同形态的釉面砖、石材、木材、铁质用料等都完美和谐地融合在一起。

大楼的主厅以其简约同时具有其装饰性的设计工艺，最初用来作商品的交易大厅。

在其建筑时期，阿姆斯特丹股票交易所一直以其创新性著称，并将它的创造者推崇备至，得到国际认可，同时还对荷兰的其他建筑师产生了影响，特别是对阿姆斯特丹学院派运动。

※ 葡萄牙犹太会堂

葡萄牙的犹太人社区是荷兰最古老的犹太社区。这个社区是1639年由西班牙和葡萄牙的犹太人建立的，在西班牙把安特卫普占领后，这些犹太人被迫离开那里。为逃避西班牙宗教法庭的审查，他们之前还曾经从西班牙和葡萄牙逃离开。这些塞法迪犹太人在包容的阿姆斯特丹找到了一个安全的栖身之所。直到第二次世界大战之前，在海牙、纳尔登、鹿特丹和米德尔堡都有葡萄牙人社区。

1665年，犹太社区决定建一座新的犹太教堂，一座世界上最大的犹太教堂。建筑师伊莱亚斯·宝曼和丹尼尔·斯塔帕尔特受以委托建造犹太教堂。建造工作在1671年开始，1675年葡萄牙的犹太教堂建成完毕，耗费了社区至少186 000枚金币。教堂在后来做了些小的修复，但看起来仍然和340年前差不多。

这是一座独立矗立在木桩之上的建筑，从运河中的航船上可以看到教堂下方的木桩地基。它是当时最大的犹太教堂，也是阿姆斯特丹最大的建筑物之一。耶路撒冷的所罗门神庙的模型启发了建筑师。通往主教堂的入口处是一小型院落，周围环绕着教堂低矮的建筑、办公室和档案馆，还有各式的官员住所、拉比、一个停尸房，以及世界上最古老的犹太图书馆之一的埃兹哈伊姆图书馆，它收藏着珍贵的西班牙语手稿。

葡萄牙的犹太人社区是荷兰最古老的犹太社区，始于1639年。

Shopping in Amsterdam 购在阿姆斯特丹

189

A city reputed for its innovation and creativity, Amsterdam is home to many established and upcoming fashion talents. Besides all the big brands, fashion chains (on Kalverstraat and Leidsestraat) and international designers, Amsterdam also boasts its fair share of new and promising Dutch designers and independent shops. Each of Amsterdam's neighbourhoods offer different shopping experienced opportunities, from the hip Nine Streets through the luxury boutiques in grand Oud Zuid to vintage delights around Waterlooplein, immerse yourself in the vibe of the area you're in and besides shopping don't forget to do some people-watching as well!

※ De Negen Straatjes

The Negen Straatjes, which translates to "Nine Little Streets" in English, is a quaint shopping area situated in the heart of Amsterdam. This quiet area is the seventh heaven for boutique lovers. As the name implies, the Negen Straatjes is comprised of nine little streets: Reestraat, Hartenstraat, Gasthuismolensteeg, Berenstraat, Wolvenstraat, Oude Spiegelstraat, Runstraat, Huidenstraat and Wijde Heisteeg. The Singel forms the border to the East, while the Prinsengracht marks the western most point. The Nine Streets intersect the main canals between the Leidsestraat and the Jordaan district, and are dotted with great restaurants, cafés, art galleries, jewellers, boutiques and vintage stores. With an exceptional array of styles, trends and prices, this area is truly a shopper's paradise.

※ The Kalverstraat and Leidsestraat

There are two main shopping streets in the city centre of Amsterdam, which are the Kalverstraat and the Leidsestraat and they are exactly what you'd hope for and expect in a major city's principal thoroughfares. There is an abounded array of exclusive shops as well as the famous high street brands known all over the world, and you'll find there is something suitable for everyone. Amsterdam's most commercial street begins left of the Royal Palace building. Its history goes back to the 14th century when this part was transformed into a cow market. Today, here you will find all the shops you would expect to find in a large European city like H&M and Zara, along with a few local stores and excellent boutiques. Do hunt around for bargains while you are here, because many places price their wares competitively. In addition to fashion clothing and accessories, Kalverstraat and the Leidsestraat also have quite a few specialty stores, which sell souvenirs, groceries and cheeses. When you want a break from rummaging through store shelves, relax in a welcoming café, bar or restaurant. The main fast food chains also have their franchises here.

※ P.C Hooftstraat

The P.C. was originally just an ordinary street in Amsterdam's Oud-Zuid neighborhood, running behind Vondelpark. But after the construction of Museumplein in the late 19th century, the area began to acclimatise to contemporary tastes. Recognising the street's growing importance the municipality renamed it after the Dutch poet Pieter Corneliszoon Hooft, which is a title that reflects the street's refined sensibility.

In the 20th century many international brands set up shops in the P.C., establishing regional outlets inside of the Netherlands. Rent has stayed particularly low in this part of Amsterdam meaning that the P.C. is exceptionally attractive to retailers.

Over 40 luxury brands have shopfronts on the P.C. including Prada, Ralph Lauren and Chanel. Each store is expertly curated and employs a team of experienced sales assistants. Retail staff are noted for their courteous and friendly etiquette, creating a welcoming atmosphere throughout the P.C. While there is plenty of choice on the P.C., the street is relatively short and can be crossed in a few minutes, making it ideal for relaxed strolls between shops.

※ The Haarlemmerstraat

The Haarlemmerstraat is a long, trendy shopping street, stretching from east to west towards Amsterdam Central Station. It is a lively strip where you will find everything from shoes, independent labels and second-hand clothes to specialty food products, interior design items and Dutch collectables. It is also a great place to spend your afternoons and evenings, with a great number of eateries, bars and other nightlife possibilities. Honest, old-fashioned amicability from early in the morning until late in the evening.

This shopping street is busy with cars, bicycles and pedestrians but still maintains a charming feel. This busy, bustling street is ideal for strolling. When traveling its length be sure to stop here and admire the view. The lovely sunsets here make it one of the city's most popular spots to photograph.

※ Albert Cuyp Market

The Albert Cuyp Market is a street market in Amsterdam, the Netherlands, on the Albert Cuypstraat between Ferdinand Bolstraat and Van Woustraat, in the De Pijp area of the Oud-Zuid district of the city. The street and market are named for Albert Cuyp, which was a painter who lived in the 17th century.

Since 1905, the "Cuyp" has fascinated Amsterdam's residents, home cooks, tourists and anyone looking for a bargain. Fresh vegetables, fruit, fish, flowers, and plants: you'll all find them at the Albert Cuyp. And also gorgeous fabrics, trendy clothing, textile, nice leather goods, and jewellery.

Enjoy a nice herring at the fish stand or get yourself a bag of fresh syrup waffles to enjoy at home. Visit a nice, old-fashioned coffee house or a super modern café for a cup of coffee. The statue of André Hazes who is famous in the Netherlands for his tear jerk songs can be found on the corner of the Eerste Sweelinckstraat.

With 260 stands, the Albert Cuyp is the largest day market in Europe. Behind the Albert Cuyp street there are other shops with good deals on computers, pets, furniture, haircuts, and more.

※ Singel Flower Market

The floating flower market at the Singel Canal surely is one of the most colourful and fragrant places of interest in Amsterdam during all four seasons. It is unique in that the merchandise is displayed on floating barges. This is a relic from the days when the flowers and plants sold at this market were shipped in from the horticultural areas around the city by barges. The market here actually dates from 1862, when flower growers would sail their wares on barges into the city centre via the Amstel River. The modern-day market is actually comprised of fixed barges, but is no less a spectacle. Each barge has a glasshouse built atop, like a mini version of the greenhouses found throughout the countryside that ensure Holland is an international hotspot for flowers all year round. Be it tulips, narcissus, snowdrops, carnations, violets, peonies or orchids, you're sure to find your favourites at the Flower Market, no matter the time of year. What's more, the sellers also offer house plants, herbs, seeds and bulbs.

At the Amsterdam Flower Market you'll find tulips in every colour imaginable—either in bouquets or as bulbs to plant at home. But the market has far more than just tulips. No matter what your favourite flower is, you're bound to find it here. Besides cut flowers, there are plenty of house plants, seeds and gardening essentials. If you plan to buy bulbs to take out of the country, be sure they have a customs cleared stamp on the packet so you won't have any trouble at the border.

Keychains, wooden tulips and postcards are also plentiful around the Flower Market, while other thoughtful gifts can be found in the Christmas Palace. This store, specialising in baubles and other festive decorations–often with an Amsterdam twist–is open every day of the year.

※ De Bijenkorf

De Bijenkorf luxury department store is a true institution of fashion and style. Defining taste and setting trends since 1870, this department store now stands in an enviable location on Amsterdam's Dam Square.

De Bijenkorf was founded in 1870 by Simon Philip Goudsmit, starting as a small haberdashery shop at 132 Nieuwendijk, one of Amsterdam's oldest streets. Initially limited to yarn and ribbons and employing a staff of four, the stock expanded gradually. After the death of Goudsmit in 1889, Goudsmit's widow expanded the business with the help of a cousin, Arthur Isaac, and her son Alfred, eventually buying adjacent buildings. In 1909, these connecting shops were replaced by a new building. That same year, a temporary building was erected on the site of the demolished Beurs van Zocher, and construction of a new store started beside it.

What started 140 years ago as a small haberdashery shop has grown into the Netherlands' largest premium department store. Today, De Bijenkorf carries the best fashion brands, designer brands and luxury products: everything you can think of, from the latest beauty products to stunning accessories and from exquisite dinnerware to the most adorable toys. You can even buy heavenly handmade chocolates. De Bijenkorf offers the highest standard of quality and always presents the latest trends, the most spectacular events and outstanding premium services.

De Bijenkorf is continuously adding new brands. Examples of the exclusive brands include Louis Vuitton, Hermès, Gucci, Chanel, Longchamp, Céline, Michael Kors, Kenzo and Jimmy Choo. At De Bijenkorf, you can shop tax free. To this end, De Bijenkorf Amsterdam has created the Tax Free Lounge, where travellers from outside the EU can claim a tax refund from their purchases. With the exception of Amsterdam Airport Schiphol, this is the only permanent location offering this service to international customers. Non-EU customers can get an instant tax refund for purchases of €50 or more. The multilingual staff will be happy to help with all inquiries. You can also pay in your own currency, and De Bijenkorf accepts all credit cards including Union Pay and Global Blue Card, and is also CNTA certified.

The surprising and breath-taking decorations in De Bijenkorf's unique shop windows make them real attractions. Live theatre, dance and music performances can be seen on a regular basis. Each year around 300 events take place such as the launch of de Dutch VOGUE magazine. Since 2008 De Bijenkorf kicks off its Christmas season with a spectacular lighting event called Turn On The Lights during which the mayor of Amsterdam turns on the façade lighting of the Amsterdam store.

※ Royal Coster Diamonds

Royal Coster Diamonds is one of the oldest and certainly one of the world's most famous diamond cutting factories and diamond jewellery retailers. It was founded in 1840 and has ever since been associated with the best and finest craftsmanship in the jewellery industry.

Coster Diamonds over its history had often been entrusted with polishing numerous famous diamonds. For example, the re-polishing of the Koh-i-Noor, which translates as The Mountain of

Light because of its oval cut and length, is the most famous and probably best known diamond around. At the moment the Koh-i-Noor can be seen in the Tower of London, as part of England's precious Crown jewels.

Royals and diamonds have always been closely connected. Back in the days emperors and rulers used jewellery and diamonds as an expression of their power and position. These days royals wear diamonds mainly as beautiful accessories to official occasions. Often we see that jewellery worn by royals passes on from generation to generation in remembrance of their ancestors.

Royal Coster Diamonds is more than just a diamond polishing factory. In 2007 they opened their own Diamond Museum. In the museum you can learn everything about the history of diamonds, you can partake in a tour and see the breath-taking diamond collection and even participate in a diamond workshop where you can actually cut your own diamond!

The majority of Coster's diamonds are GIA or HRD certified. All items feature reasonable factory prices and tax-free shopping is available for non-E.U. residents. The facility has a cosy on-site café where coffee, tea and soft drinks are served. Of course, you'll also find a gift shop on the premises.

阿姆斯特丹是一个以创新和创造力闻名的城市，它是众多知名时尚达人的故乡。除了所有的大品牌、时尚连锁店和国际设计师，阿姆斯特丹还拥有一批新的、大有前途的荷兰设计师和独立品牌商店。在阿姆斯特丹的每一个社区都能享受到不同的购物体验，从时尚的九小街到奢华的精品时装店，再到令人振奋的古着店，你会情不自禁地沉浸在你落脚的每一个地方，还有，购物之余也别忘了看看悠然自得的那些血拼客！

阿姆斯特丹有着浓重的商业氛围，特别在市中心地区，中央车站也近在咫尺。图为市中心的商业街。

※ 九小街

九小街，翻译成英文是"Nine Little Street"，是位于阿姆斯特丹市中心的一个古色古香的购物区。这个安静的区域是喜欢淘货热爱情调的购物者们的天堂。顾名思义，九小街由九条小街道组成，分别是Reestraat、Hartenstraat、Gasthuismolensteeg、Berenstraat、Wolvenstraat、Oude Spiegelstraat、Runstraat、Huidenstraat和Wijde Heisteeg。辛格运河形成了东边的边界，而王子运河则是这个区域的最西端。这九条街横亘在莱顿街与约尔丹区之间运河的主要交汇处，这里遍布着大量的餐馆、咖啡馆、画廊、珠宝店、精品店和古董店。这里的风格独特、紧跟时尚、价格合理，是不折不扣的购物天堂。

※ 卡尔弗尔大街和莱顿街

在阿姆斯特丹市中心有两处主要的购物街，那就是卡尔弗尔大街和莱顿街，它们正是在一个主要城市的主干道上你所希望和期盼的那个样子。这里有大量的高档专卖店和知名的高街时尚品牌，你会发现所有的人都能在这里找到适合自己的东西。这两条阿姆斯特丹最繁华的商业街始于王宫，其历史可以追溯到14世纪，街道的一段在那时是牛市的一部分。今天，像在欧洲很多大城市里一样，你会发现H&M和Zara这样的专卖店，还有一些当地的商店和精品店。如果来这里逛，一定要四处看看比比价格，因为店多竞争力大，很多店的商品价格都颇得人心。除了时尚服装和配饰之外，卡尔弗尔大街和莱顿街也有相当多的商店出售纪念品、杂货和奶酪。要是店逛多了东西翻累了想休息，那就找间咖啡馆、酒吧或餐馆放松一下身体和心情。一些大型的连锁快餐在这里也能找到。

※ P·C霍夫特大街

P·C霍夫特大街原来只是阿姆斯特丹Oud-Zuid老城区的一条普通的街道，在冯德尔公园的后面。但在19世纪后期博物馆广场修建之后，该地区开始迎合当时人们的品味。政府也意识到这条街的重要性，以荷兰诗人彼特·科涅利兹·霍夫特的名字重新进行了命名，这一称号也映射出了这条街道的精致和不凡的鉴赏力。

所有地方的奢侈品大街都是这么"豪"。图为某奢侈品商店门口停放的金色跑车很是吸引路人的眼球。

在20世纪，很多国际大牌都在霍夫特大街开设了门店，在荷兰境内设立了区域销售网点。在阿姆斯特丹，这一地区的租金一直处于比较低的水平，这就意味着，霍夫特大街对零售商们来说实在是具有吸引力的。

霍夫特大街上的奢侈品牌超过了40个，包括普拉达、拉夫·劳伦、香奈儿等这些炙手可热的品牌。每家商店都经过精心的陈列布置，并聘请了一批经验丰富的销售助理。商店的工作人员以彬彬有礼著称，在整条霍夫特大街营造了一种热情好客的氛围。尽管霍夫特大街的选择多，但街道相对较短，不用太久即可逛完，因此非常适合在各个商家之间放缓脚步，轻松地精挑细选。

※ 哈乐姆街

哈乐姆街是一条长长的、时尚潮流的购物街，自东向西一直延伸到阿姆斯特丹中央车站。这是一个热闹非凡的地段，从鞋子、独立品牌和二手服装到特色食品、室内设计项目和荷兰藏品，应有尽有。它同时还是一个消磨下午和夜间时刻的好地方，这里有大量的餐馆、酒吧和夜生活的各种设施。诚恳和老式的友善，从清早持续到夜晚。

这条购物街上到处是汽车、自行车和行人，但仍然散发着一种迷人的感觉。这条热闹繁华的街道也是散步的理想场所旅行之际，一定要驻足停下在这里欣赏一番风景。迷人的落日余晖使其成为这座城市最受欢迎的景点之一。

※ 艾伯特库普市场

艾伯特库普市场是荷兰阿姆斯特丹的一个街市，位于Oud-Zuid老城De Pijp区的Ferdinand Bolstraat街和Van Woustraat街之间的艾伯特库普街。这条街和集市都是以生活在17世纪的画家艾伯特·库普的名字命名的。

自1905年以来，艾伯特库普市场吸引了大批阿姆斯特丹的市民、家庭厨师、游客和任何想要便宜货的人。新鲜的蔬菜、水果、鱼、花和植物都能在艾伯特库普市场找到。还有华丽的面料、时髦的服装、纺织品、漂亮的皮具和珠宝。

在鱼摊上品尝一下美味的鲱鱼吧，或者买一袋新鲜出炉的焦糖华夫饼回家慢慢享用。要不就去一家漂亮怀旧的老式咖啡屋或超级现代的咖啡馆喝一杯咖啡。在Eerste Sweelinckstraat街的角落还竖立着荷兰著名催泪歌手安德烈·哈泽斯的雕像。

艾伯特库普市场拥有260个摊位，是欧洲最大的日间集市。在市场街的后面还有一些不错的电脑、宠物、家具、理发的店铺。

※ 辛格鲜花市场

毋庸置疑，辛格运河上的水上鲜花市场是阿姆斯特丹一年四季最丰富多彩、最芬芳艳丽的地方之一。这是独一无二的在浮动的驳船上陈列商品的地方，是从用船舶将鲜花和绿植从城市周围的园艺区运送到这里直接出售那个年代所传承下来的遗俗。这个市场起始于1862年，那时花农们通过阿姆斯特尔河将货物用船舶输送到市中心。而现今的辛格市场实际上是由固定的驳船组成的，但仍不乏是一种奇观。每一艘驳船上都有一个温室，就像在乡间所见到的温室的迷你版，它们全年都是国际花卉热点所在的可靠保障。无论是郁金香、水仙、雪花莲、康乃馨、紫罗兰、牡丹还是兰花，你一定会在花市中找到你最喜欢的，无论一年哪个时节。更重要的是，卖家还提供室内绿植、草本植物、种子以及鲜花球茎。

辛格水上鲜花市场位于运河中漂浮的船上，是个采购鲜花、花种和礼品的场所。

在阿姆斯特丹的鲜花市场，你会发现各种颜色的郁金香——无论是花束，还是可以栽种在家里的郁金香球茎。不过辛格市场上拥有的可远不止郁金香，不管你最喜欢的花是什么，你一定会在这里找到它。除了剪好的花束，还有大量的室内绿植、种子和必备的花园精品。如果你打算买球茎出境的话，请确保它们配有海关清关印章，这样你就不会在边境遇到麻烦了。

钥匙链、木质郁金香工艺品和明信片在鲜花市场上也随处可见，而其他贴心的礼物可以在旁边的Christmas Palace商店找到。这家店专门经营小玩意和一些节日装饰，通常会附带一些阿姆斯特丹的标识，全年都营业。

※ 女王百货

女王百货是中国人对De Bijenkorf百货公司的中文称呼，这是一家绝对时尚的高端百货。这家百货自1870年起就界定了潮流和时尚品位的发展趋势，现在坐落于阿姆斯特丹的水坝广场旁最显著的位置。

女王百货公司成立已经一个半世纪，是荷兰的本土百货公司，目前在七个主要的城市都有门店。图为阿姆斯特丹店。

女王百货由西蒙·菲利普·高斯密特于1870年创立，最初只是阿姆斯特丹最古老的街道之一Nieuwendijk街132号的一家小型缝纫用品商店。起初的经营只有纱线和缎带等，雇佣了4名员工，后来逐渐扩大。在1889年高斯密特死后，他的遗孀在她的堂兄亚瑟·艾萨克和她的儿子阿尔弗雷德的帮助下扩大了生意，后来还买下了邻近的建筑。1909年，这些一家接一家的商店被一幢新建筑所取代。同一年，在被拆毁的老股票交易所的地盘上竖立了一座临时建筑，并在其旁边建造了一家新店。

140年前开始的一家小缝纫用品商店已经发展成为荷兰最大的高档百货商店。今天，女王百货拥有最好的时尚品牌、设计师品牌和奢侈品，你能想到的一切，从最炙手可热的美容产品到炫目的配饰，从精致的餐具到最可爱的玩具都在他们的经营范围内，甚至还有精妙美味的手工巧克力。女王百货提供着高品质的商品、最新的潮流趋势和杰出的优质服务。

女王百货橱窗的陈列享有非常高的水准，图为2018年的圣诞节主题Bobbie's kerstspektakel，意为"Bobbie熊的圣诞奇观"。

女王百货的入驻品牌数量持续增加。包括路易威登、爱马仕、古驰、香奈儿、珑骧、赛琳、迈克高仕、Kenzo和周仰杰等品牌皆悉数收纳。在女王百货还可以免税购物，女王百货公司阿姆斯特丹店设计了免税大厅，在那里，来自欧盟以外的游客可以凭购物票据获得商品退税。除了阿姆斯特丹机场史基浦机场，这是唯一一个为全球各地的客服提供这项服务的永久地点。非欧盟顾客可以享受50欧元及以上商品的即时退税。多语种的工作人员也可以给你提供各种查询等的服务。付款方式可以使用你自己手中的各币种现钞，当然，百货公司也接受所有的信用卡，包括中国银联卡和环球蓝卡，还有中国国家旅游局的签署保付支票。

有一点令人惊奇和赞叹不已的那就是女王百货独特的橱窗陈列，这一真正的亮点你一定要看一下。这里还经常可以看到现场演出、舞蹈和音乐表演。每年大约会有300场活动在这里举行，比如荷兰版VOGUE杂志的发布会。从2008年开始，女王百货开启了圣诞季的活动仪式，届时会上演一出叫做"打开灯光"的精彩绚丽的灯光秀活动，在此期间，阿姆斯特丹的市长会亲自开启阿姆斯特丹女王百货商店的立体照明设备。

※ 皇家考斯特钻石工厂

皇家考斯特钻石是世界上最古老的钻石切割工厂和钻石首饰零售商之一。它成立于1840年，此后一直以珠宝行业中最好和最精湛的工艺著称。

在考斯特的历史上，它经常被委以重任，打磨出了许多赫赫有名的钻石。例如，对"光之山"的重新抛光，因为钻石椭圆形的切割和长度，被翻译为"光之山"，这是最有名的，也可能是最为人所知的钻石。现在，"光之山"钻石存放在伦敦塔内，是珍贵的英国皇冠珠宝的一部分。

皇室和钻石一直有着千丝万缕的联系。在过去的年代里，皇帝和统治者凭借珠宝和钻石来彰显他们至高无上的权力和地位。如今，皇室成员佩戴钻石主要是作为官方场合的装饰品。我们经常看到皇室成员将其所佩戴的珠宝代代相传，以表达他们对先辈的缅怀之情。

皇家考斯特钻石不仅仅是一个钻石抛光厂，2007年，他们开办了自己的钻石博物馆。在博物馆里，你可以了解钻石的历史，可以观看令人惊叹的钻石收藏，甚至你可以参与到一个钻石作坊中去，在那里切割你自己的钻石！

皇家考斯特的大部分钻石是GIA或HRD认证。所有商品都有着合理的出厂价格，同时也适用于非欧盟居民的免税购物。这里还有一个舒适的现场咖啡厅，提供咖啡、茶和软饮料。当然了，如果你要购买礼品的话，这里也有一个礼品商店。

Eating in Amsterdam 食在阿姆斯特丹

There are over thousands of restaurants in Amsterdam catering to everyone's taste, budget and mood. Restaurants offer everything to a hungry visitor craves for: from Asian food to Western, from Chinese to Mediterranean and modern Dutch. Whether it is for a quick bite or an extensive dinner, it's all available in Amsterdam. No matter how much money is in your pocket, no matter what your taste is, you will never have to worry that you can't find a restaurant where you can enjoy a nice meal and rest your tired feet.

Here we will only recommend a few restaurants, include a Chinese restaurant which the local Chinese as well as Chinese tourists are very fond of. Did you know that Amsterdam has also quite a few very popular Michelin restaurants.

※ FuLu Mandarijn Amsterdam

FuLu Mandarijn Amsterdam (Chinese, Asian and Sichuan restaurant Amsterdam) is one of the best and top Chinese and Asian restaurants in Amsterdam near Dam Square, Royal Palace, Central Station and Madame Tussaud's.

Mandarijn Restaurant is well known for its Sichuan Cuisine and Cantonese Cuisine, along with the best hospitality service. The specialty of the chef is the famous Peking duck, served with pancakes and a delicious sauce. The rest of the menu is very extensive, whether you want meat, fish or vegetables, spicy or not you will always find something to your liking.

Hours:　　11am–10pm (Mon–Thu, Sun)

　　　　　11am–11pm (Fri–Sat)

Address: Rokin 26，1012 KS Amsterdam

Contact: 020-6230885

www.mandarijnrokin.nl

※ Ciel Bleu Restaurant

Going to a Michelin-rated restaurant can be quite the treat, and the Netherlands certainly isn't short on options. There are over 100 Michelin restaurants across the Netherlands, Just in Amsterdam, there are more than 15 Michelin-rated restaurants carrying one (or two) of the coveted stars. And you can find the complete list of Michelin restaurants on the website of the Dutch tourism bureau (www.holland.com).

Ciel Bleu is a two-star Michelin restaurant. They offer an extensive menu, which changes four times annually. You'll find a selection of culinary creations made with fresh seasonal products. Of course, if you have a special dietary requirement or other requests, tell them when you make the reservation. You can contact restaurant reservations from Monday until Sunday from 10:00 am until 6:00 pm. Online reservations are also possible.

A friendly reminder, the restaurant has a strict dress code for customers, sneakers, ripped jeans are not allowed even if they are Prada.

Hours: 6:30pm–10:30pm, Sunday closed

Address: Ferdinand Bolstraat 333, 1072 LH Amsterdam

Contact: 020-6787450

cielbleu@okura.nl

http://www.cielbleu.nl

阿姆斯特丹有数千家餐厅，可以迎合每个人的口味、预算和心情。这些餐厅提供给每一个饥肠辘辘的游客尽可能的满足：从亚洲食物到西式食品，从传统中餐到地中海美食和现代荷兰菜。无论你只是为了匆匆忙忙填饱肚子还是想放松心情静静享受一顿丰盛的晚餐，在阿姆斯特丹你都能找得到想要的餐厅。不管你口袋里的预算有多少，不管你的品味是什么，永远都不用担心找不到能让你享受美食又让你缓解疲惫的双脚的一个去处。

这里我们仅推荐几家餐厅，包括一家荷兰当地华人和中国游客非常喜欢的中餐厅，还有一些非常受欢迎的米其林餐厅。

※ 福禄川菜

阿姆斯特丹福禄川菜，经营中餐、亚洲其他国家餐食和荷兰菜，是阿姆斯特丹最好的中餐和亚洲餐餐厅之一，离水坝广场、王宫、中央车站和杜莎夫人蜡像馆都不远。

福禄餐厅以其川菜和粤菜而闻名，并拥有非常棒的酒店式服务。主厨的特色菜是配以薄饼和美味酱汁的著名的北京烤鸭。菜单的菜色覆盖广泛，不管你是想吃肉、鱼还是蔬菜，辣还是不辣，你都能找到自己想吃的菜品。

营业时间：　周一至周四，上午11点至晚上10点

　　　　　　周五、周六，上午11点至晚上11点

地址：　　　阿姆斯特丹，Rokin 26号

联系方式：　020-6230885

　　　　　　www.mandarijnrokin.nl/

※ Ciel Bleu餐厅

　　去一家米其林星级餐厅是一件很惬意的事，荷兰人当然在这方面也不会缺少选择。在荷兰有超过100家米其林餐厅，仅在阿姆斯特丹，米其林一星和两星餐厅就超过15家。你可以在荷兰旅游局的网站（www.holland.com）上找到米其林餐厅的完整名单。

　　Ciel Bleu是一家米其林两星餐厅。他们的菜单选择性很多，每年会有四次更新。Ciel Bleu餐厅供应很多使用新鲜时令季节性食材烹饪的美食。当然，如果你有特殊的饮食需求或其他要求，在你预定餐位的时候也可以告诉他们。你可以在周一到周日，从上午10点到下午6点的时间联系餐厅进行预订，在线预订也可以。

　　友情提示，这家餐厅对食客有严格的着装要求，运动鞋、破洞牛仔裤是不被允许进入餐厅的，哪怕你穿的是普拉达也不行。

199

营业时间：　每天晚上6点半至晚上10点半，星期天不营业

地址：　　　阿姆斯特丹Ferdinand Bolstraat 333号

联系方式：　020-6787450

　　　　　　cielbleu@okura.nl/

　　　　　　http://www.cielbleu.nl/

Tijd voor Nederlands 荷兰语时间

● 单词+短语

荷 stad	荷 hoofdstad	荷 vakantie
英 city	英 capital	英 holiday
译 城市	译 首都、省会	译 假期
荷 vliegtuig	荷 halte	荷 uur
英 plane	英 stop	英 hour
译 飞机	译 车站	译 小时

荷 eerst keer	荷 blijven	荷 veranderen/wijzigen
英 first time	英 stay	英 change
译 第一次	译 停留	译 更换
荷 kamer	荷 bestemming	荷 morgen/middag/avond/nacht
英 room	英 destination	英 morning/afternoon/evening/night
译 房间	译 目的地	译 上午/下午/晚上/夜里
荷 kosten	荷 hoeveel	
英 cost	英 how many/much	
译 价值	译 多少	

● 例句

荷 Amsterdam ligt in Noord-Holland, maar is niet de hoofdstad van Noord-Holland, dat is Haarlem. 英 Amsterdam is located in North Holland, but is not the capital of North Holland, which is Haarlem. 译 阿姆斯特丹位于北荷兰省，但不是北荷兰省的省会，省会是哈勒姆。	荷 Ik ben in Nederland op vakantie. Dit is mijn eerste keer in Nederland. 英 I am in the Netherlands for holiday. This is my first time in the Netherlands. 译 我在荷兰度假，这是我第一次来荷兰。
荷 Het duurt tien uur met het vliegtuig van Beijing naar Amsterdam. 英 It takes ten hours by plane from Beijing to Amsterdam. 译 坐飞机从北京到阿姆斯特丹要10个小时。	荷 Ik zal drie dagen in Amsterdam blijven, de volgde bestemming is Den Haag. 英 I will stay in Amsterdam for three days, the next destination is The Hague. 译 我会在阿姆斯特丹停留三天，下一站是海牙。
荷 Neem tram 9 en stap uit bij de volgende halte. 英 Take tram 9 and get off at the next stop. 译 乘坐9号电车在下一站下车。	荷 Kunt u een kamer voor me ruilen? Deze kamer is te klein. 英 Can you change a room for me? This room is too small. 译 您能给我更换一个房间吗？这个房间太小了。
荷 Hoeveel kost de grote kamer per nacht? 英 How much does the big room cost per night? 译 大房间一晚多少钱？	荷 Hoe laat is het ontbijt? 英 What time is breakfast? 译 早餐在几点钟？

3. 鹿特丹
Rotterdam

Rotterdam is a city of many faces and colours: a tough port city, a trendy nightlife city, a sophisticated shopping city, and a hip and artistic city. It is a city with a lot of labels. Inner-city canal surfing, a proliferation of art, and a surge of drinking, dining and nightlife venues make Rotterdam one of Europe's most exhilarating cities right now.

Rotterdam is a veritable open-air gallery of modern, postmodern and contemporary architecture, it is the architecture capital of the Netherlands and is brimming with innovation. It's a remarkable feat for a city that was largely razed to the ground by a cowardly bomber attack of Nazi Germany in World War II. The story of the city, the bombardment and reconstruction, and the drive to innovate that locals still use today to shape their city all make Rotterdam a very fascinating place to visit.

鹿特丹是一个有着多重面孔和多重色彩的城市：它是一个刚强的港口城市、一个有着时尚夜生活的城市、一个成熟的购物中心、一个时髦的艺术中心。它是一个拥有众多标签的城市。市内的运河冲浪、艺术的普及、餐饮、杯光酒影的夜生活场所使得鹿特丹成为欧洲最令人兴奋的城市之一。

鹿特丹是一个名副其实的现代、后现代和当代建筑的露天画廊，它是荷兰的建筑之都，充满了创新。这对于一个在"二战"中被纳粹德国无耻地用炸弹夷为平地的城市来说，足一个了不起的成就。这个城市的故事，轰炸和重建，以及当地人今天仍然用来塑造城市的动力，都使鹿特丹成为一个非常吸引人的地方！

201

Sights and landmarks 景点和地标性建筑

※ Rotterdam Centraal Station

Before World War II, Rotterdam did not have a central railway station-instead there were four stations to the surrounding cities, Den Haag, Delft, Utrecht. The original Delftse Poort station was badly damaged during bombing of the Rotterdam by Nazi Germany. The new Centraal station was rebuilt just westwards of the site. Gradually, the trains from other cities were diverted to Centraal station via several other different stations.

On February 9, 1968 Princess Beatrix opened the first metro line in the Netherlands at Centraal station. The line connected the station to the south of Rotterdam and is now known as Line D.

The new Rotterdam's Central Station was completed in 2014. It is an infrastructure connecting a number of different routes through which you can access the city. Nearly 110,000 travellers pass through Central Station every day to catch a bus, tram, metro or train. Intercity trains from all across the country (including the Intercity Direct), the Thalys to Paris, and other international high-speed trains stop here several times a day, some even several times an hour.

The new station also has perfect supporting facilities, like fast-food restaurants, pharmacies, supermarkets and even clothing stores. It won't make you feel bored in transit time.

This significant example of contemporary architecture was designed by the Team CS (Benthem Crouwel Architects, MVSA Meyer & Van Schooten Architects, West 8), winners of the competition held in 2003. The roof is covered with 130,000 solar cells.

※ Markthal Rotterdam

The Markthal, which is the first covered market in the Netherlands, is a place where good food and unique housing are harmoniously combined in a spectacular arch.

New European regulations set stricter requirements on selling produce such as fish, meat and cheese in the open air. In Rotterdam, this moment was seen as an opportunity, and on November 9, 2009 work began on a highly ambitious project: a fresh food market, the like of which the world has never seen before. This iconic fresh market opened its doors for business on October 1, 2014, after nearly five years of construction.

The distinctive arch of the Markthal was built brick by brick near to the Rotte River, the very place where Rotterdam was founded in the year 1270. During construction, all sorts of medieval objects were found, from vases and tools to numerous cannonballs. These objects can currently be seen from the escalators in the Markthal and in the car park. In the interior of the building, the artist Arno Coenen and Iris Roskam created *The Horn of Plenty*, the biggest work of art in the world. Its bright colours cover an area of 11,000 m^2, resulting in this creation now being known as Rotterdam's very own Sistine Chapel.

※ Erasmus Bridge

The Erasmus Bridge is a striking feat of engineering and a must-see fixture on every Rotterdam visitor's itinerary.

Built from light-blue steel, its one-armed pylon jutting out high into the sky and throwing a row of 40 steel cables across the water, the 800-meter-long Erasmus Bridge is a remarkable sight. At its highest point, the bridge is 139 meters tall. Known as the 'Erasmusbrug' in Dutch, the bridge has also been lovingly nicknamed The Swan ("De Zwaan") by locals, thanks to its unusual shape. Rather than consisting of a simple vertical, its base runs parallel with the ground surface, then folds up at an angle before eventually bending up straight. It was designed by Ben van Berkel and opened in 1996 by Queen Beatrix.

As one of the Netherland's most famous bridges, the Erasmus Bridge spans the River Nieuwe Maas and forms an important connection between the northern and southern parts of Rotterdam. This can be explored particularly well as part of a bike tour through Rotterdam's city center.

As one of Rotterdam's key landmarks, the Erasmus Bridge is the setting for many spectacular events. A regular fixture on the city's cultural calendar is the annual World Port Days, a large-scale maritime event that celebrates Rotterdam's famous harbour–Europe's biggest seaport. Another important event is the Marathon of Rotterdam, the Netherland's largest running event. But that's not all: the bridge has also seen Hollywood movie shoots, Red Bull Air Races, dance events and featured in the Tour de France cycling race.

※ Euromast Tower

This is a landmark that many Chinese people are familiar with and have seen this tower in the text books in middle school.

The Euromast is an observation tower in Rotterdam, which was designed by Hugh Maaskant and constructed between 1958 and 1960. It was specially built for the 1960 Floriade, and is a listed monument since 2010. The tower consists of a concrete structure with an internal diameter of 9 meters and a wall thickness of 30 cm. For stability it is built on a concrete block of 1,900,000 kg so that the centre of gravity is below ground. It has a "crow's nest" observation platform 96 meters above-ground and a restaurant. Originally 101 meters in height it was the tallest building in Rotterdam. It lost this position to the high-rise of Erasmus MC (113.5 m) which was completed in 1968, but regained it when the Space Tower was added to the top of the building in 1970, giving an additional 85 meters. Euromast is a member of the World Federation of Great Towers. In 2008 and 2009, the tower hosted an extreme sports event which featured BASE jumping.

It should be noted that the Euromast is not the highest construction in Holland at present. The radio tower near Lopik has this honour: the Gerbrandy Tower is 361 meters high.

Euromast is almost one of Rotterdam's most popular attractions. Climb to the highest point and enjoy the beautiful scenery. On a clear day, you can see the Belgian city of Antwerp some 80 kilometers away. High above the city you will even find several luxury suites, where you can enjoy the most beautiful sunrise and sunset ever.

※ Kinderdijk

Kinderdijk with its beautiful windmills lies not far from the port city of Rotterdam and Dordrecht, the oldest city of the province of South-Holland. It's a popular, yet authentic, tourist destination for its large network of windmills. The windmills received their recognition as a UNESCO World Heritage Site in 1997.

The name Kinderdijk is Dutch for "Children dike". During the Saint Elizabeth flood of 1421, the Grote Hollandse Waard flooded, but the Alblasserwaard polder stayed unflooded. It is said that when the terrible storm had subsided, someone went to the dike between these two areas to see what could be saved. In the distance he saw a wooden cradle floating on the water. As it came nearer, some movement was detected. A cat was seen in the cradle trying to keep it in balance by jumping back and forth so that no water could get into it. As the cradle eventually came close enough to the dike for a bystander to pick up the cradle, he saw that a baby was quietly sleeping inside it, nice and dry. The cat had kept the cradle balanced and afloat. This folktale and legend has been published as "The Cat and the Cradle" in English.

In Alblasserwaard, problems with water became more and more apparent in the 13th century. Large canals, called "weteringen", were dug to get rid of the excess water in the polders. However, the drained soil continued to subside, while the level of the river rose due to the river's

203

sand deposits. After a few centuries, an additional way to keep the polders dry was required. It was decided to build a series of windmills, with a limited capacity to bridge water level differences, but just able to pump water into a reservoir at an intermediate level between the soil in the polder and the river; the reservoir could be pumped out into the river by other windmills whenever the river level was low enough; the river level has both seasonal and tidal variations. Although some of the windmills are still used, the main water works are provided by two diesel pumping stations near one of the entrances of the windmills site.

※ Cube House Rotterdam

Cube houses are a set of innovative houses built in Rotterdam. Dutch architect Piet Blom designed Rotterdam's Cube Houses in the late-1970s at the request of the city's planners. The building based on the concept of "living as an urban roof": high density housing with sufficient space on the ground level, since its main purpose is to optimise the space inside. Blom tilted the cube of a conventional house 45 degrees, and rested it upon a hexagon-shaped pylon. His design represents a village within a city, where each house represents a tree, and all the houses together, a forest. The residences were constructed on concrete pillars with wooden framing. Once you step inside, the first thing to get used to is that all the walls are slanted. And as you enter the top half of the structure, your initial inclination may well be to mind your head.

The houses in Rotterdam are located on Overblaak Street, right above the Blaak Subway Station. There are 38 small cubes and two so called "super-cubes", all attached to each other.

As residents are disturbed so often by curious passers-by, one house was opened be a "show cube", which is furnished as a normal house, and is making a living out of offering tours to visitors.

The living room of the "show cube" contains three floors: ground floor is the entrance, the living room and an open kitchen are on the first floor, two bedrooms and a bathroom on the second floor, the top floor is sometimes a small garden in a warm season.

The walls and windows are angled at 54.7 degrees. The total area of the apartment is around 100 square metres, but around a quarter of the space is unusable because of the walls that are under the angled ceilings.

In 2006, a museum of chess pieces was opened under the houses.

In 2009, the larger cubes were converted by Personal Architecture into a hostel run by Dutch hostel chain Stayokay.

※ Museumpark

Museumpark is an urban park in Rotterdam, the Netherlands, located between the Museum Boijmans Van Beuningen, Westersingel, Westzeedijk and the complex of the Erasmus MC, a medical centre affiliated with the Erasmus University.

The park lies on the former land of the Hoboken family, who lived in the building that is now the Natuurhistorisch Museum Rotterdam. The park was laid out in 1927 to the design of the architect Witteveen. The Museumpark is divided in five areas. The first area is the rose garden with a pond and a memorial for the prominent city architect Gerrit de Jongh. The second area contains the Kunsthal and the Natuurmuseum. The third area is a romantic garden. The fourth area is a raised event terrain on top of a underground car park. The fifth area eventually is a crossing between city and park recognisable by white shells on the ground.

There are a number of museums located in the vicinity of the park, hence the names:

- The Netherlands Architecture Institute (NAi)
- Museum Boijmans Van Beuningen
- The Chabot Museum
- The Kunsthal
- Huis Sonneveld
- Natuurhistorisch Museum Rotterdam

※ Sint Laurenskerk

The 'St. Laurenskerk' of Rotterdam was constructed between 1449 and 1525, in the late gothic period. It is the only remaining medieval structure and the first all stone building in Rotterdam. In 1621 a wooden spire was added to the tower, designed by Hendrick de Keyser. Poor quality of its wood caused the spire to be demolished in 1645. A stone cube was added to the tower, which proved too heavy for the foundation in 1650. New piles were driven under the tower and in 1655 the tower stood straight again.

During the bombing by Nazi Germany on May 14, 1940 the Laurenskerk was heavily damaged. At first there were calls to demolish the church, but that was stopped by Queen Wilhelmina of the Netherlands. In 1952, Queen Juliana of the Netherlands laid the foundation stone for the restoration, which was completed in 1968. The restoration of the Laurenskerk was viewed as a symbol of the resilience of Rotterdam's community.

In 1971 the Laurenspastoraat community was established (as part of the Reformed Church of Rotterdam) in order to resume church services. The community received a Cross of Nails replica from Coventry Cathedral in order to become a local center for peace and reconciliation. In 1981 the liberal Maaskant/Open Grenzen community joined the church and since then the two communities alternate their services.

※ Rotterdam Zoo

Rotterdam Zoo (Dutch: Diergaarde Blijdorp) is one of the most popular attractions in the Netherlands and the most visited Rotterdam attraction, because this 150-year-old zoo is one of Europe's most beautiful zoos. In 2016 and 2017 it was even elected the best zoo in the Benelux.

During your tour through Rotterdam Zoo, you discover the animal world on a voyage from the Asian Rainforest and the African Savannah to the Himalayas Highlands and the Gorilla Forest in Congo: you will travel to all of the continents in a day in Blijdorp. Dive into the Oceanium and stroll among the sharks. At Tiger Creek, you literally come face to face with these beautiful predators.

Or go and explore a jungle full of fluttering butterflies in Amazonica. In short, there is too much to do at Diergaarde Blijdorp!

Diergaarde Blijdorp was established in 1857. In 1940, the zoo was relocated from the city center to its current location in the Blijdorp district. The new zoo was designed by the architect Sybold van Ravesteyn. He tried to avoid fences and bars in his design as much as he could and created a zoo unlike any other in the world with spacious animal pens. Today, the old part of the zoo is a national monument.

Are you curious to see what the animals do after closing hours? Visiting the zoo at night is also possible, you could book the Blijdorp By Night arrangement. Several days every year, Blijdorp opens its doors at night. You can enjoy a meal and then go on a guided tour of the zoo at nightfall. It certainly will be remarkable and unforgettable experience!

※ 鹿特丹中央车站

"二战"前，鹿特丹没有一个中央火车站，但周边的城市海牙、代尔夫特、乌特勒支有四个火车站。在纳粹德国轰炸鹿特丹的时候，最初的Delftse Poort火车站遭到严重破坏。新的中央车站是在该址的西侧重建的。渐渐地，来自别的城市的列车从其他几个不同的小车站挪到了新的中央车站。

1968年2月9日，当时的贝娅特丽克丝公主在鹿特丹中央车站主持开通了第一条地铁线路。这条线连接了鹿特丹南部的车站，现在被称为"D线"。

鹿特丹中央车站是非常重要的站点，从这里可以直接途经安特卫普和布鲁塞尔前往巴黎，以及乘坐"欧洲之星"前往伦敦。

新的鹿特丹中央车站于2014年建成。这是一项接连了诸多不同线路的城市基础设施，经由这些路线你可以到达鹿特丹的各个地方。现在每天在鹿特丹中央车站乘坐、换乘公共汽车、电车、地铁或火车的客流量可达11万人。来自全国各地的城际列车（包括城际直通车）、开往巴黎的Thalys和其他国际高速列车每天都会在这里停几次，有时甚至是一小时几次。

新的车站拥有非常完善的配套设施，如快餐厅、药店、超市甚至服装店，不会让你在转乘途中感到无聊。

鹿特丹中央车站这一当代建筑的重要典范是由2003年举办的设计大赛的获胜者Team CS团队（Benthem Crouwel Architects、MVSA Meyer、Van Schooten Architects、West 8）设计的。其车站顶部由13万块太阳能电池板所覆盖着。

※ 鹿特丹拱廊市场

鹿特丹拱廊市场或缤纷菜市场是荷兰第一个有顶盖的市场，在壮观的拱形建筑中，美食与独特的住宅房屋和谐地融合在一起。

新出台的欧洲法规对在露天销售的鱼、肉和奶酪等农产品的规定提出了更严格的要求。在鹿特丹，这种新的规范成了一个机遇，2009年11月19日他们提出了一个雄心勃勃的计划：要建造一个在世界上从来没有的、一个新颖的食品市场。经过近5年的建设，这个标志性的新市场于2014年10月1日开门营业。

拱廊市场独特的拱门是由一块一块的砖砌成的，位于罗特河附近的地块，这里正是1270年鹿特丹的发源地。在建造过程中，各种各样的中世纪物品被挖掘发现，从花瓶和工具到无数的炮弹。这些物品现在可以在拱廊市场和停车场的自动扶梯上看到。在这座建筑的内部，艺术家阿诺·库恩和伊利斯·罗斯卡姆创作了世界上最大的艺术作品《丰饶之角》。它明亮的色彩覆盖了11 000平方米的面积，因此现在被称为鹿特丹的西斯廷教堂。

拱廊市场的穹顶很是抓人眼球，颜色明艳，象征着收获和喜悦。图为傍晚的拱廊市场。

※ 伊拉斯谟大桥

伊拉斯谟大桥是一项引人注目的工程壮举，是每一个到鹿特丹的游客必到的景点。

这座800米长的伊拉斯谟大桥是由浅蓝色的钢建成的，它的单臂长塔高高地耸立在天空中，在水面上映射出一排四十根钢缆，这是一幅非凡的景象。桥的至高点是139米。这座桥因其独特的外形而被当地人亲切地称为"天鹅"。它的基部与地面平行，而不是简单的垂直，然后以一个角度折起，最终向上弯曲。它由本·范·贝尔科设计，在1996年由贝娅特丽克斯女王主持开放。

作为荷兰最著名的桥梁之一，伊拉斯谟大桥跨越了新马斯河，形成了鹿特丹北部和南部的重要联系。这是在鹿特丹市中心骑自行车旅行的一部分。

作为鹿特丹的重要地标之一，伊拉斯谟大桥是许多盛大活动的举办场地。在鹿特丹的文化日历上定期举办的是一年一度的世界港口日，这是一场大型海上活动，以此庆祝欧洲最大的海港——著名的鹿特丹港；另一个重要的大型活动是荷兰最大的跑步项目鹿特丹马拉松。但这些还不是全部，这座桥还见证了好莱坞电影的拍摄、红牛竞速飞行、舞蹈活动，以及环法自行车赛等特色赛事。

※ 欧洲桅杆

这是很多中国人都熟悉的一处景点和地标建筑，在中学的教科书里看到过这座塔。

欧洲桅杆是鹿特丹的一座瞭望塔，由休·马斯康德设计，建于1958年至1960年之间。它是专门为1960年的Floriade园艺博览会建造的，是自2010年起被列为国家历史遗迹。该塔为混凝土结构，内径为9米，壁厚30厘米。为了稳固塔身，它是建在一个大约为190万公斤的巨大混凝土方块上，这样一来重力中心就转到了地下。在96米高的地方有一个"鸦巢"一般的观景台及餐厅。欧洲桅杆最初101米的高度曾是鹿特丹最高的建筑，在1968年113.5米高的伊拉斯谟大学附属医学中心完工之后便失去了第一的位置，但是在1970年，它的顶部又增加了一个"太空塔"，使总高度达到了185米，直至今日仍是荷兰最高的地标建筑之一。欧洲桅杆是世界高塔联盟的成员。在2008年和2009年，该塔举办了一项以定点跳伞为特色的极限运动。

值得注意的是，目前欧洲桅杆并不是荷兰的最高建筑。靠近洛皮克的无线电塔获得了这一殊荣：高361米的Gerbrandy tower。

欧洲桅杆几乎算是鹿特丹最受欢迎的景点之一。爬到最高点，欣赏美丽的风景。在晴朗的日子里，你可以看到大约80公里外的比利时城市安特卫普。在城市的高处甚至可以找到几间豪华套房，在那里你可以陶醉于迷人的日出和日落。

欧洲桅杆几乎算是鹿特丹最受欢迎的景点之一，晴朗时可远眺安特卫普。

※ 小孩堤防

小孩堤防有着漂亮的风车，离港口城市鹿特丹和荷兰最古老的城市多德雷赫特都不远。这是一个备受欢迎，但也真真切切的旅游目的地，全因它拥有庞大的风车网。1997年，这些风车被联合国教科文组织列为世界文化遗产。

小孩堤防的风车景象最能体验鼎盛时期的荷兰，无论什么季节来都很美。

Kinderdijk荷兰语名字的意思是"Children dike"，就是小孩堤防。在1421年的圣伊丽莎白洪水期间，大荷兰瓦德地区被洪水淹没，但阿尔布瑟瓦德的圩田却安然无恙。据说，当可怕的风暴平息后，有人去这两个地方的堤防去看看能救什么，结果在远处他看见一个木制的摇篮浮在水面上，再走近时发现了一些动静，在摇篮里看到一只猫，试图通过来回跳跃来保持摇篮的平衡，这样水就进不到里面了。最后摇篮终于靠近了堤岸，一个旁观者拎起摇篮时发现一个婴儿正静静地睡在里面，干干爽爽的。这只猫保障了摇篮没有失去平衡，从而让摇篮一直漂浮在水面上。这个民间传奇故事以"猫和摇篮"的名字被出版。

在阿尔布瑟瓦德的圩田地区，水灾的问题在13世纪变得越来越突出。人们开凿了大运河，称为"水道"，其目的为了清除圩田里多余的水。然而，排干积水的土壤却继续下沉，河流的水位也由于沙质的沉积而不断上升。几个世纪以后，人们需要另寻他法来保持这些圩田的干燥。于是人们决定建造一系列的风车，凭借有限的能力来弥合水位的差异，但只能将水注入圩区土壤和河流之间的中间水库；当河流水位足够低时，水可以被其他的风车泵入河中；河流水位既有季节性的变化，也会随着潮汐有高低变化。虽然一些风车仍在使用当中，但主要的水力运作是由两个柴油泵站提供的，在靠近风车村的一个入口处。

※ 立体方块屋

立体方块屋是一套建造在鹿特丹的创新房屋。在城市规划者的要求下，荷兰建筑师皮特·布洛姆在20世纪70年代末设计了鹿特丹的立体方块房屋。该建筑以"生活在城市的屋檐下"的概念为设计理念：地面上配备足够空间的高密度住宅，其主要目的是优化室内空间。布洛姆把传统房子的立方体倾斜了45度，把它放在一个六边形的塔上。他的设计代表了一个城市里的一个村庄，每个房子都代表一棵树，所有的房子融合在一起代表一片森林。这些住宅是用混凝土柱子和木质框架建造而成的。一旦进到建筑的上半部分时，首先要习惯所有的墙都是倾斜的，注意不要碰到头。

这些方块屋坐落在Overblaak大街上，就在布拉克地铁站的上方，由彼此相连的三十八个小方块和两个所谓的"超级立方体"组成。

居住在此的人们被充满好奇心的路人打扰简直是家常便饭，因此其中一所房子开放给公众作为展示房间，作为项目中一所普通的房子，现在主要为游客提供旅游方面的服务。

展示方块屋的大厅有三层：地面楼层（即我们习惯称的一层）是入口，客厅和开放式厨房在一楼（我们称为的二层），二楼（我们称为三层）有两间卧室和一间浴室，顶层在温暖的时节会当作一个空中小花园。

墙壁和窗户的角度为54.7度。公寓的总面积约为100平方米，但由于墙壁在倾斜的天花板下面，大约四分之一的空间无法使用。

立体方块屋很能表达鹿特丹市政府对城市规划的态度，这也是鹿特丹城市建造诸多新型尝试中的代表之作。

2006年，房子的下面开了一家国际象棋博物馆。

2009年，更大一些立方体由私人住宅结构改造成了荷兰连锁青年旅社"好住"（Stayokay）。

※ 博物馆公园

博物馆公园是荷兰鹿特丹市的一个城市公园，在博伊曼斯·范伯宁恩美术馆、韦斯特辛格、韦斯特泽迪克和伊拉斯谟大学附属的医学中心伊拉斯谟中心之间。

公园坐落在霍博肯家族以前的土地上，他们之前住在现在是鹿特丹自然历史博物馆的建筑内。

209

这座公园是建筑师维特维恩于1927年所设计的。博物馆公园分为五个区域：第一个区域是玫瑰花园，内有一个池塘和著名的城市建筑师格里特·德伊昂的纪念碑；第二个区域包括昆莎现代艺术中心或者叫昆莎美术馆和自然历史博物馆；第三个区域是一个浪漫的花园；第四个区域是建在一个地下停车场上部的活动区；第五个区域最终成为城市和公园的交叉口，地上铺着白色的贝壳，很好辨识。

博物馆公园的附近有较多的博物馆，名字如下：荷兰建筑学会、博伊曼斯·范伯宁恩美术馆、鹿特丹沙博博物馆、昆莎现代艺术中心、松内费尔德住宅家庭博物馆和自然历史博物馆。

※ 圣劳伦斯大教堂

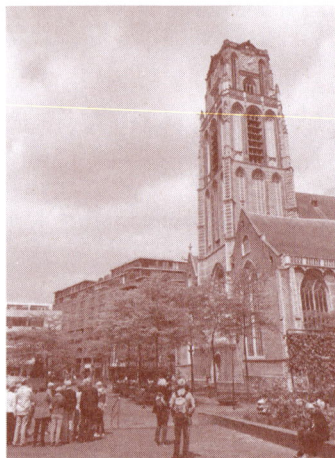

圣劳伦斯大教堂位于中心位置，代表了鹿特丹对生命的积极态度。图为圣劳伦斯大教堂。

鹿特丹圣劳伦斯大教堂是在1449年到1525年间建造的，在晚期的哥特时期，它是鹿特丹现存的唯一的中世纪建筑，也是鹿特丹第一个全石头建筑。1621年，由亨德里克·德·凯瑟设计的一座木塔被加到钟楼上。由于木材质量低劣，塔尖在1645年被拆除。1650年，一个石头立方体代替木质塔尖被安放到钟楼，但这对地基来说太沉重了。1655年，塔基又进行了加固和扶正，重新恢复笔直。

在1940年5月14日纳粹德国轰炸期间，圣劳伦斯大教堂受到严重损坏。起初，有人要求拆毁教堂，但被当时的荷兰女王威廉敏娜阻止了。1952年，荷兰女王朱莉安娜为修复工程奠定了基础，修复工作于1968年完工。圣劳伦斯大教堂的恢复被认为是鹿特丹社会韧性的象征。

1971年，作为鹿特丹改革教堂的一部分，圣劳伦斯大教堂恢复其作为教堂的服务功能。为了成为当地和平与和解的中心，教堂工会接收到了来自考文垂大教堂的十字架。1981年，自由派马斯康特和赫恩泽恩加入了教会，从那时起，便由两个社区交替为教堂服务。

※ 鹿特丹动物园

鹿特丹动物园是最受欢迎的鹿特丹景点，也是荷兰最受欢迎的景点之一，因为这个有着150年历史的动物园是欧洲最漂亮的动物园之一。在2016年和2017年，它甚至被评为比荷卢联盟的最佳动物园。

在游览鹿特丹动物园的过程中，你会经历一个从亚洲热带雨林和非洲大草原到喜马拉雅山和刚果大猩猩森林的奇幻旅程，在动物园的一天中你将"走遍"所有的大洲。潜入水族馆中，在凶猛的鲨鱼群间徜徉；在老虎溪，你将会与这些美丽的掠食者直接面对面；或者去飞满蝴蝶的亚马逊丛林来一次探险之旅。简而言之，在鹿特丹动物园有太多的事情要做！

鹿特丹动物园建于1857年。1940年，动物园从城市中心搬迁到布莱多普地区，也就是当前位置。新动物园是由建筑师赛博德·范·拉夫斯滕设计的。为尽量避免在自己的设计中使用传统的栅栏，他创造了一个与世界上其他任何动物园都极不相同的围栏。今天，旧的动物园已经成为国家纪念遗址。

你想知道动物们在闭园之后都在做什么吗？夜间造访动物园也是可以的，你可以预定动物园夜间项目。鹿特丹动物园每年都会有好几天夜间参观活动安排。你可以在享受一顿美味晚餐之后再启程前往动物园，它肯定是一种极具不同难以忘怀的体验！

Shopping in Rotterdam 购在鹿特丹

One of the befits of being in a world city is having ample chance to go shopping and Rotterdam has the best shopping experience of the Netherlands. It has many major department stores, shoe and fashion stores, but also a variety of specialised shops. Most shops are located down town Rotterdam, but there are also two huge malls just outside the city centre (Zuidplein mall and Alexandrium mall).

※ Lijnbaan

The Lijnbaan is the main shopping street of Rotterdam, it runs from the Weena street near Rotterdam Central Station to Binnenwegplein. The Lijnbaan was opened in 1953, as the main pedestrian street in the new shopping district, after the old shopping district was completely destroyed during the bombing of Rotterdam by Nazi Germany. It was designed by the firm Van den Broek & Bakema led by architects Jo van den Broek and Jacob B. Bakema.

Lijnbaan was the first modern shopping street in post-war Europe, where no cars were allowed to enter. Today, Lijnbaan is still car-free and it is still an excellent shopping area. Lijnbaan is the beating heart of Rotterdam shopping with many large stores of international fashion chains. Whether you're a fast fashion fan or a limited-edition fashion fan or just a crazy foodie, here you can satisfy all your desires. Lijnbaan is the place to be for all young people in Rotterdam.

※ Koopgoot (Beurstraverse)

The sunken shopping passage "Koopgoot", which links two important shopping streets, Lijnbaan and Hoogstraat, via the Beursplein underground metro station. It is the generally accepted nickname of what was officially named Beurstraverse and roughly translates as 'shopping Gutter', which has been the main shopping centre in the heart of Rotterdam for the last 20 years. Apart from this, it is an architectural masterpiece that has won many awards. Particularly inviting to relax and take in all the impressions are the chairs that were especially designed for the Koopgoot by Maarten Baas.

This is different from Lijnbaan. At end of the Koopgoot you find the best-known department store in the Netherlands Bijenkorf and also the very fashionable department store Peek & Cloppenburg. Inside Koopgoot, you'll find Kruidvat, the largest drugstore chain in the Netherlands, but also some boutiques and of course big brand stores like Zara and H&M.

※ Hoogstraat

Hoogstraat Rotterdam is another one of the main shopping streets in Rotterdam's city centre. Hoogstraat connects the Koopgoot shopping street with the Binnenrotte, where Rotterdam's biggest market and the huge Rotterdam Market Hall are located, it has its one character, you'll find stores in many different categories. In Holland&Barrett, Kruidvat and Etos, you can find a wide range of skincare products and cosmetics as well as some food products, through the year they have different discounts and special sales. If you have a sweet tooth, then this is the place to be, as there are many shops that sell traditional and delicious dutch waffles and sweets.

Also located in this street are several famous sporting goods stores, and on the site of the former department store V&D you will now find the famous Canadian department Hudson's Bay which sells many popular cosmetics brand such as NARS, YSL, TOMFORT. They also provide a good dining environment and is a nice place to take a break.

※ Van Oldenbarneveltstraat

Van Oldenbarneveltstraat is a little known shopping area in Rotterdam and its shops are definitely worth a visit. Although you won't find any of the big chains here, you will certainly forget the time searching and strolling through the small-scale and trendy boutiques and restaurants. Van Oldenbarneveltstraat is considered as one of the most exclusive shopping streets in Rotterdam.

Here you will find "Dorien David's" with wedding, party and evening wear. "Rings to Connect" at Van Oldenbarneveltstraat has a special collection of wedding rings. On the other side of the street you can find Filippa K for fashionable basic clothing. At the crossroads, you will find the "Wendela van Dijk boutique" with a collection of women's designer labels and "SK Edelsmid" sells jewellery with a plain and simple but elegant design. SAS/KOOKAI mainly offers exclusive KOOKAI clothing collection. Fashion boutique "Mostert & Van Leeuwen" has an exclusive collection of designer labels and Skins Cosmetics and is the right shop for real beauty fans.

Time for a shopping break? Alice in Cakeland has delicious sweets and cupcakes. At the end of the street, lunch and winebar Nostra serves a great high tea, but you could also choose to have lunch or dinner at the intimate winebar "l'Ouest". Don't miss "Mangiare", a sweet and small restaurant with daily changing dishes.

※ Binnenrotte Centrummarkt

The largest street market of Rotterdam is located in the city centre at Binnenrotte near the Blaak underground station. This weekly market covers the Binnenrotte square from Blaak to shopping street Meent and contains more than 400 stands. Near the Blaak area, you will find fresh produce such as fruit, fish, cheese, vegetables, flowers and candy. At the Rotterdam market square in the vicinity of Meent clothes, smart phone accessories, vintage goods, fabrics and souvenirs are offered. In the afternoon this market can be quite crowded, especially during the weekend. On rainy days the street market has a functional shelter by means of plastic covers, so if you're a tall person do mind your head! You can combine a visit to the Rotterdam street market with a day of shopping in Rotterdam, because the market square is connected to the Meent and Hoogstraat shopping streets.

※ Alexandrium mall

Shopping mall Alexandrium includes a Shopping Center, Megastores and a Woonmall. With almost 140 stores Alexandrium Shopping Center is one of the largest shopping malls in the Netherlands. Alexandrium Shopping Center focuses on fashion, gifts, shoes, jewellery and basically all shops you would expect in a huge indoor shopping mall are located here. The second area is the Alexandrium Megastores area and it's located next to the shopping center. The name says it all: this is a strip with a range of big flagship stores. The third area is called the Alexandrium "Woonmall", which focuses on everything related to home decoration and interior design.

作为世界性大城市的一员，鹿特丹适合购物的场所众多，且在这里也拥有荷兰最棒的购物体验，这里有众多主要的百货公司、潮流鞋店和时装店，也有各种不同类别的专门店。鹿特丹大多数商店都位于市中心，但市中心以外也有两个大型购物中心——南广场购物中心和亚历山大购物中心。

※ 莱恩班街

莱恩班街是鹿特丹的主要购物街，它从鹿特丹中央车站附近的维纳街一直延伸到快捷路广场。莱恩班街于1953年开业，是新购物区的主要步行街，此前的老购物区在"二战"时被纳粹德国炸毁。新的购物步行街是由建筑师乔·范登·布鲁克和雅各布·B.巴克马所领导的同名设计公司所设计的。

莱恩班街是战后欧洲第一条现代购物街，机动车辆一律禁止入内。今天，莱恩班街仍然是车辆禁行街道，是一个很好的购物区。莱恩班街是鹿特丹购物中心的心脏，拥有许多大型国际时装连锁店，无论你是一个时尚品的忠实用户还是一个限量版的痴迷粉丝，或是一个疯狂的美食评论家，在这里都可以满足你所有的欲望。莱恩班街是鹿特丹所有年轻人的圣地。

Lijnbaan是"二战"后第一条现代的购物街，已经超过半个世纪，遍布着许多年轻人喜爱的潮流品牌和运动品牌集合店。

※ 购物战壕

购物战壕是一条下沉式购物街道，连接着两个非常重要的购物街，莱恩班街和胡格街，并连通着Beursplein地铁站。购物战壕是一个形象的荷兰语昵称，正式的称呼为Beurstraverse，大致可以直接翻译成购物中心，在过去的20年里，这里一直是鹿特丹市内的主要购物区。除此之外，这里也是一项杰出的建筑作品，赢得了许多奖项。其中专供游人休息放松的椅子给人印象深刻，是由马汀巴斯专门为购物战壕设计的。

Koopgoot是一个下沉式的购物区，有旗舰店和百货商店，还有美妆店和甜品店。

购物战壕和莱恩班街有所不同。在购物战壕的两端，你会发现荷兰最著名的百货公司女王百货（我们在阿姆斯特丹这一篇章专门讲过，这是在鹿特丹的门店），以及非常时尚的百货商店Peek & Cloppenburg。在购物战壕还有荷兰最大的药妆连锁店Kruidbat以及多家精品店，当然也少不了年轻人们喜爱的像Zara和H&M这样的大型快时尚品牌店。

※ 胡格街

胡格街是鹿特丹市中心另一条主要的购物街。胡格街连接了购物战壕和市中心露天集市，后者是鹿特丹最大的市场，这是鹿特丹拱廊市场所在的位置，特色鲜明，各种类型的商店均能在这里找到。在著名的保健品商店花园店（现改名为Holland&Barrett）、Kruidvat和Etos，可以采购名目繁多的护肤品和化妆品，还有一些可食用商品，他们各家店全年都有不同的折扣和特价销售。如果你是个甜食控，那么这里也必须要来一趟，有很多商店出售传统美味的荷兰华夫饼（有些还是现做的）和糖果。

在这条街上还有几家非常著名的体育用品商店。在之前百货的公司V&D的旧址，现在新开了一家，著名的加拿大哈德逊湾百货公司，当前很多明星品牌和热门化妆品品牌他们都有，如NARS、YSL、TOMFORT等。百货里面还有环境非常良好的餐厅，是一个逛累了休息的绝佳去处。

※ 范·奥尔登巴内费尔特街

范·奥尔登巴内费尔特街是鹿特丹的一个鲜为人知的购物区，但它的商店绝对值得一逛。在这里找不到任何所谓的大品牌的连锁店，但你沉迷在小巧玲珑的、时髦的精品店和餐馆里时会忘了时间。奥尔登巴内费尔特街被认为是鹿特丹最高档的购物街之一。

在这里你可以看到多利安·戴维的门店，他们出售婚礼、派对和晚宴等的礼服。在 "Rings to Connect" 则能选购到特别珍藏的结婚戒指。在街道的另一边，菲利帕·K有时尚的基本款服饰。在十字路口是汶德拉·范·戴克的精品时装店，出售女设计师品牌时装，而 "SK Edelsmid" 则出售设计简洁而优雅的珠宝首饰。SAS蔻凯主要出售独家KOOKAI服装系列。时尚精品店莫斯泰特·范·鲁文独家收藏了设计师品牌和化妆品，是爱美之人真正的不二之选。

逛累了需要休息一下？爱丽丝蛋糕乐园有非常美味的甜品和纸杯蛋糕。在这条街的尽头，

Nostra供应午餐，也是个饮酒的好地方，有丰盛的下午茶。你也可以在 "l'Ouest" 享用午餐或晚餐。还有一家Mangiare不要错过，他们家每天都供应不同的餐食。

※ 鹿特丹市中心市集

鹿特丹最大的市集——市中心市集位于城市中心布拉克地铁站附近。这个每周开放的市场包括布拉克地铁站到门特购物街的整个市中心广场，包含400多个摊位。在布拉克附近，能买到新鲜的农产品，如水果、鱼、奶酪、蔬菜、鲜花和糖果。在门特街中心广场这边则是服装、智能手机配件、复古货、面料和纪念品的摊位。市场在下午的时候会很拥挤，尤其是在周末。雨天市场同样开放，会用塑料遮盖起来避雨，如果你是个大高个儿的话要注意不要碰头了！你要来市场的话也可以当天安排同时逛逛附近的街道，因为市中心广场就连接着门特街和胡格购物街。

鹿特丹市中心市集在拱廊市场前的大广场上，胡格购物街的尽头，市场上商品种类很丰富，有鲜蔬水果和衣物，还有传统小吃和日化商品。

※ 亚历山大购物中心

亚历山大购物中心包括一个购物中心、一个大卖场和一个家居大卖场。这个购物中心有约140家商铺，是荷兰最大的购物中心之一。亚历山大购物中心的店铺主要集中于时尚、礼品、鞋子、珠宝，基本上你希望在购物中心能够逛到的品类这里都涵盖了。亚历山大大卖场是购物中心的第二个部分，就在购物中心的旁边。它的名字说明了一切：这是一个集中了大型专卖店的区域。第三个区域叫做亚历山大 "Woonmall"，意思是家居卖场，专注于家居装饰产品和室内设计类的商品。

Eating in Rotterdam 食在鹿特丹

There are many places to eat in Rotterdam. People of 176 different nationalities have made Rotterdam their home, bringing with them an incredible variety of food and flavours.

From the well-known fast food chains to the best restaurants of the Netherlands, from Italian, Chinese and other Asian restaurants located in Rotterdam to the very fine French restaurants. When it's about food then Rotterdam can accommodate almost everyone. Michelin restaurants can satisfy you even if you want to eat well but not expensive. These fine restaurants in Rotterdam are listed at the Michelin Guide for their outstanding kitchen at a price below €35: restaurant Huson (international), restaurant Asian Glories (Chinese) and restaurant In den Rustwat (French).

※ Sansan

Sansan is a Sichuan restaurant that opened its doors in 2011. The restaurant specialises in Sichuan cuisine, with all its lovely and spicy tastes and flavoured. It's a real difference from the mainstream Chinese restaurants in the Netherlands which serve food that could is much milder and sweeter than real Chinese mainland cuisine.

Hours:	Daily 12pm–10pm; Tuesday closed
Address:	Hang 33, 3011 GG Rotterdam
Contact:	010- 4115681
	http://www.sansan33.nl

※ Parkheuvel

Parkheuvel in Rotterdam is one of the best restaurants in the Netherlands, their French cuisine was rewarded two Michelin stars. The restaurant is located at Heuvellaan 21 in Rotterdam, in a semicircular modern pavilion with a view over the Nieuwe Maas and Rotterdam Harbour. The pavilion is decorated in art deco style.

Restaurant Parkheuvel provides an amazing dining experience with superb wines that accompany every course. You can taste their passion for food every single bite, which is artfully presented on your plate. Restaurant Parkheuvel is definitely a must-visit restaurant for gourmets.

The wine and Kobe steaks of the restaurant and the very considerate service will not disappoint you.

Hours:	Monday & Tuesday: Closed
	Wednesday &Thursday& Friday: 12pm–3pm, 6:30pm–9:30pm
	Saturday: 6:30pm–9:30pm
	Sunday: 12:30pm–6pm
Address:	Heuvellaan 21, 3016 GL Rotterdam
Contact:	010-4360766
	http://www.parkheuvel.nl

鹿特丹吃饭的地方非常多。来自全世界176个不同民族的人把家安在了鹿特丹，同时将各自民族难以置信的多姿多样的食物和不同的口味都带到了这里。

从著名的快餐连锁店到荷兰最好的餐厅，从驻扎在鹿特丹的意大利餐、中国料理和其他亚洲餐馆到高端的法国餐厅。关于吃饭问题，鹿特丹几近能满足所有的人，即使是一家米其林餐厅也能满足你想要吃得好但又要不贵的要求。这些广受好评的餐馆被列在了米其林指南上，消费也不过人均

35欧元，如Huson（国际餐）餐厅、 Asian Glories（中餐）和In den Rustwat（法国餐）。

※ 三三川菜

三三（Sansan）是一家在2011年开业的四川餐馆。其餐厅的特色菜当然也就是川菜了，味道鲜美、麻辣，满足了你想吃川菜的需求。三三跟那些在荷兰提供口味清淡、甜腻中式菜肴的主流广式中餐馆有很大的不同，口味已经尽量在接近国内的真正川菜。

营业时间：　每天中午12点到晚上10点，周二不营业

地址：　　　鹿特丹Hang 33号

联系方式：　010-4115681

　　　　　　http://www.sansan33.nl

※ Parkheuvel

鹿特丹的Parkheuvel餐厅是荷兰最好的餐厅之一，他们的法国美食荣获了米其林两颗星的赞誉。这家餐厅位于鹿特丹的Heuvellaan21号，在一个半圆形的现代展馆中，俯瞰着新马斯河和鹿特丹港。其装饰风格散发着浓厚的艺术氛围。

在Parkheuvel餐厅用餐是一种美妙的体验，每道菜都搭配着一流的葡萄酒。盛在餐盘的食物巧妙精致，品尝每一口食物你都能感受到餐厅饱满的热情和其特别用心。Parkheuvel是美食家们不得不拜访的餐厅。

餐厅的酒和神户牛排很赞，体贴周到的服务更不会让你失望。

营业时间：　周一、周二餐厅不营业

　　　　　　周三、四、五，中午12点到下午3点，晚上6点半到9点半

　　　　　　周六晚上6点半到9点半

　　　　　　周日下午12点半到下午6点

地址：　　　鹿特丹Heuvellaan21号

联系方式：　010-4360766

　　　　　　http://www.parkheuvel.nl

217

Tijd voor Nederlands 荷兰语时间

● 单词+短语

荷 kerk	荷 windmolen	荷 strand
英 church	英 windmill	英 beach
译 教堂	译 风车	译 沙滩

荷 paleis	荷 koning	荷 plein
英 palace	英 king	英 square
译 宫殿	译 国王	译 广场
荷 gracht	荷 lopen	荷 bouwen
英 canal	英 walk	英 build
译 运河	译 走路	译 建造
荷 hoog/laag	荷 druk	荷 Tweede Wereldoorlog
英 tall/short	英 busy	英 Second World War
译 高的/矮的	译 繁忙的	译 第二次世界大战

● 例句

荷 Hoe kan ik naar deze kerk gaan?	荷 Er zijn veel grachten en pleinen in Amsterdam.
英 How can I go to this church?	英 There are many canals and squares in Amsterdam.
译 我怎么去这个教堂？	译 阿姆斯特丹有很多运河和广场。
荷 Ik ben al een week in Nederland, ik ben naar de windmolens geweest.	荷 Kan ik vanaf hier naar het strand lopen?
英 I have been in the Netherlands for a week. I have been to the windmills.	英 Can I walk to the beach from here?
译 我已经来荷兰一周了，我已经去看过风车了。	译 我从这里能走到沙滩吗？
荷 Woont de koning van Nederland in dit paleis in Den Haag?	荷 De Euromast Tower is een zeer hoog gebouw.
英 Does the king of the Netherlands live in this palace in The Hague?	英 Euromast Tower is a very tall building.
译 荷兰的国王住在海牙的这所宫殿里吗？	译 欧洲桅杆是一座非常高的建筑物。
荷 De kerk werd herbouwd na de Tweede Wereldoorlog.	
英 The church was rebuilt after the second world war.	
译 这座教堂是在第二次世界大战后重建的。	

4. 海牙
The Hague

The Hague is a city on the western coast of the Netherlands and the capital of the province of South Holland.

With a population of more than 1 million including the suburbs, it is the third-largest city in the Netherlands, after Amsterdam and Rotterdam. The Rotterdam and The Hague Metropolitan Area, with a population of approximately 2.7 million, is the 12th-largest in the European Union and the most populous in the country.

Although The Hague is the seat of government, the Staten General, the Supreme Court, and the Council of State, the city is not the capital of the Netherlands, which constitutionally is Amsterdam. Most foreign embassies in the Netherlands and 150 international organisations are located in the city, including the International Court of Justice and the International Criminal Court, which makes The Hague one of the major cities hosting the United Nations, along with New York City, Geneva, Vienna, Rome, and Nairobi. King Willem-Alexander lives at the Huis ten Bosch and works at the Noordeinde Palace in The Hague, together with Queen Máxima. The Hague is also home to the world headquarters of Royal Dutch Shell and numerous other major Dutch companies.

海牙是荷兰西部沿海的一座城市，也是南荷兰省的省会所在地。

包括郊区，海牙的人口超过了100万，是荷兰第三大城市，仅次于阿姆斯特丹和鹿特丹。鹿特丹和海牙大都会区域的人口约为270万，在欧盟排第12，也是全国人口最多的地方。

虽然海牙是荷兰中央政府所在地，也是立法委、最高法院及国务委员会所在地，但它并不是荷兰的首都，在宪法上荷兰的首都是阿姆斯特丹。大多数驻荷兰的外国大使馆和150个国际组织都驻扎在这里，包括国际法庭和国际刑事法院，这使得海牙连同纽约、日内瓦、维也纳、罗马和内罗毕，成为联合国组织的主要城市之一。荷兰国王威廉·亚历山大及其王后马克西玛所居住的豪斯登堡宫和办公用的努尔登堡宫也都坐落于海牙。海牙还是荷兰皇家壳牌和众多荷兰大型企业的总部所在地。

Sights and Landmarks 景点和地标性建筑

※ Peace Palace

The Peace Palace (Dutch: Het Vredespaleis) is an international law administrative building in The Hague. Today the building is still used by the International Court of Justice, the Permanent Court of Arbitration, the Peace Palace Library, as well as by The Hague Academy of International Law.

The Peace Palace in The Hague finds its origins in the ideals of pacifism and world peace. At the end of the 19th century, these principles were blooming as never before.

The Palace officially opened on August 28, 1913, and was originally built to provide a home for the PCA, a court created to end war by The Hague Convention of 1899. Andrew Dickson White, whose efforts were instrumental in creating the court, secured from Scottish-American steel magnate Andrew Carnegie US$1.5 million ($40,000,000 in today's money) to build the Peace Palace. The European Heritage Label was awarded to the Peace Palace on April 8,2014.

The Eternal Peace Flame burns beside the entrance to the Peace Palace. The first peace flame in the Netherlands was placed beside the entrance gates to the Peace Palace on April 18, 2002. The monument bears the inscription: "May all beings find peace". Since 2004, the monument has been surrounded by the World Peace Path, which consists of a path of 196 large and small stones from 196 countries. Some of these stones are unique: they include, for example, a piece of stone from the Berlin Wall and a stone from Robben Island where Nelson Mandela was imprisoned for many years.

The Peace Palace can be viewed under the supervision of a guide, but the visitor's centre on the palace grounds is opened every day, except on Mondays.

※ Binnenhof & Ridderzaal

The Binnenhof is situated in the heart of The Hague's city centre. It has been the location of meetings of the Dutch parliament, the Staten-Generaal, since 1446, and has been the centre of Dutch politics for many centuries. The grounds on which the Binnenhof now stands were purchased by Floris IV, Count of Holland in 1229, where he built his mansion, next to the modest lake that has been called Hofvijver or 'Court Pond' since the 13th century.

Without a doubt, the most eye-catching part of the Binnenhof is the Ridderzaal (Knights' Hall), where King Willem-Alexander holds his annual speech at Prinsjesdag (Prince's Day). This monumental building was erected in the 13th and 14th centuries as the castle of the Counts of Holland, although its current design was completed towards the end of the last century. The building that had been neglected for a long time was renovated under the leadership of Chief Government Architect Cornelis Peters, reconstructing the great timber roof. P.J.H. Cuypers was involved in the renovation as an advisor and also designed the fountain in front of the Ridderzaal, which features a statue of the Dutch Count and Elector William II.

※ Het Plein

Het Plein is situated next to the Binnenhof, the Mauritshuis Museum and the House of Representatives and lies at the political heart of the Netherlands.

Het Plein was originally a garden, forming a part of the Binnenhof castle, residence of the Counts of Holland. It was used to grow vegetables for the court. The garden was surrounded by a ring of canals and intersected by ditches. As a town square, Het Plein was constructed in 1632 and was inspired by the Place des Vosges in Paris. A statue of William the Silent, made by Dutch sculptor Lodewyk Royer, was installed in the centre of the square in 1848.

Today, it is probably the most lively, the most distinctive area in The Hague, surrounded by

lots of restaurants and bars. Even in winter, local residents and tourists alike sit outside with a cup of hot tea or coffee.

※ Madurodam

Madurodam is a miniature park and tourist attraction in the Scheveningen, a district of The Hague in the Netherlands. It is home to a range of 1:25 scale model replicas of famous Dutch landmarks, historical cities and large developments.

Princess Beatrix opened Madurodam on July 2, 1952 and has since been visited by tens of millions of visitors. Since day one, it has been more than a theme park that shows the best of the Netherlands: it was founded as a living memorial to the war hero George Maduro and as a way to raise funds for charities. The entirety of net proceeds from the park go towards various charities in the Netherlands.

Something interesting about Madurodam: On July 2, 1952, the then teenage Princess Beatrix was appointed mayor of Madurodam, and was given a tour of her town. When Beatrix became Queen, she relinquished this title. After her resignation a new tradition arose: the city council would annually select a mayor from their midst. All members of the youth council are The Hague students.

Every object in Madurodam has been built at a scale of 1:25. You can find a lot of landmarks buildings of the Netherlands, like Rijksmuseum, Airport Schiphol, Port of Rotterdam, Domtoren, etc.

※ Noordeinde Palace

There are several palaces in The Hague and 'Paleis Noordeinde' (Noordeinde Palace) is one of them. The palace originated as a medieval farmhouse, which was converted into a spacious residence by the steward of the States of Holland, Willem Goudt in 1533. From 1566 to 1591, the palace had a different owner. In 1595, it was purchased by the States of Holland for Louise de Coligny, for the widow of William of Orange, and her son Prince Frederik Hendrik. In recognition of William's service to the nation, the States presented the building to his family in 1609.

In 1948, the central section of the palace was destroyed by fire. That same year Juliana acceded to the throne. She preferred Soestdijk Palace as her official residence, though some members of the Royal Household continued to use offices in Noordeinde. Between 1952 and 1976 the Institute of Social Studies was based in the north wing of the palace. Following a thorough restoration in 1984, the Palace became the Dutch Monarch's workplace and office for all political and stately affairs. Since 2013, it has been used as the "working palace" for King Willem-Alexander.

Paleis Noordeinde is located in the center of The Hague along the street Noordeinde. You can take pictures from the street, but the palace itself is not open to the public.

On the other side of Paleis Noordeinde you can enjoy some peace and quietness in the Palace Garden. It's a small park and admission is free. Just next to the park you'll see the Royal Stables where the horses and coaches of the Royal House are kept.

※ The Pier

The famous Pier in Scheveningen is an icon on the Dutch coast, it has long been a favourite of beach lovers who want to enjoy the view.

The Pier in Scheveningen extending 400 meters into the sea was built around 1900 as a wooden promenade above the sea. It burned down in 1943, but in 1961 the Pier was rebuilt out of concrete and officially reopened. In 2015, The Pier was renovated and reopened again, it has become a true attraction for people who love good food, entertainment, and a great view.

Scheveningen is the most-visited beach resort in Holland. Its Pier is surrounded by a host of other attractions, such as SEA LIFE Scheveningen, Beelden aan Zee, the Circustheater and Holland Casino. Throughout the year the Pier offers festivals, cultural events, markets, kids' afternoons, educational activities and musical performances. Moreover, several events take place around The Pier, like the Fireworks Festival and the Scheveningen Kite Festival.

One of the Pier's latest tourist attractions is a Ferris wheel constructed over sea. The Ferris wheel is over forty meters high and has 36 closed gondolas with air conditioning, the Ferris wheel even includes a luxury VIP gondola with a glass bottom. All gondolas have comfortable seats and each gondola offers room for up to six people.

For those who think that a ride in the Ferris wheel is a little bit too tame, there is also the option to go bungee jumping from the pier.

※ 和平宫

海牙国际法庭，这是我们对它最熟悉的名称。是大多数游客都想一睹风采的一处场所。

和平宫的荷兰名称是Het Vredespaleis，它是位于海牙的国际法庭行政大楼。如今，和平宫仍被国际法庭、常设仲裁法院、和平宫图书馆以及海牙国际法学院所使用。

海牙的和平宫源于和平主义和世界和平的理想。在19世纪末，这些准则开始前所未有地盛行和繁荣。

这座宫殿是在1913年8月28日正式开放的，最初是为了给常设仲裁法院提供一处场所，这是一个由1899年的海牙公约所创建的旨在结束战争的法庭。安德鲁·迪克森·怀特通过不懈的努力促成了法庭的建立，他从苏格兰裔美国钢铁巨头安德鲁·卡内基手中获得了150万美元（约合今天的4 000万美元）的资金来建造和平宫。2014年4月8日，和平宫被授予了欧洲遗产标识。

和平宫的入口处熊熊燃烧着永恒的和平火焰。2002年4月18日，荷兰的第一个和平火炬被放置在通往和平宫的大门旁边。纪念碑上刻着："愿一切众生平安"。自2004年以来，这座纪念碑一直被世界和平之路所包围，这是一条由196个国家的196个大小石块所组成的小径。其中的一些石块是独一无二的：例如有来自柏林墙的石头和罗宾岛的石头，纳尔逊·曼德拉曾在罗宾岛被囚禁多年。

　　和平宫内部的参观需要导游带领才可以，但周一不开放，宫殿外的广场则每天都对游客开放。

※ 国会大厦和骑士厅

国会大厦位于海牙市中心的心脏位置。自1446年以来，它一直是荷兰议会的会议所在地，也是几个世纪以来荷兰政治的中心。国会大厦现在的看台位置是由荷兰伯爵弗洛里斯四世在1229年买下来的，他在那里盖起了豪华宅邸，紧紧毗邻从13世纪起就被称为Hofvijver或"廷池"的一汪湖水。

荷兰国会大厦不仅是荷兰政治的中心，也是海牙地理位置的中心，是海牙游客的必到之处。图为廷池边的国会大厦。

　　骑士厅理所应当地成为了国会大厦内最引人注目的部分，这里是一年一度的亲王日之际威廉·亚历山大国王发表年度演讲的场所。尽管骑士厅的设计和重修是在20世纪末完成的，但是这座宏伟的建筑却建造于13世纪和14世纪，原本是荷兰伯爵的城堡。这座长期被疏于照管的建筑在首席政府建筑师康尼利斯·彼得斯的领导下进行了翻修，重建了巨大的木结构屋顶。佩特鲁斯·库伯斯作为一名顾问也参与了翻修工程，他还设计了骑士厅的户外喷泉，荷兰伯爵和威廉二世的雕像是该喷泉的一大特色。

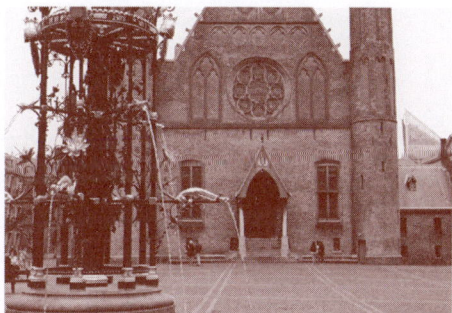

骑士厅是国会大厦最引人注目的部分，是威廉·亚历山大国王发表年度演讲的场所。

※ 海牙广场

　　海牙广场位于国会大厦、莫瑞泰斯皇家美术馆和众议院附近，处在荷兰的政治中心。

　　海牙广场原本是一个花园，是荷兰伯爵内廷城堡的一部分，以前被用来为宫廷种植蔬菜，其四周被一环形运河所萦绕，沟渠纵横交错。海牙广场作为一个城市广场建于1632年，灵感来自于巴黎的孚日广场。1848年，由荷兰雕塑家罗德维克·罗耶所创作的雕像沉默者威廉被安置在广场中心。

　　到今天，海牙广场可能是海牙最热闹、最有特色的

海牙广场紧邻众议院、莫瑞泰斯皇家美术馆，是休闲的最佳场所，也是众多活动的热门场所。

223

地方，周围林立着很多餐馆和酒吧。即使在冬天，当地的居民和游客也会坐在外面喝杯热茶或咖啡，品味一番。

※ 马德罗丹微缩公园

马德罗丹微缩公园内的建筑都是荷兰各地最具代表性或者最有特色的建筑，都按照1：25比例建造。图为公园内的建筑和远处的游人。

马德罗丹微缩公园是位于荷兰海牙席凡宁根的一个微型公园和旅游景点。它按照1:25的比例复制了一些著名的荷兰地标性建筑、历史名城和大型发展项目。

贝娅特丽克丝公主于1952年7月2日开启了马德罗丹微缩公园，至今公园已经接待了数千万前来参观的游客。从第一天开始，它就不仅仅是一个展示最好的荷兰的主题公园，它是作为纪念战争英雄乔治·马杜罗的活生生的纪念碑，也是为慈善事业筹集资金的一种方式。这个公园的全部净收入都捐给了荷兰的各种慈善机构。

这里是关于马德罗丹微缩公园的一些趣事：1952年7月2日，当时十几岁的贝娅特丽克丝公主被任命为马德罗丹市长（没错，就是这个公园/城市的市长），并参观了她自己所管理的这个微缩城镇。当贝娅特丽克丝成为女王时，她放弃了这个头衔。在她辞职后，一个新的传统出现了：市议会每年都会从他们当中选出一位市长来作为马德罗丹微缩公园的市长。而市青年理事会的所有成员都是来自海牙的学生。

马德罗丹微缩公园的每一个物体都是以1:25的比例建造的。你可以在这里看到荷兰的很多地标建筑，比如阿姆斯特丹国家博物馆、史基浦机场、鹿特丹港、乌特勒支大教堂塔楼等。

※ 努尔登堡宫

在海牙有几座宫殿，而努尔登堡宫就是其中之一。努尔登堡宫的前身是一个中世纪的农舍，在1533年由荷兰官员威廉·古特将其改建为宽敞的住宅。从1566年到1591年，努尔登堡宫几经易主。1595年，荷兰政府为威廉·奥伦治的遗孀路易丝·德科利尼和她的儿子弗雷德里克·亨德里克买下了宫殿。为了表彰威廉对国家的贡献，荷兰于1609年将这栋建筑物赠予了他的家人。

1948年，努尔登堡宫的中心部分被大火烧毁。同年，朱丽安娜公主继承了王位，尽管一些皇室成员继续以努尔登堡宫作为办公地点，但朱丽安娜女王更喜欢把索斯戴克宫作为她的官邸。1952年至1976年，海牙社会科学研究院在努尔登堡宫的北翼成立。在1984年宫殿整修完毕彻底恢复后，努尔登堡宫成为荷兰君主用于处理所有政务和庄严事务的工作场所和办公室。自2013年起，它被用作威廉·亚历山大国王的工作场所。

努尔登堡宫是荷兰国王在海牙的办公场所，需要预约才可访问，但努尔登堡宫身后的公园是开放的，随时可入内。图为努尔登堡宫门前的雕塑和身后的公园。

努尔登堡宫位于海牙的中心努尔登堡街。你可以在街上拍照，王宫本身并没有向公众开放。

在努尔登堡宫的另一侧，皇宫花园平和而宁静，难得的惬意之处。这是个不大的公园，入内并不需要任何费用。就在公园的旁边，你会看到皇家马厩，那里有皇家马匹和马车。

※ 栈桥

鼎鼎大名的栈桥是荷兰海岸的一个标志性建筑，一直以来都是海滩爱好者的最爱。

栈桥在20世纪初建在了席凡宁根的码头上，是一个木结构的海滨长廊，向水中延伸了400米的长度。木结构的栈桥在1943年被大火焚毁，于是又在1961年的时候重新修建了混凝土结构的栈桥并重新开放。2015年，栈桥又经过了焕然一新的装修重新开放，摇身一变成为了热爱美食、美景、喜欢休闲娱乐的人们竞相前往之地。

席凡宁根是荷兰最受欢迎的海滩度假胜地。栈桥的周围环绕着许多其他的景点，如席凡宁根海洋馆、海边雕塑博物馆、马戏剧场和荷兰赌场。节日庆典、文化活动、露天市集、儿童游乐场、亲子教育和音乐表演等活动更是贯穿全年。此外，还有一些大型活动也在这里举办，比如一年一度的席凡宁根烟花节和国际风筝节。

席凡宁根码头最近增加了新的旅游项目，一座建在海上的摩天轮。摩天轮的高度超过40米，有36个封闭的装有空调的吊舱，甚至还有一个VIP吊舱，吊舱的底部是透明的玻璃。吊舱的舒适度也足够，每个舱可容纳最多6个人。

席凡宁根是荷兰最受欢迎的海滩度假胜地，这里设有海上摩天轮和蹦极，不管喜欢浪漫还是刺激都能得到释放。这里还是众多国际娱乐和体育赛事的举办地，比如烟火节和风筝节。

对于那些认为乘坐摩天轮太枯燥无趣的人来说，还可以挑战从栈桥高塔往海平面蹦极的刺激。

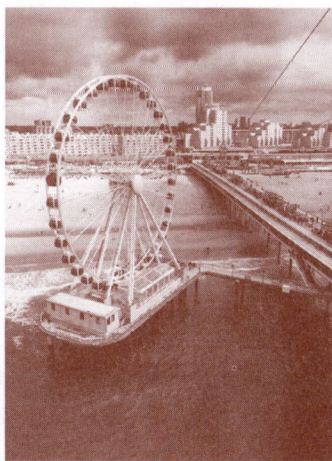

Shopping in The Hague 购在海牙

The Hague city centre is perfect for a day of shopping. The shops in the car-free historical centre are open seven days a week. You will find well-known department stores like the Bijenkorf within walking distance of hip fashion boutiques and concept stores around the royal palaces. And those who continue towards the sea, will discover all kinds of neighbourhoods with a wide range of speciality stores.

※ Grote Marktstraat (City Center)

Grote Marktstraat is one of the most important shopping areas in the centre of The Hague. The shopping street runs from the charming Grote Markt with its many cafés to Spui where you will find a large Pathé cinema. Many department stores are located here in beautiful buildings. If you are looking for top international brands, then De Bijenkorf is the place to be. Stylish clothing for any occasion for the whole family can be found at the department store Hudson's Bay, it is a new store that has opened its doors in 2017. Then there are the new and old sections of De Passage. Grote Marktstraat has stores to suit all tastes and they are open every day of the week! The tram tunnel that runs under Grote Marktstraat makes it easy to reach the stores by public transport.

※ De Passage

De Passage that opened in 1885, is a magnificent, more than 120 years old, (indoor) shopping arcade. It is the only remaining example in the Netherlands of this type of covered shopping street, popular in major European and American cities during the 19th century. The construction of The Hague Passage is designed for the ground plan by Herman Wesstra Jr. from The Hague and the architect Jan Christiaan van Wijk from Rotterdam.

A few years ago, De Passage welcomed a new section the entrance of which is on Grote Marktstraat. Again, the glass roof is pivotal. This multi-floor new area is all about modern shopping with every retail facility visitors might take for granted nowadays.

Visit the largest Mango store in the Netherlands, choose and buy perfume and cosmetics in ICI PARIS XL, eat the famous and classic croquette at Dungelmann's, there are also some classic and cosy cafés to have a rest and enjoy a nice cup of coffee with some famous Dutch apple pie.

※ Hoogstraat, Noordeinde & Plaats

This area is home to Hoogstraat, Plaats, Heulstraat and 't Noordeinde. King Willem-Alexander's work palace is at the very heart of this district, which means you are guaranteed an interesting mixture of royal elegance, brands and fashionable lunchrooms.

Noordeinde is all about galleries, which makes it the art street in all of the Netherlands. In a compact area you find an abundance of historic monuments, art galleries, high end fashion stores and many unique and original stores that you simply cannot find anywhere else. If you are looking for modern or classical art objects, custom or branded fashion, a unique gift or a special souvenir, you will find a visit to Het Noordeinde an experience well worth your time.

Hoogstraat harbours the most elegant fashion stores across the city of The Hague (jewellery, trendy design and interior shops, flagship stores). In addition, there is also a well-known bookstore, Booksellers van Hoogstraten, one of the oldest, independent bookshops in Den Haag. It is situated just a few meters from Noordeinde Palace, His Majesty King Willem-Alexander's office.

The Square Plaats has lots of terraces and it is beautifully overlooking the Hofvijver and Binnenhof.

※ Haagse Markt

The Haagse Markt with more than 500 permanent stalls is one of the largest open-air markets in Europe. The market is open 4 days a week and covers an area in the size of about 3 football fields.

The Haagse Markt was completely refurbished in 2014 and 2015. The narrow aisles were replaced with wide paths measuring about 800 metres long and the old stalls were replaced with new modern units.

It is a unique market in the Netherlands with a wide variety of products. Here you will find a large range of fresh vegetables, fruit, fish and meat, but you can also buy clothing and household items. The market is known especially for its wide range of exotic products.

The Haagse Markt is open on Monday, Wednesday, Friday and Saturday from 9:00 to 17:00.

海牙市中心是一天购物的好去处，充满历史气息的步行街商店每周七天营业。一些著名的百货公司在这里也有门店，比如在阿姆斯特丹和鹿特丹都有的女王百货，和与皇家宫殿近在咫尺的时尚精品店和概念店。要是继续往海边方向行进，还会发现各式各样的社区特色商店。

海牙的市中心购物区很集中，大市场街就在中心位置，附近分布着众多的潮流店铺和中高端百货。图为大市场街一瞥。

※ 大市场街（市中心）

大市场街是位于海牙市中心最重要的购物区之一。这条购物街一直从林立着许多小咖啡馆的大市场到达Spui，也就是Pathé电影院所在的路口位置。这里的很多百货商店都开在了漂亮的建筑物里面。如果你要找顶级的国际大牌，那么你就去女王百货。如果你是给大家庭的老老少少买买衣服，那就去哈德逊湾百货商店，这是一家在2017年才开业的新店，我们在鹿特丹也提到过。再就是海牙De Passage室内购物街了，分为新旧两个部分。大市场街的商店适合所有人的品位，关键的是这些商店一周七天全部开放营业。大市场街地下有有轨电车隧道，坐电车可以直达，非常便利。

227

※ 海牙通道室内购物街

De Passage是荷兰唯一一个还保留下来的19世纪的顶棚遮盖的室内购物街。图为早期建造的De Passage的一部分。

1885年开张的海牙通道购物街De Passage，是一个宏伟的、超过120年历史的室内购物商场。这是荷兰唯一一个还保留下来的19世纪的顶棚遮盖的室内购物街，这在当时的欧洲和美国的主要城市非常流行。海牙通道的建造是由来自海牙的赫尔曼·韦斯特拉和来自鹿特丹的建筑师扬·克里斯蒂安·范·韦克所设计的。

几年前，通道购物街增添了一个新的部分，即大市场街的入口处的一段。关键的亮点是，其屋顶的设计依然采用了玻璃。这个多楼层的新区域是实实在在的现代化购物区域，所有的零售设施都理所应当地符合人们的现代需求。

这个部分设有荷兰最大的Mango店，ICI PARIS XL是选购香水和化妆品的好地方，名声在外的荷兰经典炸肉丸则可以在Dungelmann's买到，还有一些舒适的咖啡馆可以坐下来休息一下，享受咖啡时光的同时还不要忘了点一块有名的荷兰苹果派。

※ 特色街道

Plaats附近的环境相对幽静，外面小广场的露天位置就在国会大厦的百米之处。图为Plaats及附近的环境。

这个购物区分布着胡格街（Hoogstraat）、Plaats、Heulstraat和努儿登堡街（Noordeinde）。威廉·亚历山大国王所用来办公的努儿登堡宫就位于这个地区的中心。这就意味着，在这里你既能感受到皇家优雅所带来的气息，又能找到彰显你非凡品位的品牌，还能找一家时尚餐厅享受一顿美味午餐。

努儿登堡街两旁画廊林立，这使它成为整个荷兰的一条艺术街。在并不宽松的区域内，你会发现大量的有历史纪念意义的物品、艺术画廊、高端时装店，以及许多你在其他地方找不到的独特和原始的商店。如果你正在寻找现代或古典的艺术商品，定制的或品牌性的，一份独特的礼物或特别的纪念品，那么努儿登堡街非常值得你来逛一逛。

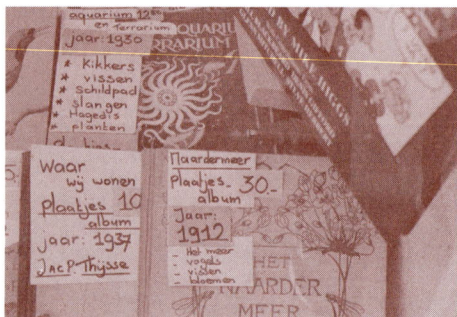

努儿登堡街就是努儿登堡宫所在的街道，是一条艺术之街，分布着众多的小画廊、艺术品店、古董和旧书店。图为一家旧书店的橱窗，显示的图书均出版自20世纪初期。

胡格街是海牙最优雅最时尚的购物去处，分布着珠宝、时尚设计和室内装饰商店和旗舰店。此外，胡格街还有一个著名的书店——胡格斯特拉顿的书店，是海牙最古老的独立书店之一，坐落在离威廉·亚历山大努儿登堡宫仅数米远的地方。

Plaats广场上有很多露台，从这里可以眺望不远处的国会大厦和廷池。

※ 海牙市场

海牙市场拥有500多个永久性摊位，是欧洲最大的露天市场之一。市场占地面积约三个足球场那么大，每周开放4天。

海牙市场在2014年和2015年进行了全部翻新。狭窄的通道被长度约800米的宽通道所取代，老旧的摊位也被新的现代化摊位所代替。

这是一个荷兰独一无二的市场，产品种类异常繁多。这里的新鲜蔬菜、水果、鱼和肉的量非常大，种类非常多，但还有很多衣服和家居用品等都能在这里买到。海牙市场还因为来自异国繁多的奇特产品和商品而闻名。

市场的开放时间是在周一、周三、周五和周六，时间从上午9点到下午5点。

Eating in The Hague 食在海牙

The Hague is famous as the seat of power in the Netherlands. It is also a cosmopolitan, cultural city that fuses many nationalities and tastes thanks to its history as the centre of the former Dutch colony of the East Indies. The tastes of The Hague, which consist of a myriad of cultures and exciting flavour combinations, can be experienced at these restaurants.

※ Full Moon City

The Hague is not very large, and most of the Chinese restaurants are concentrated in the city centre, near Chinatown. Full Moon City is too.

This restaurant specialises in Cantonese cuisine. Over the years, the name Full Moon has almost become household name within the Chinese community of The Hague. Full Moon City is the largest Cantonese restaurant in The Hague and can accommodate more than two hundred people. Dim sum and classic Cantonese seafood, grilled and stir-fried dishes here are worth a try.

Please be aware that there are two Full Moon restaurants on both sides of the street, Dim Sum Restaurant Full Moon City is buffet for Dim Sum, and Full Moon is an a la carte restaurant. Full Moon is on the second floor of the street. Dim Sum Restaurant Full Moon City is opposite to it.

Hours:　　Dim Sum Restaurant Full Moon City

Daily 11:30am–01:00am

Full Moon City

Daily 12:00pm–22:00pm；Thursday, Friday, Friday 12pm–23pm

Address: Achter Raamstraat 75，2512 BW Den Haag (Dim Sum Restaurant Full Moon City)

Gedempte Burgwal 24-26, 2512 BV Den Haag (Full Moon)

Contact: 070-3562013

http://fullmooncity.nl/

※ Baladi Manouche

The Arab restaurant in The Hague is very authentic, because here are a lot of immigrants from the Middle East countries. The owners of the restaurant are a Lebanese couple who recently moved to the Netherlands to share their love for cooking and Lebanese street food.

Baladi Manouche are flat bread that are made to order and include healthy and fresh toppings such as thyme with olive oil, strained yogurt (labneh), cheese, spinach and meat. Manouches are tasty, healthy, low in calories and most of all easy on the wallet.

They also offer a wide range of Lebanese desserts and delicacies such as Knefe and Sfouf (turmeric based cake) as well as Lebanese drinks and refreshments such as Jallab (drink made from raisins and grapes), Ayran (made from fresh yogurt) and Lemonade.

An Arab restaurant that is very rare in China, it is definitely worth trying.

Hours: Monday: Closed

Thursday: 9am–8pm

Tuesday-Sunday: 9am–6pm

Address: Torenstraat 95，2513BP Den Haag

Contact: 06-19891597

http://baladionline.nl/

海牙以荷兰权利机构中心而闻名于世，这得益于它作为前荷兰殖民地东印度群岛中心的历史，海牙融合了世界各民族及其多种口味的饮食，是一个世界性的、文化的城市。在这些餐厅里，可以体会到由无数的多元文化和令人兴奋的风味组合构成的海牙的味道。

※ 月满楼

海牙并不是很大，大多数中餐馆都集中在唐人街附近的市中心。月满楼就在这里。

这家餐馆专营粤菜。多年来，"月满楼"在海牙的华人社区里几乎成了家喻户晓的名字。月满楼是海牙最大的广东餐厅，可以容纳200多人。点心和经典的广东海鲜、烧烤和炒菜都值得一试。

请注意，在街道两侧有两个月满楼餐厅，一个也叫月满城，是吃广式点心的餐厅，另一个是单点餐厅，在街道一侧的二楼。而点心餐厅则在它的对面。

营业时间：　点心餐厅，每日上午11点半到凌晨1点

月满楼餐厅，每日中午12点到晚上10点，周四、五、六延长到晚上11点

地址：　　　点心餐厅，海牙Achter Raamstraat 75号

月满楼餐厅，海牙Gedempte Burgwal 24-26号

联系方式：　070-3562013

http://fullmooncity.nl/

※ Baladi Manouche

海牙的阿拉伯餐厅非常正宗，因为这里生活着很多来自中东国家的移民。这家餐厅的主人是一对黎巴嫩夫妇，他们前几年刚搬来荷兰，分享着他们对烹饪的兴趣和对黎巴嫩街头小吃的热爱。

Baladi Manouche是一种馕或者面饼，搭配着包括健康新鲜的配料，比如橄榄油浸过的百里香、中东浓缩酸奶、奶酪、菠菜和肉类。Manouches吃起来味道不错，食物也是美味健康、低卡路里的，关键是不用考虑钱包是否承受得了。

他们还提供各式各样的黎巴嫩甜点和美味佳肴，如Knefe（一种由酥皮、白芝士、蜂蜜、开心果仁制成非常常见的阿拉伯甜点）和Sfouf（由粗粉、姜黄、糖、鸡蛋、茴香和松子等制成的蛋糕）以及黎巴嫩饮料和茶点，如Jallab（用葡萄干和葡萄制成的饮料），Ayran（由新鲜酸奶制成）和柠檬水。

在中国很少见的阿拉伯餐厅，绝对值得一试。

营业时间：　每日早上9点到晚上6点，星期四早9点到晚上10点；星期一不营业
地址：　　　海牙Torenstraat 95号
联系方式：　06-19891597

http://baladionline.nl/

Tijd voor Nederlands 荷兰语时间

● 单词+短语

荷 winkel	荷 warenhuis	荷 winkelcentrum
英 shop	英 department store	英 shopping centre
译 商店	译 百货公司	译 购物中心

231

荷 korting	荷 cadeau	荷 schoenen
英 discount	英 present	英 shoes
译 折扣	译 礼物	译 鞋
荷 tas	荷 maat	荷 kleur
英 bag	英 size	英 colour
译 包	译 尺寸	译 颜色
荷 goedkoop/duur	荷 winkelen	荷 kopen
英 cheap/expensive	英 shopping	英 buy
译 便宜/贵的	译 购物	译 买
荷 verpakken		
英 pack		
译 包装		

● 例句

荷 Ik ga vanmiddag naar de winkels om te winkelen.	荷 Dit warenhuis heeft nu opruiming, het is goedkoop.
英 I am going to shop at the shops this afternoon.	英 This department store has a sale now, it is cheap.
译 我今天下午要去商店买东西。	译 这家百货公司正在打折，很便宜。
荷 Deze maat is te groot voor mij, en ik hou niet van de kleur.	荷 Ik heb er vijf nodig, kunt u me een korting geven?
英 This size is too big for me, and I do not like the colour.	英 I need five. Can you give me a discount?
译 这个号码对我来说太大了，我也不喜欢这个颜色。	译 我需要五个，你可以给我打折吗？
荷 Ik wil een cadeautje kopen voor mijn moeder.	荷 Kunt u het voor me verpakken?
英 I want to buy a present for my mother.	英 Can you pack it for me?
译 我想给我的妈妈买个礼物。	译 您能把它给我包装起来吗？
荷 Ik heb gisteren een goedkope tas gekocht.	荷 De sportschoenen in deze winkel zijn duur.
英 I bought a cheap bag yesterday.	英 The sports shoes in this store are expensive.
译 我昨天买了一个便宜的包。	译 这家商店里的运动鞋很贵。

5. 乌特勒支
Utrecht

Utrecht can be called the beating heart of the Netherlands, due to its central position within the country and because it is an important transport hub for both rail and road transport. It has been the religious centre of the Netherlands since the 8th century. It lost the status of prince-bishopric but remains the main religious centre of the Netherlands. Utrecht was the most important city in the Netherlands until the Dutch Golden Age, when it was surpassed by Amsterdam as the country's cultural centre and most populous city.

Utrecht was built around the Dom tower, which you can see from any point in the city, so there is no way you can get lost in the attractive, car-free city centre. Utrecht boasts beautiful canals with extraordinary wharf cellars housing cafés and terraces by the water. As well as the Dom tower, Utrecht boasts hundreds of other monuments that each contribute to the special atmosphere in this centuries-old university town.

乌特勒支被称为荷兰的心脏，这源于它在该国的中心地理位置，它是铁路和公路运输的重要交通枢纽。乌特勒支从8世纪以来一直是荷兰的宗教中心，虽然它早已失去大主教的地位，但仍然是荷兰的主要宗教中心。在荷兰黄金时代之前，乌特勒支是荷兰最重要的城市，荷兰黄金时代其地位被阿姆斯特丹超过，后者成为该国的文化中心和人口最多的城市。

乌特勒支处于荷兰的心脏位置，其中央车站是荷兰最大的火车中转站，可从此抵达全荷兰每个角落。

乌特勒支围绕圆顶大教堂钟楼而建造，你可以从城市的任何地方看到这座塔，所以在迷人的无车市中心迷失方向是不太可能的。乌特勒支拥有令人艳羡的美丽运河和非凡的码头酒窖，还有水上咖啡馆和临水畔而居的露台。除了教堂钟楼，乌特勒支还拥有数百个其他的纪念碑，它们都为这个有着几百年历史的大学城的特殊氛围做出了贡献。

Sights and landmarks 景点和地标性建筑

※ Dom Tower

Being 112 m and 32 cm (369 ft) in height, the Dom Tower is the tallest church tower in the

233

Netherlands. The highest viewpoint is at 95 m (312 ft). From this platform you have a magnificent panoramic view of the city of Utrecht and its surroundings. Utrecht's history began 2,000 years ago on the site of the Dom Square today. That is also where the tumultuous past of the city and the Dom Tower begins.

The construction of the Dom Tower began in 1321, but due to a lack of funds the construction of the church stopped between 1328 and 1342. Eventually, the Dom Tower was completed in 1382: it is the highest point of the Dom complex and symbolises the bishop's secular and ecclesiastical power. Jan van Henegouwen and Jan van den Doem were the main master builders.

In 1505, Bell-founder Geert van Wou created the 13 impressive bells that hang halfway up the tower. All of the bells have their own names and sound, and weigh more than 30,000 kilos.

A devastating tornado swept through Utrecht on August 1, 1674, and the church's nave collapsed. Elsewhere in the city, too, the storm caused significant damage. Since then the tower and the church have become permanently separated.

※ Oudegracht Utrecht

Around two kilometres long, the Oudegracht is the most famous canal in Utrecht, it is also unique in the world as it is part of an ingenious medieval dockland development with wharves and cellars connected under the streets and huge storage cellars under the canal houses. In the second half of the twelfth century, Utrecht's inhabitants decided to dig tunnels from the dock to the canal-side houses. This resulted in the double docks typical of the city.

If you like you can take a boat ride through the canals, you can choose between a round-trip with a canal cruise or set out on an exploratory expedition by pedal boat, rowing boat or canoe. Explore this city from the water and you will be treated to an entirely different view of this old city.

These days, you will find countless pleasant restaurants and cafés with a water-side terrace in the dock cellars. They make a perfect place for a drink or a bite after a great day in Utrecht!

※ Utrecht Botanical Gardens

At the very heart of the province of Utrecht there is a unique natural treasure consisting of thousands of plant species: the Botanic Gardens of Utrecht University. They were laid out on and around Fort Hoofddijk, which dates from the 19th century. As an organisation, the gardens date back to 1639, making it one of the oldest botanic gardens in the whole of the Netherlands.

To this day, the Botanic Gardens continue to serve their primary function, which is to support education and research. In addition, there has been an increasing focus on the public role played by the Botanic Gardens. Nature conservation, especially in an international context, is another important aspect.

On and around Fort Hoofddijk, different gardens and other attractions can be found, each with its own distinctive character. For example there is a Rock Garden, Evolution Garden,

Discovery Garden (Theme Garden), Tropical Greenhouses, Birders Den and Bee Hotel.

※ Trajectum Lumen

Trajectum Lumen is made for an exploration after dark, and it follows artistically lit locations throughout Utrecht's historical city centre. The works of light art are created by the most renowned national and international light artists in the world. When night falls, Trajectum Lumen leads from centrally located Vredenburg past a growing number of installations by (inter)nationally renowned light artists. The light art route leads you along all kinds of streets, objects, canals and structures. You will learn more about the city and historical events from the past and discover Utrecht from a new perspective.

Trajectum Lumen is switched on 365 nights a year until midnight. You can cover it in about 1.5 hours at a comfortable stroll. The tourists can pick up a free itinerary at the VVV tourist office on Domplein square or take a guided tour.

※ De Haar Castle

De Haar Castle is located near Haarzuilens, in the municipality of Utrecht in the Netherlands. It is the biggest and most luxurious castle in the Netherlands and also one of the top European historic houses. The current buildings, all built upon the original castle and date from 1892.

De Haar Castle fell into disrepair in the 18th and 19th centuries. Architect Petrus Cuypers (famous for his designs of the Rijksmuseum and the Central Station in Amsterdam) restored and rebuilt it for baron Etienne van Zuylen van Nijevelt van de Haar.

In the 1960s, it became a place where the Van Zuylen van Nijevelt family received the international jet set, from Coco Chanel and Maria Callas to Gregory Peck and Roger Moore. A visit to De Haar Castle will take you back to the glory days of the castle and will show you the breathtaking splendour that surrounded the international rich and famous in the early 20th century.

Next to the castle you can find a romantic chapel and beautiful parks and gardens—covering over 135 acres of land—are worth a visit in their own right. The Rose Garden, the Roman Garden, the ponds and canals, as well as the many bridges, romantic vistas and impressive avenues invite visitors to go on long walks or have a picnic. Each season in the park has its own charm.

※ 大教堂钟楼

大教堂钟楼高112.32米，是荷兰最高的教堂塔。教堂塔最高的观景处在95米处，从这个位置眺望，你可以看到整个乌特勒支城及其周边的壮丽景色。乌特勒支的历史始于两千年前今天钟楼广场的位置，这也是这座喧嚣的城市和教堂塔开始的地方。

大教堂钟楼的兴建开始于1321年，但是由于缺乏资金，教堂的建造在1328年到1342年之间曾停了下来。最终，Dom塔在1382年完工，它是Dom建筑群的最高点，象征着主教的世俗和教会权力。扬·范·埃诺和扬·范·登杜姆是其主要的建筑师。

235

1505年，吉尔特·范·沃创造了13个令人印象深刻的教堂大钟，挂在钟楼中间的高处。所有的钟都有自己的名字和音色，总共重量超过了3万公斤。

1674年8月1日，一场毁灭性的龙卷风席卷了乌特勒支，教堂的正厅倒塌了。在这座城市的其他地方，风暴也造成了严重的破坏。从那时起，这座钟楼和教堂就被永久分离开来。

※ 乌特勒支老运河

长度大约有两公里的老运河是乌特勒支最著名的运河，作为巧妙的中世纪港区码头开发项目的一部分，它也是世界上独一无二的，在街道下面的码头和酒窖紧密连接，在运河的房子下面还有巨大的储藏室。在12世纪后半叶，乌特勒支的居民决定从码头开挖隧道以贯通运河边的房子，因此形成了这个城市典型的双码头。

乌特勒支的运河有着自己独有的个性，与阿姆斯特丹非常不同，运河游览是这里最佳的参观方式，无论游船还是徒步。图为双码头的乌特勒支运河。

如果你想乘船在老运河上穿梭，你可以选择乘坐运河游船，或者租用脚力踏船、划艇或独木舟进行探险。从水中探索这个城市，你定会对这个古老的城市得出一个完全不同的看法。

现如今，你会发现无数的餐厅和酒吧都会在码头酒窖增设一个居水露台。在乌特勒支度过精彩的一天之后，这里还为你提供一个可以小酌一杯或者吃点小吃的完美场所。

※ 乌特勒支大学植物园

在乌特勒支省的心脏地带，有一个由数千种植物组成的独特的自然宝藏——乌特勒支大学植物园。这些植被栽种在胡夫德克堡及其周围，开始于19世纪。作为一个组织机构，乌特勒支大学植物园可以追溯到1639年，是整个荷兰最古老的植物园之一。

时至今日，植物园继续发挥其主要功能，即支持教育和研究。此外，人们对其作为公众角色的关注也越来越多。自然保护是另一个重要方面，特别是在国际范围内。

在胡夫德克堡及其附近，你可以观赏到不同的花园和其他景致，每个景致都有自己的独特之处。比如

乌特勒支大学植物园可以追溯到1639年，是整个荷兰最古老的植物园之一，在这里能见到来自全球各地包括中国的许多类别的树种和花卉，主题园区会让人更加赞叹。

岩石花园、进化花园、探索主题花园、热带温室、鸟巢和蜜蜂旅社。

※ 艺术灯光

Trajectum Lumen是一条开启在黑暗之后进行探索的艺术灯光路线，沿着乌特勒支历史悠久的市中心艺术照明的位置。 Trajectum Lumen灯光艺术作品是由世界上最著名的国家和国际灯光艺术家创作的。当夜幕降临时，Trajectum Lumen从市中心位置的弗里登堡桥开启，已经吸引了越来越多的国际上著名的灯光艺术家前来布展。灯光艺术路线会指引着你穿过各种街道、物体、运河和建筑。你将会了解到更多关于城市的过去和历史性的事件，从一个全新的角度认识乌特勒支。

Trajectum Lumen灯光线路全年都开放，每日持续到午夜时分。以一种自然舒适的漫步方式的话，整条路线大约花费1.5小时。游客可以在钟楼广场的VVV旅游办公室索取免费游览日程，也可以参加游览团。

※ 德哈尔城堡

德哈尔城堡位于荷兰乌特勒支市的哈泽伊伦斯附近。它是荷兰最大、最豪华的城堡，也是欧洲顶级的历史建筑之一。现在的建筑始于1892年，都是在原来的城堡基础上建造的。

在18至19世纪，德哈尔城堡失修严重。建筑师佩特鲁斯·库伯斯（以阿姆斯特丹的国家博物馆和中央车站的设计而闻名）为艾蒂安·范·泽易伦·范·尼杰威尔特·范·德哈尔男爵修复并重建了它。

在20世纪60年代，这里成为了

德哈尔城堡周围的环境让人艳美，本图选自德哈尔官方网站。

范·泽易伦·范·尼杰威尔特家族招待从可可·香奈儿和玛丽亚·卡拉斯到格里高利·派克和罗杰·摩尔等国际大腕的地方。德哈尔城堡的参观游览过程将会带你回到城堡的辉煌时期，并将向你展示在20世纪初围绕着国际富豪和名人的令人惊叹的壮观景象。

在城堡的旁边有一个浪漫的小教堂和占地超过54万平方米的美丽的公园和花园，非常值得一看。玫瑰花园、罗马花园、池塘和运河，还有许多小桥，浪漫的景色和令人印象深刻的林荫道招致很多人前往漫步或野餐。公园里的每个季节都充满了独有的魅力。

Shopping in Utrecht 购在乌特勒支

Whatever your shopping needs, Utrecht has them covered. One of the great things about Utrecht is the fact that you can shop in the old-fashioned way: strolling the city centre's street, ducking in and out of any number of high street stores and cute little boutiques. If you arrive by train you can already start at Hoog Catharijne, the biggest shopping centre in the city with more than 160 venues.

※ Hoog Catharijne

With more than 26 million visitors a year, Hoog Catharijne is the most frequently visited shopping center in the Netherlands. The shopping centre with over 160 stores is one of the largest indoor shopping centers in the Netherlands. It provides an attractive and diverse range of shops. In addition to clothing, electronics and food, it is also a cultural and entertainment center-with the Vredenburg concert hall and the Hoog Catharijne cinema.

The central location–next to Utrecht's Central Station and bus station and with extensive parking facilities within walking distance–makes Hoog Catharijne the shopping heart of the Netherlands.

※ Oudegracht

The Oudegracht is the central canal in Utrecht. It starts in the southeast of the city, you can walk all along it. The Oudegracht is the second main shopping street of Utrecht, and is characterised by its typical Dutch cosy character. The street is located on both sides of a canal and hosts many domestic and foreign retailers. Because of its location and character, its capacity is limited, as the street is relatively narrow. Nevertheless, well-known international retailers opened their stores in this location because of the character of the street.

Done shopping? Then finish up your great day of shopping in a charming café or restaurant. Go downstairs to the waterside wharves or tuck into a romantic alleyway to grab a bite, because there are not only shops in this area, but also many small eateries and restaurants.

※ Vredenburg market

The largest market of Utrecht is the large general market held at Vredenburg. This is where you can buy fish, meat, vegetables, fruit, bread, belts, jackets, accessories and electronics. You are also in the right place for a bread roll with herring, a fresh treacle waffle or a bag of Dutch liquorice.

Held on Wednesdays, Fridays and Saturdays, the Vredenburg market counts between 75 and 125 stalls! Saturdays are the busiest day of the week.

※ Lapjesmarkt (fabric market)

The fabric market at the Breedstraat has been held here for more than 400 years and is thereby the oldest and biggest fabric market in the Netherlands. On May 9, 1597, the Utrecht city council gave the Linen-weaving guild permission to hold a linen market two times each year, but today you can shop for fabric every Saturday from 8:00-13:00. More than 100 stalls are available.

You'll find stall after stall filled with assorted fabrics sold by the metre, and a variety of clothes–both new and vintage, plus some antiques and second-hand books.

无论你的购物需求是什么，乌特勒支都有。乌特勒支的一个伟大之处是，你可以以老习惯和老方式达到采购目的：在市中心的街道上漫不经心地闲逛，在林林总总的商业街和可爱的小精品店里进进出出。如果你是坐火车抵达的，那你就可以从Hoog Catharijne开始逛起，这是该市最大的购物中心，拥有160多个商家。

霍格凯瑟琳购物中心连接着荷兰最大的中央车站乌特勒支中央站，是去往市中心的必经之路。图为购物中心建筑。

※ 霍格凯瑟琳购物中心

这里每年接待超过2 600万的游客，这是荷兰人们最经常光顾的购物中心。霍格凯瑟琳购物中心拥有超过160家商店，是荷兰最大的室内购物中心之一。这里的商店很多样化，很具有吸引力。除了常规的服装、电子产品和食品之外，这里还是一个文化和娱乐的中心——一家弗里登堡音乐厅和霍格凯瑟琳电影院。

霍格凯瑟琳购物中心位于核心区域，在乌特勒支的中央火车站和公共汽车站旁边，从这里步行的范围内配备了大量的停车设施，这使得霍格凯瑟琳购物中心成为了全荷兰的购物中心。

※ 老运河购物区

老运河是乌特勒支的中央运河。它从城市的东南方向开始，你可以直接沿着运河行走。老运河购物区是乌特勒支的第二个主要购物街，这个购物区的特点就是你可以以一种典型的荷兰式逛街的舒适方式来采买。老运河购物区的街道位于运河两岸，这里开设了许多国内外知名的零售品牌。由于受运河老城区位置和特点的限制，这里店铺的数量仍旧受到了一些影响，因为街道相对都比较狭窄。但这也恰恰是这一区域的卖点，著名的国际零售商们仍然在这个地方开设了他们的门店。

乌特勒支的运河购物区是最集中的，分布在运河两侧，很多品牌是在荷兰为数不多的店铺甚至是唯一店。图为运河旁小巷的服装店。

逛够了你可以在迷人的咖啡馆或餐馆结束你的购物之旅。到楼下的水边码头，或者到一个浪漫的小巷去吃点东西，因为这里不仅有商店，还有很多小餐馆和大餐厅。

※ 弗里登堡综合集市

乌特勒支最大的市场是在弗里登堡的大型综合市场。在这里你可以买到鱼、肉、蔬菜、水果、面包、皮带、夹克、配饰和电子产品。你也可以找到相应的商铺尝一尝夹鲱鱼的面包，或者现做现卖的新鲜的焦糖华夫饼，或买一袋荷兰甘草糖大胆试上一试。

弗里登堡综合集市在周三、周五和周六开放，市场上有75～125个摊位。周六是一周中人最多最忙的一天。

※ 面料市场

布莱德街的面料市场已经在这里开了400多年，因此也是荷兰最古老和最大的面料市场。1597年5月9日，乌特勒支市议会批准了亚麻纺织工会每年可以举办两次亚麻市场的活动，但到如今每周六8点到下午1点你都可以到这里购买面料。市场开放的摊位有100多个。

在这里你会发现一个挨一个的摊位上摆满了各种类型的布料和各式各样的服装，既有新的也有二手的，还会看到一些老古董和二手书。

Eating in Utrecht 食在乌特勒支

Utrecht has a huge selection of restaurants, diners, lunch rooms, coffee corners and delicatessens both in the city centre and in the surrounding districts. Turn into a charming alleyway or establish yourself in a restaurant on the bustling squares. For a culinary snack, you can choose from among many burger bars and hip pizzerias. Due to the large amount of Asian students in Utrecht the range of Asian restaurants is larger than it has ever been before. But if you prefer an entire culinary evening, you can go anywhere in the city.

And if you are staying for dinner then do as the locals do and start off with some fingerfood and a locally brewed beer. Settle down in one of the cosy bars in Utrecht and after that spend the evening in one of the more than 200 restaurants.

※ Jasmijn & ik

At Jasmijn & ik you will get soaked up by the Asian vibe! In the melting pot of Lombok in Utrecht you can eat spicy Thai, fresh Vietnamese, Chinese dumplings and fried fresh shallots. The dishes from the colourful Jasmijn & Ik's Asian kitchen provide a nice combination of pure flavours.

The variety of textures, smells and flavours in the meat dishes can also be found in the vegetarian or vegan (100% vegetable) dishes.

Hours: Tuesday and Wednesday 5:30pm–11pm
Thursday-Saturday 5:30pm–12am
Monday and Sunday closed

Address: Kanaalstraat 219-221, 3531 CH Utrecht

Contact: 030- 2938907
http://jasmijnenik.nl/

※ Bistro Karel 5

The restaurant is located in the centre of Utrecht where you can enjoy the atmospheric setting or one of the most beautiful terraces in the city. It is an atmospheric, authentic bistro with a unique, open convent kitchen, also the oldest kitchen in the Netherlands dated from 1348. This creative kitchen gets top marks for price/quality excellence.

For good reasons, Bistro Karel 5 in Utrecht is a favourite with locals, tourists and business folk alike. Here is cooked with seasonal products from the region and you can expect classic basic recipes with a modern twist. You can also get a snack, drink or afternoon tea.

Hours: Monday-Friday 8:30am–10pm; Saturday&Sunday 9am–10pm

Address: Geertebolwerk 1, 3511 XA Utrecht

Contact: 030-2337595

http://karel5.nl/

乌特勒支在市中心和周边地区拥有大量的餐厅、小饭馆、午餐店、咖啡馆和熟食店。你可以顺势拐进一条迷人的小巷，要么就在熙熙攘攘的广场边找一家自己接受的餐馆。要是想吃点美食小吃，大量的汉堡店和披萨饼店总能找到你想要的。由于乌特勒支的亚洲学生数量庞大，因此亚洲餐厅的数量规模也比以往大很多。如果你想要整个晚上都沉浸在这些美食当中，那几乎在城市的任何地区都能找到亚洲餐馆。

要是在乌特勒支吃晚餐的话，那就学学当地人吧，找一个舒适的酒吧里放松一下，再在两百多家餐馆的其中之一享受一个奇妙夜晚。

※ Jasmijn & ik

在Jasmijn & ik，你会被亚洲的氛围所紧紧包围！在乌特勒支的龙目岛这个文化和美食的大熔炉里，你可以吃到辛辣的泰国菜、爽口的越南菜、中国饺子和新鲜的洋葱圈。Jasmijn & Ik丰富多彩的亚洲厨房与当地的纯正口味进行了完美的融合。

肉类的各种美妙的口感、气息和味道同样也能在素食甚至是百分百蔬菜的纯素菜肴中品尝到。

营业时间：　周二、周三，下午5点半到晚上11点

周四、周六，下午5点半到晚上12点

周一和周日不营业

地址：　乌特勒支Kanaalstraat 219-221号

联系方式：　030-2938907

http://jasmijnenik.nl/

※ 卡雷尔5号

这家餐厅位于乌特勒支的中心位置，是一个可以感受到这座城市的气息和欣赏到最美丽的城市露台的地点之一。这是气氛正宗的小酒馆，有一个独特的开放式的修道院厨房，也是荷兰最古老的厨房，始于1348年。这个富有创意的厨房在合理的价格和菜色品质方面都获得了很高的评价。

卡雷尔5号有充足的理由成为乌特勒支当地人、游客和商人们最爱的餐厅。这里供应采用本地区季节性食材的烹饪美食，传统的食谱配方和现代手法进行的结合，可以小小期待一下。卡雷尔5号还是个吃小吃、喝饮料或下午茶的地方。

始于14世纪的荷兰最古老的厨房就在卡雷尔5号，离繁华区不远，却是片幽静的地方。图为餐厅门口。

营业时间：　周一至周五，上午8点半到晚上10点
　　　　　　周六和周日，上午9点到晚上10点

地址：　　　乌特勒支Geertebolwerk 1号

联系方式：　030-2337595
　　　　　　http://karel5.nl/

Tijd voor Nederlands 荷兰语时间

● 单词+短语

荷 raam	荷 stoel	荷 vork
英 window	英 seat	英 fork
译 窗户	译 椅子	译 叉子
荷 zout	荷 zoet	荷 vers
英 salt	英 sweet	英 fresh
译 盐	译 甜的	译 新鲜的
荷 hoofdgerecht	荷 saus	荷 groente
英 main course	英 sauce	英 vegetable
译 主菜	译 酱汁	译 蔬菜

荷 vlees/rundvlees/varkensvlees/ kip/vis 英 meat/beef/pork/chicken/fish 译 肉/牛肉/猪肉/鸡肉/鱼	荷 bestellen 英 order 译 点（餐）	荷 wachten 英 wait 译 等待
荷 roken 英 smoke 译 吸烟	荷 de rekening 英 bill 译 账单	荷 betalen 英 pay 译 付款

● 例句

荷 Jullie moet vijftien minuten wachten, er zijn geen lege stoelen. 英 You have to wait fifteen minutes, there are no empty seats. 译 你们需要等十五分钟，现在没有空位子。	荷 Ik wil bij het raam zitten. 英 I would like to sit by the window. 译 我想坐在靠窗的位置。
荷 Mag ik nu bestellen? 英 May I order now? 译 我现在可以点餐吗？	荷 Ik denk dat het hoofdgerecht heerlijk was. We aten vandaag veel groenten. 英 I think the main course was delicious. We ate a lot of vegetables today. 译 我觉得主菜很好吃。我们今天吃了很多蔬菜。
荷 Deze vis is erg vers, maar hij is een klein beetje zout. 英 This fish is very fresh, but it is a little bit salty. 译 这个鱼肉非常新鲜，但是有一点点咸。	荷 Welke saus wil je met je frietjes? 英 What kind of sauce would you like for your fries? 译 你的薯条要什么酱汁？
荷 Kun je me nog een vork geven? 英 Can you give me another fork? 译 能再给我一把叉子吗？	荷 Dit restaurant is rookvrij. 英 This restaurant is non-smoking. 译 这家餐厅是不能吸烟的。
荷 Mag ik de rekening even zien? 英 Can I see the bill? 译 我可以看一下账单吗？	荷 Ik heb niet genoeg contant geld, Ik wil met een creditcard betalen. 英 I do not have enough cash, I want to pay with a credit card. 译 我的现金不够，我想用信用卡付款。

6. 其他主要城市
Other Important Cities

Maastricht 马斯特里赫特

Many people say that Maastricht is the least Dutch city in the Netherlands. It is a city and a municipality in the southeast of the Netherlands. It is the capital and largest city of the province of Limburg.

Maastricht developed from a Roman settlement to a Medieval religious centre. In the 16th century it became a garrison town and in the 19th century an early industrial city. Today, the town is a thriving cultural and regional hub. It became well-known through the Maastricht Treaty and as the birthplace of the Euro. Maastricht has 1,677 national heritage buildings (Rijksmonumenten), the second highest number in the Netherlands, after Amsterdam. The town is popular with tourists for shopping and recreation, and has a large international student population.

Maastricht is about two hours away from Amsterdam, and if time permits, you can explore the city and see how it is different from other cities in the Netherlands.

※ Maastricht Underground

Do you dare to go underground? Not afraid of the dark? Go exploring in the caves below the St. Pietersberg hill. No light, no sound, no smell, no radiation, no pollution, no mobile phone signal, no idea of time…

Your guide will make sure you don't get lost in the man-made galleries, which once measured 230 km in total and measure around 80 km today. Almost 50,000 Maastricht residents sheltered in the expanded cave network during the World War II. An evacuation area with electric lightning, a public address system, a bakery, chapels, toilets, a small hospital, water pumps and much more! All facilities were constructed underground, though never put into full use. Remnants of them can still be seen in the Zonneberg Caves.

Each tour route has only one English tour during the working day. At the weekends the tour of North Caves has three English visits and the tour of Fort Sint Pieter offers two. The prices for the two tours are the same, € 6.75 for adults.

※ Het Vrijthof

The Vrijthof is a square in the centre of Maastricht. It is the largest square in the capital of the province of Limburg. Many very nice restaurants and cafés encircle the square. Adjacent to the Vrijthof is the St. Servatius Basilica, a Romanesque cathedral with crypts and treasuries.

During the summer you can enjoy the outdoor cafés of Vrijthof Square. Enjoy one of the many different kinds of beers that are served in Maastricht or try a piece of Limburgse Vlaai, a fruit pie famous among the Dutch.

※ Basilica of Our Lady

The Basilica of Our Lady is a Romanesque church in the historic center of Maastricht, the Netherlands. The church is dedicated to Our Lady of the Assumption and is a Roman Catholic parish church in the Diocese of Roermond.

Besides the chapel with the statue of Our Lady, there's much more arts and crafts to be admired. The treasury of the basilica holds a large number of objects of religious arts and crafts.

The square where the Basilica of Our Lady is located was once voted the most beautiful square in the Netherlands. There are plenty of outdoor cafés where you can sit down and appreciate this distinctive Dutch city.

※ Basilica of St. Servatius

Maastricht is filled with breathtaking churches, and even has two basilicas. The Basilica of St. Servatius (Basiliek van St. Servaas), which is located on the famous Vrijthof Square, is a Romanesque basilica with crypts and treasuries.

According to the legend, Saint Servatius was the first bishop of Maastricht and a small chapel was built on the spot where he was buried. In the centuries that followed, this chapel grew into the St. Servatius Church.

The architecturally hybrid but mainly Romanesque church is situated next to the Gothic church of Saint John, backing onto the town's main square, Vrijthof.

※ Boekhandel Dominicanen

Bookstore Dominicanen, located in a former Dominican church, is one of the most beautiful bookshops in the world.

Each year an American website draws up a list of the twenty most beautiful bookshops in the world, and Maastricht's Dominicanen is always on the list! And when you see it, you'll understand exactly why. The bookshop also offers the biggest collection of new and used books in Maastricht. You can easily lose track of time wandering among the shelves looking for the latest bestseller or a one-of-a-kind gift.

Even better, there is a coffee bar in the bookstore. Enjoy a delicious cup of coffee and a sweet snack at the famous Blanche Dael Coffeelovers, that's not a wonderful experience you can not enjoy everywhere.

※ Shopping in Maastricht

Maastricht is built around Vrijthof Square. Most of the main shopping streets, like the 'Grote Staat', are connected to this square. If you would like to find some exclusive brands and unique designs, go straight to the most romantic quarter of Maastricht: "stokstraatkwartier".

245

Wyck Quarter is well-known for trendy boutiques, interior design, antiques, art galleries and delicatessen.

Rechtstraat is a sophisticated shopping street with a range of lovely boutiques, including several exclusive fashion shops stocking big, well-known brands.

※ Eating in Maastricht

Harry's is an international restaurant which is open for lunch and dinner seven days a week, and for brunch on Sundays. Harry's restaurant deals in French, seafood and creative cuisine. And it serves unpretentious food and beverages in a relaxing, comfortable setting. The restaurant has a good reputation and price is reasonable.

Hours: LUNCH

Monday-Saturday, 12pm–2:30pm

DINER

Monday-Saturday, 6pm–9:30pm

BRUNCH

Sunday, 11am–4pm

DINER

Sunday, 4pm–9pm

Address: Wycker Brugstraat 2, 6221 EC Maastricht

Contact: 043-3281366

http://www.harrysrestaurant.nl/

马斯特里赫特有别于其他荷兰城市，其国家文化遗产数量仅次于阿姆斯特丹，超过1 600处。图为从火车站通往市中心的桥横跨马斯河。

人们都说马斯特里赫特是最不像荷兰的荷兰城市。它是荷兰东南部的一个自治市，是林堡省的省会和最大城市。

马斯特里赫特从罗马人的聚居地发展成中世纪的宗教中心。在16世纪，它变成了一个要塞城镇，到了19世纪又成了一个早期的工业城市，今天的马斯特里赫特是一个繁荣的文化和区域中心。这座城市因为《马斯特里赫特条约》在此签署和作为欧元的诞生地而闻名于世。马斯特里赫特拥有1 677个国家级文化遗产建筑，是荷兰文化遗产建筑数量第二多的城市，仅次于阿姆斯特丹。这个小城受到喜爱购物和游乐的人们的热烈欢迎，也同时拥有数量庞大的国际留学生群体。

马斯特里赫特离阿姆斯特丹大约有两小时路程，如果时间允许，你可以去看看这个城市，看看它和荷兰其他城市有什么不同。

※ 马斯特里赫特地下洞穴

你敢去地下吗？不怕黑？那一定要去圣彼得山下面的洞穴探险。没有光、没有声音、没有气味、没有辐射、没有污染、没有手机信号、没有时间概念……

你的导游会确保你不会迷失在人造的画廊里，这些画廊所测量的长度一度达到了230公里，而如今的长度是80公里。在第二次世界大战期间，将近50 000名马斯特里赫特居民在这个奢华的洞穴网络中躲避灾难。一个带发电灯光的疏散区、一套公共广播系统、一个面包房、小教堂、厕所、一个小医院、水泵，以及更多！所有的这些设施都是在地下建造的，但从未完全投入使用。在桑纳堡洞穴中仍然可以看到它们的遗迹。

每一条游览路线在工作日的时候每天只有一班英语导览团。在周末，北侧洞穴每天有三班英语导览团，参观的是圣彼得要塞。这两个团的价格是相同的，每个成人6.75欧元。

※ 弗莱特霍夫广场

弗莱特霍夫是马斯特里赫特市中心的一个广场，它是林堡省首府最大的广场，在广场的周围环绕着许多非常好的餐馆和咖啡馆。与弗莱特霍夫毗连的是圣瑟法斯大教堂，这是一个内部有地下室和金库的罗马式大教堂。

夏天时节，在广场的露天咖啡馆喝上一杯真的是一种享受。马斯特里赫特本地产的各式各样的啤酒也一定要试一试，还有荷兰非常著名的水果馅饼，林堡水果馅饼必须要尝尝。

Vlaai是非常有名的来自于林堡省的甜品，虽然在全荷兰各地都能吃到，但来到林堡省怎么能错过呢！图为林堡樱桃水果馅饼。

247

※ 圣母大教堂

圣母大教堂是荷兰马斯特里赫特历史中心的罗马式教堂。这座教堂是献于圣母升天的，是鲁尔蒙德地区一个罗马天主教教区的教堂。

除了尊敬的圣母像小堂，大教堂内还有非常多的艺术和工艺品值得欣赏。大教堂的宝库也藏有大量的宗教艺术品和手工艺品。

圣母大教堂所处的广场曾经被选为荷兰最美丽的广场。这里有很多户外咖啡馆，你可以坐下来细细品味一下这个独特的荷兰城市。

※ 圣瑟法斯大教堂

马斯特里赫特市充满了令人叹为观止的教堂，甚至还有两座柱廊大厅教堂。位于著名的弗莱特霍夫广场上的圣瑟法斯大教堂，是一种罗马式的长方形基督教堂，里面有教堂地下室和金库。

根据传说，圣瑟法斯是马斯特里赫特的第一个主教，在他死后，被埋葬的地方建了一个小教堂。在随后的几个世纪里，这个小教堂逐渐发展成为圣瑟法斯大教堂。

圣瑟法斯大教堂源自马斯特里赫特第一个主教圣瑟法斯，位于城市主广场，是一座罗马式教堂。

融合了多种建筑风格但主体上仍是罗马式教堂的圣瑟法斯大教堂坐落在哥特式圣约翰教堂的旁边，北靠城市的主广场弗莱特霍夫广场。

※ 天堂书店

天堂书店位于前多米尼加教堂，是世界上最美丽的书店之一。

每年，美国的一个网站都会评选出世界上最漂亮的二十家书店，马斯特里赫特的天堂书店总是榜上有名。当你看到这个书店的时候，你就会确切地明白为什么说它是最美丽的。这家书店还提供了马斯特里赫特最大规模的新书和二手书市场。走在货架之间，寻找着最新的畅销书或独一无二的礼物，你会很容易就忘记了时间。

更赞的是，书店里有一个咖啡吧。在著名的咖啡烘培商Blanche Dael Coffeelovers的店里享受一杯美味的咖啡和甜品，这可不是随便哪里都能体验到的。

天堂书店位于前多米尼加教堂，是世界上最美丽的书店之一。图为书店内景。

※ 购在马斯特里赫特

马斯特里赫特是在弗莱特霍夫广场的周围建造的。大多数主要的购物街，如Grote Staat，都与这个广场相连。如果你想找到一些高端品牌和独一无二的设计，可以直接去马斯特里赫特最浪漫的地方Stokstraatkwartier。

Wyck Quarter是一个以新潮时装店、室内装潢设计、古董、艺术画廊和熟食店而闻名的街区。

Rechtstraat是一个高雅的购物街，有大量可爱的精品店，包括几家独有的大型知名品牌开设的专卖店。

※ 食在马斯特里赫特

Harry's是一家国际餐厅，一周七天供应午餐和晚餐，周日供应早午餐。Harry's餐厅提供法式餐、海鲜和创意料理。餐厅的环境轻松舒适，食物和饮料都朴实无华。Harry's餐厅的信誉不错，价格也是合理的。

营业时间：　午餐周一到周六，中午12点至下午2点半

晚餐周一到周六，晚上6点至晚上9点半

周日早午餐，上午11点至下午4点；晚餐，下午4点至晚上9点

地址：　　　马斯特里赫特，Wycker Brugstraat 2号

联系方式：　043-3281366

http://www.harrysrestaurant.nl/

Groningen 格罗宁根

Groningen, the capital of the eponymous province in the northern part of Holland, is the largest city in the north of the Netherlands.

As a lively university city, Groningen has the youngest average population in the Netherlands, it has much to offer in terms of culture and events. Groningen has a long and turbulent history, which becomes evident from the historic warehouses, courts and buildings. Because of its charm, it was once proclaimed the city with the best city centre in the Netherlands.

※ Martinitoren

The Martinitoren is the highest church steeple in the city of Groningen and the fourth highest tower of the Netherlands. It is the bell tower of the Martinikerk which is considered as one of the main tourist attractions of Groningen and offers a view over the city and surrounding area.

The tower is located at the north-eastern corner of the Grote Markt (Main Market Square). It contains a brick spiral staircase consisting of 260 steps, and the carillon within the tower contains 62 bells. The Martinitoren can be climbed until the third gallery, during which visitors can also communicate with the tower through their mobile telephones! Afterwards, see the Martini church, the largest church in Groningen. The building of the church began approximately around 1230, it includes frescos from the 13th century, and has one of the largest Baroque organs in northwest Europe.

※ Prinsentuin

The Prinsentuin is located with the Old City of Groningen, behind the Prinsenhof, this garden consists of a rose garden, a herb garden, a part with berceaus and a sundial on the wall above the entrance.

The letters "W" and "A", the initial letters of stadtholder Willem Frederik van Nassau and his wife Albertine Agnes van Nassau, are planted in the Prinsentuin too, using hedges.

The Prinsentuin is also known because of the annual event Dichters in de Prinsentuin (English: Poets in the Prinsentuin), where known and unknown poets read out their poems in the open air.

※ Der Aa Church

The Der Aa Church with its striking yellow tower and medieval arches is one of the most iconic buildings in Groningen. Upon entering the church, visitors immediately feel that this is a place steeped in history. In 1226, the church received its official name: Kerk van Onze Lieve Vrouwe ter A, currently Der Aa church. Today it is used as a location for receptions, concerts, symposia and exhibitions.

More options than one would expect from a medieval church, thanks to the natural light and the exceptional lay-out of the building. Book fairs, exhibitions, information markets and whisky tastings held here always create a buzz.

※ The coast of Groningen

Now that you have come to Groningen, it is necessary to take a look at Groningen's coastline, which is a part of the Wadden Sea World Heritage Site and offers a level of peace and space that are difficult to find anywhere else in Holland.

This part of the Groningen coast is one of the rare parts of Holland where nature is allowed to go entirely its own way. Partly for this reason the Wadden Sea is known as the nursery of the North Sea, with many seals, coastal birds, special fish and plenty of crustaceans and shellfish.

There is also the brackish water area called the Dollard, where unique (salt tolerant) plants flourish and rare bird species like the avocet and redshank breed.

※ Shopping in Groningen

Grote Markt Square, with the famous Martinitoren, is the beating heart of Groningen. On and especially around the edges of this beautiful square, you will find a variety of shops, cafés and restaurants. Here is the best choice for shopping. And nearby, Vismarkt and Herestraat are home to various large chain stores and exclusive boutiques.

If you want to visit an art store or a jewellery store, then Kromme Elleboog is a good place to go.

There is always some kind of market going on in Groningen's city centre from Tuesdays to Saturdays, generally on the Grote Markt or the Vismarkt squares. You will find fresh food and flowers here, enjoy the aroma of food in the air and savour the moment.

※ Eating in Groningen

On Grote Markt Square, in one of Groningen's most unique buildings, lies café restaurant Goudkantoor. Dinner on the upper floor is particularly memorable, as it offers a beautiful view of the city, sit at the table and see the Martinitoren.

The restaurant serves both lunch and dinner, and is reasonably priced. They serve traditional Dutch cuisine and street food, such as French fries. Many diners recommend their veggie burgers and Italian sandwiches, make up your own mind and taste it for your yourself.

Hours: Daily, 10am–10pm; Monday 12pm–10pm; Sunday 12pm–6pm

Address: Waagplein 1,9712 JZ Groningen

Contact: 050-5891888

http://www.goudkantoor.nl/

格罗宁根是荷兰北部同名省份的省会，是荷兰北部最大的城市。

作为一个充满活力的大学城，格罗宁根是荷兰人口平均年龄最年轻的地方，在文化和活动方面做出了很多贡献。格罗宁根有一段漫长而动荡的历史，从历史悠久的店铺、法院和建筑物中就可见一斑。也因为它的魅力所在，它曾经被宣称为拥有最好的市中心的荷兰城市。

※ 马提尼塔

马提尼塔是格罗宁根市最高的教堂尖塔，也是荷兰的第四高塔，它是马提尼教堂的钟楼，被视为是格罗宁根的主要旅游景点之一，可以俯瞰整个城市和周边地区。

该塔位于主要的市场广场大市场的东北角。它包含一个由260个台阶组成的螺旋楼梯，在塔内悬挂着62个大钟。马提尼塔可以攀爬到第三层眺望台，这里是游客们拿手机拍拍照，与高塔交流的很好的平台。然后，看看格罗宁根最大的教堂马提尼教堂，这座教堂始建于1230年左右，包括13世纪的壁画，是欧洲西北部最大的巴洛克艺术机构之一。

马提尼塔是格罗宁根最知名的建筑，马提尼教堂是欧洲西北部最大的巴洛克艺术机构之一。

※ 王子花园

王子花园位于格罗宁根的老城区，在格罗宁根王子酒店的后面，有一个玫瑰园、一个药草园和带储藏区的一部分，还有一个日晷镶嵌在入口上方的墙上。

花园中所呈现的字母"W"和"A"是省督威廉·弗雷德里克·范·纳索和他的妻子艾尔柏缇娜·阿涅斯·范·纳索的名字首字母，它们都是用树篱种植在花园中的。

王子花园之所以为众人所知，是因为在花园中举办的一年一度的"王子花园诗歌活动"，那些知名的和不知名的诗人都曾在这里朗诵他们的诗歌作品。

251

※ 阿教堂

这座有着引人注目的黄塔和中世纪拱门的阿教堂是格罗宁根最具标志性的建筑之一。进入教堂后，游客们立刻觉得这是一个浸透历史的地方。1226年，这教堂被正式命名为：Kerk van Onze Lieve Vrouwe ter A（英文译为：Chapel of Our Lady at the river Aa），意思是"A河畔的圣母教堂"，目前是"Der Aa"，即"A教堂"。如今这座教堂被用作接待、音乐会、座谈会和展览的场所。

由于自然光和建筑的特殊布局，中世纪教堂的使用远比人们能想到的要多得多。在这里举办的图书博览会、展览、信息市场和威士忌品酒会总会引起一番轰动。

※ 格罗宁根海岸线

现在你已经来到格罗宁根，有必要看一看格罗宁根的海岸线，它是瓦登海洋世界遗产的一部分，呈现出在荷兰其他地方很难见到的和平与空间的平衡。

格罗宁根海岸的这部分是荷兰少有的地方，在这里大自然可以不受干预自我发展。从某种程度上也正是由于这个原因，瓦登海栖息着非常多的海豹、海岸鸟类、特殊鱼类和大量甲壳类动物和贝类，被称为"北海的育婴室"。

格罗宁根的海岸线是瓦登海洋世界遗产的一部分。图为栖息在此的成群海豹。

还有一片叫多拉德的盐水区域，这里生长着非常繁茂的独特的耐盐植物，还栖息着大量的鸟类如反嘴鹬和红脚鹬。

※ 购在格罗宁根

大市场广场及著名的马提尼塔是格罗宁根的心脏地带。在这个美丽的广场周围，你会发现各种各样的商店、咖啡馆和餐馆，这里是购物的最佳选择。而附近的Vismarkt和Herestraat则是各种大型连锁店和专卖店的所在地。

如果你想去艺术品商店或珠宝店，那么Kromme Elleboog是一个不错的去处。

从周二到周六，格罗宁根市的市中心总会有一些集市，通常是在主广场和Vismarkt广场上。你会在这里买到各种现加工的食物和新鲜的花卉，美食的香气弥漫在空气，吸一吸，享受北海的此刻吧！

※ 食在格罗宁根

在格罗宁根最独特的建筑之一的城市主广场，有一家名为Goudkantoor的餐厅。在餐厅的楼上吃一顿晚餐是让人难以忘怀的，因为这个位置的城市景观实在迷人，就坐于自己的餐桌旁，便可以看到马提尼高塔。

Goudkantoor餐厅供应午餐和晚餐，价格也合理。在这里能吃到传统的荷兰美食和街头的一些小吃，比如炸大薯条。许多食客推荐他们的素食汉堡和意大利三明治，不过每个人的口味有别，还是要自己拿主意多尝试哦！

营业时间：　　每天上午10点到晚上10点

周一中午12点到晚上10点

周日中午12点到晚上6点

地址：　　　　格罗宁根，Waagplein 1号

联系方式：　　050-5891888

http://www.goudkantoor.nl/

Delft 代尔夫特

Founded around 1100, Delft grew rich from weaving and trade in the 13th and 14th centuries, known for its historic town centre with canals, Delft Blue pottery, the Delft University of Technology, jurist Hugo Grotius, painter Johannes Vermeer and scientist Antony van Leeuwenhoek, and its association with the royal House of Orange-Nassau. It is located in the province of South Holland, to the north of Rotterdam and south of The Hague.

※ The canals of Delft

Delft is a picturesque city, and the delft canal is the flowing blood of this painting. The canals of Delft were incorporated into the original city planning. They served as defence and lifelines throughout the city, delivering goods, people, and supplies. The oldest canal line is the Old Delft, but the other city canals are still central to city life.

A walking tour will give you the background of the buildings as you pass them, but a tour from the water, will give you a true feel for the city's history and culture. You can rent a canal taxi boat to take you to the main tourist spots.

※ Nieuwe Kerk

The Nieuwe Kerk is a Protestant church in the city of Delft in the Netherlands, the construction of church began in 1381; the church was finally completed in 1655. The building is located on Delft Market Square, opposite to the City Hall. In 1584, William the Silent was entombed here in a mausoleum designed by Hendrick and Pieter de Keyser. Since then members of the House of Orange-Nassau have been entombed in the royal crypt. From the 108.75m-high tower, you can see as far as Rotterdam and The Hague on a clear day, after climbing its 376 spiralling steps.

※ Oude Kerk

The Oude Kerk started with a wooden church in 1050, which grew out to be a 75-metre high building with a gothic tower, a fact that runs the shivers down many tourists' back is the fact that its 75m-high tower leans nearly 2m from the vertical due to subsidence caused by its canal location, hence its nickname Scheve Jan ('Leaning Jan').

The church has beautiful stained glass windows and two organs. It also holds several mausoleums and graves of important people, such as admirals Piet Hein and Maarten Tromp and the painter Johannes Vermeer.

253

※ Delft City Hall

Delft City Hall is a perfectly balanced, virtually symmetrical building in the Renaissance style and was completed by Hendrick de Keyser in 1620. It was built around the late Gothic count's tower that dates from the 13th century.

The City Hall is opposite the Nieuwe Kerk. It is the former seat of the city's government, and today is still the place where residents hold their civic wedding ceremonies. The building underwent many changes over the centuries but was restored in the 20th century to its Renaissance appearance.

※ Shopping in Delft

The main shopping street in Delft is mostly around the Market Square, such as Oude Delft, Choorstraat, Wijnhaven and Vrouw Juttenland. The shops here are varied: art galleries, gift boutiques, exclusive fashion shops and lovely vintage shops.

Attractive shopping streets like Gasthuislaan, Molslaan and Breestraat offer a broad range of fashion boutiques, delicious food and trendy cosmetics. And 'In de Veste' and 'Zuidpoort' are modern shopping areas. This is where you will find big department and chain stores.

※ Eating in Delft

Spijshuis De Dis is situated on a beautiful square, The Beestenmarkt, which distinguishes itself from other restaurants, Spijshuis De Dis and offers you Dutch specialties.

Fresh fish and amazing soups served in bread bowls take centre stage at this romantic foodie haven, but meat eaters and vegetarians are also welcome here. Smoked, marinated mackerel on sliced apple with horseradish, these innovative dishes are well worth trying.

If you're a picky eater, they also have custom menus. Being able to eat well should not be too difficult.

Hours: Daily, 5pm–10pm; Monday, Sunday closed

Address: Beestenmarkt 36, 2611 GC Delft

Contact: 015-2131782
http://www.spijshuisdedis.com/en/

代尔夫特成立于1100年左右，在13世纪和14世纪，由于织造业和贸易的繁荣昌盛积累了大量财富，并以其历史悠久的市中心和运河、代尔夫特蓝陶器、代尔夫特理工大学、法学家胡果·格劳秀斯、画家约翰内斯·维米尔和科学家安东尼·范·列文虎克及其与皇室奥伦治·拿骚的故居而闻名。代尔夫特位于南荷兰省，在鹿特丹北边，海牙南边。

※ 代尔夫特运河

代尔夫特是一个风景如画的城市，代尔夫特运河是这幅画流动的血液。代尔夫特运河最初就被纳入了城市规划，他们在整个城市中充当着防御和城市生命线的功能和作用，用以运送货物、人员流动和物资配送。最古老的运河段在代尔夫特的老城，但是城市的其他运河段仍然是其城市生活的中心。

在城市中徒步游览会让你深刻了解到建筑物背后的故事，但若选择运河乘船游览，你便会对代尔夫特这座小城的历史和文化有一个切实的感受和体验。你可以租用一艘运河小船，城市主要的旅游景点都可到达。

※ 新教堂

代尔夫特新教堂始建于1381年，在1655年建造完成，是荷兰代尔夫特市的新教教堂。该建筑位于代尔夫特市场广场，也就是城市主广场，与市政厅相对。1584年，亨德里克·德·凯泽和彼得·德·凯泽设计了陵墓，沉默的威廉被埋葬在这里。也就是从那时起，奥兰冶·拿骚家族的成员都被安葬在了皇家墓穴里。爬上376级螺旋阶梯，在天气晴好的时候，你可以在108.75米高的教堂塔上看到鹿特丹和海牙。

代尔夫特对于荷兰皇家来说非常重要，新教堂埋葬着荷兰国父威廉一世，他被刺杀的地方也是在这座城市。图为从新教堂塔楼俯视代尔夫特小城，靠左侧的教堂是老教堂。

※ 老教堂

代尔夫特老教堂，这座75米高的哥特式建筑高塔，始于1050年所建造的一个木制结构教堂。让许多游客胆战的是，这座75米高的教堂塔由于所处运河位置的路面下陷，高塔倾斜了近2米，因此给予其"Scheve Jan"的昵称，意思是"倾斜的Jan"。

老教堂有着非常漂亮的彩色花窗和两大管风琴。它还保存着一些重要人物的陵墓，如海军上将皮特·海恩和马顿·特龙普以及画家约翰内斯·维米尔。

※ 代尔夫特市政厅

代尔夫特市政厅是一座文艺复兴风格的建筑，由亨德里克·德·凯泽在1620年完成，这是一个完全平衡的几乎完美对称的文艺复兴风格建筑。它建立在13世纪晚期哥特式建筑的遗址之上。

市政厅在新教堂的正对面，它是市政府的前身，至今仍是市民举行婚礼仪式的地方。这座建筑在几个世纪里经历了许多变化，但在20世纪又恢复到文艺复兴时期的面貌。

代尔夫特市政厅是一座几乎完全对称的文艺复兴建筑，与新教堂正面相对，位于城市主广场两端。图为从新教堂看市政厅。

255

※ 购在代尔夫特

代尔夫特的主要购物街大多围绕着城市主广场，像代尔夫特旧运河街、Choorstraat街、葡萄酒港和Vrouw Juttenland。这里的商店种类繁多，有艺术画廊、礼物精品店、高档专卖店和可爱的古董店。

还有一些引人注目的购物街如Gasthuislaan、Molslaan和Breestraat，这些街上有着各种各样的时尚精品店、美味的食品和潮流化妆品。而De Veste和Zuidpoort则是现代的购物区，在这里你可以到大的百货公司和连锁店去逛逛。

※ 食在代尔夫特

这家餐厅坐落在代尔夫特非常漂亮的Beestenmarkt广场上，与其他餐厅不同的是，Spijshuis de Dis餐厅供应的是非常传统的荷兰特色菜。

在这个浪漫的美食天堂，你可以品尝到新鲜的鱼肉，他们还用面包做成了汤碗，里面盛着味道鲜美的热汤，这是一特色主打。不管你是视肉如命者还是素食者，这家餐厅都有人们可选择的。烟熏再腌制过的鲭鱼和辣根配苹果片，这样的创新菜肴非常值得一试。

如果你是一个挑剔的食客，他们还有定制菜单。总之，在这里吃好并不是什么难事。

营业时间：　周二到周六，下午5点至晚上10点；周一、周日不营业

地址：　　　代尔夫特，beestenmarkt36号

联系方式：　015-2131782

http://www.spijshuisdedis.com/en/

购在荷兰

Shopping in the Netherlands

When planning your visit to the Netherlands or one of its cities, the first thing that comes to mind are probably the excellent museums, the special architecture or nice restaurants. For many people the Netherlands would not be their first choice as shopping destination, however fitting in an afternoon of shopping is rather worthwhile. Whether you like to shop for fashion, shoes and jewellery, or if you are a lover of art and design or maybe rather prefer literature and music, the Netherlands has them all, the cities harbour countless shops specialising in products related to food, cosmetics, handicrafts, clothing, all kinds of gadgets, art and antiques etc. Of course there are also a lot of stores that can help you to find that special souvenir for your loved ones. Luckily many big cities open their shops on Sunday as well.

在你打算到荷兰或者去荷兰某个城市旅行时，首先想到的可能是那些优秀的博物馆、特殊的建筑或不错的餐馆。对于许多人来说，荷兰并不是他们购物的首选目的地，但花上一个下午转一转买买东西仍然很有必要。不管你热衷于时尚的服装、漂亮的鞋子、不菲的珠宝，还是热爱艺术和设计或者喜欢文学和音乐，都能在荷兰尽享其中，食品专营店、化妆品店、工艺品店、服装店、卖各式小玩意的商店、古董店等，市内各类专门商店数之不尽。当然还可以从很多商店给自己爱的人买一些特殊的纪念品。好消息是，现在很多大城市的商店在星期天也开门营业（欧洲大部分国家商店在周末不营业）。

1. 荷兰标签
Dutch Label

✿ Cheese 奶酪

The Dutch dairy factories and local dairy farmers produce and export hundreds of millions of tons of cheese every year. The Dutch probably love cheese more than anything else and eat about 15kg to 20kg of it annually per person. There are five cheese markets operating in the Netherlands, they are Woerden (which is an commercial one and operating all year round), Alkmaar, Gouda, Edam and Hoorn (operating during the tourist season from spring to fall). Besides selling cheese, these markets have also become a tourist attraction and are a great promotion for the Netherlands as an tourist destination.

If you want to taste or buy cheese, here are a few things you need to pay attention to:

※ Types of Dutch cheese

● **Gouda Cheese.** This cheese is a Dutch cheese par excellence. Almost half of the cheese production in Holland is devoted to this iconic cheese, which makes it the Netherlands' most important and best-known cheese. Gouda is a semi-hard cheese with a 48 % milk fat content and has a mild to piquant taste.

● **Edam Cheese.** Edam cheese is the second best known cheese in the Netherlands, making up 27% of the country's total cheese production. This semi-hard cheese with a fat content of about 40% has a very mellow, salty taste. This cheese is produced in a typical round shape and many export versions often have a very recognisable red paraffin coating as well.

● **Leidsekaas.** This cheese is a kind of yellow cheese "laden" with cumin, originally from the region of Leiden. Leidsekaas does resemble Gouda a bit, in terms of form, but is less round and has sharp edges on the sides. It has also lower fat content (30-40%) so if you are minding your waist this is a weight-conscious choice.

● **Maasdam Cheese.** The outside shell of this cheese is smooth, with a waxed yellow or naturally polished rind, which is similar to that of the Gouda Cheese. Inside the pate is a semi-firm, pale yellow with big eyes (holes that are created by special bacteria which release gases during the maturation process). The cheese has a sweet, buttery, nutty taste with a fruity background, the texture of the pate is creamy and soft. It goes very well with a sandwich or as a snack when eaten young.

● **Boerenkaas.** This is a kind of artisanal cheese by law: It is made of raw milk cheese and at least half the milk used to produce this cheese needs to come from the farm's own cows, and the rest is allowed to be provided by no more than two other farms.

● **Goat Cheese.** Goat Cheese in Holland comes in two types: the well-known soft goat's cheese and in the semi-hard Gouda style. A big advantage of goat's cheese is that it needs a

259

shorter maturation process than cheese made from cow milk. The semi-hard goat's cheese is rather pale, and has an interesting slightly piquant taste, its creamy melt-in-the-mouth texture certainly will win you over to try more.

● **Frisian Clove Cheese.** This is a kind of cheese made with skimmed mild and has a fat percentage of 20% to 44%, it is native to Friesland, a Northern Dutch province. It is a tangy cheese with a firm texture and is studded with cumin seeds and aromatic cloves, hence it got its name.

※ Dutch cheese brands

The most famous cheese brands in the Netherlands are by far Gouda and Edam. Both these cheeses are named after their place of origin. Today, Gouda and Edam are made the world over. Edam Holland and Gouda Holland, however, are protected brand names as they include the additional "Holland", indicating they are made locally. So if you want to make sure you have the real stuff, check for this addition.

Besides these brands there are also other internationally renowned brands, for example, Uniekaas, Hollandse Chèvre, Mimolette, just to name a few.

Dutch people like to go to their local cheese shops instead of the supermarket to purchase their favourite cheese. Many smaller brands, like Reypenaer, which sells artisanal cheeses, are available only in Dutch cheese shops. And then there is a children's brand cheese called Miffy Dutch cheese, which sports the friendly character from a series of Dutch picture books called Nijntje in Dutch, but is better known as Miffy the world over.

荷兰的奶业工厂和当地奶农们每年可生产和出口数亿吨的奶酪。荷兰人可能是对奶酪最情有独钟的了，平均每人每年消耗的奶酪在15公斤到20公斤。荷兰有5个奶酪市场，分别是商业运作全年营业的武尔登，以及传统运作只在春季到秋季开放的阿尔克马尔、豪达、艾登和霍恩奶酪市场。除了卖奶酪，这些市场现在也成了旅游景点，对促进荷兰旅游起到了一个很大的提升作用。

如果你想品尝或购买奶酪，以下是几件需要注意的事：

※ 荷兰奶酪的种类

豪达奶酪（**Gouda**）：这是荷兰奶酪的一个杰作。几乎半数的荷兰奶酪市场都被这一标志性的奶酪占据，这使得它成为荷兰最重要和最著名的奶酪。豪达奶酪是一种半硬奶酪，脂肪含量有48%，有轻微的辛辣味。

左图为艾登奶酪，右图是小城艾登人家。

艾登奶酪（**Edam**）：艾登奶酪是荷兰第二著名的奶酪，占到全荷兰奶酪总产量的27%。属半硬奶酪，脂肪含量约为40%，口感醇香、有咸味。这种奶酪是典型的圆形奶酪，许多出口产品通常带有一种非常容易辨认的红色石蜡涂层。

莱顿奶酪（**Leidsekaas**）：这是一种最初源自莱顿地区的黄色奶酪，含有茴香籽。莱顿奶酪跟豪达奶酪有点儿相似，但它的形状比较小，边缘也要锋利一些。它的脂肪含量也要低一些，大概有30%～40%，所以如果你担心体重超重，腰围变粗，那莱顿奶酪会是个不错选择。

马士丹奶酪（**Maasdam**）：这种奶酪的表面比较光滑，有蜡黄色或自然抛光的外皮，类似于豪达奶酪。奶酪内部呈半硬状态、带有淡黄色的大眼睛，这些如眼睛般的气孔是由特殊的细菌产生的，可以在奶酪逐渐成熟过程中释放气体。这种奶酪有一种甜的，是黄油和坚果的味道，还有一种水果味的，摸起来的手感绵软而细腻。发酵时间短的奶酪很适合配三明治吃或者当零食吃。

农夫奶酪（**Boerenkaas**）：根据规定，农夫奶酪是一种手工奶酪，由生奶酪制成，且制作这种奶酪的原料奶必须至少有一半来自于农场自己饲养的奶牛，其余的原料奶可以由最多两个另外的农场供应。

山羊奶酪（**Goatt Cheese**）：荷兰的山羊奶酪有两种类型——著名的山羊软奶酪和半硬的豪达山羊奶酪。山羊奶酪的一大优点是它的成熟过程要比牛奶奶酪的成熟过程要短。半硬的山羊奶酪颜色苍白，有一种让人喜欢的轻微的辛辣味儿，入口的感觉软软绵绵，透着丝丝甜气，会忍不住再尝上第二口。

弗里斯兰丁香奶酪（**Frisian Clove Cheese**）：这是一种用脱脂牛奶制成的奶酪，脂肪含量在20%～44%之间，它的原产地是荷兰北部的弗里斯兰省。它的味道浓郁，质地坚硬，上面点缀着茴香籽和丁香，因此得名。

※ 荷兰的奶酪品牌

荷兰最著名的奶酪品牌是豪达和艾登，这两种奶酪都是以原产地命名的，如今的豪达和艾登已经遍布世界各地。现在，这两种品牌名称是受保护的，因为其中包含了"荷兰"两个字，表明它们是荷兰本地生产的。所以如果你想买最正宗的豪达和艾登的话，那么你就要看一下有没有这一标志了。

除了这两个品牌，荷兰奶酪还有其他国际知名品牌，如Unie kaas、Hollandse Chèvre、Mimolette等，不逐一列出。

要想买自己最爱吃的奶酪的话，荷兰人更喜欢去当地的奶酪店，而不是去超市。有很多较小的品牌店，比如销售手工奶酪的Reypenaer，只能在荷兰的奶酪专卖店买到。还有专卖儿童奶酪的荷兰米菲兔，在荷兰米菲兔系列图画书上塑造出了一个温暖友好的人物性格，不过Nijntje这一称号在世界各地都被称为"Miffy"。

Windmills and Its Products 风车及周边产品

The first things that come to mind when you think of the Netherlands most probably are windmills. The Dutch love their windmills and every year a day or a weekend is designated as National Mill Day, when all windmills over the country are open to the public. A trip to the Netherlands wouldn't be complete without stopping by at least one of these iconic windmills. Fortunately for those who are eager to visit one of these impressive monumental machines there are hundreds dotted around the country which are open to visit for a small fee.

If you would like to buy your own little windmill then you can do that at one of the small shops in a windmill village like Zaanse Schans or in the souvenir shops in cities, all over the Netherlands but certainly in the big cities as Amsterdam and The Hague, where there are ample shops selling products with an iconic image of a windmill on it.

If you go to Zaanse Schans, you will find that the windmills here are not just for tourists to visit, some are still used for normal production. Windmills used to grind flour or as refinery and have been in production for centuries, the traditional goods they produce, like all kinds of oils for cooking as for painting, pigments for traditional oil painting, spices from the orient and of course all kinds of flour that are used to bake the lovely Dutch artesian breads are sold directly to tourists at acceptable prices.

当你想到荷兰时，脑袋里闪过的第一个印象可能是风车。荷兰人热爱自己的风车，每年的某一天或其中一个周末都被指定为"国家磨坊日"，届时全国各地的风车都向公众开放。到荷兰旅行，至少也要去看一次这些标志性的风车，否则整个旅程都是不完整的。幸运的是，对于那些渴望参观这些令人印象深刻的巨型机器的人来说，风车遍布整个国家，并且参观费用也非常便宜。

怎么跟没有亲眼见过风车的朋友描述呢！这些小摆件、小玩意总是很好的伴手礼，物美价廉。图为礼品店中的风车小摆件。

如果你想买个属于自己的小风车，也是可行的，在风车村的小商店里，比如说像桑斯安斯风车村，或者在城市的纪念品商店里，尤其是像阿姆斯特丹和海牙这样的大城市，都能买到琳琅满目的各式带有风车形象的商品。

如果你去桑斯安斯风车村，你会发现这里的风车不仅仅是供游客参观的，有些还用于正常生产。风车用来磨面粉或炼油已经持续了好几个世纪，一些传统的产品，像绘画颜料一样的各种烹调油、传统的油画颜料、来自东方的香料，当然还有用于烘烤美味的荷兰面包的各种面粉，都在以合理的价格出售给游客们。

Tulip 郁金香

Although tulips are now mostly associated with Holland, they originally are found in a band stretching from Southern Europe to Central Asia, but have become widely naturalised and cultivated even before the 17th century when they arrived in the Netherlands.The Ottoman rulers enjoyed the beauty of this gorgeous and mysterious flowers, and while tulips probably already have been cultivated in Asia from the loth century, they did not come to the attention of the west till the 16th century, when western diplomats to the Ottoman court observed and reported on them. In 17th century the Netherlands, during the time of the well-known Dutch Golden Age an infection of tulip bulbs by a virus created variegated patterns in the tulip flowers that were much admired and valued. This phenomenon was referred to as "broken". They were rapidly introduced into Europe and cultivated. They soon became a frenzied commodity which lead to the tulip mania and eventually to what is called the first example of an economic bubble.

Tulips were frequently depicted in paintings during the Dutch Golden Age, and although they ever since have become associated with the Netherlands, the name "tulip" as we now know it still reminds us of its Persian roots as the name is thought to have been derived from a Persian word for turban, which it may have been thought to resemble.

For Dutch people the first thing to come to mind when you mention tulips is "De Keukenhof" ("Kitchen garden"), also known as the Garden of Europe. De keukenhof is one of the world's largest flower gardens, situated in Lisse in the Netherlands.

According to the official website for De Keukenhof, approximately 7 million flower bulbs are planted annually in the park, which covers an area of about 32 hectares (79 acres).

The history of Keukenhof dates all the way back to the 15th century. At that time Countess Jacoba van Beieren would gather her fruit and vegetables from "De Keukenduin " (kitchen dunes) for the kitchen at her court at Teylingen Castle. Keukenhof Castle was built in 1641 and the estate grew to encompass an area of over 200 hectares.

In 1949 by the then-mayor of Lisse established the park which opened its gates to the public in 1950. De Keukenhof was an instant success, with 236,000 visitors in the first year alone. During the past 68 years De Keukenhof has developed into a world-famous attraction.

The Keukenhof features a variety of different gardens and garden styles. For example, the English landscape garden features winding paths and unexpected see-through points (designed by Jan David Zocher in 1830, who is also the garden architect of the famous Vondelpark in Amsterdam, among others). Then there is the historical garden which is an enclosed garden where you can see many old types of tulips. The nature garden consists of a water garden where shrubs and perennials are combined with bulbous plants. The Japanese country garden is a non-traditional garden in a natural environment.

The park usually opens from March to May every year and every year the park is redesigned according to a new theme.

The Keukenhof is of course the ideal place to buy your flower bulbs, but the Singel Flower Market is also a great place for tourists who want to buy tulips. (See "shopping in Amsterdam" for more information). Many other cities around the country also have flower markets, such as the Bloemenmarkt Janskerkhof in Utrecht.

Friendship tips, due to Chinese customs regulations, tulip bulbs cannot be brought into the country unless quarantine reports are provided.

虽说郁金香现在和荷兰密不可分，但郁金香最初却是在欧洲南部延伸到中亚这一带被发现的，且在17世纪引进到荷兰之前，已经被广泛地推广和培育。郁金香大概从10世纪就已经在亚洲地区种植，当时奥斯曼帝国的统治者沉醉于这种华丽而神秘的花，但是直到16世纪西方的外交官在奥斯曼帝国的法庭观察提到这种花，这才引起了西方的注意。在17世纪，在荷兰著名的黄金时代，郁金香球茎被一种病毒感染，却在其花朵中呈现出来各种各样的花纹，于是变异的花朵受到了人们的赞叹及重视。这种现象被称为"裂变"现象。人们迅速地将郁金香引进到欧洲并加以栽培。很快，郁金香就成了一种让人们趋之若鹜的商品并导致了郁金香热，最终成了被称做经济泡沫的第一个例子。

郁金香的千姿百态原本是因花朵被病毒感染产生，因此引入欧洲后引起人们趋之若鹜，导致经济泡沫。图为电影《狂热郁金香》剧照，便描述了这件事情。

在荷兰黄金时代的绘画中经常能见到郁金香的踪迹，虽然它们和荷兰已经紧密相连，但是"tulip"这个名字仍然提醒着我们，它本是起源于波斯语中人们所包裹的头巾"turban"，可能是因为这种花的形态和头巾包裹的样子太相似了吧！

当你和荷兰人提到郁金香的时候，那么让人首先想到的是库肯霍夫公园（厨房花园），它可算得上是欧洲的花园。库肯霍夫是世界上最大的花园之一，位于荷兰的利瑟。

根据库肯霍夫官方网站的信息描述，库肯霍夫公园的占地面积约32公顷，每年种植的花卉数量约有700万株。

库肯霍夫的历史可以追溯到15世纪。当时，来自巴伐利亚州的雅可布·范·贝伦伯爵夫人从"De Keukenduin"（厨房沙丘）采集她位于泰灵恩城堡的厨房所需要的蔬菜和水果。库肯霍夫城堡修建于1641年，庄园的面积则扩大到200多公顷。

图中如同葱头般的便是郁金香和风信子球茎，从超市到花店，处处可以买到，但要带回国内一定要提前准备好检疫报告。

1949年，利瑟当时的市长建立了这座公园，并于1950年向公众开放。库肯霍夫公园建成后马上就获得了成功，仅第一年就有23.6万名游客前往游览。在过去的68年时间里，库肯霍夫已经发展成为举世闻名的旅游景点。

库肯霍夫公园的特色就是对不同的花园及其风格的包容。例如，英国的景观花园有蜿蜒的小径和意想不到的透视点（其由Jan David Zocher在1830年设计，阿姆斯特丹著名的冯德尔公园也出自他的手笔）；还有一个封闭的历史花园，在那里可以看到许多古老品种的郁金香；自然花园则是一个流水花园，栽满了灌木、各种多年生植物和球茎植物；还有日本乡村花园，是一个自然环境下的非传统花园。

库肯霍夫公园可谓是欧洲花园，每年3到5月份，这里是彩色海洋。图为库肯霍夫公园的美景。

264

公园通常在每年的3月到5月开放，公园的主题设计每年也都会不同。

库肯霍夫公园自然是购买花卉的理想场所，但是对于想买郁金香的游客来说，辛格鲜花市场也是个不错的去处（可详见"购在阿姆斯特丹"这一章节）。荷兰全国很多的其他城市也有花卉市场，如乌得勒支的Bloemenmarkt Janskerkhof。

友情提示，由于中国的海关规定，除非提供检疫报告，否则不能携带郁金香球茎入境。

Klompen (Clogs) 木鞋

Prior to the 16th century, poor people wore no shoes at all. Shoes were expensive and worn only by the rich to protect their feet and prove that they could afford such a luxury.

The early versions of clogs featured clogs and leather tops, however eventually the entire shoe was made of wood to better protect feet, as many people who wore them were fisherman, farmers, and factory workers.

Nowadays it is almost impossible to find a Dutch person wearing clogs in the city, but for some special occupations, such as farmers in the countryside, gardeners, tradesmen, and fishermen, or special occasions people still wear clogs and in some villages wearing clogs is still a treasured tradition.

Approximately 3 million pairs of clogs are made each year. They are sold throughout the Netherlands. A large part of the market is for tourist souvenirs. Outside the tourist industry, clogs can be found in local tool shops and garden centres.

If you are interested in knowing how clogs are made then you certainly have to visit the Zaanse Schans open air museum as "The Wooden Shoe Workshop" is located in this open air museum. This is a company which was founded in 1974, and it is specialising in the production of clogs. Using antique machines, they demonstrate how they still make clogs in the same way as they were made a hundred years ago. The whole process of making clogs is open, and all visitors can see. They provide an explanation service and all the clogs are unique and make a perfect Dutch souvenir, which can be bought directly at the store.

在16世纪以前，穷人根本不穿鞋。鞋子是昂贵商品，只有富人才会穿，以保护他们的双足，这样才能证明他们买得起这样的奢侈品。

早期的木鞋是木质的鞋底和皮革的外帮，最后发展成整只鞋都是用木头做的，以更好地保护双脚，因为许多穿木鞋的人都是渔民、农民和工厂的工人。

如今，要想在城市里找到一个尚穿木鞋的荷兰人几乎是不太可能的，但有一些特殊的职业，比如农村的农民、园丁、商人、渔夫，或者在特殊的场合，人们还是会穿木鞋的，在一些村子里，穿木鞋仍然是一项值得珍惜和延续的传统。

每年大约有300万双木鞋被生产出来，它们在整个荷兰都有销售，市场的很大一部分是旅游纪念品。在旅游业之外，当地的工具商店和花园中心也能看到木鞋，这些地方也在对外销售。

如果你有兴趣了解木鞋是如何被制作出来的，那么你一定要去桑斯安斯风车村的露天博物馆去参观一下，如位于露天博物馆的"木鞋作坊"。这家公司成立于1974年，是一家专业制作木鞋的公司。他们仍在延续使用着老古董的机器，向人们展示着一百年前是如何制作木鞋的。制作木鞋的整个过程都是开放的，所有的游客和参观的人都能亲眼目睹。商店也配有讲解人员给人们做流程的讲解，所有制作出来的木鞋都是独一无二的，是个极其完美的荷兰纪念品，可以直接在商店里选购。

木鞋是荷兰的标签之一，在桑斯安斯风车村的"The Wooden Shoe Workshop"，除了能够购买木鞋之外，现场还能看到工匠们制作木鞋的整个流程。

Delft Blue 代尔夫特蓝

Delft Blue is blue and white pottery made in Delft and the surrounding region, this tin-glazed pottery has been produced in the Netherlands from about the 16th century.

Delft Blue is one of the types of tin-glazed earthenware or faience in which a white glaze is applied, and is usually decorated with metal oxides, it forms part of the worldwide family of blue and white pottery and are inspired by Chinese originals which persisted from about 1630 to the mid-18th century alongside the European patterns.

Between 1600 and 1800, Delft was one of the most important pottery producers in Europe. The Delft Blue pottery was immensely popular, and was collected by rich families throughout the world. Unfortunately, for many potters, Delft Blue also went out of fashion, and one by one, they had to close their doors. The only one that has remained in operation since 1653 is de Koninklijke Porceleyne Fles, known as Royal Dutch, a company that continues to produce the Delft Blue pottery according to the traditional methods.

Delft Blue was inspired by Chinese porcelain, but during the course of history Delft Blue has formed its own major characteristics. You can find ample examples of Delft Blue pottery at many souvenir shops around the central market square in Delft. There are also stores selling Delft Blue in other cities.

代尔夫特蓝是代尔夫特及周边地区制造的一种融合了蓝色和白色的瓷器，这是自大约16世纪以来在荷兰生产的一种锡釉陶器。

代尔夫特蓝借鉴中国瓷器的制作方式，但发展出了自己的特色，曾经盛极一时。左图为二手市场上的蓝陶，右图为博物馆中陈列的蓝陶。

代尔夫特蓝是呈现白色釉面的锡釉陶器或彩陶的一种，通常配以金属氧化物加以装饰，是世界上蓝白陶器大家庭的一员，其灵感最早来自中国，从1630年到18世纪中叶进行了欧洲模式的改良并一直持续下去。

在1600年到1800年间，代尔夫特是欧洲最重要的陶器生产商之一。代尔夫特蓝陶器非常受欢迎，并被世界各地的有钱人所收藏。不幸的是，对于许多陶工来说，代尔夫特蓝也过时了，制陶工厂接二连三地关门。从1653年以来，只有荷兰皇家代尔夫特蓝瓷工厂一直维持着运作生产，其使用的仍然是传统的代尔夫特蓝的制陶工艺。

代尔夫特蓝的产生受到了中国瓷器的启发，但在历史的演变过程中，代尔夫特蓝形成了自己的独有的特征。在代尔夫特城市的中央市场广场附近的许多纪念品商店都能发现大量的代尔夫特蓝陶器。还有专门售卖代尔夫特蓝的商店，在其他城市也能看到。

Tijd voor Nederlands 荷兰语时间

● 单词+短语

荷 kaas 英 cheese 译 奶酪	荷 bloemen 英 flowers 译 花	荷 dorp 英 village 译 村庄
荷 tuin 英 garden 译 花园	荷 porselein 英 porcelain 译 瓷器	荷 tulp 英 tulip 译 郁金香
荷 rood/groen/blauw/geel/wit/zwart 英 red/green/blue/yellow/white/black 译 红色/绿色/蓝色/黄色/白色/黑色	荷 banaan/appel/sinaasappel/aardbei 英 banana/apple/orange/strawberry 译 香蕉/苹果/橙子/草莓	荷 bakkerij 英 bakery 译 面包店

267

荷 boekwinkel	荷 apotheek	荷 medicijnen
英 bookstore	英 pharmacy	英 medicine
译 书店	译 药店	译 药品
荷 hoofdpijn	荷 wegen	
英 headache	英 weigh	
译 头疼	译 称重	

● 例句

荷 Ik wil naar de boekwinkel om een boek te kopen.	荷 U moet aan de kassa betalen.
英 I want to go to the bookstore to buy a book.	英 You need to pay at the cashier.
译 我想去书店买本书。	译 你需要在收款台付款。
荷 Sorry, ik hou niet echt van kaas.	荷 Delfts Blauw is porselein geproduceerd in Delft, Nederland.
英 Sorry, I don't really like cheese.	英 Delft Blue is porcelain produced in Delft, the Netherlands.
译 对不起，我不是很喜欢奶酪。	译 代尔夫特蓝是一种产自荷兰代尔夫特的瓷器。
荷 De tulp is een zeer mooie bloem.	荷 Er is een grote tuin naast dat dorp.
英 The tulip is a very beautiful flower.	英 There is a large garden beside that village.
译 郁金香是很漂亮的一种花。	译 那个村子旁边有一个大花园。
荷 Waar kan ik deze appels wegen?	荷 Ik heb hoofdpijn, ik ga naar de apotheek om medicijnen te kopen.
英 Where can I weigh these apples?	英 I have a headache. I'm going to a pharmacy to buy medicine.
译 我在哪里可以称一下这些苹果？	译 我头疼，我要去药店买药。
荷 Nederlanders eten veel brood en Nederland heeft veel bakkerijen.	
英 The Dutch eat a lot of bread, the Netherlands has a lot of bakeries.	
译 荷兰人吃面包很多，荷兰有很多面包店。	

2. 游客这样购
Shopping as a Tourist

There are many great places to shop around the country and you can read about these in the chapters concerning the different cities in the Netherlands. In this paragraph we only want to provide some supplementation to the mentioned information.

For many tourists, the city centre provides the most convenient and easiest shopping experience, most cities in the Netherlands have a major shopping street at the heart of their city centre. If you have the chance to stay in the Netherlands for a longer period of time, let's say a week then we highly recommend you to visit one of the weekly open markets, some cities have even an open market on more than one day a week. The best known open markets are the "Albert Cuyp Markt" in Amsterdam, the "Binnenrotte Centrummarkt" and "Markthal" in Rotterdam, the "Haagse Markt" in The Hague and the "Vredenburg Markt" in Utrecht.

在荷兰全国各地都分布着很多很棒的购物场所，我们在荷兰各个城市的相关章节中做了介绍。这一部分是作为购物信息的补充和附加。

对于许多游客来说，在每个城市的市中心购物是最便利也最容易找到的，荷兰的大多数城市都在市中心的核心区域有一条主要的购物街道。如果你有机会在荷兰停留的时间稍长一些，如一周，那么我们强烈建议你去一下每周开放的市场，有些城市的市场每周开放还不止一天。最著名的开放市场是阿姆斯特丹的艾伯特库普市场、鹿特丹的市中心集市和缤纷菜市场，以及海牙的海牙市场和乌特勒支的弗里登堡市场。

Kaasmarkt Alkmaar 阿尔克马尔奶酪市场

Despite being slightly overshadowed by Edam and Gouda, Alkmaar actually has the largest cheese market in the Netherlands, which has taken place almost uninterrupted for over 300 years. Trading starts at 10am every Friday between April and September and continues until around 13pm. By then, every participant at the market is adorned in traditional Dutch attire and the cheese is unloaded, sampled and weighed according to historical methods.

The cheese market is surrounded by a fun art and craft market. This is where you can find real Dutch "poffertjes", herring, farm cheese, a clog maker, craft stalls and much more!

Hours:　　Every Friday from April to September every year

　　　　　　　Every Friday 10am–1pm, March 30th-September 28th

Address:　　　Kaasmarkt Alkmaar, Waagplein 2, Alkmaar

Contact:　　　http://www.kaasmarkt.nl/

　　尽管光芒被艾登和豪达所遮挡，但实际上，阿尔克马尔才是荷兰最大的奶酪市场，在三百多年的时间里其运营几乎没有间断过。阿尔克马尔奶酪市场从每年的4月到9月的每星期五上午10点开放，一直到下午1点左右。在交易的时间，市场上的每个参与者都穿着传统的荷兰服装，奶酪被卸下、取样，并根据传统的方法进行称重。

　　奶酪市场被一个有趣的工艺艺术市场包围着。在这里，你可以发现真正的荷兰小煎饼、鲱鱼、农场奶酪、木鞋制造商、手工艺摊位等。

阿尔克马尔是荷兰最大的奶酪市场，依然保留着传统的称重方式。

开放时间：　4月到9月的每个星期五上午10点到下午1点

地址：　　　阿尔克马尔，Waagplein 2号

网站：　　　http://www.kaasmarkt.nl/

270

IJ-Hallen 跳蚤市场

　　Once every month, legions of shoppers flock to Amsterdam's NDSM-Werf in order to rummage through the thousands of vintage treasures contained within IJ-Hallen flea market. It is among the largest flea markets in the world that sells almost everything. Two industrial warehouses are filled with 750 stands that sell second-hand clothes, shoes, antiquities, jewellery, books, and even furniture. But it usually spills out into the open air, due to the sheer volume of goods on sale.

Tips: Bring a backpack or some extra bags with you to carry your purchases. Not all vendors will be able to provide a bag for that vintage coat or antique vase.

Sunday afternoon is the best time to shop at IJ-Hallen. Vendors usually start discounting their stock an hour before closing time.

Tickets:　　The market is charged, adults €5, children under 11 €2

Hours:　　Open every month at the weekend, and the website is detailed

Address:　　IJ-Hallen, Tt. Neveritaweg 15, Amsterdam

Contact:　　https://ijhallen.nl/

每个月都会有大批购物者蜂拥而至阿姆斯特丹的NDSM-Werf艺术区，到IJ-Hallen跳蚤市场成千上万的古董珍品里翻找自己的渴求之物。IJ-Hallen是世界上最大的跳蚤市场之一，几乎无所不售。两个工业仓库里遍布着出售二手衣服、鞋子、古董、珠宝、书籍甚至家具等750个摊位。但是由于出售的商品数量过多，摊位通常会摆到大仓库的外面。

小贴士：记得随身携带一个背包或带几个袋子来装你的战利品，并不是所有的摊位老板都提供包或袋子装那些古董大衣或古董花瓶。

周日下午是去IJ-Hallen购物的最佳时间，摊主通常在关门前一小时会进行打折。

门票：　　　市场需要买票才能入内，票价成年人5欧元，11岁以下的儿童2欧元

开放时间：　每个月的周末开放，确切的时间建议查看网站

地址：　　　阿姆斯特丹，Tt. Neveritaweg 15号

网站：　　　https://ijhallen.nl/

Markets in Delft 代尔夫特集市

On every Thursday and Saturday between April and October Delft hosts a large outdoor market which usually trails well beyond the city's Nieuwe Kerk into several nearby streets. This event is an absolute haven for antique lovers and is among the best places in the Netherlands to search for rare or unique items such as paintings, candlesticks and authentic Delftware pottery.

Foodies should also definitely check out the market, as there is always plenty of local produce and traditional Dutch delicacies on offer.

The merchants don't just offer fresh products; the market also features clothing, bicycle accessories and electronic gadgets. Around the market, pubs and open-air terraces are happy to serve a cup of coffee if you need to rest your feet.

Hours:　　From April to October every year on Thursdays and Saturdays

Address:　Markt, Delft

在每年4月到10月之间的每一个周四和周六，代尔夫特的大型户外市场都开放，通常从新教堂一直蔓延到周遭的几条街道上。这个市场绝对是古董爱好者的天堂，也是荷兰寻找稀有或独特物品的最佳场所之一，比如绘画、烛台和真正的代尔夫特蓝。

美食家们也应该去市场看上一看，这里总是在卖一些本地的农产品和最传统的荷兰美食。

新鲜的产品可不是代尔夫特集市唯一交易的，还有其他像服装、自行车配件和电子产品也是这里的交易品类。如果你需要小憩小酌，在市场周围还散落着酒吧和户外露台，都提供咖啡饮品，可坐下来放松一下。

开放时间： 每年的4月到10月，每周四和周六

地址： 代尔夫特市中心广场

De Bazaar 德巴扎市场

Located approximately twenty kilometres north-west of Amsterdam, Beverwijk is famous for its Bazaar, Europe's largest ethnic market with 2,000-plus vendors and 65 eateries.

Beverwijk Bazaar offers a hustling and bustling atmosphere, multicultural visitors—local and tourists—over fifty restaurants in and around the bazaar, multiple languages, fresh fruit and flowers, computers and IT-related applications, nail salons and beauty parlours, clothing ranging from lingerie to leather jackets, shoes and the list goes on and on. De Bazaar is huge. Covering the entire market in one day is impossible, so plan a whole weekend for exploring, or return another weekend.

Hours: 9:30am–7pm on every Saturday and Sunday; Major festivals open hours, please check the website

Address: Montageweg 35, Beverwijk

Contact: https://www.debazaar.nl/

贝弗韦克位于阿姆斯特丹西北约20公里处，以德巴扎市场而闻名，这里是欧洲最大的民族市场，拥有2 000多家供应商和65家餐馆。

贝弗韦克德巴扎市场弥漫着一派繁忙景象，拥挤着来自海内外四面八方的游客，这里分布着超过50家餐馆，多种语言交汇于此，新鲜水果和鲜花、电脑及周边产品、美甲店和美容沙龙、从内衣到皮夹克的各类服装、鞋子，品类繁多，不胜枚举。德巴扎市场非常大，想要一天之内逛遍整个市场是不可能的，所以值得花上整个周末，或者过上一周再返回来。

贝弗韦克德巴扎市场是非常值得搜寻好物的，图为迎接圣诞节安置的超大盒子，上写荷兰语"荷兰最大的圣诞礼包"。

开放时间： 每个星期六和星期天的上午9点半到晚上7点开放（节假日的开放时间请查询官网）

地址： Montageweg 35, Beverwijk

网站： https://www.debazaar.nl/

3. 本地人这样购
Shopping as a Local

In 2016, more than 70 percent of the Dutch shopped online, which makes the Netherlands the fifth country in the European Union when it comes to the share of consumers shopping online. But, consumers in the Netherlands still buy the lion's share of their groceries in physical supermarkets and this isn't about to change soon. The Netherlands has a well-developed retail system, and a wide range of goods. If you want to shop as a pay reasonable prices for your food items or something, then we advise you to leave the tourist trail for a moment and visit the local shops.

2016年，在网上购物的荷兰人超过了70%，这使得荷兰成为欧盟第五大网购国家。但是，人们的绝大部分日常生活用品仍然会在实体超市购买，而且这种情况不会很快改变。荷兰拥有完善的零售体系和非常广泛的商品种类。如果你想以合理的价格买一些食品或其他东西，我们建议你还是暂时放弃那些游客蜂拥而至的场所，去当地的商店看看吧。

273

Supermarket 超市

Across the Netherlands, there are more than 20 major supermarket chain brands and for a country that is not bigger than two and a half times the area of Beijing. The Dutch shopping habits are a bit different from those of Chinese people, the Dutch go grocery shopping at least 3 to 4 times a week and many people go to the supermarket every day.

Albert Heijn is one of the largest Dutch supermarket chains, and can indisputably be called the National supermarket of the Netherlands. With 1,000 stores in the Netherlands they have a branch in almost every city and village in the Netherlands and in many train stations.

Besides having stores in the Netherlands, Albert Heijn also has hundreds of stores in Belgium, Germany, France and Spain. In 2015, Albert Heijn also opened an online store on tmall.com.

Jumbo is the second largest supermarket brand in the Netherlands, together with Albert Heijn they account for more than half of the Dutch supermarket market share. As of 2017, Jumbo has about 600 supermarkets. The big yellow and white logo is very striking, they are well worth a visit if you want to prepare your own meal, or if you want to stock up on supplies for a long train journey.

Aldi and Lidl are also two very well-known cheap food supermarkets, and both are German brands. The two supermarket brands are well-known, largely because of the low prices for their products. These supermarkets sell their now brands so don't expect well-known brands to be sold here.

There are also some other supermarket brands, they are not as big as the ones mentioned above, but still just as convenient, SPAR, PLUS, EKOPLAZA, DIRK, MAKRO, etc.These are all closely related to local life.

这就是分大小号的荷兰国民超市，这是一家XL店，还有XXL超级店。超市商品常年轮番折扣，力度颇大。

在荷兰，有超过20家大型连锁超市，要知道这个国家也不过只有两个半北京区域那么大。荷兰人的购物习惯与中国人有一点不同，荷兰人每周去超市购物的次数至少三到四次，而很多人是每天都去超市。

Albert Heijn是荷兰最大的连锁超市，毫无疑问，这是荷兰的国民超市。在荷兰有1 000家Albert Heijn，分布在几乎每一个城市和村庄，在很多火车站也有门店。除了遍布在荷兰的门店，Albert Heijn还在比利时、德国、法国和西班牙拥有数百家分店。2015年，Albert Heijn还在阿里巴巴天猫上开了一家网店。

Jumbo是荷兰第二大超市品牌，与Albert Heijn一起占据了荷兰超市市场份额的一半以上。截至2017年，Jumbo拥有大约600家超市。超市黄白的LOGO标识非常醒目，如果你要自己做饭或者想为即将开启的长途旅行储备吃吃喝喝的食物，它们很值得一逛。

Aldi和Lidl也是两家非常知名的廉价食品超市，都是德国品牌。这两个超市品牌知名度很高，很大程度上是因为他们的产品价格低廉。这些超市所出售的商品很多都是自有品牌，所以不要抱太大期望在这里能买到一些名牌商品。

还有一些其他的超市品牌，它们没有上面提到的这几个连锁品牌那么大，但是仍然提供了很大的便利度，如SPAR、PLUS、 EKOPLAZA、DIRK、MAKRO等，这些都与当地老百姓的生活息息相关。

Commodity and Cosmetics Stores 日用品和化妆品商店

Many Chinese coming to the Netherlands have probably heard of Kruidvat, better known in Chinese as K-Store. This is a Dutch retail, pharmacy and drugstore chain specialised in health and beauty products, which also has branches in Belgium. The first Kruidvat was opened in 1975 by Ed During and Dick Siebrand. In addition to Kruidvat itself, Kruidvat company also owns ICI Paris XL and Trekpleister in the Netherlands and Belgium. Kruidvat was acquired by the Watson in 2002 and now operates over 1,000 Kruidvat stores in the Netherlands and Belgium. The range of goods sold in in Kruidvat stores exceeds those of Watson stores, in addition to cosmetics and beauty products they also sell medicines, food, mobile phone accessories, toys and even furniture. Kruidvat also offers self-service photo printing services.

De Tuinen has now been renamed Holland & Barrett. In 1980 the first health shop of De Tuinen opened its doors in the city center of The Hague under the name The Garden of Babylon. In May 2003 De Tuinen became part of the British Holland & Barrett. A subsidiary of the American NBTY. In June 2017, it was announced that Holland & Barrett was acquired by the LetterOne investment group of the Russian oligarch Michaïl Fridman. Holland&Barrett (De tuinen) is different from Kruidvat, which mainly focuses on health products, health foods, organic foods and cosmetics.

Etos is a store that sells many of the cosmetics and beauty that you can find at Kruidvat. It was founded in 1918 by Philips to create a grocery and drugstore where Philips employees could benefit from lower priced products than the average stores. In 1973 Etos was bought by Ahold which reformed the grocery stores to the Albert Heijn formula. The drug stores went on as Etos. Etos has more than 500 stores, often next to Albert Heijn, and which are located in most shopping centers and train stations. Etos has some unique brands, the reputation of its own brand is also very good.

ICI Paris XL is a perfume shop chain founded in the late 1960s in Belgium. The company was acquired by the Kruidvat Group in 1996, which then in-turn became part of the A.S. Watson Group in 2002. Perfume is ICI Paris XL's core business, it is also a good choice to buy major skin care and make-up products. The company has about 250 stores spread over three countries, Belgium, Netherlands and Luxembourg. Douglas is another important perfume store. Douglas stores are a little bigger, with more focus on makeup and skincare products. In the business district of most cities around the Netherlands you can find their stores.

很多中国人可能听说过Kruidvat，或者说K店这一称号更为人知。这是一家荷兰零售、医药和化妆品连锁店，专门经营健康美容产品，在比利时也有分支机构。第一家Kruidvat是在1975年由Ed和Dick Siebrand创立的。除了Kruidvat同名品牌店，Kruidvat集团在荷兰和比利时还拥有ICI Paris XL和Trekpleister，2002年的时候，Kruidvat被香港屈臣氏收购，目前在荷兰和比利时经营着1000多家Kuidvat门店。在Kruidvat商店销售的商品种类超过了屈臣氏，除了化妆品和美容产品之外，他们还销售药品、食品、手机配件、玩具甚至家具。Kruidvat还提供自助式照片打印服务。

花园店（De Tuinen，店名荷兰语意为花园）现在已经改名叫做Holland & Barrett了。1980年，De Tuinen的第一家健康商店在海牙市中心以"巴比伦花园"的名称开门营业。2003年5月，De Tuinen成了美国NBTY公司的子公司，英国Holland & Barrett的一部分。在2017年6月，Holland & Barrett宣称又被俄罗斯寡头Michail Fridman的LetterOne投资集团收购。Holland & Barrett / De tuinen与Kruidvat不同，它主营业务主要集中在保健产品、健康食品、有机食品和个人护理品。

De Tuinen 大概是最受中国游客欢迎的健康护理品商店，有机护肤品牌、保健品和有机食品是主营。图为De Tuinen店内进行买一送一的活动。

Etos商店出售很多能在Kruidvat见到的化妆品和美容产品，它是由飞利浦公司在1918年创立的一家食品、杂货、药品商店，这样飞利浦的员工可以从比普通商店价格更低的产品中受益。1973年Etos被Albert Heijn的母公司阿霍德集团收购，店铺被改造成Albert Heijn的标配店，而Etos药店业务继续保持不变。Etos的门店数量超过了500家，通常在Albert Heijn超市旁边，这些店位于大多数购物中心和火车站。Etos里有一些独有的品牌，其自有品牌的声誉也非常好。

ICI Paris XL是一家香水连锁店，成立于20世纪60年代末的比利时。该公司于1996年被Kruidvat集团收购，并在2002年成为屈臣氏集团的一部分。香水是ICI Paris XL的核心业务，但购买一些主流的护肤品和化妆品，ICI Paris XL商店也是极佳的选择。该商店目前在比利时、荷兰和卢森堡三个国家拥有大约250家门店。还有一家很重要的香水店Douglas。Douglas商店一般要更大一些，更加侧重于化妆品和护肤品。在荷兰大部分城市的商业区，你都会见到他们的商店。

Household Items 家居用品

Your home is your castle is definitely a saying that is applicable on the Dutch. The Dutch are constantly busy with making their homes more cosy and enjoyable.

● **Blokker Holding.** Blokker Holding is a Dutch retail group and active in the household and living sector, with approximately 1,450 stores and over 14,000 employees in eight countries. Brands that belong to Blokker holding are Blokker, Xenos, Intertoys, and Big Bazar store formulas.

Blokker itself focuses on household items and kitchen appliances, Xenos is a store where all kinds of things can be bought, from stationary to furniture. Intertoys is the national brand toy store of the Netherlands. Big Bazar is a sort of outlet shop for all kinds of things used in and around the house.

● **HEMA.** The Hollandsche Eenheidsprijzen Maatschappij Amsterdam, or HEMA., opened its first department store in Amsterdam on November 4, 1926. The founders wanted to open a department store for "ordinary" people. Before this, department stores were mainly aimed at wealthy people and most store personnel spoke French. HEMA, as it would later become known, was the first department store of its kind in the Netherlands. Products were priced at 10, 25 or 50 cents. Since its establishment HEMA has become an indispensable part of every household in the Netherlands. In the 1950s, HEMA was the first franchise organisation in the Netherlands and is still the largest franchise operator in the Netherlands. Today, HEMA has almost 700 stores in seven countries, with 10,000 employees serving over six million visitors every week. All the products at HEMA are developed in house, are sustainable and range from food to non-food articles. Which is why their products can be found in every Dutch household. At HEMA you will find things you never knew you needed. The pastries at HEMA are worth well trying, they are cheap and super delicious.

你的家就是你的城堡，简直没有比这个说法更能生动地描述荷兰人了，荷兰人总是忙于让他们的家变得更加舒适和充满欢快。

Blokker Holding是一家荷兰零售集团，活跃于家庭和生活领域，在8个国家拥有大约1 450家店铺和超过14 000名员工。属于Blokker Holding的品牌有Blokker、Xenos、Intertoys和Big Bazar。

Blokker品牌店本身专注于家居用品和厨房用具，而Xenos商店则包罗万象，从家饰到家具等各种物品。Intertoys是荷兰的国民品牌玩具店，而Big Bazar是一家尾货商店，出售房子里里外外的装饰、工具、用具等物品。

HEMA，荷兰语Hollandsche Eenheidsprijzen Maatschappij的缩写，或是H.E.M.A.。1926年11月4日，HEMA在阿姆斯特丹开设了第一家百货公司。创始人想为"普通人"开一家百货商店。在此之前，百货商店主要是服务于一些有钱人，且大多数商店的员工都说法语。HEMA这个称号是后来得来的，它是荷兰的第一家此类百货公司。当时产品的定价大多为10美分、25美分或50美分。自成立以来，HEMA已然成为荷兰每个家庭不可缺少的一部分。在20世纪50年代，HEMA是荷兰第一家特许经营机构，到现在仍然是荷兰最大的特许经营商。如今，HEMA在七个国家拥有近700家门店，每周HEMA的一万名员工为超过600万人的进店顾客提供着服务。HEMA的所有产品都由内部开发，具有可持续性，商品种类从食品到非食品类全覆盖，这也是为什么每个荷兰家庭必然消耗着来自HEMA的商品的原因。HEMA的商品种类齐全到让人叹为观止，你总会在那里发现一些你永远都不知道自己所需要的东西。还有，HEMA的糕点绝对值得一试，价格便宜，美味绝伦。

HEMA是荷兰最知名的生活品牌之一，商品品类包罗万象，并且一直会推陈出新，上架节日商品。图为一家HEMA店铺。

乐在荷兰

Entertainment in the Netherlands

Live like a Dutchman, but how does a Dutch person live? The outside world has its own prejudices about the Dutch and their way of life. The Dutch have their habits and they are reflected in all aspects of social life, in terms of work, family, social activities, consumption, ideas, and social hierarchy and so on. In this chapter we will talk about Dutch traditional festivals and social activities.

要像一个荷兰人那般生活，但荷兰人是如何生活的呢？外界对荷兰人和他们的生活方式产生了很多误解和偏见。荷兰人有他们自己的一套生活习惯，反映在社会生活的各个方面，比如工作、家庭、社会活动、消费方式、价值观念、社会等级等。在这一章我们就讨论一下荷兰人热衷的传统节日和他们热衷参与的社会活动。

1. 节假日
Celebrations and Holidays

Like China, the Netherlands also has a variety of colourful festivals, some of which are unique to the Netherlands and some are the same as those in other parts of the world.

※ Sinterklaas

The feast of Sinterklaas celebrates the name day of Saint Nicholas on December 6. The feast is celebrated annually with the giving of gifts on St. Nicholas' Eve (December 5) in the northern parts of the Netherlands and on the morning of December 6, Saint Nicholas Day, in the southern provinces of the Netherlands, as well as Belgium, Luxembourg and northern France.

Sinterklaas is based on the historical figure of Saint Nicholas (270–343), a Greek bishop of Myra in present-day Turkey. He is depicted as an elderly, stately and serious man with white hair and a long, full beard. He wears a long red cape or chasuble over a traditional white bishop's Alb and sometimes red stola, dons a red mitre and ruby ring, and holds a gold-coloured crosier, a long ceremonial shepherd's staff with a fancy curled top. He traditionally rides a white horse. Saint Nicholas carries a big, red book in which is written whether each child has been good or naughty in the past year.

The festivities traditionally begin each year in mid-November (the first Saturday after 11 November), when Sinterklaas "arrives" by a steamboat at a designated seaside town, supposedly from Spain. In the Netherlands this takes place in a different port each year, whereas in Belgium it always takes place in the city of Antwerp.

In the Netherlands, Saint Nicholas' Eve, 5 December, became the chief occasion for gift-giving during the winter holiday season. The evening is called Sinterklaasavond ("Sinterklaas evening") or Pakjesavond ("gifts evening", or literally "packages evening"). The main presents will somehow arrive, or a note will be "found" that explains where in house the presents were hidden by Zwarte Piet who left a burlap sack with them. Sometimes a neighbour will knock on the door (Pretend to be Zwarte Piet, a servant of Sinterklaas) and leave the sack outside for the children to retrieve. On December 6, Sinterklaas departs without any ado, and all festivities are over.

In the two months before Sinterklaas you will find a lot of traditional delicacies in the supermarkets around the country, spiced cookies in all shapes, marzipan, as well as chocolate letters. These foods are only available during this season Sinterklaas.

※ Christmas

Like many countries, including China, Christmas is not a traditional Dutch festival, many people still celebrate Christmas. Among the Dutch, Christmas is a time of togetherness. Gifts were generally not exchanged, but is becoming a general practise. Usually it is celebrated with

281

one's direct, and not extended, family. It's celebrated on December 25 and 26.

※ New Year

New Year is a festival celebrated all around the world. The Dutch generally celebrate New Year's Eve, which is called Old Years' Night in Dutch, with friends and family. On this day, traditional New Year's pastries like Oliebollen (This traditional Dutch food has already been mentioned in "Dutch traditional food") are eaten. At mid-night the Dutch wish all the best to all in their presence with three kisses and lots of hugs also fireworks are set off. Following these activities it is customary to express a good intention for the next year. The following morning is marked by visits to family, usually parents. It's celebrated on December 31.

But across the Netherlands, there are also many unique traditional activities, such as a 'new year's dive', a tradition that started in 1965. There are over 200 locations in the Netherlands where you can jump into the stone cold sea or a lake. The New Year's dive is cold, bold and the best way to start the year fresh. The largest dive is held at the beach of Scheveningen, where 10,000 people plunge into the sea each year. This spectacle is also great to watch from the side line.

※ Carnival

In Holland, carnival is a holiday mainly celebrated in the south of the country. The provinces of Limburg and Noord-Brabant are the predominantly Catholic provinces of the Netherlands, where most inhabitants celebrate Carnival.

Carnival was originally a religious activity, many people in modern times do not relate the holiday at all with religion. The first day of Carnaval is six weeks before Easter Sunday. Carnaval officially begins on Sunday and lasts three days until the start of Ash Wednesday at midnight. Nowadays the celebrations often start on Thursday evening though, which makes it in practice a six-day celebration.

Although the carnival tradition is to dress up to attend the celebrations, but most people keep it simple and just drink, sing and dance wearing a colourful outfit. Another tradition of the carnival is the "key handover". The Carnival celebrations start after the mayor symbolically hands over the key to the city to Prince Carnival. For three days, the Carnival Prince has control of the city and, together with his subjects, celebrates the temporary establishment of their Kingdom of Fools.

※ Easter

Easter is a time to celebrate for many people. Observant Christians make a special effort to attend a church service. Easter Sunday church services are often longer than usual and may conclude with a festive meal. Easter fires (paasvuren) are held in rural areas in the northern and eastern parts of the Netherlands.

Many people prepare an Easter breakfast, brunch or lunch with a range of seasonal and luxurious foods to share with family members, friends or neighbours. Easter food variety is very rich: boiled, poached or fried eggs; paasstol (a rich loaf of bread filled with raisins, nuts and marzipan); butter made into the shape of a lamb; butter flavoured with herbs; bread; croissants;

282

cheese; ham; shrimps; smoked fish; and sweets or chocolates in the shape of eggs or hares.

Families with children may decorate boiled eggs and hide boiled or chocolate eggs around the house or garden. Children are told that these eggs have been delivered and/or hidden by the mythical Easter hare (paashaas).

※ King's Day

Another traditional feast of the Netherlands used to be "Koninginnedag" ("Queen's day"). This was celebrated in honour of the Queen's birthday on April 30. Since April 2013 the Netherlands has a king so Queen's Day has been renamed "Koningsdag" ("King's Day") and is celebrated on April 27, unless this date is on a Sunday, then it's celebrated on the preceding Saturday.

The most famous and crowded places during King's Day are the countless free markets of various places. These free markets are scattered on the main streets of the city centre, open to all, crowded and chaotic. Many people try to sell their second-hand clothing, furniture on these flea markets, also many children sell their own paintings, toys here. For them, the joy is far more important than the income from these sales.

On King's Day, people wear orange clothes or orange hats, at least something with orange elements. This is the colour of the Royal Dutch family as it is their surname. The King and his family visit two places somewhere in the country. These places will organise a special program displaying local folklore.

※ Liberation Day

On Liberation Day, also known as Freedom Day, the Dutch celebrate the capitulation of Nazi Germany. For the Netherlands, this marked the end of World War II, even though the war had not yet ended in the rest of Europe and Asia. Liberation Day celebrations will be held in the capital of each province, these activities include the Liberation Festival in Amsterdam and Liberation Day festival in Wageningen. Many officials visit Wageningen, because it was in this small town that the Germans troops in the Netherlands capitulated in 1945. In Amsterdam, thousands of people gather to see the free concerts at Museum Square.

Throughout the country two minutes of silence are observed at 8:00pm on the day before Liberation Day, so on the fourth of May, trains will stop, radio shows are stopped, cars and busses will stop next to the road, the whole country will come to a standstill during these two minutes. You are advised to respect this custom as it is considered highly insulting to answer your phone or have a chat in public during these two minutes of silence, you can even get arrested for this.

※ Ascension Day

In the months of March, April, May and June, many Christian feast days commemorate important events at the end of Jesus' life. Good Friday commemorates his crucifixion, Easter Sunday celebrates his resurrection and Ascension Day remembers his bodily ascension to heaven. Ascension Day is an important feast in the Christian liturgical year.

如同中国一样，荷兰的节日庆典也是极其丰富多彩的，其中一些节日是荷兰特有的，当然还有些与世界其他地区一样的节日。

※ 圣尼古拉节

圣尼古拉节是于每年12月6日举行的，庆祝圣·尼古拉斯这个名字的节日。圣尼古拉节每年的庆祝活动在荷兰北方一般在节日的前一夜即12月5日开始，在荷兰南方省份，以及比利时、卢森堡和法国北部地区一般在12月6日当天早上开始。

圣尼古拉节源于古代的历史人物圣·尼古拉斯（公元270—公元343），他是现今土耳其米拉的一位希腊主教。在这个有着浓郁宗教色彩的盛大节日里，他被描绘成一个满头华发，留着长长的络腮胡子的上了年纪的、优雅却又严肃的人。圣·尼古拉斯身披一件红色的斗篷，或者穿着一件传统的白色主教Alb——一种宗教法衣，有时是红色的斯托拉——一种古罗马披肩服饰，头上戴着一顶红色的主教冠，戴着红宝石大戒指，手握金色的主教权杖——一柄高高长长，顶部有着精美弯曲类似于羊角的用于典仪的棍杖。按照一般的传统，圣·尼古拉斯会骑着一匹白马，衣服里还会揣着一本大红的书，上面写着在过去一年里每个孩子是乖乖的还是太淘气了。

传统的圣尼古拉斯庆祝活动早在每年11月中旬，确切说是11月11日之后的第一个周六就已经开始了，届时将有一艘汽船在指定的海边城镇"抵达"，据说是从西班牙远道而来的。在荷兰，这艘汽船每年都会停靠在不同的城市港口，而比利时的传统则是，汽船每年都会抵达安特卫普。

圣尼古拉节并不是圣诞节，而是荷比地区最重要的节日。左图为圣尼古拉和乘汽船抵达荷兰南部。右图是黑彼得的传统装扮。

在荷兰，12月5日的圣尼古拉节前一天，即Saint Nicholas' Eve是冬日时节里很重要的一个送礼的时机。这天晚上被称为"Sinterklaasavond"，意思是"圣尼古拉节之夜"，或者趣味一点叫"Pakjesavond"，字面意思是"包裹之夜"，也就是礼物的包装袋或包装盒之类。节日的礼物大都会以某种方式送到你手里或者让你自己根据线索来找，有时会"意外发现"一张纸条，上面会说明黑彼得在屋子里留下了一个麻布袋，里面藏着礼物。有时邻居还会敲门（他们假装是黑彼得，圣尼古拉斯的一个黑人仆人），他们把袋子放在外面让孩子们去拿。12月6日，圣尼古拉斯就离开了，所有相关的庆祝活动也就结束了。

在圣尼古拉节之前的两个月里，你会在荷兰全国各地的超市里找到品目繁多的传统食物，有各种形状的趣味饼干、杏仁糖，当然还有必不可少的最经典的字母巧克力，所有的这些食物平时都不会有，只在每年的圣尼古拉节期间可以买到。

※ 圣诞节

和许多国家，包括中国都一样，虽然圣诞节不是传统的荷兰节日，但在这里仍然有许多人庆祝圣诞节。在荷兰人当中，圣诞节是团聚的日子。一般没有像圣尼古拉节交换礼物的习俗，过圣诞节也因人而异，想过则过，没有什么家庭庆祝活动。圣诞节的庆典活动在每年的12月25日和26日，荷兰的圣诞节也不例外，也有圣诞树的装点，也会备好圣诞礼物，当然了，在这期间更吸引人的是商店各种各样的折扣活动。

※ 新年

新年是一个世界性的节日。荷兰人通常会在新的一年的前一夜和家人或朋友进行庆祝活动，荷兰人把它叫做Old Years' Night，意为过去的或旧的一年的夜晚。在这一天，荷兰人吃的传统糕点是炸面团，这是一种传统的荷兰新年专供食品（在"荷兰传统食品"这一篇章中已经讲过）。在新的一年钟声敲响之时，荷兰人会和身边的人进行荷兰式的三吻脸颊祝福礼仪互动，还有深深的拥抱。一系列过后，人们通常会表达在来年有什么新的期许和愿望，并表示诚挚的祝福。第二天早上，一般会去拜访一下家人，大多是父母。新年的庆祝性活动和仪式也多是安排在12月31日。

但在荷兰，新年的庆祝方式还有很多独特的传统活动，比如"新年跳水"，这一传统始于1965年。每年的新年第一天荷兰都会有超过200个地点举行这项跳水活动——跳入冬季冰冷的海水或湖水中，以这种冰冷、大胆的新年跳水活动迎接全新一年的到来无疑是最好的。冬季最大的新年跳水活动是在席凡宁根海滩举行的，每年都会有一万人跳入刺骨的海水中。不过如果胆量不足以下水，那么在岸边观摩这一奇观也非常不错！

※ 狂欢节

狂欢节主要是荷兰南部地区的一个节日庆祝活动。荷兰林堡省和北布拉班特省是荷兰天主教分部的主要省份，这两个地区的大多数居民会庆祝狂欢节。

狂欢节原本是一种宗教活动，但是现在很多人并不会把这个节日与宗教联系起来。狂欢节的第一天是复活节前的六个星期。狂欢节从周日正式开始，然后持续三天，直到圣灰星期三午夜开始。现在很多庆祝活动通常在周四晚上就开始了，这也使得狂欢节的活动延长到六天。

狂欢节的传统是盛装出席，但实际上大多数人都还是穿着简简单单的五颜六色的服装，只是喝酒、唱歌、跳舞。狂欢节还有另一个传统是"钥匙交接"。狂欢节开始以后，城市的市长象征性地将城市的钥匙交给"狂欢国王"。在接下来的三天，"狂欢国王"便会掌控这座城市，并与他的臣民们一起庆祝他们"愚人王国"的临时建立。

※ 复活节

复活节是许多人会庆祝的节日，虔诚的基督徒还会专程去参加礼拜。复活节的时候，星期日教堂的礼拜仪式通常比平常要长，而且结束可能还会有丰富的圣餐。荷兰北部和东部的农村地区还会举行复活节焰火活动。

许多人会准备一份极其丰盛的复活节早餐、早午餐或午餐，搭配一系列节日性和奢华的食物、食材，并与家人、朋友或邻居分享食用。复活节的食物种类繁多，有水煮的、清蒸的或者油煎的蛋、荷兰复活节Paasstol（一种含有葡萄干、坚果和包裹着杏仁馅儿的复活节面包）、做成羔羊形状的黄油、香料植物调味的黄油、普通白面包；可颂面包（羊角面包）、干酪、火腿、虾、熏鱼，还有糖果或鸡蛋和兔子造型的巧克力。

有孩子的家庭还可能用煮鸡蛋来装饰，把鸡蛋或者复活节彩蛋巧克力藏在房子或花园周围，然后告诉孩子们，这些鸡蛋是由神秘的复活节兔子送过来的或者藏起来的。

※ 国王节

另一个重要的荷兰传统节日是女王节，这是为了庆祝荷兰前女王的生日在每年的4月30日举行的。自2013年4月起，女王退位，荷兰便有了国王，因此女王节也被改成了"国王节"，在每年的4月27日，若是碰上这个日期是在周日，那么节日便在周六举行。

国王节的时候，最著名、最拥挤的地方就是遍布各地的跳蚤市场了。这些自由市场分散在市中心的主要街道上，向所有人开放，拥挤而混乱。很多人都会把他们的二手衣服、家具拿到这些跳蚤市场上来卖，还有许多孩子把自己画的画和玩具拿来换成钱。对人们来说，在市场上买卖的快乐远比能换来多少钱更加重要。

在国王节，人们都会穿上橙色的衣服或戴着橙色的帽子，通身上下至少有点儿橙色的元素。橙色是荷兰皇室家族的颜色，因为Orange，即橙色是荷兰皇室的姓氏。国王节的时候，荷兰国王会带领家人前往荷兰的两处地区参观访问，这些地方将会通过特别编排的节目来展示当地的风俗民情。

国王节是荷兰最重要的节日之一，自由市场是看点。图为市场上的小摊主，商品主要出自谁手不是重点，培养孩子的自立沟通能力最重要。

※ 解放日

解放日，也称自由日，是荷兰人庆祝纳粹德国投降而建立的。对荷兰而言，这是第二次世界大战结束的标志，尽管当时在欧洲和亚洲的其他地区的局部战争仍然在继续。荷兰每个省的省会都会举行解放日的庆祝活动，这些丰富多彩的活动包括在阿姆斯特丹举行的解放日活动和瓦格宁根的解放日活动。届时很多政府官员都会造访瓦格宁根，因为在1945年，纳粹德军就是在这个小城投降的。在阿姆斯特丹，这一天会在博物馆广场举办免费音乐会，吸引成千上万的人前往。

在解放日前一天晚上，也就是5月4日，在8点钟会有一个全荷兰默哀两分钟的活动，所以这一刻所有的列车运营都会停止、广播节目暂停、私家车和公共汽车也会停在马路旁边，整个国家在这两分钟时间内完全是停滞的。如果恰巧这期间你在荷兰，请一定要尊重这项传统活动，因为在这两分钟内于公共场合讨论、接电话等是非常无礼的行为，严重情况下甚至可能遭到逮捕。

※ 耶稣升天节

在三月、四月、五月和六月，有很多基督教宗教节日都是为了纪念耶稣生命的终结。耶稣受难日是为了纪念耶稣在这一天受苦受难，被钉在了十字架上；复活节是庆祝他的复活；而耶稣升天节，顾名思义就是纪念他升天成神；耶稣升天节是基督教会年历中非常重要的一个节日。

2. 娱乐和大型活动
Entertainment and Events

The life of the Dutch is colourful. Culture and entertainment are a very important part in their daily lives. In addition to the traditional holidays, the Netherlands also has a wide variety of festivals, markets, parades, expositions and events. These large-scale activities are distributed in various small and medium-sized cities in the Netherlands. Spring mainly offers flower parades and cheese markets. In summer, there's a wealth of dance, music and theatre festivals; autumn is the time for art and culture, and Sinterklaas and the Christmas markets bring warmth to cold winter months. Because of the variety of activities, here are just a few of the more representative ones.

※ January&February

● Eurosonic Noorderslag

Eurosonic Noorderslag is an annual four-day music showcase festival and conference held in January in Groningen, the Netherlands. With over 300 performances and some 150 panels, the festival draws more than 30,000 visitors from some 40 countries. And these are not just music lovers, but also professionals who come here to headhunt new talents. The first three days of the festival feature artists from all over Europe, the last day of the festival features only Dutch artists.

In addition to many performances and panels, the festival presents a range of awards and represents an exchange programme for talents from different European countries.

Eurosonic Noorderslag presents: the European Border Breakers Awards (EBBA) , the European Festivals Awards, the Buma Cultuur Pop Award (Popprijs), the Pop Media Award (Pop Media Prijs), The Feather (De Veer) and the Buma Music Meets Tech Award.

● National Tulip Day

Witness the official start of tulip season on National Tulip Day. The event is organised by Dutch tulip growers. Every year, they build a huge garden with tens of thousands of tulips on Dam Square in Amsterdam. The biggest garden of Amsterdam transforms Dam Square into a sea of colours, where thousands of people come to pick a free bouquet of flowers every year. In addition to the garden the tulip growers organise countless surprises and promotions.

Tulip season is the period from January until the end of April in which most tulip varieties are available from florists, supermarkets and flower stands. Thousands of tulip variants in every colour of the rainbow find their way from auctions in Holland to vases around the world. As a result, tulips have truly become Holland's trademark flower.

● International Film Festival Rotterdam

International Film Festival Rotterdam (IFFR) is one of the largest public film events in the world. Since its founding in 1972, it has become one of the most important events in the film world. Every year, hundreds of film makers and other artists present their work to a large audience in Rotterdam. Twelve days in a row, twenty-four screening venues are fully programmed. The festival attracts many interested visitors, plus up to 3,000 press and film industry representatives.

The International Film Festival Rotterdam focues on independent and experimental filmmaking by emerging talents and established auteurs. The festival also has a unique focus on presenting cutting edge media art and artist's film. The highlight of the International Film Festival is the VPRO Tiger Awards. Not the established film makers, but new talents receive awards for their promising work. The awards are an important encouragement for young directors. IFFR also hosts CineMart, for film producers to seek funding.

The International Film Festival Rotterdam management emphasises diversity in its film programming and on building relationships with and between filmmakers and audiences. The festival claims having "a unique atmosphere" and a "fiercely loyal following" locally and internationally—around 90% of tickets are sold to regular supporters.

● ABN AMRO World Tennis Tournament

The Rotterdam Open (also known by its sponsored name ABN AMRO World Tennis Tournament) is a professional tennis tournament played on indoor hard courts. It is part of the 500 series of the ATP World Tour and has been held annually at the Ahoy Rotterdam in Rotterdam, Netherlands.

The first Rotterdam Open tennis tournament was held in November 1972 and was won by Arthur Ashe. The following year the tournament was not organised because it switched to a March date. Originally the Rotterdam Open was an event of the World Championship Tennis circuit and in 1978 became part of the Grand Prix tennis circuit. Since 1990 it has been part of the ATP Tour.

You won't just see the tennis players on the court, some will also participate in a series of surprise activities that take place amid the bars, terraces and shops. There's even time to shop for fashion, sportswear, tennis accessories and luxury items at the shopping promenade.

※ March&April

● Keukenhof

Some of the information about Keukenhof has been already mentioned in Chapter "shopping in the Netherlands", this is a small supplement to this chapter.

Keukenhof lies in Lisse, between Amsterdam and The Hague, in the heart of the Bollenstreek (Bulb Region). More than 7 million flower bulbs are planted every year in the park. Gardens and four pavilions show a fantastic collection of: tulips, hyacinths, daffodils, orchids, roses, carnations, irises, lilies and many other flowers. Take a photo readily, this is the most widely circulated and the highest appearance of the beauty on the social network.

At Keukenhof, you will be overwhelmed by a spectacle of colours and perfumes. Divided across various gardens and pavilions, the tulips and other flowers number in the millions. Keukenhof has a different theme each year, meaning that it is never the same. Unique in the world, this park attracts over a million visitors every year.

Note that the tulips bloom only from mid-March to mid-May, meaning that the park is only open during this period. If you want to see the Dutch tulip fields in bloom, you have to go during this period.

● NN Marathon in Rotterdam

The Rotterdam Marathon, currently branded NN Rotterdam Marathon, is an annual marathon that has been held in Rotterdam, the Netherlands since 1981. It has been held in April every year since the third edition in 1984, it is without doubt Holland's largest running event. Every year, over 20,000 runners show up for this sportive event. Among them are some of the greatest runners in the world.

The Rotterdam Marathon has also been ranked as one of the top 10 marathons in the world by Runner's World magazine. The event is the most popular marathon in the Netherlands, followed by the marathons of Amsterdam and Eindhoven.

The Rotterdam Marathon often produces very fast times, as the course is flat and weather conditions are typically favourable. Between April 1985 and September 1998 the world best time were been set at Rotterdam, by Carlos Lopes and Belayneh Dinsamo respectively. As of April 2012 six different runners ran a sub 2:05:00 time and four of the ten fastest marathon runners ever ran their fastest time in the Rotterdam Marathon.

● Flower Parade

The annual Flower Parade of the Bollenstreek is a feast brimming with beautiful colours and delicious perfumes, It is one of the many flower parades in the Netherlands and also one of the largest editions of the world.

The origins of Flower Parade of the Bollenstreek took place in the end of the 1940s, just after World War II. When the World War was over, the need for parties and socialising was great. Organising parades began. The procession consisted then of a couple with flower garlands and flower lingers, decorated trucks and handcarts.

The event takes place at the end of April, with twenty huge floats and thirty lavishly decorated cars follow a 42-kilometre route from Noordwijk to Haarlem. Hundreds of thousands of visitors from Holland and abroad are drawn to the colourful flower spectacle every year.

● Some tips

Travel as EARLY as possible! Every year there is a big traffic jam to Keukenhof from 10:00am onwards. If you are traveling after 9:00am, be aware of this traffic jam it can take 2-3 hours one way to get from the train stations (Haarlem, Sassenheim, Hillegom, Leiden, Schiphol) by bus to the Keukenhof area!

This is a slow moving parade and it takes around 45-60 mins. Most people are lining up 1-1.5 hours before and some people sit next to the roads all day. Bring snacks, drinks and something to kill time.

If you want to return to the Keukenhof after the Bloemencorso Flower parade make sure you have your entrance tickets with you.

※ May&June

● Open-Air Theatres

The Netherlands has over 60 open-air theatres, about 50 of which are active. Annually, these theatres organise about 600 performances that are enjoyed by 250,000 to 300,000 visitors between May and September.

In addition to drama, you can experience a very extensive program including children's shows, concerts, cabaret, musicals, opera, classical music, jazz, open-air movies, dance festivals (ranging from African festivals to contemporary dance festivals), and even drama workshops for primary schools. There are performances both by amateur and professional groups and both well-known and unknown artists. There are programs for young and old, modern and classic.

One of the most famous open-air theatres in the Netherlands is the Vondelpark Open-air Theatre in Amsterdam. The theatre is in the open air, freely accessible and for 75% of the performances language is no problem! On Friday evening you can enjoy contemporary and modern dance performances, Saturday afternoon the theatre presents performances by and for children and Saturday evenings are marked by stand-up comedy and music.

● PINKPOP Festival

The PINKPOP Festival is a large, annual music festival held at Landgraaf, the Netherlands. It is usually held in the Pentecost weekend. Started in 1970, at Burgemeester Damen Sportpark in the town of Geleen, PINKPOP is the oldest and longest running annual dedicated pop and rock music festival in the world.

Nowadays, PINKPOP is a three-day festival, from Saturday through Monday, with different stages where (inter) national artists put on spectacular shows. The tickets to PINKPOP are sold out almost every year.

The great line-up of musicians that have performed at PINKPOP since it started in 1970 proves how special this festival is. Bruce Springsteen, the Foo Fighters, Fleetwood Mac, Dire Straits, Pearl Jam, Golden Earring, Red Hot Chili Peppers and many other artists have performed at PINKPOP. Apart from being Holland's biggest outdoor festival, PINKPOP is also the longest-running pop festival of its kind in the world.

Another great feature of PINKPOP is that the festival area has a camping site that meets your needs and demands as well as those of 50,000 other campers. This makes it possible to dance and enjoy the best concerts while taking a nap in between.

● Parkpop The Hague

Parkpop was presented for the first time in 1981 in The Hague and attended by 35,000 visitors. Today up to 350,000 people visit the festival every year, is one of the largest free pop music festivals in Europe and one of the longest running festivals in the Netherlands.

Parkpop is a great success, each and every year. It is more than just beer and pop music, it's about the atmosphere in the park, about bringing people together. Besides, every year the program, which contains great national and international acts, is composed with great care.

Every year on the last Sunday in June, the Parkpop pop festival is held in The Hague. Every since its beginnings, this free event has become ever more popular, drawing increasingly big names to the stage.

※ July&August

● North Sea Jazz Festival

The North Sea Jazz Festival is an annual festival held each second weekend of July in the Netherlands at the Ahoy venue. It used to be in The Hague but since 2006 it has been held in Rotterdam. This is because the Statenhal, where the festival was held before, was demolished in 2006. As of 2017 the festival officially will be known as the NN North Sea Jazz Festival.

The founder of the three-day festival was Paul Acket, a businessman and jazz lover, he desired to present a great diversity of jazz music to the public, from American jazz to European avant-garde. In 1976 the first edition of the North Sea Jazz Festival took place. It was an immediate success: six stages, thirty hours of music and 300 performances drew over 9,000 visitors. Many great jazz legends were presented, like Benny Goodman, Miles Davis, Billy Eckstine, Sarah Vaughan, Count Basie, Dizzy Gillespie and Stan Getz.

Several significant awards, such as the Edison Jazz Award, and since 1985, the Bird Awards, are presented at the North Sea Jazz Festival. From 1998 onward the Edison Jazz Awards are presented at the festival. The Edison is the award of the Dutch music industry for albums of a special quality.

In 1990, two sub-festivals were introduced: "North Sea Jazz Heats", a free festival performed in pubs throughout The Hague, and the more exclusive "Midsummer Jazz Gala". Artists that have performed at the Midsummer Jazz Gala include Tony Bennett, Herbie Hancock and Oscar Peterson.

In 2004, late singer Amy Winehouse who was well-known for her jazzy vocal performed at the festival, following her debut album Frank (2003).

The festival is known worldwide for the many music styles it presents, from traditional New Orleans jazz to Swing, bebop, fusion, blues, gospel music, funk music, soul music and drum & bass. It is acknowledged as the "biggest indoor jazz festival in the world".

● The Four Days Marches

The International Four Day Marches Nijmegen is the largest multiple day marching event in the world. It took place in 1909, being based at Nijmegen since 1916 as a means of promoting sport and exercise.

Depending on age group and category, walkers have to walk 30, 40 or 50 kilometres each day for four days. Originally a military event with a few civilians, now it is a mainly civilian event. Numbers have risen in recent years, with over 40,000 taking part in including about 5,000 military. It is now the world's largest walking event. Due to crowds on the route, since 2004 the organizers have limited the number of participants. The first day of walking is always the 3rd Tuesday in July. Many participants take part every year, including several that have taken part in 50, and even 60 different annual marches.

291

Each day of the marches is named after the biggest town it goes through. Tuesday is the day of Elst, Wednesday the day of Wijchen, Thursday the day of Groesbeek and Friday the day of Cuijk. The routes always stay the same unless there is a specific need to change, as it did in 2007 (route changed in 2006 but cancelled) when the walkers went through the Waalkade on Wednesday for the first time since the original route got too crowded and walkers had to wait for over an hour at some times. 2006 was the first year to be cancelled in 90 years (apart from World War II). After the first day's march there were thousands of drop-outs and two deaths because of extreme heat.

On the Friday, as participants near the finish, the public awards the walkers with gladioli, a symbol of force and victory since Roman times, when gladiators were likewise showered with these flowers. The entry into the city and towards the finish, the St. Annastraat, is for that reason called Via Gladiola during the Nijmegen Marches.

Standard categories:

30 km x 4 days

40 km x 4 days

50 km x 4 days

55 km x 4 days—reinstated specially for the 100th edition.

Military category:

40 km x 4 days—Wearing uniform + at least 10 kg (+ water, etc.) marching weight for males aged 18–49, for females the weight is optional.

● International Fireworks Festival in Scheveningen

Every year the International Fireworks Festival in Scheveningen draws tens of thousands of visitors. In the course of the festival several countries try to put on the best fireworks display.

The International Fireworks Festival is a serious competition with strict rules. Participating countries have the same budget to spend, must ensure that at least 80% of their fireworks are produced in their own country, and have 11 to 13 minutes to display their fireworks prowess. Teams from several countries brandish the most vivid kaleidoscopic creations of colour and light with the accompanying ear splitting sound in an effort to outdo each other and take home the Fireworks Trophy Scheveningen.

The International Fireworks Festival in Scheveningen spans several evenings (generally 4) on the Scheveningen beach, offers two crackling shows of fireworks per evening. In addition to the fireworks displays, you can also enjoy various side events and performances on different stages on the Scheveningen Boulevard, such as fire eaters, dance groups and live performances by Crazy Piano's.

※ September&October

● Scheveningen Kite Festival

International Kite Festival Scheveningen is an annual event that proves just how much fun kites can be for adults and children alike. The kite festival is held in Scheveningen in September every year. Over 100 participants from around the world come to fly every shape and size of kite on the beach. The organisers have invited also several international teams, which they hope will be supplemented by thousands of amateur kite enthusiasts. The international teams will be competing for the European Sport Kite Championship.

The largest event of its kind in the Netherlands, the festival fills the beach with enthusiastic viewers while the sky is flooded with flying colours and designs by the kite-flyers from around the world, who will perform demonstrations and stunts. The kites range from the everyday to more intricate designs like whales, lobsters, pandas and more, don't seem to be affected by gravity.

Throughout the day there will be all kinds of kite demonstrations, if you like you can learn how to fly a kite. You will also be able to join in by purchasing your own kite at a nearby stall. There's even a workshop where children can make their own kite!

● Amsterdam Marathon

Wanting to go for a 42 km and 195 metre run through and around Amsterdam? Join the Amsterdam Marathon I would say. The Amsterdam Marathon attracts thousands of runners from all over the country and all over the world every year, with some of the world's very best among them.

The first marathon in Amsterdam was held on August 5, 1928, during the 1928 Summer Olympics. It was won by Boughera El Ouafi in 2:32:57. After the Olympics there were no marathons in Amsterdam until 1975. Since that year the marathon was held annually, with the exception of 1978.

The 1980 course record of 2:09:01 ran by Dutchman Gerard Nijboer could be considered an unofficial world record as the generally recognised record at that time, 2:08:34 in Antwerp, had been run on a course that was 500 meters short. However, IAAF doesn't recognise Nijboer time as any record.

In 2005, the former world record holder on the marathon, Haile Gebrselassie, earned his first win in the Amsterdam Marathon in the fastest marathon time in the world for the 2006 season (2:06:20).

In 2012, the Kenyan Wilson Chebet won the race by a time of 2:05:41 and broke the previous course record by three seconds. In the same year, Ethiopian Meseret Hailu broke the women's course record with a time of 2:21:09.

In 2017, Kenya's Lawrence Cherono was the surprise winner of the TCS Amsterdam Marathon, taking more than a minute off his PB to set a new course record of 2:05:09.

The route of the Amsterdam marathon goes past many beautiful sites, including the Amstel Hotel and Tropenmuseum (museum of the tropics). The runners speed through the attractive Vondelpark, over Leidseplein square and along the Amstel river with its beautiful windmills and views. Another special feature on the itinerary is the run through the passage beneath the Rijksmuseum.

※ November&December

• Amsterdam Light Festival

Amsterdam Light Festival is a public-private collaboration between the municipality, the cultural sector and numerous businesses. Exhibiting more than 200 light art installations in recent years, Amsterdam Light Festival has become one of Europe's most important light art festivals. It has been able to bring light art to a wide audience while providing artists with an international platform to present their work.

The sculptures can be spotted all over Amsterdam city centre for the duration of the festival, illuminating and transforming its familiar monuments in magical and surprising new ways. It's possible to find your own way around, but in order to view the festival in its best possible light two recommended routes have been created—a boat route and a walking route.

The Water Colours boat tour introduces you to Amsterdam in a unique way. Board one of the tour boats embellished with lights and sail through the famous 17th century canals to see the beautiful Water Colours exhibition. The latest light innovations make you look at the historical heritage of the city in an entirely new way. Amsterdam Light Festival has a host of great partners offering cruises, all of which are easy to recognise by their "official partner" flag—including specialist canal cruise company Stromma. For the 2017/18 event, 900 submissions were submitted by designers, architects and artists from 45 different countries. These submissions were whittled down to 35 artworks which make up the festival's installations.

Illuminade, the land exhibition, shows interactive and innovative installations from designers. In previous years Illuminade consisted of a walking route was in the Plantage neighbourhood, in the centre of Amsterdam. The Illuminade walking itinerary leads past over 20 light installations every year. The exhibition shows off the masterpieces created especially for the festival by international top artists. Examples are brightly coloured projections on historical architecture, dynamic light installations in city parks, and works that you can literally walk through.

荷兰人的生活真的是多姿多彩。文化和娱乐是他们日常生活中非常重要的一部分。除了传统的节日，荷兰还非常频繁地举办各种各样的节日、集市、游行、博览会和各种大型活动。这些大型活

动分布在荷兰的各个中小城市。春天时节，有鲜花游行和奶酪市场；炎炎夏天，有丰富的舞蹈、音乐和戏剧节；秋日时分，是艺术节和文化节的天堂；而寒冬季节里丝丝的暖意则由圣尼古拉集市和圣诞集市带来。因为各类活动繁多，在这里仅给出一些比较有代表性活动的介绍。

※ 一月和二月

● 欧洲音乐大会

ESNS欧洲音乐大会是一年一度的为期四天的音乐表演节，于每年1月在荷兰格罗宁根举行。音乐节有超过150个乐队和小组的300场演出和表演，每年能吸引来自40多个国家的3万多游客。来这里的可不仅仅是音乐迷们，还有一些专业人士到此来挖掘潜在的新新艺人。音乐节的前三天展现的是来自欧洲各地的艺术家们的演出，最后一天的表演嘉宾只有荷兰本地艺术家。

除了大量的节目表演和乐队，这个音乐节还会颁发一系列音乐奖项，为来自欧洲不同国家的音乐人才提供了非常棒的交流空间。

欧洲音乐节上颁发的奖项有："欧洲跨国界音乐奖 (EBBA)"、"欧洲艺术节奖"、荷兰最富盛名的"布玛流行乐大奖"、"流行乐媒体大奖"、"羽毛奖"和"布玛音乐技术交流奖"。

● 全国郁金香节

郁金香节标志着郁金香季节的正式开始。该活动是由荷兰郁金香种植者们组织的。每逢郁金香节，他们就会在阿姆斯特丹的大坝广场上建造一个巨大的花园，里面有成千上万的各色鲜活郁金香。阿姆斯特丹最大的花园将水坝广场变成了一片五彩缤纷的海洋，每年都有成千上万的人来这里采摘免费的花束。除了搭建了临时花园外，郁金香种植者还会举办很多促销活动，给采花的人们带来重重惊喜。

郁金香节是尚在春寒时节的一场生机勃勃的活动，大坝广场的带株郁金香都是免费领取的，可以来年接着种植。图为群众还未入场的活动区。

郁金香季是从每年的1月持续到4月底，大多数郁金香品种都可以从花店、超市和花架上买到。从荷兰的郁金香拍卖行到世界各地千家万户人们的花瓶里，有着数千的郁金香变种，彩虹里的任何一种颜色都能找到。郁金香真正成为了荷兰的标志性花卉。

● 鹿特丹国际电影节

鹿特丹国际电影节 (IFFR) 是世界上最大的公共电影盛事之一，自1972年成立以来，它已成为电影界最重要的事件之一。每年，数以百计的电影制作人和其他艺术家都会在鹿特丹的大批观众面前展示他们的作品。连续12天的电影节，24块荧幕排得满满当当。每年的鹿特丹国际电影节吸引了一众的电影爱好者和多达3 000个新闻和电影行业的代表。

鹿特丹国际电影节专注于新兴人才和成熟导演的独立和视觉实验的电影制作，该电影节还特别关注呈现尖端媒体艺术和艺术家电影。这个国际电影的亮点是金虎奖 (VPRO Tiger Awards)，这是一个不只是针对那些老牌的电影制作人的奖项，此奖还会颁发给那些新兴的电影制作人和导演，以资表达对他们作品的肯定并对其进行鼓励，这些奖项对年轻导演是非常重要的鼓舞。IFFR还会举办电影集市（CineMart），旨在为电影制片人寻求资金援助。

鹿特丹国际电影节强调电影制作的多样性，以及建立制片人和观众之间的联系。电影节宣称是一个拥有"独特的氛围"和在当地与国际上拥有一大批"忠实的追随者"的电影节——鹿特丹电影节大约90%的门票都被卖给了普通的观影群众和拥趸。

● 鹿特丹网球公开赛

鹿特丹网球公开赛——因为冠名商的缘故，故也被称为荷兰银行世界网球锦标赛，这是在室内硬地球场举行的职业网球锦标赛。它是ATP世界巡回赛500系列赛事的一部分，每年在荷兰鹿特丹的Ahoy体育馆举行。

第一届鹿特丹网球公开赛于1972年11月举行，由阿瑟·阿什赢得。接下来的一年，因为赛事改到3月份，鹿特丹锦标赛没有组织起来。最初，鹿特丹网球公开赛是世界锦标赛网球巡回赛的一项赛事，1978年成为大奖赛网球巡回赛的一部分。自1990年以来，它一直是ATP巡回赛的一部分。

在鹿特丹的Ahoy体育馆网球赛场，你不仅能亲眼目睹网球选手激烈的争夺赛，还可以参加一系列在酒吧、露台和商店中举行的惊喜活动，甚至还有时间在购物区选择喜爱的时装、运动装、网球配饰和奢侈品。

※ 三月和四月

● 库肯霍夫

关于库肯霍夫的一些信息已经在"购在荷兰"一章中提到过，这是对这一章的小补充。

库肯霍夫位于阿姆斯特丹和海牙之间的利瑟，在球茎花田区的中心位置，公园每年种植的花卉可达700多万株。库肯霍夫园区和四个展厅是一个奇妙的花卉集合地：郁金香、风信子、水仙花、兰花、玫瑰、康乃馨、鸢尾、百合和许多其他的花。信手拍来，就是一张在网络世界广泛流传、曝光率极高的美照。

在库肯霍夫，你会被壮观的色彩和花的芳香所淹没。整个园区把花园含展厅划分成了不同的部分，郁金香和其他各类花株数量达到上百万。库肯霍夫每年的展览都有不同的主题，也就意味着你看到的库肯霍夫永远都是不一样的。这个公园在世界上独一无二，每年都会有超过一百万的游客来这里游览赏花。

需要注意的是，郁金香只在3月中旬到5月中旬开放，也就意味着公园只会在这段时间开放。如果你想感受开满郁金香花的荷兰田野，那你必须在这一时期走一遭了。

● 鹿特丹马拉松

鹿特丹马拉松目前被命名为NN鹿特丹马拉松，是一项一年一度的马拉松比赛，从1981年开始就在荷兰鹿特丹落地生根了。从1984年的第三届开始，鹿特丹马拉松每年4月份举行，毋庸置疑地成为荷兰最大的跑步活动。参与鹿特丹马拉松赛事的跑步爱好者每年都超过2万人，其中还有一些世界顶级的赛跑运动员。

鹿特丹马拉松是荷兰最受欢迎的马拉松比赛，被《跑步者世界》杂志评为世界十大马拉松之一。图为参赛者通过伊拉斯莫斯大桥。图片提供方Pim Ras Fotografie。

鹿特丹马拉松被《跑步者世界》杂志评为世界十大马拉松之一。这是荷兰最受欢迎的马拉松比赛，紧随其后的是阿姆斯特丹和埃因霍温的马拉松比赛。

因为赛道平坦，天气状况通常良好，鹿特丹马拉松经常会诞生新的纪录。在1985年4月到1998年9月之间，世界最好的成绩是由卡洛斯·洛佩斯和贝雷内·迪萨摩分别在鹿特丹赛事中所创下的。截至2012年4月，6名不同的运动员跑出了2小时5分的成绩，而10名跑得最快的马拉松选手中有4人在鹿特丹马拉松比赛中创造了最佳成绩。

● 花车游行

一年一度的Bollenstreek花车游行是一场充满了绚丽的色彩和鲜花芳香的盛宴，它是荷兰众多的花车游行活动之一，也是世界上最大的花车游行之一。

Bollenstreek的花车游行始于20世纪40年代末，在"二战"结束以后。当时世界大战刚刚结束，人们迫切需要聚集庆祝和社会交际，于是就开始组织游行活动。当时的游行队伍由一对夫妇组成，他们带着花环和鲜花，卡车和手推车也都进行了装饰。

Bollenstreek的游行活动于4月底举行，届时将有20辆巨大的彩车和30辆豪华的装饰车辆从诺德韦克出发，一路行进42公里到达哈乐姆。每年都有成千上万来自荷兰和国外的游客被吸引到五彩缤纷的花展上。

● 建议和提示

若要参加，尽早出行！每年这个时候，前往库肯霍夫的路上从早上10点开始就会交通大堵塞。要是你在9点才出发，你就会知道交通拥堵有多可怕了，从哈乐姆、萨森海姆、希勒霍姆、莱顿、史基浦机场等地到库肯霍夫地区单程都要花上2～3小时。

花车游行非常缓慢，大约需要45～60分钟。大多数人提前1小时到1.5小时就开始排队了，还有些人会坐在马路旁边等一整天，最好是带上零食、饮料和打发时间的玩意儿！

如果你想在花车游行之后再回到库肯霍夫公园，那一定要保存好入园门票！

※ 五月和六月

● 露天剧场

荷兰的露天剧场超过了60个，其中比较活跃的约有50个。每年的5月到9月间，这些露天剧场就会组织大约600场演出活动，吸引了25万到30万的观众前往观看。

露天剧场带来的可不止是戏剧表演，这些节目的类型非常广泛，包括儿童节目、音乐会、歌舞表演、音乐剧、歌剧、古典音乐、爵士乐、露天电影、从非洲音乐到当代舞蹈的舞蹈节，甚至还有专门针对学校孩子们的戏剧班。露天剧场的表演者们有业余爱好者也有专业团体，有鼎鼎大名的艺术家也有不为众人所知的普通表演者。其节目安排贯穿现代和古典，老少咸宜。

荷兰最著名的一个露天剧场是阿姆斯特丹的冯德尔公园露天剧场。剧院是露天的，可以自由出入，75%的表演都不会受到语言的限制。在星期五晚上，你可以欣赏到当代和现代的舞蹈表演，星期六下午是孩子们的时间，星期六晚上的表演则是喜剧类和音乐类。

● PINKPOP音乐节

PINKPOP音乐节是在荷兰兰德赫拉夫举行的大型音乐节，通常在五旬节的周末举行。PINKPOP始于1970年小城赫伦的达门市长健身公园，是世界上最古老、持续时间最长的年度流行音乐和摇滚音乐节。

现在的PINKPOP音乐节是一个为期3天的音乐活动，从周六到周一，来自荷兰国内外的艺术家们在不同的舞台上轮番上演精彩的音乐节目。PINKPOP的门票几乎每年都销售一空。

从1970年音乐节一成立，就有一众的大牌音乐家们来到PINKPOP的舞台上进行表演，足以证明PINKPOP音乐节是多么的与众不同。布鲁斯·斯普林斯汀、喷火战机乐队、弗利伍麦克、恐怖海峡乐队、珍珠果酱乐队、金耳环乐队、红辣椒乐队以及其他许多伟大的艺术家都在PINKPOP表演过。除了是荷兰最大的户外音乐节，PINKPOP也是世界上历史最悠久的流行音乐节。

PINKPOP音乐节还有一大特点，在活动的区域专门有一个露营场地，可以满足你的需求，5万名参与音乐节的人都可以在此安营扎寨。中场休息间隙，欣赏着悠扬动听的音乐翩翩起舞当然也是完全可行的。

● 海牙Parkpop音乐节

1981年，Parkpop首次在海牙举办，有3.5万名观众参与活动。而现在的Parkpop每年会吸引35万人前来参加，这是欧洲最大的免费流行音乐节之一，也是荷兰历史最悠久的音乐节之一。

Parkpop每年的活动都是一个巨大的成功，不仅仅因为是啤酒和流行音乐，而是活动现场公园里热闹的氛围，它以此让人们聚集在一起。此外，每年音乐节上来自国内外艺术家们的表演节目都经过了精心安排。

Parkpop流行音乐节每年6月的最后一个星期天都会在海牙举行，自从它成立以来，这项免费的音乐活动变得越来越流行，越来越多的大牌表演者出现在了活动的舞台上。

※ 七月和八月

● 北海爵士音乐节

北海爵士音乐节是每年7月第二个周末在荷兰Ahoy体育场举办的年度节日，这个音乐节以前在海牙举办，但自2006年起就挪到了鹿特丹举行，因为2006年举办这项活动的场馆Statenhal被拆除。在2017年，音乐节正式改称为"NN北海爵士音乐节"。

这个为期3天的音乐节是由保罗·艾克特创立的，他是一位商人，同时也是一名爵士乐爱好者，从美国爵士到欧洲先锋，他希望向公众展示爵士乐的多样性。1976年，第一届北海爵士音乐节举行，活动立即获得了成功：6个舞台、30小时的音乐和300场演出，吸引了9 000多名观众。许多伟大的爵士传奇人物都参加了演出，比如本尼·古德曼、迈尔斯·戴维斯、比利·埃克斯丁、莎拉·沃恩、康特·贝西、迪兹·吉莱斯皮和斯坦·格茨。

许多伟大的爵士传奇人物都在北海爵士音乐节留下了足迹，也诞生了爱迪生爵士奖。图为2018年在鹿特丹举办的北海爵士音乐节。

一些重要的奖项，比如爱迪生爵士奖，还有1985年开始的菜鸟奖都会在北海爵士音乐节上颁发。爱迪生爵士奖是1998年在音乐节上推出的，是荷兰音乐产业颁发给特殊质量专辑的奖项。

1990年，两个小型的节日庆典被吸纳进来："北海爵士热"，一个全海牙酒吧的自由表演活动，以及一个更高档些的"仲夏爵士晚会"。托尼·班奈特和奥斯卡·彼得森都曾在仲夏爵士晚会上进行过表演。

已故歌手艾米·怀恩豪斯在首张专辑《Frank》（2003年）发行之后，于2004年凭借在音乐节上的爵士表演名声大振。

北海爵士音乐节在全世界范围内都以它所呈现的多种音乐曲风而闻名，从传统的新奥尔良爵士音乐到摇摆乐、波普、融合、蓝调、福音音乐、放克音乐、灵魂乐、鼓和贝司，它被公认为"世界上最大的室内爵士音乐节"。

● 奈梅亨四日徒步行

奈梅亨四日徒步行是世界上最大的多日徒步行活动。它开始于1909年，从1916年开始作为促进体育运动发展的一种方式落户在奈梅亨。

这项徒步行活动根据年龄和参与者类别的不同，分为每天走30公里、40公里或50公里的行进路线，持续时间都是4天。最初，这主要是针对军人而设立的一项活动。但随着活动的发展，越来越多的普通民众参与其中。近年来，参与徒步行的人数超过了40 000人，其中包括了5 000名军人，现在它是世界上最大规模的徒步活动。由于人数众多导致路线拥挤，自2004年以来，组织者限制了参与者的数量。奈梅亨四日徒步行每年7月的第三个星期二开始，每年都吸引大批徒步爱好者，其中有些人已经参加了不同年度的50次甚至60次徒步活动。

299

徒步行的每一天都以它经过的最大城镇命名。星期二是埃尔斯特日，星期三是韦亨日，星期四和星期五分别是赫鲁斯贝克日和柯埃克日。活动的路线一般是固定不变的，除非有特殊情况，如2007年（2006年路线也发生了改变，但被取消了），因为原来的路线过于拥挤，参赛者有时不得不在途中等上一个多小时，于是将周三的路线改到了瓦尔卡德。2006年，活动被取消，除了"二战"期间，这还是90年来第一次。当时由于天气酷热难耐，在第一天行进之后，有成千上万人被迫放弃，还造成两人死亡。

在周五快接近终点时，人们会给参赛者们献上剑兰，这是自罗马时代以来的一种力量和胜利的象征，当时的角斗士们也同样沐浴在这些鲜花中。最后的终点是奈梅亨的圣安娜街，也正是因为这个原因，在活动的期间这里又被称作"Via Gladiola"（这个表述可以追溯到罗马时代，有"死亡和剑兰"之意）。

奈梅亨四日徒步行的赛别：

30公里x4天

40公里x4天

50公里x4天

55公里x4天，这是在第100届活动中特别划定的；

军人参与者行程：

40公里x4天

穿制服及至少10公斤负荷（饮用水等），这是18～49岁的男性军人参与者的标准；女性军人参与重量是可选的。

● **席凡宁根国际烟花节**

席凡宁根每年的国际烟花节都会吸引成千上万的游客。在烟花节的表演中，各个参与国家八仙过海，各显其能，把最好的烟火表演呈现给大家。

国际烟花节是一个严肃的比赛，有严格的规定。每个参与的国家预算相同，且必须确保至少80%的烟花是自己的国家生产的，表演环节仅有11～13分钟的时间来展示他们的烟花魅力。来自多个国家的团队挥舞着最鲜艳的万花筒般的由色彩和光线构成的作品，伴随着烟花绽放的噼里啪啦声，努力想超越彼此，将席凡宁根烟花奖杯抱回家。

席凡宁根的国际烟花节虽欢乐，但也是个正规的比赛，前几年中国均有参加。图为烟花和海上摩天轮及蹦极。图片由Chris Reichard Photography提供。

在席凡宁根海滩举行的国际烟花节通常会持续4个晚上，每天晚上都有两场烟花表演。除了烟花表演，席凡宁根的海滨大道上还可以欣赏到各种精彩绝伦的活动和演出，比如吞火表演、舞蹈团体和疯狂钢琴Live演奏。

※ 九月和十月

● 席凡宁根国际风筝节

席凡宁根国际风筝节是一个年度活动，不管对成人还是孩子而言，都会在这里看到异常多有趣的风筝。风筝节在每年的9月份举行，来自世界各地的100多名参赛者带上各种形状和大小的风筝放飞在席凡宁根的上空。主办方还邀请了几只国际团队作为对数以千计业余风筝爱好者的补充。这些国际参赛队伍还将参加欧洲体育风筝锦标赛。

席凡宁根国际风筝节是荷兰同类活动中最盛大的一次，海滩上满是热情饱满的观众，而天空中则充斥着来自世界各地的风筝人所设计的五彩缤纷的风筝，他们会做各种示范操作和特技表演。这些风筝从日常的设计到如鲸鱼、龙虾、熊猫等复杂造型的设计，似乎都不受重力的影响，高高地在天上翱翔。

风筝的示范演示会全天都有，如果你喜欢的话也可以学一学如何放风筝。在附近找个摊位，买个属于你自己的风筝，然后加入进来。这里还有一个小作坊，孩子们可以学着自己制作风筝！

● 阿姆斯特丹马拉松

想横穿阿姆斯特丹跑上42公里又195米吗？那么加入阿姆斯特丹马拉松吧！阿姆斯特丹的马拉松比赛每年都吸引着来自全国各地和世界各地的成千上万的参赛者，其中一些还是世界上最棒的跑手。

阿姆斯特丹首届马拉松比赛在1928年8月5日举行，当时是在1928年夏季奥运会期间。这次马拉松由Boughera El Ouafi以2小时32分57秒的成绩赢得比赛。在这次奥运会之后，阿姆斯特丹直到1975年才开始定期举办马拉松比赛，自此，马拉松比赛每年举行一次，1978年除外。

1980年荷兰人杰拉德·尼布尔所创造的2小时9分1秒的比赛纪录被认为是一个非官方的世界纪录，因为当时公认的纪录是安特卫普的2小时8分34秒，这个时间是在一条短了500米的赛道上创下的，即便如此，国际田联（IAAF）仍没有将尼布尔创造的时间视为任何纪录。

2005年，前世界纪录保持者，马拉松选手海勒·格布雷西拉西耶在2006年赛季阿姆斯特丹马拉松比赛中第一次取得胜利，跑出了2小时6分20秒的世界最好成绩。

2012年，肯尼亚的威尔逊·切贝特以2小时5分41秒的成绩赢得了比赛，凭3秒优势打破了之前的纪录。同年，埃塞俄比亚的梅塞特·海鲁打破了女性纪录，时间为2小时21分9秒。

2017年，肯尼亚的劳伦斯·切罗诺出人意料地赢得了TCS阿姆斯特丹马拉松赛的冠军，以快一分多钟的速度刷新了他的个人纪录，创下了2小时5分9秒的新纪录。

阿姆斯特丹马拉松的路线途经许多环境优美的地点，包括阿姆斯特尔酒店和热带博物馆。穿越迷人的冯德尔公园，通过莱顿广场，沿着耸立着美丽的风车和拥有优美景致的阿姆斯特尔河前行。路线中还有一大特色，那就是会从国立博物馆下方通道跑过。

※ 十一月和十二月

● 阿姆斯特丹灯光艺术节

阿姆斯特丹灯光艺术节是市政、文化部门和众多企业之间的公私合作。近年来，阿姆斯特丹的灯光艺术节已成为欧洲最重要的灯光艺术节之一，在为艺术家们提供一个展示他们作品的国际平台的同时还能给人民大众带来一场灯光艺术盛宴。

节日期间，在阿姆斯特丹市中心各处都能看到雕塑，这些平日熟悉的雕塑和纪念碑，在灯光的映衬下会以一种惊奇的形象出现。你可以以自己的一种舒适的方式规划游览路线，但要想尽善尽美地完成参观，那就看一下这两条推荐的路线，分别是运河游船路线和步行路线。

灯光是场震撼的视觉展示，阿姆斯特丹灯光艺术节每年都能将最优秀的创作展现出来。图为灯光节期间的运河桥梁。

水上灯光游览船以一种独特的方式向你介绍着阿姆斯特丹，其中一艘游船装饰着灯，穿过著名的17世纪运河，观看美丽的水上灯光展览，新颖的灯光创意会让你以全新的视角瞻仰着这座城市的历史遗产。阿姆斯特丹灯光艺术节的很多合作伙伴都有游船提供，上面有明确的 "official partner（官方合作）" 的旗帜标识，很容易找到——包括像Stromma这样的专业运河游船运营商。在2017年到2018年的活动中，来自45个不同国家的设计师、建筑师和艺术家提交了900份参展作品，最后从中筛选了35项艺术作品在本届灯光艺术节中亮相。

Illuminade是一项陆上照明展览，展示了来自设计师的互动和创新装置。往年，陆上照明由阿姆斯特丹中心Plantage附近的步行路线组成。Illuminade陆上灯光线路每年安装的照明装置都会超过20个，这些作品装置都是国际顶尖艺术家特别为灯光艺术节制作的，例如历史建筑上色彩鲜明的投影、城市公园里的动态灯光装置，以及与游人融为一体可以在光影中穿行的作品。

Tijd voor Nederlands 荷兰语时间

● 单词+短语

荷 cultuur	荷 feest	荷 Evenement
英 culture	英 party	英 event
译 文化	译 聚会	译 活动
荷 feestdag	荷 muziekfestival	荷 bioscoop
英 holiday	英 music festival	英 cinema
译 节日	译 音乐节	译 电影院

荷 voorstelling	荷 wedstrijd	荷 dragen
英 performance	英 match	英 wear
译 演出	译 比赛	译 穿
荷 vieren	荷 deelnemen	荷 winnen
英 celebrate	英 join	英 win
译 庆祝	译 参加	译 赢得

● 例句

荷 De Nederlandse cultuur is heel anders dan de Chinese. 英 Dutch culture is very different from the Chinese culture. 译 荷兰的文化跟中国很不一样。	荷 Het is nu een feestdag, mensen hebben veel feesten. 英 It's a holiday now, people have a lot of parties. 译 现在是节日，人们有很多聚会。
荷 Het Vondelpark heft volgende week een evenement. 英 Vondel park has an event next week. 译 冯德尔公园下周有一场活动。	荷 Is dit muziekfestival gratis? 英 Is this music festival for frec? 译 这个音乐节是免费的吗？
荷 Wil je naar de bioscoop of wil je graag naar een voorstelling? 英 Do you want to go to the cinema or want to go to a performance? 译 你想去电影院还是想看演出？	荷 Vanavond is er een voetbalwedstrijd. 英 There is a football match this evening. 译 今天晚上有一场足球比赛。
荷 Mensen vieren carnaval en je kunt de mooiste kleding dragen. 英 People are celebrating Carnival and you can wear the best-looking clothes. 译 人们正在庆祝狂欢节，你可以穿上最好看的衣服。	荷 Wil je morgen aan het feestje in Amsterdam deelnemen? 英 Do you want to join the party in Amsterdam tomorrow? 译 你要参加明天在阿姆斯特丹的聚会吗？
荷 Welk team heeft deze wedstrijd gewonnen? 英 Which team won this game? 译 哪个队伍赢得了这场比赛？	

303

3. 荷兰人的社交文化
Dutch Social Culture

The Netherlands is a society of etiquette and order. If you deal with Dutch people, whether it is for business or for friendship, some social etiquettes should be kept in mind.

荷兰是一个讲究礼仪和秩序的国家，如果你和荷兰人打交道，不管是生意上的合作还是个人人际关系交往，一些社交礼仪必须要谨记在心。

※ Meeting and Greeting

Shake hands with everyone present—men, women, and children—at business and social meetings. Shake hands again when leaving. Introduce yourself if no one is present to introduce you. The Dutch consider it rude not to identify yourself.

The Dutch will shake hands and say their last name, not "Hello." They also answer the telephone with their last name.

※ Business occasions

The Dutch take punctuality for business meetings very seriously and expect that you will do likewise; call with an explanation if you are delayed.

Lateness, missed appointments, postponements, changing the time of an appointment or a late delivery deteriorates trust and can ruin relationships.

The Dutch tend to be direct, giving straight "yes" and "no" answers.

In many companies the decision-making process is slow and ponderous, involving wide consultation. Consensus is vital. The Dutch will keep talking until all parties agree.

Once decisions are made, implementation is fast and efficient.

In the Netherlands, commitments are taken seriously and are honoured. Do not promise anything or make an offer you are not planning to deliver on.

※ Dining and Entertainment

To beckon a waiter or waitress, raise your hand, make eye contact, and say ober (waiter) or mevrouw (waitress).

It is appropriate to discuss business during lunch. Business breakfasts are not very common.

Most business entertaining is done in restaurants, but the Dutch do a fair amount of entertaining at home as well.

The Dutch will make it clear that you are their guest if they intend to pay the bill, otherwise expect to "go Dutch" and pay your fair share. No one will be embarrassed at splitting the bill.

Dutch manners are frank-no-nonsense informality combined with strict adherence to basic etiquette.

Parties may go very late. Plan to stay for an hour or so after dinner.

※ Gifts

Gifts are generally not given or expected at business meetings.

Gifts are exchanged in business only once a close, personal relationship has developed.

The Dutch find any form of ostentation a bit embarrassing. A grand gesture of generosity will only make them uncomfortable. Lavish displays of wealth are considered bad taste.

Give books, art objects, wine, and liquor. Do not give knives.

When invited to someone's home, bring a small gift for the hostess. Bring children a small gift or candy. Sending flowers before or after the party is also appropriate.

※ 会面及招待

参加商业性质活动或者社交活动时，要与在场的每个人握手，不管是男人、女人还是孩子。在离开时要再次握手。要是没有人在场介绍你的情况下，记得介绍你自己，如果不做自我介绍会被荷兰人认为是没礼貌的行为。

初次会面，和荷兰人握手时记得说出自己的姓名，也就是自我介绍，而不是我们通常认为的说"你好"。荷兰人接电话的时候第一时间也是要说出自己的姓氏。

※ 商业场合

荷兰人非常看重商务会议的准时守时，也希望与会的每个人都一样，如果你因事务被耽搁了，记得打电话说明。

迟到、错过约定时间、推迟、更改约定时间都有可能降低对方的信任度，并有可能破坏人际关系。

荷兰人倾向于直截了当，请直接给出"是"或"不是"的答案。

在很多公司，决策过程缓慢而冗长，需要全面的研讨和商议。共识是至关重要的，荷兰人会反复讨论下去，直到各方都同意。

一旦做出决定，就要迅速而高效实施。

在荷兰，承诺是件严肃的事情，需要履行。不要随便承诺任何事情，不打算兑现的提议和决策就不要答应。

※ 饮食与休闲

招呼服务人员的时候请举手示意，直视对方，并称呼先生或女士。

午餐时间可以适当讨论下商业话题，但早餐最好不要。

大多数情况下荷兰人会把商务性休闲活动安排在餐厅进行，但安排在家的情况也较为常见。

要是荷兰人当你是客人要替你付账的话，他们会明确表示，否则的话就是"AA制"，那你就付自己那份就好了。不会有人为平分账单感到尴尬的。

荷兰人讲究有礼坦率，严格遵守基本礼仪，不喜欢冠冕堂皇无意义的客套。

聚会通常会进行到很晚，一般在晚饭后需要再逗留一小时左右，请提前做好准备。

※ 礼物

一般来说，在商务会议上，既不送礼也不收礼。

商业合作中，如果双方人际关系比较密切之后可以相互送礼物。

炫耀这事对荷兰人来说是很尴尬的。举动过于慷慨可能会让他们感到不舒服。奢侈、炫富的举动会让荷兰人觉得你的品位很糟。

礼物可以送书、艺术品、红酒和烈性酒。不要送刀具类。

要是荷兰人邀请你到家中做客时，记得给女主人带个小礼物，给孩子们带个小礼物或糖果。在聚会前后送花也是一件合乎时宜的事。